OPERATION VICTORY

The Personal Record of Field-Marshal Montgomery's Chief of Staff from Alamein to the Final Surrender in Germany

Major-General Sir Francis De Guingand
K.B.E., C.B., D.S.O.
Chief of Staff, Eighth Army, 1942-43
Chief of Staff, 21st Army Group, 1944-45

OPERATION VICTORY

Published by Sapere Books.
24 Trafalgar Road, Ilkley, LS29 8HH
United Kingdom

saperebooks.com

Copyright © The Estate of Sir Francis de Guingand, 1947, 2024.
First published by Hodder & Stoughton, 1947, 2024.
The Estate of Sir Francis de Guingand asserted its right to be identified as the author of this work.
All rights reserved.

No part of this publication may be reproduced, stored in any retrieval system, or transmitted, in any form, or by any means, electronic, mechanical, photocopying, recording, or otherwise, without the prior written permission of the publishers.

ISBN: 978-0-85495-171-0.

To Arlie

TABLE OF CONTENTS

FOREWORD 11
CHAPTER I: A WARNING 13
CHAPTER II: MILITARY ASSISTANT TO THE SECRETARY OF STATE FOR WAR — SOME REFLECTIONS 20
CHAPTER III: GREEK ADVENTURE 51
CHAPTER IV: THE MIDDLE EAST — 1941 94
CHAPTER V: THE MIDDLE EAST — DIRECTOR OF MILITARY INTELLIGENCE 118
CHAPTER VI: WITH EIGHTH ARMY UNTIL THE BATTLE OF EL ALAMEIN 142
CHAPTER VII: MONTGOMERY 179
CHAPTER VIII: THE BATTLE OF EL ALAMEIN 216
CHAPTER IX: THE PURSUIT FROM AGHEILA TO TRIPOLI, AND THE BATTLE OF MEDENINE 239
CHAPTER X: THE BATTLE OF MARETH TO THE END IN NORTH AFRICA 268
CHAPTER XI: PREPARATIONS FOR AND THE INVASION OF SICILY 296
CHAPTER XII: ITALY — SEPTEMBER. 1943, TO JANUARY, 1944 338
CHAPTER XIII: BUSY DAYS 369
CHAPTER XIV: THE PRESS IN WAR 409
CHAPTER XV: NORTH-WEST EUROPE — I 424
CHAPTER XVI: NORTH-WEST EUROPE — II 453
CHAPTER XVII: THE END 487
CHAPTER XVIII: CONCLUSIONS 508
APPENDIX A 518

APPENDIX B (1)	520
APPENDIX B (2)	522
APPENDIX B (3)	524
APPENDIX B (4)	526
ACKNOWLEDGMENTS	527
A NOTE TO THE READER	528

FOREWORD

IN writing this book I have aimed at giving an accurate account of some of the great events of the war as I saw them. I have tried to blend history with a measure of personal reminiscence. I have stuck to that part of the war of which I had first-hand knowledge, and have refrained from probing into affairs about which I would have had to rely upon the opinions of others. As the days pass by it becomes more and more apparent how easy it is for commentators and writers, who rely upon hearsay, to produce inaccurate contributions to the war's history.

I fully realise that because of this self-imposed restriction the reader is on occasions left guessing as to what is happening elsewhere, and may not get as full a picture as he would wish. For instance, the story of the campaign in Italy stops abruptly about the Sangro River, and only touches upon the activities of the U.S. Fifth Army. In spite of these drawbacks, I feel it is better this way.

Because of the various appointments which I held, I claim to have been in a unique position for witnessing many of the war's highlights. I have no decisions to justify — I was just a staff officer. It is very natural that commanders when describing their experiences are apt to interpret events with a view to vindicating their own particular action. I am unfettered by such influences, and to the best of my belief I have been both frank and fair.

It would have been so easy for me, when dealing with the war's leading personalities, to have produced sensation by describing isolated incidents and by quoting remarks made under the stress and strain of battle. Such actions might have a certain commercial value, but would convey a wrong impression as well as being grossly unfair. Amongst strong men carrying great responsibilities there was bound to have been an occasional conflict of views — this was indeed a healthy sign. We must not forget that these men — this team of Allied Commanders — together led us to complete and final victory.

It will be seen that I am a great admirer of America — of her Commanders and her fighting men; as well as of her equipment and "go-getter" methods. I regret that some British soldiers never quite appreciated the extent of our Ally's contribution. And it seemed to surprise them and sometimes annoy them, that she should wish to run her own affairs, and take the leadership in Allied policy.

This book therefore aims at giving a true and unbiased account of the war as I saw it. I bring out the various lessons that seem to me important, and I describe the various processes and ingredients that contributed to "Operation Victory."

I give a list of acknowledgments elsewhere, but I must not fail to mention here all those commanders whom I served, and those officers on the staff who worked with me; who together made life so vivid, so interesting, and yet so bearable during those unforgettable years. This is something I shall for ever remember and cherish.

Finally, I would emphasise that this book is not an "Official History," but deals with events as I saw them — the comments and conclusions being entirely my own.

F. W. de G.
London,
October, 1946.

CHAPTER I: A WARNING

I

IN 1937 I was told that my first staff appointment was to be Brigade-Major to the Commandant of the Small Arms Schools. Before joining I thought it would be a good plan to visit our ally France, and our potential enemy, Germany, and see how they were training their infantry. By doing so I should become better equipped for my new job. I approached the War Office with this end in view. The reception my request received was not encouraging. Their attitude was at its best "very sticky."

"It would be such a business to lay on."

"No funds exist to cover such a tour."

"If you go to France or Germany, then the Germans and French will demand reciprocal visits."

I persisted in my efforts, and only after several weeks was I given the necessary permission to proceed. It was made very clear to me that any payment from Army funds to cover such a trip was quite out of the question — not even a railway warrant to Dover was permitted!

I was delighted that at long last I had the matter fixed, and willingly accepted the expenses involved. The plan was to spend two or three days with the French at Mourmelon near Chalons-sur-Marne, and then go to Germany and visit the German Infantry School at Dobrietz.

The day before I was due to leave for Paris, I bumped into an old friend of mine from King's African Rifles days — Vans Agnew. He agreed to accompany me to the Continent.

After a couple of days in Paris I left for Chalons-sur-Marne, putting up at a small and rather uncomfortable hotel in the town.

The Small Arms Schools at Mourmelon were based upon a training brigade, which was situated amongst a maze of very old, very untidy, and very depressing looking huts. Barracks of any type, wherever they may be, are often eyesores, but this collection of buildings, with the dilapidated roads around them were quite the most miserable I had struck.

This first glimpse of the general set-up was characteristic of most things I saw during my stay. Everything done on a very cheap basis, and improvisation had to be resorted to in order to offset lack of funds and equipment.

I was received with the greatest kindness, frankness and consideration. I do not mean to be patronising when I say I felt a very genuine wave of sympathy for these French soldiers who were being starved for so many of the sinews of war. Many times I was told in answer to an enquiry, "Oh, we understand there are plenty in the mobilization stores."

It was interesting that one of the few days I had available was devoted to a tour of the devastated areas. This was obviously done for a purpose, to show what France had suffered in the last war. My guides on several occasions expressed the opinion that the next war must not be fought on French soil. One had every sympathy with this view, but it did perhaps symbolise the attitude of some of the leaders of France a year or two later.

In spite of having seen only a small corner of the French Army, the general picture based upon much talk and the various things I saw, suggested that France had a long way to go before she could say she possessed a really modern Army.

And now from Lazarus to Dives.

II

This was my first visit to Germany since the occupation of the Rhineland, and even in the train we sensed how things had changed. The railways were very clean, the railway employees correct and alive. The food in the restaurant cars was simple — rationing was in progress — and the stewards most efficient. After the meals a tin box was handed round to collect subscriptions for Hitler's Winter Relief Fund. I'm afraid we contributed handsomely!

We did not arrive in Berlin until close upon 1 a.m., and drove straight to our hotel, the Esplanada. Upon arrival I was surprised to see General, then Brigadier, Mason Macfarlane, our Military Attaché. He took me aside and said he had one or two things to say before I settled in. He warned me about taking care of any documents I possessed, and also about discretion when using the telephones. He said, "Any telephone conversation can be listened to, and it is certain your room will be searched."

In spite of what I had heard of current conditions in Germany I was a bit shaken by this. However, within the next two days I was to learn how right he was.

I handed over my report upon the things I had seen in France, so that he could lock it up in the Embassy safe.

Two days later, Vans Agnew and I laid a trap to see whether our belongings were being tampered with. We put various quite unimportant papers in the drawer of a cupboard which had a very formidable sort of Yale lock. We placed the papers in a none too tidy heap, and then drew very faint lines in pencil so that we could see at once whether one particular item had been moved in relation to another. We also listed the order in which they rested. After my return from a visit to the German Infantry School I opened the drawer and found that the papers had been moved about and were not even in the order in which they had been stacked. It was a little thing, but it certainly gave me a queer turn, and made me realise what a different world this was to the one from which we came.

The two days I spent at the German Infantry School at Dobrietz were intensely interesting — but also intensely frightening and depressing. Mason Macfarlane came with me, and he was, I believe, very glad to get this opportunity of seeing the school for the first time. The Germans were not very liberal with their invitations to Military Attachés in those days.

The Army were extremely lucky to have this wonderful school at Dobrietz. It was situated a few miles west of Berlin, on the edge of an enormous training area. It used to be the Olympic Village. This was built especially to accommodate and feed all the competitors during the Olympic Games held recently in Germany. There were large modern houses, gymnasiums, cookhouses, etc., etc. Artificial lakes had been constructed, woods planted, and the whole place resembled a charming garden city. After the Games the Army asked Hitler if they could have the "Village," and so it was given to the Wehrmacht.

We were received with great cordiality and shown all forms of training and types of equipment. I was very impressed with the relationship between officer and man — it was excellent, and from the smartness and general tone of the place, it was easy to see that the German Army had lost none of its discipline.

The German small arms weapons and their training methods were well in advance of ours. There was no sign of financial restriction, and everything was being done on a particularly lavish scale.

It was obvious, for instance, how seriously the Germans were taking the threat from low-flying aircraft. They had learned their lessons in the Spanish Civil War, and were evolving methods and equipment for dealing with it.

One day we were given luncheon in the principal mess. It was a delightful building with many fine oil paintings of famous soldiers adorning the walls. These had been loaned by various well-known German families. I remember one particularly fine picture of Blucher which was pointed out to me with some such remark as: "From the days when we fought together!"

We had a simple but extremely well-cooked lunch, and the menu cards had the Nazi flag and Union Jack displayed together. At the end of the meal the Commandant made a very pretty little speech, referring to those foolish days when we fought each other in the last war, and how both nations realised the other's sterling soldierly qualities. Frequently during lunch my neighbours made somewhat disparaging remarks about the French, and once it was suggested that "next time" it would be better if we tackled that nation together.

I came away from Dobrietz thoroughly disturbed. I felt that if this was a true specimen of the efficiency of the German Army, then we were indeed in a sad position.

Whilst I was in Berlin celebrations took place on the fourth anniversary of Hitler's election as Chancellor. I spent a very interesting and yet depressing day.

I left the hotel early and took up my position in the crowd just opposite the Chancellery in the Wilhelmstrasse. I was only a few yards from the balcony, and facing it. For an hour or two squads of storm-troopers marched past with their standards — machine-like, wooden, and inspiring. The crowd were very enthusiastic. There were two types of enthusiasm. The first was organised and semi-artificial, and produced by expert cheer leaders. The other was wholly spontaneous. This latter type was in evidence around me. People went quite mad cheering the troops and shouting for Hitler. One elderly woman, shouting "Fuehrer, Fuehrer, Fuehrer," scrambled up a lamp post next door to us and sat perched upon the cross bar waving her umbrella, a feat I would have had no hope of achieving. I remember thinking what an extraordinary creed this was, which could give this old lady the agility of an ape.

When Hitler and his gang appeared in person on the veranda the crowd became delirious and shortly after this I felt I had had enough of mass hysteria and pushed my way back to the hotel. But even here we got no peace. All that afternoon and into the night and early morning the marching went on. Wherever one went one heard the tramp, tramp, tramp of feet. You saw these chunks of machinelike humanity moving through the streets, a never-ending procession of storm troopers singing their marching songs with deep throated rhythm. As night fell torches were carried which gave added significance to the scene. Here were the men who would shortly set all Europe and the world alight. I hated it all, and I felt frightened.

I think it was the next night that the "old Germany" gathered for a party in the Esplanada Hotel. It was a brave effort. "Little Willie" headed the list and was dressed as a cavalryman in his sabre-rattling uniform. We could see many frocks had been brought out from lavender-scented boxes, and stout and proud-looking dowagers were displaying the remnants from their now depleted jewel cases. As onlookers at this somewhat sordid array, we felt the regime which they represented had rightly had its day.

When waiting to catch our train and sitting sipping champagne with the German officer who had accompanied me throughout the visit, he suddenly turned to me and said: "If we soldiers could get together and muzzle our politicians then we should have peace." It was a strange parting shot.

I was glad I had obtained these very limited glimpses of the French and German Armies, and I was sure the trip had been of value. Besides the various technical matters connected with my new post which I had gleaned, there was the "feel" of things to come. If the storm were to burst, comparisons of our preparedness with that of Germany were certainly very odious.

CHAPTER II: MILITARY ASSISTANT TO THE SECRETARY OF STATE FOR WAR — SOME REFLECTIONS

I

ONE morning in June, 1939, I arrived in my office at Netheravon to find a letter from the Military Secretary asking whether I wished to be considered with some others for the appointment of Military Assistant to the Secretary of State for War. I like changes, and felt it was about time that I was removed from this peaceful existence on Salisbury Plain. To leave the realms of minor tactics and infantry weapons for that of the high political and strategical strata was certainly an intriguing proposition. I therefore replied that I should like to be considered, and was duly summoned to the War office for an interview with Hore-Belisha.

I was shown into the Secretary of State's room and was put into a chair facing the full glare from the window. We talked for twenty minutes about such subjects as my regiment, my present job, the militia, and the training of officers. The interview was then terminated and appeared quite inconclusive, and the particular appointment for which I was being considered was not even mentioned. I then returned to Netheravon once again, and after nearly three weeks — by which time I thought another applicant had been successful — I received orders to hand over and report at the War Office the very next day.

Hore-Belisha I found a most colourful character. Initially I did not take to him very much, but later I developed a great affection and regard for my new master. One was made to work very hard indeed, and those first few weeks were a nightmare. Gradually, however, I managed to get my head above water, and in October or November I was allowed to have an assistant in order to ease the strain.

The thing that struck me most about the Secretary of State was his extreme sensitiveness to the Press. He had started life as a journalist, and the Press had been largely responsible for making him into a public figure. He had all the morning dailies and would browse through them in bed before he got up. Criticism, whether in the Press or in the House, upset him, and I am sure he will now admit that he occupied far too much of his time in dealing with such matters. For instance, a letter in the *Daily Mirror* from a soldier asking how he was expected to live on half a sausage for breakfast, would take up a considerable amount of his time, and that of other high officials.

He was undoubtedly an ambitious man, and when discussing this subject with me one day he said: "Well, surely a carpenter wishes to be successful at his own particular job!"

I am convinced, however, that he had a burning desire to popularise the Army in the eyes of the nation, for he realised that unless this could be done we should continue to suffer at the expense of the Royal Navy and the Royal Air Force. The major reforms which are associated with his name, as well as some of the smaller matters in which he took an interest, were instrumental in achieving this aim. In referring to these reforms one often hears such remarks as: "Oh, these were nothing to do with Hore-Belisha, they had all been worked out by the War Office long before he arrived." I agree that to some extent this was true, but on the other hand it was Hore-Belisha who gave them his blessing, and it was he who had the courage to see them through. To him, therefore, must go the credit.

The biggest single factor in his life had been his mother, and when she died he was for a time quite lost. When discussing her one night he said: "Since my mother died, I have lost much of my ambition."

He is an extremely charitable man, of that I am quite certain, and he has often suffered criticism merely because he was so determined that some individual should be given a "fair do." And this applied to high and low alike.

He possessed great drive, and when convinced that he was right, would fight whatever the opposition. Most of the top soldiers in the War Office were frightened of him, although they would not admit it. On one occasion a certain distinguished soldier had asked me to get the Secretary of State to agree to some proposal for sending divisions out with the Expeditionary Force with a modified scale of equipment. I knew his views on this matter and said I had little hope of success. I returned with the answer I had expected. "Good God, man," said the soldier, "give me the paper, I'll see he does," and off he rushed. Being interested to see how he could succeed where I had failed, I shortly followed him into the office, and was amused to hear, "Yes, Sir" and "No, Sir" and "I quite agree, Sir." There was no change in Hore-Belisha's decision!

Delay infuriated him, and he never understood the rather cumbersome War Office machinery, why he had to wait until a question had been passed through the "proper channels" before he could get the answer. Why couldn't he speak at once to the officer who had the information? He would, however, sometimes send for the officer, and this would infuriate the more senior soldiers, and led to a lot of criticism. Because of this I would often find myself in a difficult position, and had to spend a lot of my time smoothing out such troubles.

I had a very full day. At 7 a.m. would arrive the night's telegrams, and any Cabinet papers that were still outstanding. These I would have to scan through whilst dressing and breakfasting. By 8.15 I had to be at Hore-Belisha's house, where I would spend an hour or so giving him a verbal synopsis of the various papers and telegrams. Like Montgomery he disliked reading such things. I would sometimes start in the bedroom, move on to the bathroom, and then to the breakfast table. We would then drive to the War Office where I would finish off my business, during which time he would see such people as the C.I.G.S. and the Permanent Under Secretary of State. These verbal summaries of Cabinet and other papers were by no means easy for a mere soldier; for besides dealing with strictly military matters, a variety of other subjects would be included. There were, for instance, papers submitted by the Chancellor of the Exchequer on high finance, and others by, say, the Minister of Agriculture on such subjects as Milk Marketing Schemes; and I had to know sufficient to withstand cross-examination.

I would, of course, accompany my master when he visited troops, or when he attended service dinners, and other functions. In addition, I would attend at the House when he was making a speech or taking part in some debate. I enjoyed all this immensely, for to my mind there are few orators who can equal Hore-Belisha. And this brings me to the preparation of his speeches. I used to have the idea that the professional politician could prepare and deliver speeches with little effort, but I soon found this was not the case. The majority took an immense amount of trouble over what they were going to say. We used to work in the Secretary of State's room at the War Office until the early hours of the morning building up his speeches. Each sentence and phrase would be tested and rehearsed. Sometimes after a hard day's work I would begin to nod over the table, but I was soon brought to full consciousness by Hore-Belisha who might be at that moment rehearsing a phrase, with "My boy, I can see that didn't move you — we must change it!"

But Hore-Belisha could, however, make the most delightful impromptu speeches, and could also deliver a big oration without his notes. I used to "twit" him about his inability to do the latter, but he proved me wrong. He had taken a lot of trouble over a speech he was to make at the Guildhall at the opening of an Army Welfare Week in London. In the car driving there he glanced through the notes, and then handed them back to me. After we had arrived, and the necessary introductions had taken place, he was asked to proceed to the platform to make his speech. I then took the script from my pocket and handed it to him. He, however, waved it aside and moved away. Everything went off extremely well, the speech was a success, but was not exactly in accordance with the original. After we had got into the car to drive back, he turned to me and said: "Well, you see I can make a speech without my notes."

He was possessed of a fine sense of humour, and when off duty would sometimes describe meetings which he had attended, taking off the various personalities with delightful ease.

After the war started, I moved into the office of the Secretary of State's Principal Private Secretary. I enjoyed the change, for Roseway was a delightful companion, and he taught me a great deal. Later we took it in turns to take the minutes at meetings of the Army Council, and in spite of the extra work, I welcomed the arrangement, for it kept me fully in the picture.

II

When the war started, there was great speculation as to who would command the British Expeditionary Force. Gort, Ironside, Kirke and Dill were names mentioned. Ironside, in view of his existing appointment as Inspector of Overseas Forces, undoubtedly thought he might be selected. He would often breeze into our office and ask to see the Secretary of State, would be most friendly, and then on occasions would leave one of his strategic studies behind him with some such remark as "You might like to read this little paper I've written." Hore-Belisha took a great liking to Ironside, and once said to me, "There is a man I could work with."

Finally Gort was appointed Commander-in-Chief and Ironside took his place as Chief of the Imperial General Staff.

August was an exciting month for me. On, I think, the 4th of August Parliament adjourned, and the Ministers dispersed on holiday. Our Military Intelligence were convinced that war against Poland was certain, and yet in Government circles there was undoubtedly a feeling that something would turn up to prevent it. I suppose it was the after effect of Munich.

I was up in Scotland and Hore-Belisha was in France when a full Cabinet meeting was called for August 21st. The situation was reviewed, and on the 23rd Chamberlain sent his letter to Hitler making it quite clear that we would fulfil our obligations if Poland was attacked.

Hitler's reply was breathlessly awaited. He had behaved very badly when Neville Henderson had presented the letter to him, but on the 25th he replied. It was in this letter that he made an effort to keep us out, more or less guaranteeing the British Empire if we did not fight.

I was sitting in the Secretary of State's office when a message from the Foreign Office said that Hitler's reply was on its way, and was now being deciphered. I was sent over in order to get the gist. I was shown the various sections as they came up from the decoding room, and I was delighted to note how firm were the Foreign Office officials that this time there must be no appeasement.

The Cabinet's reply went off, and it now looked as if war was certain. There was, however, one more development which raised some people's hopes. This was Goering's effort which recently was discussed at the Nuremberg trials. He had a talk with our Ambassador on August 31st, and then about the same time a report was circulated that a "go between" was flying to London. This was the Swedish business man Dahlerus. The aircraft was routed in, and our anti-aircraft guns were warned not to fire. But hopes soon petered out, nothing came of the last-minute effort, and Germany attacked Poland on the 1st of September.

All kinds of rumours were now in circulation. Here are some examples. The German plan was to remain on the defensive in the West, and to bomb London and Paris immediately war broke out. German public opinion was against the war, the morale of the German Army was bad, and their general staff was much concerned. Many German generals had resigned. When Hitler interviewed his generals immediately after his Reichstag speech he broke down and left the room without completing what he had to say.

I was lucky enough to have attended the House of Commons during those momentous days, and in particular the 2nd of September was a day I shall long remember. After an afternoon's Cabinet meeting it was announced that a statement would be made in the House by the Prime Minister at about 6 p.m. It was expected, of course, that this would be the announcement of our declaration of war. I thought of the scene at Westminster in 1914 when Sir Edward Grey made his historic speech. I therefore got to my seat in plenty of time. At first there was a subdued atmosphere, but by about 7 p.m. the House became excited as it was obvious that something unexpected must have happened. About 8 p.m. the Prime Minister appeared, and at once all was quiet.

Chamberlain's speech was anything but impressive. He appeared still unconvinced that war was inevitable. He had appealed to Mussolini to save Europe from disaster. He looked ill at ease, and his words brought protests from all over the House. The opposition speeches showed that there was genuine anxiety that there might be another "Munich" around the corner. The House then adjourned and Hore-Belisha took me along to dinner.

There was an air of gaiety in the House of Commons dining-room. I sat next to Dalton, the present Chancellor. But underlying this cheerful exterior, lobbying was going on to make certain that this time there would be no backing out. Hore-Belisha and others arranged to see the Prime Minister later that night to impress upon him the need for firmness.

At 11 o'clock the next morning Chamberlain announced our declaration of war. Not so long afterwards I was sitting in my office when the air raid sirens wailed, and I wondered whether the rumour about the German intention to attack London and Paris immediately war was declared was true. I looked out of the window and watched the people in Whitehall. Some started running, some looked up into the sky, whilst others went quietly on their way. The die was cast, and I wondered what was in store for us all.

III

Hore-Belisha has been blamed for the delay with which our Army was got into the field, and also for his decision to double the Territorial Army in 1939. I will describe the problems and process of expansion as I saw them.

One should bear in mind that it was not until April, 1939, that conscription was finally accepted by the nation, and then only against considerable opposition. In fact Hore-Belisha had to threaten Chamberlain with his resignation unless he agreed to let the Bill go before the House. By the middle of July the first batch of Militiamen were being trained, and six weeks later this vast organisation had to be scrapped when mobilisation plans were put into effect. This transition worked remarkably smoothly.

From the strictly military point of view, the doubling of the Territorial Army was most unsatisfactory, because it denuded existing regular and T.A. units of trained personnel and in some cases of weapons as well. The new units were mostly composed of inexperienced and untrained officers and men.

There is, however, something to be said for the scheme: —

(a) Politically at that time it was a necessary step towards conscription — a means to an end.
(b) It meant financial approval for the extra money required for building additional barracks, ranges, etc.
(c) It gave the necessary authority for ordering the weapons and equipment for the new units.
(d) As the availability of weapons and war material were the major factors limiting the rate at which units could be got ready for war, this plan did not really interfere with the production of trained formations as much as some people made out.

Immediately war broke out a body called the "Land Forces Committee" was set up with Sir Samuel Hoare in the chair. Their object was to make recommendations to the War Cabinet as to the expansion of the Army. To cut a long story short they asked that approval should be given to the following programme: —

(a) To raise, train and equip X divisions during the first year of war.
(b) To raise, train and equip Y divisions by the end of the second year of war.
(c) To aim at Z divisions by the end of the third year of war.[1]

The War Cabinet approved, but as sometimes happens the Cabinet decision was not sufficiently cut and dried to beat the Treasury.

The result of this was a series of arguments between the War Office, the Ministry of Supply and the Treasury, as to how far industry could be organised and materials purchased for the expansion of the Army. The first year presented no difficulties and so far as I recollect the second year requirements were more or less agreed to, but the third year requirements met considerable opposition.

The R.A.F. demands added to the Army's difficulties. The War Cabinet had agreed that they should have first priority, and so rather naturally they were apprehensive lest the Army's bids should interfere with their own production.

Yet another difficulty which the Army experienced was the question of the skilled labour which had already been called up. In spite of the reserved occupations decision, a large number of skilled workmen were called up and *required* by the Army.

---

[1] I cannot remember the exact numbers. I think the total aimed at was between fifty and sixty divisions.

Soon after the war started the Navy, the R.A.F. and munition industries started crying out for the release of these men. Some of these requests were sound and others appeared to have little justification. Each competitor naturally thought his own demands were paramount. Some cases had to go up to the Cabinet for decision, whilst others were settled mutually between departments. The Adjutant-General's[2] and General Wemyss's relations with the Ministry of National Service were excellent and many snags were removed by their efforts.

I always felt that there were many people in high places who thought that we could get through the war without any real fighting on land, and the poison of complacency was rife. No doubt because of this there did seem to be a reluctance to commit industry to such a gigantic change as would be necessitated if rapid production in the equipping of the (third year) divisions were set in motion. Another reason was the difficulty of deciding upon the correct balance between the Services at this early stage of the war. There would obviously not be sufficient manpower and industrial resources to meet all demands; therefore there was a tendency to go slow for a bit.

The Chamberlain Government was always faced with the difficulty of obtaining wholehearted labour co-operation. It was obvious that the Trade Unions would go all out if they had some share in the Government; and it was certain that the Labour Members would refuse to serve in a Government of which Chamberlain was the Prime Minister. This question of allocation of material to the Army was only tackled in earnest when Churchill started the "Military Co-ordination" Committee which examined all requirements of the three Services in detail. In unofficial circles this Committee was known as "The Crazy Gang."

---

[2] Gordon Finlayson.

I rarely attended these meetings, but I read all the minutes and the various papers issued. It was very clear that Churchill, who was then First Lord of the Admiralty, was the driving force, and he produced a logical approach to planning on the basis of a long war. Without his efforts at this time, I shudder to think where we might have been.

IV

The Army's air needs were another matter in which Hore-Belisha took a great personal interest.

When the war broke out a Joint War Office/Air Ministry Committee was sitting to consider the Army's air requirements. But as far as one could see the results generally led to compromises, delay and recommendations far below our real needs. It must be realised, however, that the R.A.F. were embarked upon a colossal plan of expansion, and so had their hands full. Aircraft of any type were in very short supply. Nevertheless I am certain the Air Ministry never appreciated what the Army would eventually require in the way of tactical support. It needed great pressure from Hore-Belisha, with the inevitable friction in the process, before a sound planning policy was accepted.

After the end of the short German campaign in Poland, the Secretary of State for War decided to start a campaign for increased air support for the Army, and he even hinted at the need for an Army Air Arm. The matter was first considered by the Land Forces Committee, and papers were prepared for the Cabinet setting out the Army's case. When we went into back history, it was sad to see how the Army had let things slide after the R.A.F. had its responsibilities defined under Army Order 100 of 1918. For instance, we were supposed to have a major say in the type, design and numbers of the aircraft we required.

Several well-known people interested themselves in our problems and various projects were produced whereby it was alleged aircraft could be built for the Army at great speed, by firms who were not as yet required by the Air Ministry. I don't believe any of these plans materialised, but it certainly got the light focused upon our needs.

Other papers were produced by the Air Ministry setting out their case. With so much lee-way to make up themselves, they were naturally loath to produce specialised aircraft which would be of use only to the Army. That is why they were so opposed to the dive-bomber. There was quite a strong body of opinion who were even against the use of aircraft in the close tactical support role. "Why not use your artillery?" they said.

Eventually a meeting was arranged between the two Secretaries of State — Hore-Belisha and Kingsley Wood. They each brought along their advisers, and soon the discussion centred around the use of aircraft in the low-flying or close support role. Before the meeting I had been lucky enough to have had access to a report by one of the Air Ministry observers in Poland, and in this document the officer concerned had stressed the successful employment of the German aircraft in the most intimate role of close support. I think to a large extent he attributed the speed of the German advance to this use of air power. I showed this report to Hore-Belisha before the meeting, and he told me to keep it handy. At a convenient moment Hore-Belisha asked his colleague how the Germans used their aircraft in Poland. Kingsley-Wood asked one of his advisers to answer the question. This officer made a little speech about the strategic role, and how the rail centres had been attacked, but he kept clear of the very close support given to the Army. Having heard him out the Secretary of State said, "Well, how do you account for these views expressed by your own observer in your own report?" and passed over the extract to Kingsley Wood. There was no adequate answer, and so Hore-Belisha said he thought there was no useful purpose in arguing any further, and that he would now have to refer the whole matter to the Prime Minister.

After an effort at compromise, Chamberlain ordered Chatfield[3] to deal with the question and produce an agreed solution. Eventually an agreement was reached which was a great step forward insofar as we were concerned. The main decisions reached were: —

(a) An improvement in the control of the R.A.F. component with the British Expeditionary Force in France.
(b) A certain number of medium bomber squadrons were *earmarked* for use with the B.E.F.
(c) The Army was to have a say in the design and type of aircraft that would operate in its support.
(d) Inter-service training in direct support would be carried out.
(e) Two new branches would be started at the War Office and at the Air Ministry, their task being to study all matters relating to the air support of the Army, and to make recommendations.

Later, of course, there were other changes, until we eventually got what we wanted, i.e. specialised tactical groups working with each Army.

Let me say in conclusion that I don't blame the Air Ministry for the lack of adequate air resources for the support of the

---

[3] Minister for the Co-ordination of Defence.

Army. We as a Service never gave sufficient thought to the whole problem. We never grasped the lessons that were there to be learnt during the Spanish Civil War. And we certainly never pressed our claims. This was just another sphere in which we found ourselves unprepared owing to the complacent attitude of the nation as a whole.

V

In view of our present relations with Russia it is very interesting to look back upon the negotiations which we carried out with that country just before the war in an effort to get her to join in an alliance with France and ourselves against Germany.

Shortly after leaving the War Office in early 1940 I was lecturing at the Haifa Staff College on the "General Situation," and I have found the notes which I used. The following is what I said about this rather sad story, and because of subsequent history I think it is not without interest.

The courting of Russia was one of the major pre-war events and we are still asking each other, "Did Russia wish for a pact with the Western Democracies?" A study of the negotiations which we conducted with Russia is therefore interesting.

There appeared to be a strong element who hoped we would not have to go as far as a military alliance, and Russia realised this, and knew what we first wanted, i.e. a political victory over Germany, which I am sure many people felt would be sufficient to deter Hitler in his schemes for expansion.

Now Russia was a realist and still is. She knew what we were after, and she very naturally wanted something in return. Very soon in our negotiations with her it became clear that her eyes were focused on the Baltic States, Western Poland up to the Curzon Line, and even Bessarabia. Negotiations proved a pitiful tale. They were conducted by our Ambassador in Moscow and a Foreign Office official.[4] I am told this was a mistake, for Russia had expected a more important delegation to discuss such high affairs of state. The sequence of events followed these lines:

Russia made certain requests; we refused and then later gave way, after which Molotov said the bidding in the meantime had been raised, and so it went on.

Public opinion gradually overwhelmed the anti-Russian feeling at home, and great efforts were made to reach an agreement, and by July 18th matters had boiled down to two main questions:

(*a*) The definition of indirect aggression, and

(*b*) Military conversations.

With regard to (*a*) Molotov wished to be allowed, with our backing, to enter the neighbouring States if in the Russian opinion indirect aggression had taken place. In view of the German technique in Norway one feels rather sympathetic to Russian foresight. They could legitimately say such action was merely in the interests of their security. On the other hand, we felt we would be signing the death warrant of those States.

Molotov said that without a military convention coming into force at the same time as the political agreement, the whole thing would be worthless. I can hardly blame him for this. He was determined that we would not get political kudos without giving him military support in return. However we stuck out against this indirect aggression clause, but agreed to start military conversations.

The composition of the Anglo-French Mission was possibly a mistake. No one higher than a Major-General was at the head

---

[4] Sir William Strang.

of our section of it, and the ranks of the Navy and Air Force members were equivalent. It was mutually agreed that the French should lead as regards Army matters, whilst we would lead with the Naval and Air matters.

Of course these conversations were full of pitfalls. To be of any value we had to be frank; in doing so we found difficulty in disguising our weaknesses and also in avoiding giving away our plans.

Molotov was very careful to see that the world was not given any encouragement to think Britain and Russia were collaborating. For instance, when we suggested that a joint *communiqué* should be issued in the three capitals saying that the conversations had now reached the stage when military discussions were to take place, Molotov would have nothing to do with such a proposal, nor was he in favour of unilateral ones. He said it might tend to "mislead the public." On August 19th and 20th a crisis occurred when the question of the Russians entering Poland was raised, but the Polish attitude remained solidly against such action. On August 21st, Voroshilov, who was head of the Russian delegation, said he was ready to meet us whenever an affirmative answer to their request regarding entry into Poland was available, but in the event of a negative reply there was no purpose in holding further meetings. And so the conference adjourned *sine die*.

On August 22nd the bomb burst and the German-Soviet pact became known.

In summing up I said:

> I think to start with Russia was prepared to come to an agreement with us against German expansion provided:
> (i) She was allowed to strengthen her position strategically by the absorption of the Baltic States and Western Poland.

To do this — with our backing and support — was the purpose of the definition of "indirect aggression." This we were not prepared to agree to.

The question is whether we should have agreed. I am sure that public opinion in all parties at the time would never have allowed us to do so. But as I have already said, the Russians did appreciate the extent to which a State could be captured even before the soldiers entered.

Undoubtedly Germany agreed to these Russian demands. (ii) The second factor which Russian co-operation depended upon was the extent of support France and Britain could give in the West. Russia — rather naturally — did not want to bear the full weight of the German attack.

I'm afraid she was not encouraged by the information she gleaned during the military conversations. Our help for some time would be in the naval and economic fields. We had already decided that our initial strategy must be defensive in character, and so we could not start an air or land offensive.

VI

During my time at the War Office we only had one major scare concerning a German offensive in the West. This occurred in November, 1939. To appreciate fully Belgium's attitude in the early part of the war, it is necessary to look back to 1937. In this year she changed her policy from that of a defensive alliance to one of strict neutrality. From then onwards she took great care not to do anything that might be construed as unneutral. For instance, when building fortifications around Brussels to protect her from a German advance, she built similar defences sited to oppose a possible attack by France. Naturally at the same time all contacts between the Belgian General Staff and the French and British ceased.

It was, I think, at the end of August, 1939, that our Government declared her acceptance of Belgian neutrality, and in the latter's reply it was stated that if contrary to expectations Belgium was to be the object of aggression she would not hesitate to appeal to the United Kingdom, and she would expect immediate assistance. This was rather like having your cake and eating it, and so about the middle of September we pointed out to the Belgian Government the dangers that might ensue if no staff talks took place, and no reconnaissances were permitted. Without these very necessary preliminaries we could hold out very little hope that the "immediate assistance" referred to would be very effective.

Gamelin was from the beginning very keen on a move into Belgium for the simple reason that it would shorten the line the Allies held in the West and save some forty divisions. Our estimates of the coming German strength were frightening when compared with our own, and so such a saving would be much to our advantage. The Belgian Government, however, would not budge from its former attitude.

Having finished off the Polish campaign the Germans immediately started to build up their forces opposite the frontiers of Holland, Belgium and France. And before long they were in a position to launch a major offensive at very short notice, and without any great change in their dispositions. During October many rumours were circulating about German action in the West, and these were reinforced by air photos showing that several extra bridges had been constructed across the Rhine.

About November 7th, Holland and Belgium became acutely alarmed about German intentions, for, besides the massing of troops opposite their borders, many reconnaissance flights were being carried out over their territory. But still there was no move from the Belgian Government. There was, however, a difference of opinion within that government as to what action they should take.

Eventually on November 11th, they agreed to listen to any information which we were prepared to impart, but even this change of heart was of little use, for there were several restrictions, particularly with regard to whom we were allowed to contact, and there was reluctance in allowing the French to participate. As the B.E.F. was under command of a French general — Georges — this was a most unreasonable stipulation. It was at this stage that Admiral Keyes, who was a close personal friend of the King of the Belgians, went over to see what he could do.

November 12th was an exciting day. We expected at any moment that the Belgians would co-operate, and Gamelin was waiting ready to carry out his plan.

Hore-Belisha was somewhat apprehensive regarding the hazards of advancing into Belgium to the chosen line, and wishing to satisfy himself that we could attain our object without major German ground and air interference, asked the Air Ministry for an exposé of our air plan for delaying a German move from the east.

In answer to his request two or three R.A.F. officers arrived with an enormous map. After some trouble this was hoisted up against the wall in the Secretary of State's office, and then we gathered round to hear the plan.

The map embraced the various routes by which the enemy could advance, and it was covered with a great number of black spots — some large, some small. It was explained that these represented potential targets which when hit would either interfere with the enemy's advance, or prevent supplies reaching his forces. The targets selected were bridges, crossroads and defiles which constituted bottle-necks along the various routes.

The plot was explained in a confident manner. The enemy could only advance by the following routes — these were explained. If he came this way then targets Nos. 000 to 000 would be attacked — if by that route another series would be engaged. In theory it was all very nice, but there appeared to be many major snags in practice. The targets had to be hit accurately, and even then it was questionable whether much harm would have been done. To achieve any prolonged effect, sustained attacks would have been necessary. How were we going to fulfil these heavy commitments? Had we the right type of aircraft for both day and night attacks, and had we enough of them? Would they survive the enemy's fighters and A.A. defence? These were some of the questions which I'm sure those who were watching turned over in their minds.

The exposé came to an end, and silence descended upon the room. After a pause Hore-Belisha asked: "In view of our shortage of medium bombers, what do you propose to use against these numerous targets by day?" There was no satisfactory answer.

The large map was rolled up again — the R.A.F. staff officers departed, and we were left with an uneasy foreboding as to the dangers of a policy which dictated a move of our forces into Belgium. The R.A.F. could not be blamed — the tools were just not available to implement such an ambitious plan.

Still the Belgians would not "play," and Gamelin became very impatient and more or less issued an ultimatum on the lines of "Now or never." One must appreciate his feelings, for he had concentrated large forces close to the Belgian frontier ready to move across; and this presented a very vulnerable target to the German Air Force.

Two days later the scare died down and the Allied troops returned to their previous positions.

I am not clear from studying the German records whether this November threat was anything more than "cover." It undoubtedly gave them the knowledge that we hoped to move forward into Belgium when the moment arrived. This was most valuable information for them. It was not, however, a very good time from the climatic point of view to start an offensive. This factor would have diminished to a large degree the strength of the German Air Force.

In May, 1940, we left our strong defensive position and came out into the open to oppose the advance of the stronger German forces. And the weather was perfect from the attackers' point of view, and allowed the German Air Force to develop their full weight of attack. Our action in going forward can be criticised from the strictly military angle, but we undoubtedly derived a measure of political kudos from it, and in any case I very much doubt whether the ultimate result of the campaign would have been altered if we had remained where we were and waited for the enemy in our well prepared positions.

VII

I was not at the War Office when we despatched our ill-fated expedition to Norway; but I saw the way things were shaping before I left. It is such a good example of how political factors dictate an unsound military policy that I think it is worth recording what I know.

Certainly early on the soldier was entirely opposed to any action on our part in Scandinavia. The reasons were obvious.

At that stage of the war we were lamentably short of troops and equipment, and in addition France was pressing us to send more forces to the main front.

But the public's eyes were focussed upon Finland's fight against Russia. Gradually a great wave of sympathy was built up for this modern "David" who was holding his own against a big power which was in alliance with our enemy. The Government was being pressed on every side to send assistance to the Finns.

With the early Finnish successes against what we now know to have been second class formations of the Red Army, the pressure increased. There was a call for volunteers and for material to be sent. Then the economist got busy and pointed out the advantages of stopping the Swedish iron ore supplies from reaching Germany. Could we not gain a footing in that area, and so achieve this desirable object? Many people now became obsessed with this idea. If successful, our intervention in Scandinavia might undermine Germany's industrial strength by reducing its iron ore supplies, and at the same time it would weaken Russia — our potential enemy.

The Services were now told to study and prepare plans for sending men and material to help Finland. This would of course involve the use of Norwegian bases, and sufficient troops to help Norway in the most likely event of Germany taking counter measures.

The Navy, I believe, said that they could guarantee the forces across and their subsequent supply. But as far as I know, any action on our part was always dependent upon Norway agreeing to our arrival. *No opposed landings were contemplated.* On this premise, the Joint Planners got down to working out detailed plans.

Norway would not, however, agree to our intervention, and Finland collapsed. And I guess the old plan was then put away.

Subsequently the Germans invaded Norway and popular clamour demanded that we take some counter-action. The ill-fated expedition sailed and achieved no useful purpose. I must presume that the soldiers still opposed the expedition on strictly military grounds, and were forced to act by the politicians. If, on the other hand, the politician was led by the soldier to think that it was a reasonable military risk, then those at the War Office can be held very much to blame. For never was an expedition more doomed to failure; neither was it equipped nor organised for the task it was meant to play. It possessed none of the ingredients that would give it any chance of success. The only other excuse could be that our Intelligence of the enemy's intentions and strength in Norway was hopelessly at fault. I will leave the detailed historian to fathom out the story.

VIII

I now come to the events leading up to Hore-Belisha's resignation from the appointment of Secretary of State for War. Few people know any of the inner story of an event which caused a colossal sensation in the country, and featured as headline news for several days. "Hore-Belisha ousted by the Brass-hats" was typical of the posters one saw. In my view this was nearer the truth than many believed. For rightly or wrongly some of the "Brass-hats" were not favourably disposed towards the Secretary of State, and a visit he paid to the B.E.F. in November produced the ammunition for which some were waiting. I will describe this visit as I saw it.

We left London on November 16th by air, and as foggy conditions persisted on the Continent, we were unable to fly direct to Arras, but had to make for Paris instead. We landed at Le Bourget about 4 p.m. and drove straight to the British Embassy, where we all had tea. After this we took a train to Arras, arriving there rather late. We fed on the train and drove to the Commander-in-Chief's château where after a short talk and a drink we went to bed. Our late arrival, which was due to no fault of Hore-Belisha's, I could see was not very popular! The next two days we were up early and toured the British front. The weather was bad and wet, but the original programme was adhered to. The Secretary of State had designed a special pair of boots for the visit. They were a sort of Wellington — wool lined, with a zip fastener up the back. He was very pleased with them at first, but before long the water got in through the zip, and the inside became very unpleasant. He never showed his discomfort during the day, but confided his disappointment at the failure of his design that evening when we got in.

The front which we had been given to hold was a long one for the available troops, and the winter conditions had caused a great deal of flooding. A large anti-tank obstacle had been constructed, which in most places consisted of a deep ditch. Blockhouses, built by the French, were sited every thousand yards or so, and from them anti-tank weapons and machine guns could cover the obstacle. Everyone appeared very pleased with this arrangement, but we now know what little reliance can be placed upon this type of defence. The line was held in as much depth as was possible, and the sappers were constructing concrete pill-boxes, to form strong points in the defensive system. They were not to be seen in large numbers, and the winter conditions made work rather slow and difficult.

We met most of the formation commanders, including the present Viscounts Alanbrooke and Montgomery. On the 18th we returned to Lord Gort's château in time for dinner, after which there took place a sort of conference at which members of the Commander-in-Chief's staff described their particular problems. It all seemed to me to be very friendly. After this we went up to our rooms to bed. I called in to say good night to the Secretary of State and we discussed what we had seen. He told me he would see what he could do to procure more resources for building pill-boxes, as he thought we could do with a lot more.

The following day we spent the morning visiting a sector garrisoned by French troops, and we were not encouraged by what we saw. In the afternoon we drove to Paris and stayed there the night.

The next morning Hore-Belisha had a meeting with Gamelin at his Headquarters. I met the French General, but did not attend the actual meeting. I spent the time talking to his staff. Apparently Gamelin was very interested in some new machine they were developing. It was a wireless-controlled vehicle which carried a heavy charge of explosive, and was intended for tackling heavily fortified lines, pill-boxes, etc. These were probably the machines used by the Germans which we met in Normandy and elsewhere.

We flew back to London that afternoon and Hore-Belisha attended a meeting of the Army Council, and gave his colleagues a description of his tour. Several days later another meeting of the Army Council took place at which the "Pill-Box" question was again discussed.

About November 30th the C.I.G.S. (Ironside) went over to France to examine the situation for himself, having expressed dissatisfaction concerning the report of the defences. At the time it was said that a signal had been sent to say that he was coming to "inspect the defences at the request of the War Cabinet."

On his return Ironside appeared very upset, and I went to see him. He said that Gort was angry about this criticism, and that there was considerable feeling against the Secretary of State. This change of attitude was interesting, for before his departure the C.I.G.S. had given the impression that he was going out to put these defences right. After some time spent in discussion, I persuaded Ironside to come and talk to the Secretary of State. But the meeting was not a very satisfactory one. I realised now that the relationship was hardly one that was of much value to the Army.

I felt very strongly on this matter of the pill-boxes, for from what I knew, I was convinced Hore-Belisha was trying to help, and that some people were making capital out of things he had said. I don't know what he had said to the Cabinet or to the Army Council, but to me he had always shown his desire to help the British Commander-in-Chief.

After Hore-Belisha's resignation, I wrote down my impressions of the "Pill-Box" controversy as I knew it. Here are some extracts:

> I accompanied the S. of S. to France on his visit to the B.E.F. and to the best of my knowledge was present or was told firsthand concerning all stages of the controversy.
>
> After a long conference at "The Chateau" conducted in a very friendly atmosphere, I went to say good night to the S. of S. in his room. We discussed the tour of the front which had been carried out during the day. He said he would love to see more concrete pill-boxes and made such remarks as: "We must see what can be done to accelerate the work — we must procure extra labour and machines."
>
> The S. of S. discussed pill-boxes with the C.-in-C.

I never gained the impression that these conversations were carried out in the sense of criticism, but merely as an endeavour to explore ways and means to help.

S. of S. held an Army Council on the evening of his return from France, and described his visit to the B.E.F., mentioning his impressions regarding the scarcity of pill-boxes.

Several times during the next few days S. of S. mentioned the pill-box question to me. His whole attitude was one of endeavouring to help rather than one of criticism.

He also had talks with the Chief Engineer B.E.F. and Colonel French. I was not present at these interviews.

At a subsequent meeting of the Army Council the pill-box question was again discussed. General Pakenham Walsh[5] was present and also Generals Collins and Riddell-Webster.[6] S. of S. had just returned from seeing the Prime Minister, who had drawn his attention to some comments made to him by some Dominion representatives who had returned from a visit to France. These representatives had criticised the defences as not being strong enough to withstand a German onslaught. S. of S. said he felt bound to tell the Army Council about the interview. A discussion then took place on ways and means of increasing numbers and speed of pill-box construction.

Later the S. of S. gave the War Cabinet an account of his visit.

About November 30th the C.I.G.S. went to France to look at the defences of the B.E.F. I understand that a wire was sent to G.H.Q. saying that he was coming to "inspect the defences on instructions of the War Cabinet."

On the C.I.G.S.'s return he reported that the defences were very strong and that work on pill-boxes was going along well. He also reported that the C.-in-C. was very worked up about enquiries *re* the pill-boxes, and had taken them as criticisms against the B.E.F. C.I.G.S. said the feeling in France and even

---

[5] Chief Engineer, B.E.F
[6] Deputy Q.M.G.S

in London was very strong and widespread. S. of S. asked C.I.G.S. how. the matter had been given such wide publication.

S. of S. sent a letter to the C.-in-C. explaining the whole question.

During December I could feel that sinister moves were going on to de-frock the Secretary of State. There must have been something brewing, for the Prime Minister sent for Hore-Belisha one day, and told him that he had complete confidence in him, and would support any changes in the Army hierarchy which he felt necessary. Hore-Belisha replied that he was quite satisfied with the leading army personalities.

Early in the New Year things came to a head, for Chamberlain offered Hore-Belisha the Board of Trade. He asked him to "make this sacrifice," but the Secretary of State for War refused the new appointment and resigned.

For a few weeks before this a campaign of malicious stories aimed at undermining Hore-Belisha's position had been going on in London. The "Pill-Box" controversy brought matters to a climax. Apparently the Prime Minister had in a short space of time changed his opinion as to Hore-Belisha's suitability for his existing job. What was the cause of this change of attitude? It is obvious that the reason was not connected with inefficiency, otherwise another appointment would not have been on offer.

The answer is pretty clear. Strong pressure must have been brought on the Prime Minister. Hore-Belisha could not have been considered the right man by the other Ministers in the War Cabinet. Further, there must have been those at the War Office who wished for his removal, and had not been backward in making known their views.

This turn of events was a bitter blow to my chief, for he had a very genuine love of the army. What I disliked was the scheming that went on, and how capital for bringing about his downfall was made from his very genuine efforts to help Gort.

That evening following the Prime Minister's offer I went back with Hore-Belisha to his house. We discussed at length whether he should accept the Board of Trade. After dinner Beaverbrook's advice was sought, and on hearing the story he immediately put through a call to Churchill who was then on a visit to Paris. He asked him to intervene, but got no response. The future Prime Minister, who had himself experienced a long period "in the wilderness," advised Hore-Belisha to accept the Board of Trade — a very significant fact.

During the following week-end Hore-Belisha's house near Wimbledon was besieged by the press. The papers were full of this development, and he was no doubt tempted to make a fight of it. He was expected to deliver a resignation speech in the House in a few days' time, and he was trying to decide what line he would take. He decided very rightly that he would make no trouble "One must not do that sort of thing in time of war," he said.

I listened to his speech, and it was all very correct and harmless. Yet I, more than most people, knew how deeply he felt it all. I'm glad he took it that way.

My last official task as Military Assistant to the Secretary of State for War was to drive to the Palace with Hore-Belisha when he handed in his seals of office.

I stayed on at the War Office for a week or two — until the new Secretary of State, Oliver Stanley, had decided that no M.A. was required! I had asked Ironside if I might go when the change took place. He agreed, and told me he would see that I got the job I liked. I did as all young officers would do at the beginning of a war — I asked to go back to my regiment. In due course I received my orders to report to a Training Centre in Yorkshire, and on the evening before I was due to leave I had a call from the War Office to say I must see the Military Secretary the next morning. I did so, and was told that I had been posted as a "teacher" at the new Staff College at Haifa in Palestine. I looked upon this as banishment, and was very depressed, for the official view then taken was that Italy would not go to war.

I sailed from Marseilles in late February, leaving war-time Europe for the peaceful Middle East. No black-out, no rationing, and peace-time hours of work. But before long Italy, thinking she was backing a certainty, came in, and war had come our way. But it took us some time to notice it in lovely Haifa. A few silvery Italian planes would fly over now and again to drop their bombs on the oil refinery, but that was the only reminder of a state of war that we received.

In November I was appointed, for no apparent reason, as I possessed none of the right credentials, as Commandant of the new School of Combined Operations. Having worked out the syllabus and commandeered a large building in Haifa, my appointment was cancelled, and I returned to the Staff College. But I was only to be there for a very short time for, in early December, I was posted as a planner to the Joint Planning Staff in Cairo. I was now to become more intimate with the war, but I still lived in a comfortable flat.

CHAPTER III: GREEK ADVENTURE

I

OUR intervention and failure in Greece was, at the time, the subject of heated argument and controversy. Since those days, far greater decisions and campaigns have tended to relegate these events into comparative obscurity. But it is a good example of a test case in respect of the adoption of a correct strategy after assessing the true merits of the political and military factors. I think, therefore, a somewhat detailed account as I knew it might be of value. I don't claim to know the whole story by any means, and if I did I probably would not be allowed to describe it all. I was, however, rather intimately associated with the general background, and sometimes took quite an active part in the happenings at that time.

In the first part of this chapter I will endeavour to describe the story as I know it. I shall not deal with operations at any length, my object being to give the best first-hand evidence available in order that conclusions as to the rights and wrongs of the case can be made. The chapter will finish with these conclusions. I would stress again that I don't know the whole story or the whole background to the decisions, but I do claim to be able to piece together the key-stones of this difficult and delicate subject.

I will go back to an evening at G.H.Q. Cairo in early January, 1941. We were sitting in the Joint Planning room, and had just agreed upon the final draft of a planning paper. The title of this paper was "Future Policy in North Africa," or "Advance to Tripoli," or some such name.

General O'Connor, who commanded the Western Desert Force, had certainly kept us busy during the last few weeks. We had written many papers relating to our future policy in North Africa ever since the offensive started in December. Should we cross the Egyptian frontier? Should we capture Bardia, or Tobruk, or Benghazi, etc.? I'm afraid in many cases by the time we had produced our somewhat academic studies in their final form, General O'Connor had already shown us how right or how wrong we were!

At this time the Italians had been soundly thrashed, and the major portion of their armies had ceased to exist. Preparations were being made to capture Tobruk, and General Wavell and his Commanders were looking far to the westward. In the Sudan and East Africa intensive preparations were being made for the coming campaigns against the Italian colonies of Eritrea and Italian Somaliland. About this time, General Wavell made a bold and far-seeing decision which certainly had a great influence upon the rapid clearing up of the Italian East African commitment. Once he saw that we had the measure of the Italians, he switched an Indian Division and other forces from the Western Desert to the Sudan.

Outside Africa the Allied picture was anything but rosy. Rumours were coming in regarding German infiltrations and preparations in the Balkans. Whether Turkey or other Balkan countries were their objectives no one knew. Some people were very optimistic about obtaining active help from Turkey. Why they should have thought this, many of us — especially the J.P.S. — could never understand. Vichy France had now full control of Syria, whilst Iraq and Iran were certainly being influenced by the tremendous Axis successes. Then the Dodecanese islands were a source of great trouble to us, and strategically their capture became a high priority. Without them in our hands, major assistance to Turkey was very difficult, as they controlled the Aegean Sea. Further, air bases on these islands provided a constant threat to our shipping in the Eastern Mediterranean.

Against these numerous commitments and desirable aims, what were our resources? The cupboard was terribly bare in practically every commodity. The Army possessed few tanks, were short of transport, and lacked much modern equipment. The R.A.F. were equipped with obsolescent machines, and few of them at that. The Navy were holding their own, but were under considerable pressure, and shipping affected everything — whether for the carriage of troops, supplies and equipment, or for operations outside the Middle East base.

II

Meanwhile in the Joint Planning room at G.H.Q., we had convinced ourselves that once Tobruk and Benghazi were captured we could, after a pause of a week or two, advance with adequate forces to capture Tripoli. The prize was great. It would mean that we should be in a position to avoid further major campaigns in North Africa. We would be able to link up with the French in Tunis, which might well lead to active collaboration. The shipping route through the Mediterranean might be kept open without great difficulty. There were uncertainties — inherent in all bold military ventures. For instance, subsequent maintenance of the forces in Tripolitania might well have proved very difficult. On the other hand, I seem to remember that General O'Connor's own staff were studying the same problem and were very hopeful. There was very little, if any, useful Italian opposition left, and at the time the decision had to be made, the Germans had not decided upon major intervention across the Mediterranean. In order to maintain the comparatively small force that would have been necessary to capture Tripoli, all but this striking force would have had to be grounded and its transport formed into supply echelons. All this, however, had been worked out and was by no means impossible.

Just as the secretary was collecting papers together an orderly arrived at the door and produced a "Most Urgent" signal. We read it together and our faces fell. The news meant that our paper and our high hopes could now be relegated to the waste paper basket. I might add, a not unusual fate to many of our papers!

The message changed the whole framework of our strategy. Greece was now to become top priority. Forces must be collected to enable us to help Greece. The future campaign in North Africa was to be strictly limited. The capture of Benghazi was to be the final scope of the advance, and then only provided that it could be done on the cheap. All this to us was a bitter blow, and we felt deflated and sad. We did not at that moment know anything of the high policy behind this decision, but we felt there must be pretty weighty factors which robbed us of a prize which to us sitting in Cairo glittered so brightly and appeared so desirable.

I think this might be a suitable moment to digress from the main story so that I can deal with the problem of the "Benghazi Bulge." The shape of Cyrenaica had a great influence upon the strategy and tactics of the North African campaigns. I think this all-important factor was never correctly appreciated until we were thrown back after General Auchinleck's successful offensive in 1942. General Montgomery was quite clear about it all, and realised to the full the weakness of halting in Cyrenaica, and how important it was to undertake a rapid advance into Tripolitania with adequate resources behind him.

Supply was the predominating factor in determining the scope of operations in the vast spaces of the desert. The ports of Bardia, Tobruk, Derna and Benghazi, therefore, played an all-important part in our own and the enemy's plans. Having captured Tobruk our forces were given a new lease of life. Benghazi was, however, essential if a move out of Cyrenaica were contemplated.

Between Tmimi and Benghazi is the high Jebel country. This belt stretched about fifty miles southward from the coast. In this area good roads existed, in spite of the somewhat hilly terrain. To the south of this country was desert. Water was scarce, but with modern motor transport, movement across it was comparatively easy. It will be seen that the port of Benghazi is tucked up in the North-West corner of Cyrenaica and therefore could be outflanked and cut off by mobile forces operating from the Agheila area towards Tobruk. Herein lay the inherent weakness of our army's position after the capture of Benghazi. This basic weakness could, however, be offset by any, or by a combination of the following:

(a) Having so defeated the enemy that he had not the power to launch a counter-stroke.
(b) Making certain of having strong forces available to protect Benghazi as well as mobile reserves which could strike at the enemy's L. of C. if he attempted to by-pass that port.
(c) An adequate force available to deny the enemy Tobruk and Derna; for without those ports it would not be easy for the enemy to maintain a real and sustained threat to our positions.
(d) The rapid development of the port of Benghazi was of course essential to any plan.

To stick out one's neck in the Agheila area without these necessary requirements behind, was not sound tactics. We learnt our lesson twice in this respect, and very costly lessons they were. But we survived in the end, and it was for Montgomery finally to cast aside this bugbear, and at long last to advance far beyond the Gulf of Sirte.

III

From the moment that this strategical switch was heralded, intensive planning went on in Cairo. The examination of the situation in the Balkans became of paramount importance. We concentrated on the German capabilities in this area, assessed possible strengths, objectives, routes, and all the other factors connected with the employment of our forces in Greece. The part that Turkey might play was naturally all important. If that country were prepared to co-operate actively, then intervention in the Balkans became a far more attractive proposition. But Turkey's attitude was extremely difficult to assess. Commonsense dictated that we should never count upon her active support until we showed ourselves capable of defeating Germany; until the German Air Force could no longer hope to destroy Turkish cities, such as Istanbul; and until the Turkish forces had been reequipped upon modern lines. It always appeared extraordinary to me how during this period the politician was so optimistic as to Turkey's attitude. Neutrality, yes — but not active participation. I suppose it was the old story of a man in difficulties clutching at a straw.

Besides the strategical examinations being undertaken, a vast amount of detailed planning took place. The collection of a suitable expeditionary force; the earmarking of shipping; the preparation of movement tables, and the hundred and one other things connected with a great project of this nature. And in the meantime Western Desert Force was gradually stripped of its power — in the air and on the ground — and was left a mere skeleton of its former self. No one felt happy about this, and I know the new Commander, General Neame,[7] expressed his anxiety concerning the situation. Having made his protests he loyally did what he could with the inadequate resources at his disposal. All this must be remembered by those critics of our army in North Africa when it fell back upon Tobruk in front of Rommel a few weeks later.

The more we examined the problem, the more unsound the venture appeared. There were so many uncertain quantities. What would Turkey do? Would Yugo-Slavia resist an Axis move through her country? Would Germany attack Turkey before Greece? The answer to any of these questions would have a decided influence upon our plans. One thing was quite certain, and that was if Germany decided to attack Greece, it would be in full strength, and by all practicable routes.

I don't know what the Greek attitude to our intervention was at that time. I presume that in view of our alliance she felt she had a call upon our help. To what extent she genuinely wished us to send forces to Greece I do not know. I had an impression at the time that Metaxas foresaw certain disadvantages. The gallant Greek Army was fighting a heroic campaign against the Italians in Albania, fighting with an ill-equipped army in appalling conditions. In spite of this, it had achieved great successes. But the German Army was a very different proposition. The crux of the matter appeared to be — would the arrival of Allied forces precipitate a German attack, with the result that the Greek Army would be swamped long before sufficient forces had arrived to remedy the

---

[7] General O'Connor had handed over command when Benghazi was captured — he became G.O.C. British troops in Egypt.

situation? I may be wrong, but I think this vital factor weighed very heavily with Metaxas. But Metaxas died at this momentous hour in his country's fortunes.

German infiltration had certainly begun in Bulgaria. Large numbers of Germans in plain clothes had arrived and were busily engaged in preparing the way for a large scale campaign. Roads were being built by the Todt organisation, airfields constructed, and quantities of munitions and supplies were being built up. Bridging material was being dumped, and later bridges were built across the Danube. With characteristic thoroughness the enemy was paving the way for a rapid campaign against Greece or Turkey, or against both these countries. There were no doubts about the signs.

Before describing the defensive problem facing Greece in the event of a German attack, I propose to mention some of the basic weaknesses from the strictly military angle which this policy produced.

The Greek Army had suffered enormous losses in men and equipment. Their successes had not been won cheaply. Greece as a country did not have the industrial power either to replace material losses or to keep her armies supplied and equipped without a considerable measure of assistance from the Allies. Morale against the Italians was high, but the results of the long winter campaign might well affect the Army's spirit if suddenly required to face the German Army as well. Equipment and munitions were anything but plentiful as far as we were concerned, and practically the only handy source of supply was that derived from the defeated Italian armies in North Africa. Without a strong Greek Army with full fighting powers, any force that we could afford to send was doomed to disaster. It would not be lack of spirit, but lack of *matériel* that would prevent the Greek Army from playing its part.

The forces which we could muster were not numerous; neither were they well provided with the most modern implements of war. We were particularly short of such items as tanks, aircraft, transport and anti-aircraft guns. Compare this with the colossal weight of equipment that the Germans could muster. They had many and better tanks and an enormous air force which could swamp anything we could produce. In addition, they had a number of troops and leaders who had great experience of modern war in Europe.

The time factor was difficult to assess. The weather and the extent of German preparations would probably give us until April before an attack was launched. But on the other hand, we had a great deal to do, when once the final decision to send an Expeditionary Force had been made. The flow over was strictly limited by shipping and port capacity. We had to build our bases and accommodate adequate reserves of all commodities. Would we have sufficient time to do all this before the enemy crossed the Greek frontier?

The L. of C. was very vulnerable. Ships had to pass close to enemy bases in the Aegean. Initially we would be solely dependent upon Piraeus as our base port. The communications northwards from here were meagre to say the least of it, one small single line railway and one main road. It has always been difficult to understand why the Axis allowed us to sail our forces and supplies to Greece for so long before they commenced attacks upon them.

The one bright spot appeared to be the terrain. This by all the teaching was most suitable for defence. In spite of this, however, the many defiles might prove nightmares when fighting an enemy with so great an air force.

Of the many military problems I have studied during this war, I never came across one which appeared so unattractive.

A planner is often apt to foresee too many difficulties, but with this problem the military advantages appeared to be nil. The one factor which might weight the scales in our favour was the intervention of Turkey and/or Yugo-Slavia. But these were long shots — both most uncertain quantities.

IV

The very shape of Greece produced a major defence problem. Western Thrace and Macedonia consist of a narrow strip of country stretching out towards Turkey with the sea on the southern flank, and its northern side open to potential attacks in varying strength along its border. Comparatively small and rapid success would cut off chunks of territory at will. To make matters worse the great port of Salonika, upon which Greece relied for the maintenance of her forces fighting in Albania, was situated in this vulnerable stretch of country.

If Germany attacked through Yugo-Slavia, then Salonika would be cut off from the rest of Greece. If she attacked to the east of Salonika, then the forces to the east would be cut off from their base and isolated from the remainder of the army. What a problem — particularly when one considers the political implications of losing such important territory so soon.

An examination at once showed that it would be impossible to bring into the Salonika area sufficient forces before the enemy could launch his attack. It was not hard to see how Salonika could be isolated by German attacks and then the port and town dealt with by the air from bases just across the frontier. Under no circumstances could it be considered as a secure base.

Another great weakness respecting the Greek defence problem was the fact that their army was fighting in Albania.

This produced the main disadvantage. First, it meant we were committed to a long and difficult line; whilst if the Germans attacked through Yugo-Slavia, the Greek position in Albania was in danger of being turned. Secondly, whilst Salonika was denied them, the maintenance problem — especially in winter — became acute.

Political and morale reasons alone obviously made any plan involving a voluntary withdrawal from Albania unacceptable. The problem, therefore, resolved itself into finding the best defensive line exclusive of Salonika. After a careful study of the map, this was not hard to find. In the area of Mount Olympus suitable country appeared to exist, for besides the defensive value of the hills there existed several rivers which would form good obstacles to a German advance. The line would have to run north-westwards from, say, about Katerine through Verria to the Edessa-Florina area. This position became known as the "Aliakmon Line." Another important factor was that it protected the vitally important communication centre of Larissa. There was also a large airfield in the vicinity.

So if to Greece we must go, then the Aliakmon Line was the obvious one to hold.

V

In February, 1941, a very high-powered party arrived in Cairo. There were Eden (then Secretary of State for War), Dill (Chief of the Imperial General Staff), and their advisers. Discussions took place behind closed doors and we on the lower levels were all agog to know what was happening, and what decisions were being made. As far as I can remember the Planners were not asked to produce a paper giving their views as to the feasibility of the project. We certainly held some very decided ones.

The D.M.I., Brigadier Shearer, did produce a paper drawing attention to the great dangers of this campaign in view of the German resources and methods. I remember this paper coming back from the C.-in-C., General Wavell. There was a short note written in his own hand across the top — it said:

"'War is an option of difficulties.' — Wolfe. A. P. W."

We admired the spirit but questioned — in so far as junior officers are allowed to question — the judgment!

VI

The time had now come to make a definite offer to send a force into Greece and so help to repel the Germans — if and when they attacked. I was detailed to accompany the party that left for Athens. It consisted of Eden, Dill, Wavell, Naval and Air Chiefs and their advisers. We travelled in two Lockheed aircraft and after taking off from Cairo, landed to re-fuel at El Adem before proceeding across the Mediterranean to Greece.

Whilst waiting at El Adem airfield we toured some very dilapidated hangars and looked at specimens of Italian aircraft in various stages of decomposition. It reminded us of what can happen when one side has the measure of the other in the air.

From El Adem we flew over the blue Mediterranean, skirting Crete, over the glorious Aegean Sea, and made a safe landing at Tatoi, an airfield north of Athens. We were taken straight off to the King's country residence and there had tea. Arrangements were then made for the meetings which were to decide Greece's fate. I forget where everyone stayed — the Palace or the Legation — but I was very comfortably housed with the First Secretary and his wife in their charming apartment in Athens.

After a really good English tea with the King, served on a long and beautifully polished table, subsequent procedure was decided upon. The Big Ones were, I believe, to start meetings at about 5.30 p.m. A full-scale assembly was to take place some time after dinner and this I was ordered to attend.

Some of us were asked to dinner at the Legation. Here we spent a delightful couple of hours. Dining with our charming host and hostess in the sanctuary of the British Legation building will always remain a very pleasant recollection. We were well fed and wined and then drove back to the King's residence for the coming session.

Some time between our arrival and the time I left for dinner, a small meeting took place to discuss the provision of equipment and munitions for the Greek Army. Their staff had produced a formidable list. No one could deny that the items were necessary, but it was obvious we should have great difficulty in meeting anything like their full demands. I had brought with me a mass of documents on the subject, but as it was not my line of business, I'm afraid I hardly knew my way about. This lack of knowledge earned me a mild "rocket" from Wavell, but I'm glad to say that the whole matter was now handed over to General Heywood's Mission, whose task this rightly was.

The conference took place in the big room in which we had had tea. It was now looking more sombre with the table cleared of the beautiful china, which had been replaced by inkwells and paper. Being a very low form of life amongst this great constellation, I only took my place at the table during discussions which turned upon the purely military angle. I am, therefore, not in a position to describe the whole scene, nor was I in a position to hear all the arguments used, both political and military, in favour of our policy. I was, however, present when three important items were discussed. First was the question of the aid which we were prepared to give the Greeks

— men and weapons. Secondly, was the military opinion of what we hoped to achieve, in the event of a German invasion. And thirdly, the Greek acceptance to our offer.

When I took my place at the table it was getting very late, and I noticed that everyone looked very grave — particularly the Greek Prime Minister. In all discussions the King appeared to take a leading part, and he certainly impressed me with his attitude and knowledge of the problems involved. Prince Paul, the King's brother, looked somewhat disinterested, and I don't think he was enjoying the party, and certainly not the subject. He sat at the flank of the Greek delegates with his chair slightly away from everyone. General Papagos was an impressive figure. His name had become a byword, and he was considered a national hero and a fine soldier. His strategy and leadership in Albania had been of a high order. The successes, however, had been achieved at a great price, and he, above all, knew how much more the Greek Army could stand. I watched him often during these discussions.

Rather frightened I sat down and put my massive file on the table. It contained details regarding the force we proposed to send: number of men, guns and tanks, as well as a great deal of other things.

I think it was Eden who stressed and enumerated the "formidable" resources which we were prepared to send over. It sounded pretty good, but if a real expert had carried out a more detailed investigation, I doubt whether those present would have been so satisfied. Totals of men and guns are generally impressive. In the aircraft flying over I had been asked to produce a list showing totals of items we were proposing to send. My first manpower figures excluded such categories as pioneers, and in the gun totals I only produced artillery pieces. This was nothing like good enough for one of

Mr. Eden's party who was preparing the brief. He asked that the figures should be swelled with what to my mind were doubtful values. I felt that this was hardly a fair do, and bordering upon dishonesty. I don't know, however, whether figures meant very much to the Greeks by the time they were produced.

Our assistance was to be sent over in three echelons, the initial contribution in fighting troops being one infantry division, an armoured brigade group and some extra artillery. Naturally a large number of Base and L. of C. units would have to precede this contribution. Two contingents were to arrive, each consisting — so far as I can remember — of a division and something extra. But the process was a slow one owing to shipping and port capacity.

As far as I could gather, there seemed to be general acceptance of the British offer of help, but the plan was still being considered. Discussion went on as to where the Germans should be held, and naturally Salonika's part in such a plan was stressed. Papagos explained that the troops holding the static defences in Western Thrace and Macedonia possessed no mobility, and therefore were unsuitable for fighting a withdrawal from their far-flung positions. It was generally accepted that the holding of Salonika was not a practicable proposition and that the Aliakmon Line was the right answer under the circumstances. The political disadvantages and dangers of giving up so much Greek territory were mentioned. As far as I understood the discussion, it appeared that the Greeks agreed that the troops holding these isolated positions should be withdrawn as early as possible. This would prevent their being cut off, and at the same time, provide much-needed reinforcements to man the defensive line decided upon.

The Greeks referred frequently to the question of Turkey and Yugo-Slavia. The danger of a German advance through the latter was brought up on many occasions. If either or both these countries came in against Germany, the whole outlook would be vastly improved.

And so the Aliakmon Line was decided upon as the strategic plan in the event of our sending our expeditionary force to Greece. There were further discussions as to the weight of the German attack when it came. The number of divisions required to hold the Aliakmon Line was also brought up — nine was, I think, the planning figure. To me sitting there with the facts in front of me, the prospect of producing the requirements from Greek and British resources looked rather remote. My impression was that Papagos looked none too happy. He had a lot on his hands already.

I was now asked to leave the room, and I left the assembly endeavouring to draft the signal that was to be sent to London, which, of course, would include the agreement for us to send forces to Greece.

The night was passing by. I wandered about the anteroom trying to see the whole venture in a different light. I couldn't — I still considered the project a bad one. There may have been strong political reasons of which I was not fully aware, but from the purely military point of view, the whole thing looked terribly unsound.

The hours went by and at about 3 a.m. I went in search of coffee, and some kindly palace servant produced some for me. I then relaxed in a chair. Some minutes later noises came from the next room and the party broke up. I think the Greek Prime Minister was to report to his Cabinet that day, and the "big shots" were to return to Egypt later in the morning, whilst Eden was to leave for discussions with the Turks.

I remained in the ante-room for a few minutes whilst the party dispersed. Eden came in looking buoyant. He strode over to the fire and warmed his hands, and then stood with his back to it dictating signals to his staff. They in turn looked nearly as triumphant as he did, and were positively oozing congratulations.

Presumably he had done his job, and accomplished what he had set out to achieve. He was, therefore, no doubt entitled to be pleased with himself. But whether it was a job worth doing and in our best interests seemed to me very doubtful.

I was glad when my host came along to drive me back to his house.

VII

At some period during the evening, or it may have been the next morning — when exactly I don't remember — I had a lucky break. General Wavell came up to me and said:

"What are you going to do now?"

"Going back to Cairo, sir," I said.

"Well, I think you had better stay behind and carry out a reconnaissance of the Aliakmon position with the Greeks," he replied.

I was simply delighted at this news, for not only did it mean that I could test our conclusions arrived at from studies of maps, but I would also see Greece, and get a break from office routine in Cairo. Our Mission gave me a very nice room at their hotel in Athens, and I began to consider the problem in front of me. General Heywood, who was head of the Mission, was most helpful and we had long talks. He was to distinguish himself some weeks later when he took a leading part in saving an ammunition ship, which was in danger of blowing up, during a heavy raid on Piraeus harbour.

In the afternoon I was taken round a Greek Military Hospital. It was a pathetic visit. Several wards were filled with men who had lost, or were losing, their feet from the effects of frostbite contracted on the Albanian battlefields. They were cheerful, as soldiers of all countries are under similar circumstances. After hearing some of their tales and fitting these into the bigger picture I had gleaned from other contacts, I left this rather primitive hospital feeling anything but cheerful, and wondering whether we were going to be instrumental in helping to make these poor, brave, people suffer more than their legitimate share.

I was ordered to appear at a meeting which General Papagos had called that evening at his headquarters. We were to discuss the plans for the reconnaissance.

The office in which the meeting was held was a very dismal one. Besides Papagos there were three or four other officers. They were to accompany me on this mission.

Papagos started by stressing the secrecy of our task, and then proceeded to describe his views as to the best positions to be held. He talked about the various water obstacles and their influence upon the problem.

It was decided that I should be dressed up as a War Correspondent visiting the Albanian front and other parts of Greece. I was to wear mufti. Papagos then left and we got down to planning our reconnaissance. We decided to make straight for Larissa the next day. We were to start at ten o'clock, and would be away about five or six days. Documents were to be produced to show that I was a correspondent, and these would be given me next morning.

After dinner that night I had to chase around to find some mufti. I had, of course, got nothing but uniform with me. Luckily, Peter Smith-Dorrien of the Mission offered to let me choose from his wardrobe. We were hardly of a similar figure, and our ability to carry off certain types of clothes was very different. I took eventually a wonderful check suit — very loud I would call it. I looked like nothing on earth; not an ornament to the fraternity of war correspondents, I'm afraid. My proper place was in the silver ring! Our heads were of different sizes, so I had to buy a very low-looking mufti hat in Athens the next morning. So about ten o'clock on the morrow I stepped into my car. There were three cars altogether: one for myself, another for the Greeks, and one for the baggage. I took with me a small bag and camera. The Greek officers were those who had attended the previous evening's meeting. I think they consisted of a general staff officer, a sapper and a gunner.

Eden went off to pay a visit to Turkey, after which he was to come back to Athens. I believe that on his return he did receive a great ovation — I often wonder whether he deserved it!

VIII

With my pressman's pass (written in Greek to my ultimate cost) in my pocket, we started up the road to Larissa. It was a long journey of some eight hours. The weather was bad, which unfortunately spoilt some of the beautiful vistas we would otherwise have seen.

Larissa was anything but a modern town. In fact one of the only really modern buildings was the principal hotel in which we stayed the night. This was a reinforced concrete building. The town was full of soldiers, but owing to the Italian air raids a number of the civilians had been evacuated. This, as later events will show, was an act of providence. There was a large airfield nearby from which operated several squadrons of the R.A.F.

Early the next day we started on our task. Our method was to drive to various view-points and so get a general impression of the defensive capabilities of the country. We paid particular attention to the river crossings, to the main passes through the hills, and to possible airfield sites. There was no doubt that defensively the country was strong. There was also no doubt that with the extensive front that would have to be held, a great number of troops would be required.

I don't propose to embark upon a detailed description of our journeys, nor upon an account of the various conclusions we reached. In short, we managed to produce sufficient data to enable us to recommend the general line that should be held, together with information as to the water obstacles, bridges, and mountain passes. I managed to write up a fairly comprehensive route report covering the various roads over which we traversed. Besides the question of the number of troops required to defend this area, one was very struck with the vulnerability of the many defiles to an enemy such as Germany, possessing an efficient and numerous air force.

Our travels took us into Albania, to the Florina area. It was a ghastly sort of day with a bitterly cold blizzard blowing. Only with the full use of chains were we able to drive along the extremely indifferent roads. We called upon a unit in a reserve brigade area, where we were given a very welcome mug of steaming hot punch. The poor soldiers looked terribly ill-equipped and miserable. Their clothing and footwear was of a deplorable quality. I felt a wave of sympathy surge through me for this gallant little army which had defied and soundly thrashed Mussolini's hordes. We spoke a lot of the recent fighting, and I tried to be as inquisitive as a good war correspondent should be. But we never spoke of Germany and of the chances of an attack on Greece from that direction. I found on every side that this subject was not welcomed. They had their hands very full as it was: the other possibility required something more than a burning national pride, guts, and the will for sacrifice.

What a miserably poor country is Greece. The standard of living is so very low. No wonder it did not take long after the Germans arrived for starvation to set in upon a pitiable scale. We could not have received greater kindness from the people amongst whom we mixed; whether it was in quest for information, for a meal *en route*, or for a place to lay our heads. On one night we put up in a peasant's cottage, a very primitive little building, but very clean. We were welcomed with that characteristic friendliness of the countryman. There was one good bedroom with a large double bed which took up most of the available space. The room was full of knick-knacks, religious emblems and pictures. It was not hard to appreciate how a people who live under such conditions of poverty must find it easy to turn to God; to seek His mercy, and to pray for a better time hereafter.

Our host and hostess insisted upon giving up the bedroom to us, and I was a bit shaken when I realised that I was going to share the bed with one of my Greek colleagues. I felt tired, however, after my long day in the fresh air, turned in by candle-light, and was soon asleep. The night passed without any untoward incident, and I found that the additional body in the bed did not disturb my slumbers. On the other hand, I hope my colleague did not find me an inconvenience!

We were up early the next morning, and our hosts were there to greet us, having brewed some hot syrup to warm us on our way. As a special treat we were each given a spoonful of a great delicacy which consisted of a confection made of rose leaves and sugar. It was rather good.

Food was obviously not easy to come by, and the meals we had during our journeys were of a very meagre and unappetising type.

Another night we spent with a bishop, or was it an archbishop? Servia was, I think, the name of the place. Here was a higher standard of living and we were treated to clean sheets and pleasant meals. Our host was a charming and fatherly man, and I have often wondered how he fared under German rule. I said I would send him some tea as a small return for his kindness, but I'm afraid it could never have reached him. From Servia I decided that I had seen enough, and that before returning to Athens and Cairo to write up my reports I would have to fly over some of the area, particularly the coastal sector. The object was to get some idea of what the country was like between the roads, and also between Mount Olympus and the sea. A secure flank here was naturally of paramount importance. My colleagues still had certain tasks to complete, and so I said good-bye, arranging to meet them again in Athens.

The next twenty-four hours were to be, to say the least of it, exciting ones for me. I was arrested as a spy, nearly killed in a very bad earthquake, and all but crashed in an aircraft during that short period.

It was a lovely day, and I settled down in my car prepared to enjoy to the full the long drive to Larissa, where I proposed to spend the night. Every now and again I stopped and took photographs of subjects which I thought would be of interest to the planners. All the big bridges were guarded, but upon showing my correspondent's pass, I was always allowed to proceed without hindrance. After crossing one particularly large bridge, I decided that a photo might be of value, so I stopped the car, got out and took my picture. I re-entered the car immediately afterwards, and proceeded peacefully on my way. On arriving at the village which I had selected for a luncheon halt, I was surprised to see a collection of police and soldiers with a barricade across the road. We stopped, and I was asked for my papers. I produced them at once and waited for the usual permission to move on. This time, however, something appeared to have gone wrong. Various people were brought to read my pass, and I was then asked if I possessed a camera. Without blushing I replied "Yes," and showed them my Contax. The next question shook me a little:

"Did you take a picture of the bridge at —?" Again, with not quite so much complacency, I answered "Yes."

Then a terrific amount of talking took place, and as nothing constructive appeared to be happening, I got rather angry and, with the help of my driver, managed to find out what was the matter. It appeared that my correspondent's pass did not entitle me to take photos! This was a bit of a blow, particularly as I was getting very hungry. I then behaved, I suppose, as Englishmen do under such circumstances. I asked the Greeks how dare they stop me when I had a pass from General Papagos' Headquarters itself. I was a war correspondent, and what was the good of being one unless a camera could be used. This appeared to have some effect, and after a lot of talk and gesticulations I was allowed to proceed on my way.

I felt smugly satisfied with the way I had handled the situation and smiled quietly to myself. Soon, however, that self-satisfied smile was to be removed rapidly from my face.

We drove on to Larissa. On approaching the outskirts I received something of a shock. There, drawn up alongside a barricade, was a squad of soldiers. They barred the way. I soon realised what had happened. News had been phoned through to Larissa, and so I had not got away with it after all. A smartly dressed officer stepped over to the car, saluted and asked for my papers. He spoke a little English, and was very correct and polite. After a rapid glance at my pass, he asked me to hand over my camera and then got into the car beside me. He apologised at any inconvenience he was causing me, but his instructions were that I must be taken into custody. I had to be a bit careful here, for my true identity and mission were supposed to be secrets; therefore I asked to be brought in front of the local commander. He replied: "All in good time."

This obviously did not suit my plans, for I wished to make arrangements that evening for my flight over the Aliakmon area the next day. So I put in a demand to see the General Commanding at once; the time now being about 2 p.m. My escort replied that this would be quite out of the question, as the General was lunching at the Officers' Club. I assured him that a meeting there would suit admirably, and I insisted upon being taken there at once. After a lot of argument, I was at long last taken along. We entered the Club, and one of the waiters told us that the General was still feeding. I was left in the passage, and my friend sent into the dining-room to find out the form. There was no doubt about the form; for a few seconds later out came the Greek officer, rather red in the face to say that his master refused to see me, and that he was not in the habit of being disturbed at his meals. I had visions of a long confinement and wondered whether the Greeks had a Habeas Corpus Act! I was determined to make a firm stand, and so when my escort motioned me to proceed down the stairs, I refused to do so. I became very angry, made a lot of noise, and said that, as an Englishman, I demanded to see the General, lunch or no lunch. Once again in went the officer to the dining-room, looking very uncomfortable and worried. This time it worked, for out roared a short and plump little

General, with his mouth full of food and a napkin in his hand. He said: "Lock him up at once, I'm fed up with these bloody journalists!" or at least that was what I understood him to say. I told him that I wished for an interview in private, and that he should ring up G.H.Q., in Athens and find out something about me. He relaxed slightly, but made it clear that until he had finished his food he had no intention of talking to me.

I was then led away and driven to the hotel in which I had stayed during my last visit; placed in a room and told to remain there until further notice. Fortunately I had not long to wait, for within an hour my escort arrived to say the General was ready to see me. We drove to the headquarters, and I was shown into his office. I was asked to explain what I had been doing and why I had carried a camera without permission. Also, why had I taken a photo of that bridge? I thought the only thing to do was to take up the offensive myself, and so attacked the General for the way an Englishman had been treated. I had asked him to see me alone. I had also asked him to ring up Headquarters in Athens to find out more about me. Neither of these things he had done. He had behaved in an extremely rude manner, and I would make it my business to report the whole thing personally to General Papagos on my return to Athens.

At last he seemed to lose some confidence and put a call through to his Headquarters at Athens. He apparently got through to the right department, and soon I saw his expression changing. The poor little man looked very uncomfortable. He had been told who I was, and that every possible assistance must be given me. The atmosphere had now, of course, completely changed. Coffee and brandy were ordered, and we both vied with each other over our apologies. I told the General that he had only done his duty, and I had been remiss in failing to see that my papers were in order. He, on the other hand, insisted that he had been at fault in not having rung up Athens sooner and so saved me an embarrassing hour or two. Any information I wanted was made available, and this allowed me to check up on several doubtful items in my report. After assurances of our mutual esteem, and carrying my returned camera, I left the General sitting in his office. Little did I know that he would be killed early next morning in an earthquake. I was told he had lost his life before I left Larissa next day.

The airfield was a mile or two out of Larissa. It consisted of a very large grass meadow, but the drainage was not all that could be desired. There were some "Gladiator" fighters and some "Blenheim" machines stationed there. In addition to the R.A.F. squadrons there was a unit of the Greek Air Force, but they were terribly poorly equipped. I sought out the R.A.F. Station Commander, and put my request. He was very helpful, and produced the pilot who would fly me, and together we discussed the course we would take the next day. We decided to set off at 7 a.m. in order that I could reach Athens at a reasonable time.

Back at the hotel, I spent the time writing up my various reports, had an omelette for dinner, and turned in at 9 p.m. in view of my early rise the next morning.

I was sleeping soundly when I was awakened by being thrown from my bed. I fell over and hit the opposite wall. An awful noise was to be heard all around me, and lumps of wall and ceiling were breaking away. All the furniture had fallen over, and I soon realised that the hotel was swaying from side to side. It felt as if we were swinging at least a yard or two either side of centre. Immediately upon waking up I thought it must be an Italian air raid and that we had sustained a direct hit. But in a second or two it was obvious this was an earthquake. As I was on the sixth and top floor, I was convinced that it was only a matter of moments before the whole building would collapse. It did not seem possible that any structure could withstand this strain. One could hear buildings crashing in every direction, and the shrieks of the people were frightening. I remember well my reactions at the time. I felt certain that I was doomed to die within the next few seconds, and there was nothing one could do about it. I recollect thinking to myself what a stupid way to get killed — if be killed one must — during a war. But the worst was not to happen. The swaying became less and less, and stopped. One could still hear cries and the noise of buildings breaking up, but by what seemed a miracle this hotel had more or less stood up to the shock.

What should I do next? It was still very dark and, of course, there was no electricity working. Even if it had been, all the lamps and fittings had been smashed to pieces. I felt an intense desire to be down below, right out in the centre of the square. I crawled about the room and found my suitcase, in which I knew reposed an electric torch. On switching on its beam a particularly unpleasant scene presented itself. The room was a complete shambles, and the remaining portions of the walls and ceilings looked anything but secure. I managed to find my shoes and an overcoat, and after putting these on, I ventured out into the passage. Here I found one or two fellow guests and we made a joint reconnaissance. The main staircase was badly damaged, but could no doubt be used. So, with our hearts in our mouths, we gingerly made our way downstairs. I can't say how thankful I felt upon reaching the open square outside the hotel.

By this time it was beginning to get light, and one began to get some impression of the devastation. It was very bad indeed. Hardly a house appeared to have survived. Various Greek officers were making attempts to organise rescue parties, and I and the little party from the hotel joined one of these. I can't say I enjoyed the next hour. I had not yet seen the unpleasant side of war; the foulness of a battlefield after the fighting had passed by; the destruction and the misery caused to towns by bomb and shell. In the remains of a building in which we started work there were various limbs showing from out of the debris. I'm afraid most of their owners were dead by this time, but we couldn't be quite certain. It was a ticklish job, for we hardly dared to move away a brick or piece of stone. The parts that still stood looked very insecure. Then there was the chance of a secondary shock — but that was too horrible a thought.

At the end of an hour I'm afraid I gladly accepted the excuse of having to go out to the airfield. I was already late. On my way back to the hotel I noticed the Officers' Club which I had entered yesterday — a sorry sight of gaping holes and rubble. After a few minutes' search I was lucky enough to find my car and driver. He had been doing useful work in taking victims to a hastily improvised dressing station. I told him to wait in the square, and decided to make a dash for my suitcase which was still in my bedroom. How I hated that journey as I threaded my way up those rickety stairs! Having reached my room, I moved like lightning, collected my belongings and rapidly changed into my clothes. Just as I was closing the suitcase, another shock commenced. I felt I wanted to kick myself. Why go and worry about a few old clothes and thereby run the risk of being killed. In retrospect it looked as if I had just asked for it. I waited, feeling terrified whilst this loathsome swaying went on. A lot more damage was done; but the hotel, thank heavens, having stood up to the initial shock took this new one like a good 'un. Immediately after it was over, I grabbed up my suitcase and dashed down to the square, feeling rather disgusted with myself.

At the door I met the hotel proprietor, a fat little Greek. He stood quite dazed, looking at the debris of his home. Rather foolishly I went up and offered him a few drachma in payment for my room. With a hopeless and pathetic gesture he mechanically took the notes. What a drop in the ocean! I felt I wanted to hand him many thousands so that he could re-build his wrecked hotel.

The airfield buildings had not got away with it by any means. Many of them had suffered badly, and an *alfresco* breakfast was being served to everyone as the cookhouse had been destroyed. How I welcomed that hot mug of tea and those sandwiches. Here amongst the crowd I met my pilot. He was a bit shaken as he had jumped out of the first-story window, and by doing so, I think, had saved his life.

Business as usual was the order of the day for, in spite of the dislocation caused by the earthquake, scheduled sorties were being flown.

We had a very pleasant flight, starting off for Mount Olympus and circling around her unsullied snowfields which glistened in the morning sunlight. We flew up close to Salonika and from our position we could see the great Struma and Varda rivers stretching away to the far horizon. The flight did not, I'm afraid, dispel my doubts about our ability to conduct a successful defence of the Aliakmon position — in fact it increased them. The extent of the front appeared so immense. The country along the coast was by no means too difficult to make a turning movement in this area impossible. We flew over at a very low altitude and combed the various roads and tracks.

After about an hour and a half's flying, the old Blenheim circled in to land. The landing wasn't a good one, and on first touching down, we bounced high in the air and came down again with a nasty bang. We managed to keep upright, suffered a few bruises, and the aircraft sustained a broken tail. By this time my nerves were getting a bit frayed, and when alighting upon the grass the whole ground seemed to rock under us, I thought it time I left for Athens, and even Cairo. We had just coincided with another earthquake shock!

The earthquake was hushed up, for it was thought that the people would take it as an ill omen. It was lucky that so many civilians had been evacuated already, but even so, many hundreds lost their lives and the material damage was great.

The journey back to Athens on February 28th was pleasant. The sun shone and I looked at one or two potential ports on the way, arriving back late in the evening. A very few weeks later this road was to be the scene of a retreating army — an army heavily outnumbered, with little air support and short of heavy weapons. Above this army roamed Stukas more or less as they pleased. Behind it was the sea, and another Dunkirk to be attempted. Poor old Army, not yet given a fair do, but despite that, these gallant soldiers from all over the Empire did not lose their morale. They were beginning, however, to lose their confidence in the higher direction of the war.

I spent the next couple of days in writing up my report.

By the evening of March 2nd it was obvious that a crisis had occurred. Eden and Dill had returned to Athens and conferences had been taking place throughout the day and well on into the night. Wavell was in Cairo, but his Chief of Staff, General Arthur Smith was over in Greece.

The plans for moving over our Expeditionary Force were going at full blast, but I don't think more than "advanced parties" had landed up-to-date. The German preparations had gained in momentum and barring the weather, it did not appear that they required much more time before they could attempt a move.

I turned in at about 11 p.m., but was rung up at 1 a.m. to hear that General Smith wished to see me downstairs. I slipped on some clothes and found him in his room. He told me that complications had set in and that I must fly back early that morning to Cairo and report matters to General Wavell. He then proceeded to dictate to me a memorandum setting out the salient difficulties that had emerged. Apparently Papagos was not happy with the military situation; he was a realist, and as the time drew near, he must have had grave doubts as to the soundness of the plan. I think there were about four major issues which worried him.

First, was the prospect of fighting the Germans without any assistance from the Turks and Yugo-Slavs. Then, there was the question of the withdrawal of troops from North-Eastern Greece. This movement had not started, and Papagos was worried at the effect such a move would have upon the Army's morale and upon Greek public opinion. The time factor was another problem. Could this withdrawal take place before the Germans attacked? And would sufficient British forces arrive before that critical moment arose? Finally, there appeared to be some divergence of views as to whether, under the circumstances, the Aliakmon Line was in fact the best line to hold. Here indeed was a crisis, and I remember a significant sentence towards the end of General Smith's clear account which ran something like this:

"From the strictly military point of view this would provide us with the opportunity of withdrawing from what appears now to be an unsound venture."

I took this to mean that the Greeks did not consider our help could save them.

I found that an aircraft was leaving for Cairo at about 9 a.m. and managed to get a seat. On arrival in Cairo I heard that General Wavell had left for Athens that very morning, and so the special object of my journey was not accomplished.

IX

I don't know what happened in Athens after my return to Cairo, but apparently the difficulties were smoothed out, and our forces commenced arriving in Greece.

In spite of this firm decision many of us felt extremely unhappy. In the J.P.S. we considered we should be failing in our duty if we did not start writing a paper dealing with an evacuation. We started this in the utmost secrecy very soon after my return from Greece, i.e. whilst our forces were in the process of being transported over to that country. But more of this anon.

About the third week in March we asked for a discussion with one of Dill's advisers in order to hear of any further political or other factors which might justify this strategy. I'm afraid it was a most unsatisfactory meeting, for there did not appear to be any answers to some of the questions that were asked:

"How could we deal with the weight of air and armour that we must expect against us?"

"Were we going to get over sufficient forces in time to hold the Aliakmon Line?"

"In view of the hardships and losses sustained by the Greek Army, and their acute munition problems, could we rely upon them for a sustained effort against a German attack?"

"How could the Greek and British forces be maintained after Salonika was given up?"

These were some of the questions asked, and to which there was no sound answer. The political factors seemed to have been given too much weight in framing our policy.

Yugo-Slavia appeared to be the one potential bright spot. If they really fought the Germans, then the whole thing might be worth while.

X

Now what of the situation in North Africa whilst all these activities were taking place? Information now available shows that Hitler decided to reinforce the Italian troops in Africa about the middle of January. Initially the intention was to bolster up the Italians with a Panzer division. The first German troops must have started landing about a month later. On March 31st Rommel attacked our positions about Agheila. The forces employed were comparatively few, but forceful leadership made up for small numbers. Our forces in Gyrenaica were caught off their balance, and did not possess adequate resources to hold the Gyrenaica bulge. The result was disastrous and our forces came tumbling back upon Tobruk. Rommel exploited the weakness of our position and with light forces struck across the country to the south of the Jebel, performing a series of "right hooks" which thoroughly disrupted our positions and our L. of C.

Sunday April 6th in Cairo was indeed a black day. That morning news arrived that the German attack against Greece had begun. The sketch map shows the routes and forces used by the enemy. Not only was Salonika immediately threatened, but in view of the threat through Yugo-Slavia towards the Monastir gap, an immediate danger existed to the Greek forces in Albania. In addition the news from the Desert was very bad. A very grave decision had to be made. Should we, or should we not attempt to hold Tobruk? Our losses had been great, we possessed little armour, and locking up forces in an isolated fortress was always an expensive decision in war. That afternoon a meeting took place at which the Commander-in-Chief, Eden and Dill were present. The atmosphere was certainly tense. The subject was Tobruk. I noticed Eden's fingers drumming on the table; he looked nervous and a very different person to the Eden at the Palace in Athens. After the problem had been discussed from each service point of view, Wavell was asked to give his views. I admired him tremendously at that moment. He had a very heavy load to carry but he looked calm and collected, and said that in his view we must hold Tobruk, and that he considered that this was possible. One could feel the sense of relief that this decision produced, and the other Commanders-in-Chief agreed, and it was decided to send Air Marshal Tedder and myself up the next day to Tobruk to report on the situation and to discuss possible reinforcements.

There is no doubt that this decision was the right one, and that Tobruk in enemy hands would have given Rommel the means to undertake an advance deep into Egypt. The valiant garrison of Australians,[8] Poles and English troops held out with the greatest courage until relieved by General Auchinleck's offensive in November of that year.

The next day, April 7th, I left in Tedder's aircraft with the object of reaching Tobruk. The situation was very fluid and information was scanty. Enemy armoured patrols had been reported in the vicinity of the frontier about Solium. Just

---

[8] The Australian Division was withdrawn from Tobruk by the Royal Navy a few weeks before the relief took place.

before take-off, we received a message that we could land at Solium airfield, and so Tedder decided to do so and find out the latest form. I had a liaison officer with me who was to be dropped there with some orders from G.H.Q. They related to the line of action that should be taken on the frontier; for communications appeared to have broken down between this area and Headquarters of the Western Desert Force. Certain reinforcements were on their way up from the Delta and it was important that they should be stopped at the frontier and organised as a "long-stop" in the Solium area.

I should mention here that General Wavell had sent General O'Connor up as a sort of adviser to General Neame, in view of his past experience in desert warfare.

We touched down at Solium and found everything quite peaceful, but no one seemed to know what was happening in the Tobruk direction. Tedder therefore flew on to Gambut which was about midway between Solium and Tobruk. We found the R.A.F. in the process of evacuating the airfield. The transport was moving off and bombs were being blown up. Here a car was requisitioned and we drove to Tobruk, telling our pilot to try and make its airfield if he got an all clear.

We first called at the R.A.F. Control Headquarters just outside the town, and they were more or less in ignorance of the general situation. No one had heard where the Force Headquarters was now situated, nor the whereabouts of Neame or O'Connor. We drove along the road leading westward from Tobruk and a mile or two out met a D.R. who indicated a group of transport and tents which he said was Force Headquarters. On reaching the area it was only to find that this was "Rear H.Q.'s" and they knew nothing much of what was happening. They thought "Main H.Q.'s" were moving into Tobruk itself.

The whole atmosphere was typical of a situation of this sort. No one knew anything and odd bodies of troops and vehicles were moving rather aimlessly about. The 6th Australian Division was on its way into Tobruk, having marched a long distance from the Jebel. They looked very tired. The whole area was very naked, and if the enemy had had the forces available to send to Tobruk I'm afraid there was nothing much to stop him. We could hear a battle raging to the south-west which turned out to be the fight at Mekili between the enemy and an Indian Motor Brigade and a sadly depleted British armoured division.

We drove back into Tobruk and soon found signs of a headquarters taking up a new location. Signal cables were being run out, motor transport arriving and sign boards being fixed up. We were told the B.G.S.[9] was inside a certain building, and so in we went to hear the news and deliver our message.

Here in one of the rooms we found Brigadier John Harding. He looked terribly tired but cheerful. We were told that news had just come in showing that both Generals Neame and O'Connor had been captured the day before. They had been ambushed in the Jebel country. This was indeed a bitter blow, for we could ill afford to lose such generals, especially one with such desert experience as O'Connor's. Harding, despite all these misfortunes, was behaving splendidly. He assumed temporary command and had already made up his mind how he was going to organise Tobruk's defence and sort things out. He had arranged to meet the Commander of the Australian division later that afternoon. John Harding ran true to form right through the war, doing brilliant work wherever he might be. Bad wounds sustained during the final advance to Tripoli put him out of the hunt, but he was back in the fight again

---

[9] B.G.S. = Brigadier General Staff, virtually Chief of Staff.

before very long. I remember how tremendously impressed I was with his behaviour that day, and to me, a very junior and inexperienced officer, it was truly magnificent.

I went through the list of reinforcements which were being sent up from Egypt and, although they were not very formidable, they nevertheless acted as a tonic.

Later on we heard that our aircraft had managed to make Tobruk airfield and so drove out there to emplane for Cairo. Our plane was one of the last to use that airstrip for many a day, and we felt pretty wretched at leaving our friends to an uncertain fate, whilst we were on our way back to sleep in a comfortable bed in Cairo.

On arrival back we went round to the A.O.C.-in-C.'s house where General Wavell joined the party. The news of the capture of both Neame and O'Connor came as a real shock to the C.-in-C., and I have never seen him so moved. He listened to my report, asked a few questions and then left to go back to his house. As Commander-in-Chief he was bearing a very heavy load at this time, and to lose a close personal friend such as O'Connor was an added burden.

XI

I mentioned earlier on the paper which we were preparing dealing with evacuation plans for Greece. General Wavell realised very rightly that no mention of such a course should reach the fighting soldiers, and the study was therefore kept strictly within the orbit of the planners. Later, however, when the troops came under the full weight of the German attack, and it became patently clear that the Aliakmon Line could never be held for very long, the planners asked their respective Chiefs to be allowed to set certain preparatory arrangements for evacuation in action. As far as the Navy was concerned work must now be done, such as the collection of shipping, the selection of beaches, signal arrangements, and a host of other matters. There was also a great deal of useful work and preparation that might be done by the Army. Our hands were, however, tied in this respect on account of the reasons given above. Nothing must be said or done in Greece suggesting such an end to the campaign. It is easy to be wise after the event, nevertheless it did appear to many of us that a more realistic view should have been taken. The Navy and the R.A.F. decided that the time had now come to set certain machinery for evacuation in motion, but the Army's hands were tied.

At one of our meetings it was agreed that we must send representatives to Greece to start clewing up inter-service plans, and so prepare for the worst case. General Smith gave me permission to go as a member of the Joint Planning Staff, but the veto upon raising any matters with the Army still stood.

The next morning I arrived at the banks of the Nile to embark in the Sunderland flying boat. General Wavell was travelling in the same machine. He happened to see me and called me over to ask what I was doing. I explained and was allowed to go — but only upon pain of death if I mentioned anything to the Army in Greece.

After an uneventful journey we arrived at Piraeus and I allowed the big ones to disembark and get safely away. Wigglesworth, representing the R.A.F., and I discussed our plans with Air Vice-Marshal D'Albiac[10] and others. General Wavell had flown straight up to see General Wilson who was commanding the British Forces.

The next morning I received a telephone message to say that General Wavell wished to see me in Athens that afternoon. It

---

[10] Commander R.A.F. in Greece.

was obvious at this meeting that he had decided that evacuation was inevitable. He allowed me to discuss all our plans with certain officers whom he nominated. This I did right into the small hours of the morning. I left Piraeus about 7 a.m. for Cairo.

The end of the story is well known; how the evacuation took place, and all our valuable equipment and transport was left behind in Greece. How a gallant attempt was made to hold Crete; how we lost most things other than our honour. As I did not take part in the Greek campaign itself, and so was not involved in these tragic happenings, I shall not describe them in these pages. I will attempt, however, to draw the conclusions as I see them.

XII

As I have already said, our strategy in Greece can be looked upon as a test case respecting the relationship between the political and the military factors. Therein lies its great interest to those who wish to sift out the lessons of this war.

I have told the tale as known to me, but I realise that a lot may have happened outside my knowledge. On the other hand, I believe the principal features affecting the issue are correctly described. Were we right or were we wrong in sending our forces to Greece? That is the question to decide. It is not usually a crime to make a few mistakes during a long and difficult war like the last. It is important, however, that if mistakes are made, we should admit them and so be better prepared for the future.

At the time I felt very strongly about the Greek affair, and as time went by my initial reactions have been confirmed, especially as so many conflicting versions have seeped out into the public arena.

Surely the only way to assess the rights and wrongs of a case such as this is to examine the decision made *in the light of the situation as it appeared at the time*. I believe Eden when justifying our intervention in Greece to the House, stated that our action had delayed Germany's attack on Russia by several weeks. Whether this is true or not, I suggest such a method of justification is similar to a punter who, having bought by mistake the wrong ticket at the tote, finds that horse wins, and then goes about saying "What a clever boy am I"! For at the time we possessed no evidence to suggest that Germany's intentions were directed to this end.

It is interesting, however, with the information now available, to see what delay was in fact imposed upon Germany in her attack on Russia.[11]

There is evidence to show that the Balkan campaign did make the German High Command put back the *"planning date"* for their offensive by three or four weeks. But in the event the weather conditions would not have allowed the offensive to take place any earlier than it did. This fact is *admitted* by Halder, then the German Chief of Staff. Without doubt, in view of average weather statistics, the original planning date was far too optimistic. It is also not unknown that Planners like to find some suitable excuse when their forecasts do not turn out as expected. Here was an easy one!

We must ask ourselves whether intervention in Greece was *necessary* at that time from either the political or the military

---

[11] The Germans employed the following formations in Greece:
Three Panzer Divisions.
Four Infantry Divisions.
Two Mountain Divisions.
An Independent Brigade.
Compare the above with the 150 divisions used in their offensive against Russia.

angle. Then there is the question of whether our forces were committed to Greece with any hope of success — in other words, was the task a feasible one, and did it suit our best interests?

We can dispose of the military necessity business quite shortly. We were not in a position to start large scale operations in the Balkans at that time. We did not have the military resources. We would, therefore, not have been in a position to exploit a lodgment gained in Greece. We would be killing Germans, which in itself was a desirable object, but not a good one if in the process we were likely to lose far more than the enemy. This was in fact the case. Germany was now virtually master of Europe and we needed time to build up our strength, and for America to come to our aid. This demanded a defensive strategy unless some cheap success were possible.

The political necessity obviously hinged around our Treaty of Alliance with Greece. Initially I don't doubt that the Greeks wished for our help, but presumably the acceptance was conditioned by whether the assistance that could be given would be of any real value. In early March, however, there was undoubtedly a period when the Greeks were convinced that our assistance would either be insufficient or would not arrive in time. They were also extremely worried because it looked as if neither Turkey nor Yugo-Slavia would fight the Germans. I feel sure that if we had agreed that our intervention would be ineffective, Greece would have let us off any obligations.

Non-intervention *might* have had a serious effect in America, but I do not consider failures — even gallant ones — in the long run help a nation at war in the eyes of neutrals. *Success* is the thing that matters. I can't believe that the United States would have remained out of the war if we had kept out of Greece.

There seemed to be few grounds at that time to support the expectation of Turkish and Yugo-Slav active co-operation. As regards Turkey, surely nothing would have acted more as a damper upon her help than a demonstration of our impotence in Greece. It is also very doubtful whether the eventual partisan fight in Yugo-Slavia against their German oppressors was due to our action in Greece.

I contend that from the military point of view an intervention in Greece never had any chance of success. There were so many disturbing elements present. These are briefly summarised below:

(a) Germany's great strength *vis-a-vis* the Allies' available resources.
(b) The poor state of the Greek Army, especially their munition situation.
(c) We were very short of modern and specialist equipment.
(d) The R.A.F. were almost bound to be swamped by the German Air Force in a very short time.
(e) Our L. of C. from Egypt was very vulnerable.
(f) The communications in Greece were inadequate to supply both the Greek Army and our own, once Salonika fell.
(g) If the enemy achieved success in the Monastir Gap area, disaster would face the Greek formations in Albania. The roads were few and bad and were totally inadequate in winter to allow a successful withdrawal, and in any case their troops did not possess the necessary mobility.
(h) The Navy was stretched already and shipping was very scarce.
(i) We could not expect active co-operation from Turkey or Yugo-Slavia.
(j) It was extremely doubtful whether we should get our full strength deployed in Greece before the German attack commenced.

Perhaps the most serious risk involved was the danger to morale. It will always remain an undying testimony to the men of the British Commonwealth that in spite of Dunkirk and Greece they maintained their fighting qualities.

If Greece had asked for assistance then we were in honour bound to do our best, but I contend we misled her as to our ability to help. We led her to believe that this help would be effective. The grounds for arriving at this view appeared extremely scanty. And the result was that we lost many lives, all our valuable equipment, and jeopardised our whole position in the Middle East. We brought about disaster in the Western Desert and threw away a chance of clearing up as far as Tripoli. Whether the politician forced the soldier's hand I do not know.

This brings me to the end of a sorry tale. But the real sufferings of brave little Greece had only just begun. Her valiant efforts against Italy, her readiness for sacrifice, and her trust in our ability to protect her country from the ravages of war, were of no avail.

CHAPTER IV: THE MIDDLE EAST — 1941

I

FOR those who were stationed in the Middle East, 1941 was to prove an anxious and yet on the whole a satisfactory year. There were many ups and many downs, some failures and some successes. On balance substantial gains were to be found at the close of the year. And what is more, these successes were achieved with very meagre resources and considerable risks were taken in order to accomplish our ends. It will help if I tabulate the various milestones of this fateful year in their chronological order. They were:

(a) The reverse south of Benghazi leading to the withdrawal to the fortress of Tobruk and to the Egyptian frontier. March 31st to April 11th.

(b) The landing of our forces at Basra. April 18th.

(c) The disastrous Greek campaign, which finished on May 1st.

(d) The loss of Crete. June 1st.

(e) The campaign in Syria. June 8th to July 14th.

(f) The abortive "Battle-axe" operation in the Western Desert. June 15th/17th.

(g) The change of command in Cairo. Auchinleck replaces Wavell. July 5th.

(h) Concern over our security in the area between India and Syria, in view of the German successes against Russia. October and November.

(i) Start of General Auchinleck's offensive, after the formation of Eighth Army. November 18th.

In the last chapter I touched upon the successful Axis offensive in Cyrenaica, and also dealt with certain aspects of the disastrous Greek campaign. As this book aims at giving a first-hand account of the war, I will not attempt to describe these operations in detail.

As a planner I did, however, witness the evolution of the defence arrangements in Crete. Whether Crete could have been held once Greece was lost is a very doubtful question. The Germans were sitting in the Aegean with their extremely strong Air Force within easy range of the island. There were no really good ports, and those that existed were situated on the northern coast. To reach these, ships had to run the gauntlet through the narrow and dangerous passages round the north-east and north-west corners of Crete, and on arrival they were easy meat for the German aircraft. Then the few airfields that existed were within range of Axis air bases. At the time of the German attack there were none in the area south of the central mountain range that runs east and west across the island, or in fact inland of the northern coast. The reserves of munitions were small. And when the German airborne attack started the small but gallant garrison, consisting largely of New Zealand troops, was tired after its adventures in Greece, and ill-provided with supporting arms and anti-aircraft defence. In addition, the defences were hastily prepared. Finally, our air support had to come from the mainland of Africa. Rarely have a Commander and his troops been given a more difficult task. Under that great fighter. General Freyburg, they behaved magnificently against the first major airborne attack of the war, in which were used the very flower of the German Army and the German Air Force. Yet how near they were to defeating this first attempt. Things hung in the balance for some time, and the cost of success to the enemy was very great.

The Germans had relied upon the success of their airborne attack, and I don't know what they would have done had this phase of the operations failed. Would they have attempted a major assault by sea alone? Equipped with modern landing craft, and given modern combined operation technique, I am sure the Axis would have had no difficulty in capturing Crete, even after the initial failure of the airborne assault. But they were not well equipped for this purpose, although their great air strength would have neutralised our naval effort.

My view is that had the major airborne assault failed, the enemy would have hesitated before attempting to capture Crete with another plan. Without the necessary equipment for a big seaborne operation there would have been a grave risk of failure. The enemy had backed the "airborne horse" and Student, the German Parachute Commander, had sold his wares most successfully to his High Command. It is pretty certain that considerable extra time would have been required to carry out another plan. Would this have interfered with the attack on Russia? Not I think from the Army point of view, but very likely from the Air Force angle. Considerable air forces would have been required for the task, and it is difficult to see how these could have been spared from other future needs.

How important was Crete to the Axis, or alternatively, how important was the denial of its use to us as a base? The acquisition of the island to the Axis meant the sealing of the Aegean area — a defensive requirement. It also gave the enemy air and sea bases which helped them to dominate the Eastern Mediterranean — an offensive requirement. Air attack against targets in Egypt and North Africa was also assisted a great deal. The enemy certainly made good use of Crete, but I do not think its capture was vital to him, for in view of the weaknesses of our preparations, I believe it would have been a comparatively simple matter to have neutralised our position there. I don't see how we could have been a threat to the Axis from the Cretan base, certainly not until our strength had increased enormously. But it would, of course, eventually have proved most valuable in any operations we undertook in south-east Europe. It might, however, have proved itself a dominating influence in planning our future war strategy, and have given ammunition to those who favoured that area for our big effort in southern Europe. I think they would have been wrong, but who knows?

One thing is certain, holding on to Crete under these conditions would have been a very big drain on our resources. Under the constant threat of the German Air Force, with poor port facilities, with little anti-aircraft defence, with meagre reserves of munitions, and with the unlikelihood of the R.A.F. being able to operate from the island, our position would have been very difficult. It might have reached a state when re-supply or reinforcement became too expensive, and the subsequent capture of the island by the enemy a comparatively easy affair.

The big question which we must ask ourselves — so that we may learn a lesson for the future — is, could we have done more to ensure that Crete was adequately defended? This resolves itself into: did we appreciate its importance early enough, and could we have arranged things so that the defence of the island became a practicable proposition?

Whether it would have been better strategy to have concentrated on Crete instead of committing ourselves to Greece is a big question, and one that I am not going to argue about here. I have already given my views about the Greece expedition, arriving at the conclusion that from the military angle we backed a loser from the start.

The importance of Crete in Middle East strategy was continually cropping up in all our planning studies, and the Royal Navy never ceased to stress this point. However, I'm afraid little was done to prepare the island for defence in the time available. It must not be forgotten that the Greeks allowed us to send troops to Crete *in December*, 1940. In order to allow the fine 5th Cretan Division to be used against the Italians in Albania we assumed the responsibility for the defence of the island. Later when it was decided that our Expeditionary Force should sail to Greece itself, our strength did not permit a diversion of resources being made to Crete. But there were over two months available before this decision was made, during which, efforts could have been concentrated on organising the defence of the Island. Did we take full advantage of these precious weeks?

I'm afraid our defence policy never had great drive behind it. The Commanders we put there were often changed, and the method of defending Crete was never studied sufficiently on a high level. Each Commander considered the method of his predecessor was not good enough, or even faulty and so changed it. Being told to defend a very large island like Crete, unless one has numerous resources allotted one, is not an attractive proposition. On the other hand, I am certain, given similar conditions, the Germans would have done better. There was plenty of labour available. With this, a lot of useful work could have been done with a comparatively small professional backing. Roads could have been made; ports could have been improved; development of the small harbours on the southern coast would have proved a great asset; more airstrips could have been built to eliminate the weakness of relying upon coastal airfields; and finally, reserves of munitions could have been built up. It is easier to say these things than do them, particularly as the time available was so short. But remembering the small margin between failure and success, as well as what was achieved in a last-minute endeavour to put the defences of Crete in order, I have a feeling that we might have defeated this first Axis attempt at capture. It seemed so sad that such magnificent troops were not given a better chance. And it also seemed sad that the Greek people were led to believe in the strength of the "Fortress of Crete," because we — their powerful ally — had taken over its defence.

To sum up:

> (*a*) The Crete campaign was a very gallant affair. It gave the German Air Force, and particularly their Airborne Army, a nasty shock. Their losses were great.
>
> (*N.B.* — It is interesting to remember that the Germans never again attempted an airborne operation on such a scale.)
>
> (*b*) The defence of Crete was made extremely difficult by the decision to go all out in Greece.
>
> (*c*) More could have been done if a firmer grip had been taken at the first opportunity. Inland airstrips could have been built, landing places on the south coast exploited, and additional reserves of munitions accumulated. A Cretan Home Guard might also have been formed. Such action might well have spelt the defeat of the German attack. Whether a subsequent attempt would have been repelled, or whether we could have kept our forces supplied and maintained in Crete is questionable. This would have depended upon what effort the enemy were prepared to expend in this direction.

II

I will say very little about the campaigns in Iraq and Syria, as I took no part in them. I believe I am correct in saying that it required a good deal of pressure from London to persuade the Commander-in-Chief, Wavell, to undertake these projects.

The Iraq operations started with a landing at Basra, well planned and executed by India on April 18th. General Auchinleck, the Commander-in-Chief at Delhi, behaved with great vigour, and his management, firm direction and optimism throughout was most welcome. The object of the operation was to remove Axis influence from Iraq and so assist in the general security of the Middle East. The security of the Anglo-Iranian oilfields had also, of course, a big influence upon our action.

The campaign under General Wilson to wrest Syria from the Vichy French commenced on June 8th. Resources were small and the operations were protracted and quite costly. Had we been able to commence with a really powerful punch, it looks as if the French would have capitulated at an early date. As it was, they took heart from the weakness of our attack, and it was not until July 14th — that memorable date in French history — that the final surrender occurred.

Wavell, I believe, was very much against this venture. One can sympathise with him, for he had a great deal "on his plate" at the time. He had no doubt been shaken by the reverses in Cyrenaica and the disaster in Greece, a campaign which had received his backing. He still had active fronts in Eritrea and Abyssinia, in Cyrenaica and Iraq. He was also planning a limited offensive in the Western Desert. This is a good example of when a Government may be right in "persuading" a Commander-in-Chief to undertake a commitment against his inclination. There is no question that many of us working at

G.H.Q. Cairo about then felt that the Commander-in-Chief was losing his grip and wanted a rest. A change in command did in fact take place on July 5th, when Wavell and Auchinleck changed places.

III

The operation which went by the code name "Battleaxe" was a sorry affair. The name was symbolic, for it achieved just about as much as that ancient weapon would have done if used in a modern battle. The object was to try and gain mastery over the area of desert about the frontier, with the hope that a link-up with Tobruk might become possible. The aim was a laudable one, but the tools with which to carry it out were terribly weak. It is strange that Wavell should have pressed on with this attack. In the first place he was so busy elsewhere, and he had little or nothing in reserve. It may have been that he had hoped to create one by forcing an improvement in the situation in the Desert; it may, of course, have been the result of pressure from home. As it was, there did not appear to be either enthusiasm or optimism behind the project. The troops, however, as always, embarked on this attack with their usual spirit of sacrifice. In view of how much was asked of them during this period, it is a wonderful thing that they retained their basic morale, and so were ready later to reap their reward in the years of plenty.

I hope someone will go into this battle in detail, for to my mind it was wrong in every way, and it should be studied at the Staff College for this very reason. The one redeeming feature was the fact that Wavell flew up to see how things were going on the second day, made up his mind quickly that the operation was a failure, ordered its discontinuance, and so prevented any further loss.

We had accumulated something in the region of two hundred tanks by then, mostly of the obsolete Valentine type. Slow and armed with the two-pounder "pop-gun," they were easy prey for the enemy. Rommel used his 88-mm. guns most effectively, protecting them with his tanks and artillery, and killed our tanks long before they could get into range. I can't remember our exact losses, but they were about a hundred tanks — a very serious figure at that stage of the war. The only benefit I can see that we derived from this attack was the fact that we were now left in no doubt as to how far behind we were in both tank and anti-tank gun design.

IV

It is interesting to compare the three Commanders-in-Chief under whom I directly served — Wavell, Auchinleck and Montgomery.

Wavell had obtained tremendous kudos and prestige from the success of his Western Desert offensive. After that we all felt we had a shrewd and able commander. The reverses in the early part of 1941 did something to shake this confidence. Victories are, of course, the means by which a commander endears himself to the troops, and he was undoubtedly very popular amongst them. I never knew what effect the subsequent failures had upon their attitude. We in the lower grades of the staff saw very little of our Commander-in-Chief. Whilst I was at G.H.Q., I never remember attending an address by him. He dealt only with the highest level of staff officers, and high commanders have little time to do anything else. He used his Chief of General Staff very nearly as Montgomery used his Chief of Staff. He was the channel through which most things were done. Arthur Smith held this appointment, and I can't say enough for the kindly help and guidance he gave to staff officers like myself. He had a wonderful spirit and morale, and excelled himself when things were really black. I realise how difficult it must be for Commanders-in-Chief to find the time to make themselves known to their staff, but a very small effort in this direction produces a very big dividend. It is extraordinary how susceptible a staff officer is to a little notice taken, or by an occasional personal contact with his Commander. It is human nature. The staff usually get very little praise and all the kicks. They deserve encouragement.

Montgomery used to keep in touch with the staff as a whole by periodical talks. After some particularly successful operation he would send me charming messages of thanks and appreciation which would be circulated to all concerned. In addition, he used to walk round various branches of the headquarters at intervals. He would chat easily with high and low, and such visits had a visible effect upon the output of that particular section. Further on in the book I devote a complete chapter to my former Chief and describe in detail how he worked.

Auchinleck's arrival in Cairo was like a breath of fresh air. It luckily coincided with an improvement in the general situation and the promise of reinforcements of troops and material. But in addition, he had an engaging personality, was most accessible, and appeared amazingly alert and competent. He certainly managed to get his personality around his headquarters in a very short time. If I may be allowed to express my views as to his methods of working, and I would not do so unless I had later become a Chief of Staff, I would say that he listened to too many people. The object was, of course, to make certain that everything possible was being done. It is a dangerous procedure, and I am sure better results are produced by keeping to the recognised channels, and let the experts advise on their own particular subject; and if the experts are no good, change them. We certainly all liked working for the "Auk" and I developed a great personal affection for my Chief. He was very human and a delightful companion. He was rather in favour of the "Brains Trust" principle, and would like to gather around him various members of his staff and argue out the merits or otherwise of a certain plan. He would run little "war games" with an "enemy" and "own troops" to test out some new idea.

Force of circumstances, as I will explain later, led the Commander-in-Chief to exercise a large measure of control of Eighth Army's fortunes from Cairo.

Auchinleck attempted to find a solution to the vexed problem of where should the General Headquarters be housed, and how should the staff live. By a gradual process of evolution from the days of peace, through the period of semi-war prior to Italy's entry, and then into active war conditions, an enormous headquarters had been gathered together. Yet we all lived and worked under peace conditions — except of course for the hours we put in. We were in a foreign country that was not at war. From the communication point of view alone we had to be either in, or very near to Cairo itself. I won't deny that we all had something of a guilty feeling. Delightful flats with servants, and plenty of food and drink. Every sort of entertainment, either by day or night, numberless wealthy Egyptians only too pleased to dispense hospitality. It was undoubtedly a bad set-up, particularly when we considered the conditions and hardships at home, and those of the fighting troops. But a solution was very hard to find — things had really gone too far. Wavell, I think, wisely let things be; Auchinleck was determined to move the headquarters to the desert and get all the staff out of their flats into messes[12] and tents. He soon found that the full object was not possible, and so went for a modified scheme, whereby the staff would live out in the desert at Mena, a few miles from Cairo, and come in each day to work in the great buildings that had been requisitioned for G.H.Q., Even this plan had some major snags. The transport required to move us all in and out would be very great, a shortage of tentage, the provision of Egyptian cooks and servants willing to live out there, were some of the troubles that arose. The date for the move was gradually put back month by month, and as far as I remember by the time I left Cairo for Eighth Army, only the Commander-in-Chief himself and a few "buddies" had taken up the austere life!

How the staff should work and live is a very difficult question. Undoubtedly a great deal of harm is done by reports reaching the fighting troops of the staff living in luxury behind them. We know the results of this in the 1914-18 war, and we know how Montgomery's rigid rules regarding this matter helped to ensure confidence and mutual esteem between the troops and the staff. We must on the other hand keep a balanced view in these matters. In the first place, I do think it important that a really large headquarters should have good conditions to work under. There is no reason why they should not go into buildings. They are far more convenient and make for increased efficiency and are altogether preferable to tents and caravans. In Eighth Army and 21st Army Group we remained on a tent/caravan basis from El Alamein until we reached Brussels — then we took over the German

---

[12] I am told that the lack of messes for the large number of officers at the various Headquarters in Egypt, has created a considerable problem in connection with the move of cur forces from the cities to the Canal Zone, under the proposed terms of the revised Anglo-Egyptian Treaty (August, 1946).

headquarters. I would say, therefore, that if buildings are available a big headquarters should make use of them. The argument that the fighting troops would object should not be accepted. As far as I know the Germans, the Americans, and all other armies do so, and I won't believe that we are so sensitive a nation that we must sacrifice efficiency for sentiment. Where the staff live is another matter. Here we must be most careful. In Cairo we should have been in messes, but I admit the proposal at the time filled us with horror. The trouble was we had become too used to the existing state of affairs. Personally I do not see any harm in eating and drinking the good things that are available, or of taking recreation and accepting hospitality. But this must not be overdone, and so you come to the difficult question of how to control it. The easiest way is naturally to forbid it altogether. I'm sure Montgomery would have done this if he had been Commander-in-Chief in Cairo, and I am also certain he would have insisted upon the Headquarters moving out of that city, whatever the difficulties and whatever the opposition. I think the Egyptians would have thought us quite mad if we had not accepted their hospitality, and in many ways this did a lot of good, and helped to cement firm and cordial relations between the two Allies. I for one cannot say enough for the treatment I received, for the many acts of kindness that were shown me, and for their open-handed generosity. There must be many thousands who feel as I do.

I must admit I had to pay for sticking on to my Cairo flat when General Auchinleck went out to live in the desert at Mena. I was then Director of Military Intelligence in the Middle East, and it meant that on occasions I had to discuss matters with my Chief at odd times during the night. It meant therefore that I had to take a car out to Mena and trek across the sand to his tent, where rather dreary conferences took place. These conditions did not, however, last long, for soon I was to be sent out to the Desert myself — to Eighth Army.

V

With the change of command in Cairo and the promise of reinforcements great optimism prevailed. Two major preoccupations existed. The first was the formation of Eighth Army and the planning of an offensive, and secondly the tying up of defensive arrangements in the area between India and Syria, owing to the German advance into Russia.

The old Western Desert Force was now reorganised into a proper Army and given the number "Eighth." General Cunningham, fresh from his victories in East Africa and Abyssinia, was appointed its first Commander. Galloway took over the appointment of Brigadier General Staff. The target date for the offensive was mid-November, and its object was to destroy Rommel's Army, relieving Tobruk in the process. There was no limit put to the ultimate exploitation, and the planning staffs were busy collecting data which would take our forces to Tripoli and even beyond. The new Army came into being early in October and there was a great deal to be done. Enthusiasm was generated from the top, and feverish activity was to be seen both in the Desert and at G.H.Q. in Cairo. We were still considerably behind the Germans in respect of tanks and anti-tank guns; but we were now receiving the American "Honey" or Stuart tank, which, though small and thin-skinned, was yet a great improvement upon most of our own models. This tank was also very fast and manoeuvrable and had excellent mechanical reliability.

The planners were told to produce staff studies and suggest courses of action. Out of these two main conceptions emerged. One was to hold the enemy in the area between the frontier and Tobruk, whilst a large force was sent round on the general axis Giarubub Gialo, with the object of capturing Benghazi, and so cutting the enemy's lines of communication. The other was by carrying out a short "left hook" from the Maddelena direction towards Tobruk — which was of course still invested — and force Rommel to give battle. We hoped to possess considerable numerical superiority in tanks, guns and troops. Our air force was also in good fettle.

On a small scale map the first alternative looked attractive. But this was only so in theory, for there were so many snags and uncertainties. Here are some of them. It meant an advance of some 400 miles across a stretch of desert that we knew very little about. We did have some reports of the "going" from the Long Range Desert Group patrols, but the information available was nothing like enough. At that time of the year rain could be expected, and this might interfere with movement at a critical time. The supply of this large force would be a colossal problem, and one that, even if everything went well, would tax our available transport to the full. It would mean that little if anything could be done on the other sector of the front. Then Rommel might, with comparative ease, cut our supply line. Finally, air support would be most difficult, for at that time the Desert Air Force had not the equipment, nor had they developed sufficiently their magnificent technique for building and using airfields in the very van of the advance. The risks were enormous, and certainly not justified. Further, the object was a "woolly" one, for it was not certain that the main enemy forces would be defeated. Even if our force got to the Benghazi area our troubles would not be over, and Rommel might still be able to keep his Army further east supplied. The result of such a plan might have meant a large portion of our army being stranded without supplies 400-500 miles from any help, and incapable of achieving any useful purpose. In the event a small column was sent along this southern route to capture Gialo, and also to act as a diversion. It had a bad time, ran into extremely bad going, and I don't think paid a dividend. It took strength away from our main effort and Rommel virtually ignored it.

Unfortunately this plan found a certain amount of favour in high places. The staff officer who sponsored it was young and without any practical experience. He had a good way of serving up such studies. I am sure that Cunningham was a good enough soldier never to have accepted such a plan, but there was certainly a danger that a great deal of trouble and work would be undertaken unless it was killed once and for all. I'm afraid I did a lot of lobbying with this end in view. I went through it with "Sandy" Galloway and he was quite clear as to the dangers. Eventually the other and sounder plan was adopted and everything went full speed ahead.

The bulk of Eighth Army was concentrated about half-way between the frontier and the Delta. Rehearsals were held for the move forward, and on November 18th we started. Rain made the advance via Maddelena somewhat difficult, but generally speaking the Army was launched most favourably. Our armoured brigades were commanded with great dash, but perhaps not with comparable skill. When once they came into contact with Rommel's main forces very heavy casualties occurred. The tank "returns" that came in to Army Headquarters were positively frightening. Some units hardly had a "runner" At this stage Rommel undertook a very bold and well-timed armoured raid deep into our area. The spearhead crossed the frontier wire, and was not far short of rail-head and important supply dumps. Army H.Q., was also threatened. Eighth Army did not react to this as Rommel had hoped, and went on with their task of gaining control of the tactical area south of Tobruk with a view to a link up with that garrison, as well as taking considerable toll of the enemy. During this fighting a New Zealand Casualty Clearing Station was overrun by the enemy. Rommel found time to walk round and talk to some of the patients. He certainly had something about him, this German General. We always felt he was a fitting and chivalrous opponent.

After about nine days' fighting our losses had been so heavy — our tanks being no match for the enemy anti-tank guns and tanks — that doubts arose in the Army Commander's mind as to the advisability of pursuing the original plan at such a cost. General Auchinleck decided to fly up to Eighth Army Headquarters to study the situation. I understand that he arrived at a moment when orders had actually been issued for the move of the Headquarters back into Egypt. Galloway, the B.G.S., deserves great credit for his part at this juncture. He was convinced that a move back of the Army's Headquarters would most certainly mean the end of the offensive. He therefore played for time until the Commander-in-Chief arrived. Some caravans and tents were taking an exceptionally long time to get packed up! It is, I'm sure, not betraying a confidence when I say that when asked his opinion of the situation by Auchinleck he advised strongly in favour of the continuance of the offensive in its original form. Galloway had seen far worse situations when holding the appointment as B.G.S. to General Wilson in Greece. It was then that the Commander-in-Chief showed great courage and leadership. He decided to make a change in command, and to drive the Army forward in spite of what they had suffered. Our Intelligence showed that the enemy's situation was anything but good. This must have been a most bitter blow to Cunningham. He had done magnificently in East Africa, but the strain of the campaign had told on his health, and he was not allowed a day's rest between his old and new commands. At the opening of the battle he was not fit, and unless a commander is so at moments like this he is at a grave disadvantage.

The selection of a new Army Commander was no easy matter. He had to be found at once, and there were no commanders immediately available who really had the requisite experience. The choice fell upon Major-General Ritchie, who was at that time Deputy Chief of the General Staff at G.H.Q., Cairo. He was young, forceful and efficient, but had never held high command in the field. He had, however, served in Auchinleck's staff in England. It was an incredible responsibility to throw on his shoulders, but Ritchie accepted it and, in spite of his newness to desert conditions and his inexperience, grew from strength to strength. His Commander-in-Chief stayed up to see him into the saddle, and was always in the background for him to lean upon for advice and help. This combination remained until the issue was certain, and Rommel was being soundly beaten.

It is the way of life that so little is heard of Eighth Army's successful offensive against Rommel *before* Montgomery took over command. Admittedly one can't really call an offensive successful unless the victory is consummated. This one ended in a major reverse. But it is only right that full credit should be given to this gallant army who, although equipped with inferior tools, by sheer courage, dogged determination and spirit, defeated some of the finest and most experienced troops in the German Army. It was a wonderful achievement and should not be forgotten. Tobruk was relieved, Benghazi captured, and our forces advanced well towards Agheila. But once again the significance of the Cyrenaica bulge had not been sufficiently appreciated. Our position was very weak until Benghazi had become a major supply base, and we had gathered strong forces in the area between Tobruk and Tmini. Rommel once again saw his opportunity and took it. He attacked strongly on a narrow front on January 21st, 1942, and Eighth Army, stretched and weak in supplies, fell back to avoid a disaster. The Army was caught off its balance, and things did not go too well. Rommel captured valuable supplies of petrol and stores which helped him maintain his momentum. He also managed to cut off a chunk of our forces in the Benghazi area. There were some epic tales of how some formations, units and individuals avoided the net, and it does great credit to Ritchie, his commanders and staff, that they managed to overcome the initial confusion and difficulties, and so formed a solid front in the area south of Gazala. Here the army stayed until Rommel started his great effort to drive us out of Egypt some four months later.

VI

With the rapid advance of the German forces into Russia, it soon became evident that a potential threat existed to our security in the Middle East, Iraq and Iran. This threat might develop through Turkey or via Caucasia. In the summer of 1941, therefore, the planning staffs in Cairo and New Delhi were giving a lot of attention to the problem. By this time we had cleared up the pro-Axis element in both Iraq and Iran, and the Vichy French had capitulated in Syria. Turkey was still an unknown factor, and in spite of the somewhat optimistic reports we received from our representatives in that country, we did not feel any reliance could be placed upon either Turkey's resistance to an Axis advance through her country, or to her eventual agreement to a move of our forces into Anatolia which would give greater depth to our defence in the Middle East.

I don't see how Turkey can really be blamed for her attitude at this time. The equipment of her forces was mostly out of date, and in spite of many half-promises we found ourselves unable to deliver the very equipments of which we were ourselves too much in need. We had been allowed to build a number of airfields in Turkey and also to start accumulating stores and petrol for their possible use by us. I therefore find it hard to see what other action could have been taken. She had seen the result of resistance to the Axis might all around her. She had also seen how ineffective our assistance had proved to be. Unless her forces were modernised, opposition would be a farce. Then the question of allowing our forces into Anatolia, if the Axis attacked, was not quite so simple as it sounded. We had little that we could send to stop a determined German advance, and so we would only have been using Turkish territory for fighting our battles to give us better security in the Middle East. The result would almost certainly have been the devastation of their country, with no compensating advantage.

Our lack of resources did not allow us to contemplate a successful initial holding up of a large scale enemy advance either against the Middle East or towards the Persian Gulf. We therefore accepted the fact that we should have to give much ground, and our ability to stretch the enemy's L. of C. became the main strength in any of our plans. We produced staff studies and held war games to test out various lines of withdrawal, and areas suitable for delaying action. The whole region was reconnoitred for potential airfields. Complete demolition schemes were worked out; in fact scorched earth action — always much easier to carry out in a country other than one's own — was envisaged. In addition steps were being taken to enlist the support of the various fighting tribes, with a view to carrying out guerrilla activities against the enemy's communications. All these plans looked quite good when set out in our papers, but I'm afraid I didn't feel very sanguine about their success if the Axis really meant business.

There was, of course, a great deal of "clewing-up" between the various commands — e.g. Syria, Iraq and Iran — and then there was the difficult matter of co-ordination between India and the Middle East.

In October 1941 it was decided to send a party of staff officers from G.H.Q. Cairo, to discuss plans and co-ordination with our commands in Syria, Palestine, Iraq and Iran. This was to be followed up later on with a visit to India itself. The mission was inter-Service and I was lucky enough to be put in charge. My old friend, Claude Pelly of the R.A.F. planning staff, came with me and we numbered about eight all told. We were loaned a Lockheed aircraft by the Air Commander-in-Chief, Tedder, which was a great treat in those days of short supply, and this alone showed the importance attached to our work.

We flew first to Baghdad and held a series of conferences with General Quinan and his staff. These proved most useful, and we were able to obtain considerable agreement to our proposals. In addition, we naturally benefited from the views and information given by the experts on the spot. We possessed very scanty information about the area just inside Russia. We considered it important that we should have the latest data concerning the roads, railways, shipping and ports on the Caspian Sea, and general description of the terrain and the climate. We required all this to help us determine the strength, speed and direction of a potential enemy advance. As a Russian mission had recently arrived in Baghdad, I had asked before leaving Cairo for a meeting with its members to be arranged. On arrival at the Iraqi capital, I was told that I should get precious little from our Russian Allies. I was conceited enough to think that they might be wrong; but they were right. The meeting was a complete and utter failure. I will describe it.

I and two others and three Russians sat round a table, and after the usual cordial introductions had taken place, I was asked what was the purpose of the meeting. I had prepared a nice little speech which, as tactfully as possible explained that as a prudent staff we were engaged in producing studies dealing with all possible eventualities. Now that Germany had attacked Russia there was always the possibility — admittedly a very unlikely possibility — of a threat developing via Caucasia to our security further south. In view of our reliance upon the Iranian oil, the development of such a threat would be a very serious matter. I was hoping that they would be able to supply me with certain information which would assist us in framing our plans. Having heard me through most courteously, the Russian spokesman, after a preliminary exchange of views with his colleagues, got up and said roughly as follows: "We find it difficult to understand your requests, for the Germans have not reached the Caucasus. If by any chance such an event did take place, and the Red Army could not stop them, how in the name of heaven could you?" It was a most shattering riposte, especially as at the time there was probably a lot of truth in it. We had a good laugh, and then I tried in vain to put across our point of view. Eventually I was invited to explain some of the things about which I required information. I mentioned some of these, but the answer was always the same: "The matter must be referred to Moscow." I soon saw it was quite useless to pursue the business, and the evening finished up in drinking and eating rather more than was good for us.

From Baghdad we flew to Teheran, where I had meetings with our Minister and various other individuals. The time was spent chiefly in checking up the information which we had compiled, and going into demolition plans, and the potentialities of guerrilla warfare. We spent a delightful two days living in a very comfortable hotel a few miles from the capital in a charming garden city. We ate a great deal of caviar. On the third day we were due to fly back to Baghdad to hold other meetings, but on the way to the airfield I had an unfortunate accident. The sepoy driver of the truck which was carrying us increased speed as he started to go round a steep bend in the road, and the truck crashed into some trees. My arm got caught between the vehicle and a tree, and the result was a rather nasty mess. I was eventually taken to a funny little nursing home, and was attended to by the Legation doctor. I am so very grateful for the kindness which I received from the little Armenian nurses. I was put under, and the arm set — not an easy matter, as the elbow had been badly smashed. After a day in hospital we all flew off to Baghdad where we concluded our business. From there we visited Jerusalem to discuss the defence of Syria and Iraq. This completed, we returned to Cairo to compile our massive paper. My broken arm was compensated to some extent by an addition to my luggage of eight kilos of caviar and a dozen bottles of vodka!

My arm did not behave too well on my return to Cairo, and this necessitated a period in hospital and a long stretch with my arm in plaster. It did not stop me, however, from being able to carry out the complementary mission to New Delhi. I found this visit a most valuable and pleasant experience. Everyone was extraordinarily kind and helpful, and solutions to most of the complicated problems were found. It was the perfect time of the year in India — November/December, and as my arm still gave trouble, I was sent down to Poona to see an expert in those matters. Here I spent a delightful week's leave with a very old friend of mine, before flying back by comfortable B.O.A.C. flying boat to Cairo.

VII

In the Middle East the year 1941 closed upon a relatively high note. Our offensive into Cyrenaica had been a great success. The Russians, fighting with the greatest valour and determination, had saved Moscow from being captured. The Italian colonies in East Africa had been finally reduced. Abyssinia had been liberated. There was no immediate danger to Turkey or to Iran/Iraq. Promises of reinforcements and new material were most encouraging. But Japan's entry into the war on the side of the Axis rather offset this satisfactory picture; and we were already beginning to feel the effects of this additional commitment which the sorely tried British Empire had been made to shoulder. India had now to look to her own defence; we were no longer the only customers for reinforcement and supplies. Our expectations were curtailed, and all three services were forced even to despatch resources already in the Middle East to help deal with the menace from Japan. Stout hearts and clear heads were required to see us through the next few months.

CHAPTER V: THE MIDDLE EAST — DIRECTOR OF MILITARY INTELLIGENCE

I

ONE evening in the planning room at G.H.Q., Cairo, in late February of 1942, I was browsing over some rather depressing papers we had just written when the phone rang, and I was told the Commander-in-Chief, General Auchinleck, wanted to see me at 7.30. In due course I arrived at his office and reported. He looked up from his desk and said: "Freddie, I want you to take over D.M.I."[13] This was a shattering thing for a lieutenant-colonel with no previous Intelligence experience to be told. When I recovered my breath I replied: "But I have never done anything of that sort before, sir." "Excellent," said the Auk, "that's just why I've chosen you, you'll do it all right. I want you to take over at once. Good night."

I left the office very dazed. It was a great step up. I had never even thought about becoming a Brigadier — I had hoped the war wasn't going to last as long as all that! But I was really worried how I could master the job, particularly as the Intelligence problems were very difficult at that moment. The enemy was doing his very best to confuse us. All sorts of reports and rumours were being circulated. Cyprus was to be attacked. An airborne invasion of Egypt was under preparation. Rommel was soon to continue his drive eastwards. It was all very bewildering, and I was like a fish out of water, and I believe felt just as unhappy.

---

[13] Director of Military Intelligence.

My new Directorate were very nice to me — an inexperienced interloper. My Commander-in-Chief also could not have been kinder. In fact, I was allowed to ease myself into the saddle very gently, and for this I was most grateful. Early on I spotted two young officers as being exceptionally able, one was Ewart and the other Williams. A junior major and a junior captain respectively, I made a lot of use of them and pushed them on, and what a dividend they paid. Bill Williams became G.S.O.2 Eighth Army; Head of Intelligence Eighth Army, and finally Field-Marshal Montgomery's Chief Intelligence Staff Officer in 21 Army Group. The most able and clear-headed occupier of such a post I have ever met. He was my friend and colleague for the last three and a half years of war. Joe Ewart, somehow with a little help from me, used to find himself visiting Eighth Army for very long periods, whether he was stationed at home or in the Middle East. Ewart and Williams were an ideal combination. They understood each other perfectly. Both had first class brains, and both were University dons, and hated soldiering as a profession! Towards the end of the war Ewart was William's representative at Montgomery's Tactical Headquarters. By a cruel turn of fate Ewart lost his life in a car accident after we had achieved victory in Europe.

It took me several weeks before I felt that I was not a passenger, and once having passed this stage, I really began to enjoy my work. It was intensely exciting at times, and the diversity of one's activities was refreshing. I managed to get away for a ten day tour of Palestine, Syria and Iraq, in order to visit the Intelligence staffs in those areas. Other than this, I only found the time to visit Eighth Army, and this I did with increasing regularity. Auchinleck had given me as my first priority task, that of establishing the greatest measure of confidence between the Commanders and Staffs of Eighth Army and Military Intelligence. We all worked hard to achieve this object, and I really believe we didn't fall far short of our objective. I enjoyed these visits very much indeed. Ritchie and his B.G.S. were both "I" minded, and were ever ready to give me any amount of their time. A trip to Eighth Army acted as a wonderful tonic after Cairo; the freshness of the desert and the great friendliness one met there was a fine experience, and I always felt a bit guilty on arriving back at my comfortable flat after only two or three hours' flight from the Army area.

March, April and May were exciting months. We were planning another offensive, and we well knew that Rommel was doing the same thing. Who would be ready first? What was our plan to be? What form would the enemy's plan take? These were vital questions, and naturally the last was the one that concerned me most.

There was considerable pressure from home to get our offensive off at an early date. Our present positions about Gazala were not good, and the sooner we got going the better. But this was easier said than done. It was going to take a considerable time to recover and make good the losses from our recent reverse, and it was no good undertaking an offensive unless we were strong enough to exploit success and ensure that the usual "swan" back was not to take place this time after we reached Benghazi!

We were getting bigger and better tanks, and the new six-pounder anti-tank gun was on its way. Time was, however, required in order that we could re-equip units with these new and most necessary weapons. I consider that in this case the Commander-in-Chief was pressed too hard, and as one who was in daily and intimate contact with him, I noticed that he was feeling the strain of fighting this battle in order to give his own troops a fair chance.

To evolve a plan that would ensure success was no easy matter. All sorts of theories were put forward. New arrivals to the Middle East saw an easy solution in a dash to Benghazi across the desert to the south of the Jebel country. We were neither strong enough nor equipped adequately for such a plan, and I am sure Rommel would have thanked God for the opportunity such an operation might give him. His main army would have been able to play havoc with our L. of C. and in any case, when one worked out the detail, the bill for the transport and supply services was immense and really beyond our capacity. Auchinleck used to hold discussions and war games to test out these theories. At one moment the "cow-pat" scheme was finding some favour. This was the term given to establishing a series of supply bases one by one in front of our present positions. Strong armoured forces were to be based upon these administrative areas, and they in turn would be protected by infantry and artillery. The idea was to force the enemy to attack us, as he could not go on ignoring these thrusts into his territory. It had a fundamental weakness, and that was that it automatically made us disperse our forces, whilst it gave the enemy the opportunity of concentrating against these detachments. The "cow-pat" theory finally died at a war game in which McCreery — a future Commander of Eighth Army — took part. His efforts, I think, assisted to some extent by mine as controller of the enemy, did the trick. Before a firm plan had been decided upon, it became obvious that Rommel would be in a position to strike first, and so our thoughts were switched to devising means of holding this attack when it came, and then to launch at the right moment a counter stroke.

The collecting and collating of all the evidence about the enemy intentions were full of interest. Suffice to say that we were in a position to forecast with reasonable accuracy the date of the Axis attack. We had to guess more or less, however, the plan he would adopt, and the scope of the offensive. We now know that it was part of a grandiose scheme in which two great pincers were directed against our positions in the Middle East, one via North Africa and the other through Turkey or Russia. I remember with the help of my staff preparing a list of the various signs which we considered would appear in the course of the enemy's preparations. It was a long list including matters connected with supply, reinforcements, activity at the ports, air photography, types of wireless traffic, and periods of wireless silence. It was intriguing how many of these items we were able to tick off before that fateful day, the 27th May.

In assessing our relative strengths, the number of tanks possessed by each side was at that time taken as the basis for calculation. We went to tremendous pains to ensure that we had the enemy figures. As books have already been written on this subject, I will mention one of the methods we adopted. It was the use of the Long Range Desert Group. This magnificent and well-trained body of men kept a constant watch — by day and by night — on the road between Tripoli and Benghazi. They were experts in identification of enemy equipment, and had wireless communication with us in Cairo. It was extraordinary that they escaped detection, and this in itself is a striking tribute to their efficiency. I think we used to receive two reports per twenty-four hours. All heavy reinforcements used to be sent to Tripoli, and from there along this one road to Rommel's Army. The reports proved most accurate, and provided a first-class check on all other information concerning moves of troops and material.

Whilst on this subject of enemy intelligence I must mention a small but important matter in which I did not see eye to eye with my Commander-in-Chief. At one time he pressed me to form what he called a "German cell," whose job would be to live in an enemy atmosphere and try and read into the enemy's mind. This small body of officers were to be chosen because of their knowledge of Germany and Germans. They were to be fed with the Directorate's information, but divorced from it. They would be guided to a large extent upon "hunches" of what the German would do when faced with this or that situation. I had a horror of such a set-up. To begin with it would mean a rival firm that was not under my control. The Commander-in-Chief would therefore be getting his advice from two quarters, and these might often conflict. Then there would be a great danger of basing our plans upon "hunches" and not upon sound evidence. I had in the Directorate a first-class team, and a very large team. They were for the most part experienced Intelligence staff officers, and I could not see what this suggested innovation could do that we could not. I know that the idea had been sold to Auchinleck by an attractive and fertile, but not always very sound, "brain." I played for time, explained my difficulty in selecting the right officers, accommodation problems held it up, and finally the matter was allowed to drop. I am sure Auchinleck will agree now that we did not let him down, and that the proposal would have been a mistake.

One must be careful in war not to upset the normal staff arrangements. I do not mean that we should be "Blimpish," but we must not fall into the trap of relying upon brilliant but theoretical people. I have seen so much harm done in this way. Early on in the war there was a body of such officers in London who, as far as I know, had no real experience of war

— at least I sincerely hope they had not, judging by the stuff they turned out! I think they were called "Future operational planners," or some such name. Some of their studies arrived out in the Middle East for us to examine. For the most part they were futuristic and impracticable, and I shudder to think what might have happened if their plans had ever been adopted. They may have produced good ones which we never saw. At that time everyone was looking for cheap victories, and attractive-looking paper schemes of this sort found favour in some places, though not, I think, within the Services. This organisation was disbanded before long.

The efforts of the Royal Navy and the R.A.F. to help the Army in its forthcoming struggle were during this period, truly magnificent. The more Rommel's supplies were interfered with, the less would he be able to achieve. A very carefully worked out plan was laid on to cause the maximum damage. Attacks were made against enemy ships at sea and in harbours, against the ports at which he loaded in Europe and unloaded in Africa. His dumps and petrol reserves were attacked where possible. His transport was shot up along the roads. It must have been trying for some of the gallant personnel who had achieved so much in these attacks to hear later on of considerable quantities of transport and petrol falling into the enemy's hands, and so compensating to some extent for the losses they had caused.

I happened to spend a few days touring the Eighth Army just before Rommel attacked. Preparations were going on for an ultimate offensive on our part. On the other hand, everything was being done to increase our defences to receive the enemy when he struck. Extensive minefields were laid to a great depth from north to south of the sector which we held.

There were several courses open to the enemy. He could concentrate everything in a terrific punch along the coastal axis. He could carry out a big "right hook" around our southern flank about Bir Hachim, or he could undertake a combination of these two methods. In addition we expected he would try and worry us with mobile columns far back in our rear administrative areas. We never knew for certain which we must expect, and so prepared to the best of our ability for all eventualities.

II

On the night of May 27th/28th Rommel started in moonlight. Broadly speaking he moved the Afrika Korps in a "short right hook" around our southern flank, and at the same time attacked frontally in the coastal sector. This latter operation was entrusted to the Italians, and was never pressed very strongly against the concentrated artillery fire we could bring to bear against it. It wasn't for some time that we thought it anything but a feint! Poor old Italians, they were certainly given a sticky job.

This out-flanking march by the Afrika Korps supported by other troops, including Italians, was a spectacular, and to my mind, even a romantic affair. In the clear moonlight it was carried out with machine-like precision. We subsequently captured the operation order with a diagram showing the exact pattern of the movement. There were halts for refuelling and rest, and by dawn they expected to have turned northwards, eating into our defences from the rear. We received air reports of the move during the night and so a short warning was possible. An Indian Motor Brigade had just arrived on the southern flank in the very line of the enemy's advance, and before they knew what had happened were subjected to the full force of this terrific onslaught. They managed, however, to inflict very severe punishment, and the Afrika Korps received a sharp jab to the jaw. This was coupled by another unpleasant surprise from Keonig's Frenchmen at Bir Hachim. The Italians also got into trouble around this area, and suffered heavily in the minefields. Once the main enemy thrust had been appreciated, Ritchie moved some of his mobile reserves to face the German armour, and some bitter fighting took place.

Rommel's forces were somewhat taken aback by the fierceness of our defence, by the meeting with the new Grant American-built tank, and also by the six-pounder anti-tank gun. This latter weapon had in some cases only just been issued before the battle started. It was, however, easy to handle. We found out later that the enemy had cherished hopes of capturing the El Adem airfield that first day.

By the evening, Eighth Army were feeling quite pleased with themselves, and everyone was quietly confident. We knew that the enemy's tank losses had been considerable, that his advance had been held up and that the coastal attack had been defeated. The enemy's main column stretched for miles, and quantities of soft-skinned transport was moving backwards and forwards supplying the fighting element. Here the Desert Air Force found great opportunities and reports of hundreds of burning vehicles came pouring in. Our great belt of minefields had not been penetrated. So far so good.

The next day or two's fighting was very intense. The enemy could not achieve his object of breaking up our defensive system from behind, of linking up with the coastal thrust, or of obtaining an airfield to the east of our static positions. The 50th Division and the South Africans were quite happy holding the main defences in the north, whilst a great armoured battle was going on in their rear. At times their artillery could assist our armoured divisions in their task.

After a day or two Rommel realised he had failed to achieve his initial object and must pull in his horns and re-organise. His tank losses had been very severe, many were awaiting repair, and his supply and petrol situation was fast becoming acute. He decided, therefore, to pull back the Afrika Korps into our minefield area north of Bir Hachim. He did this under cover of his 88-mm. guns. We had I think, placed too much reliance upon our minefields, and on part of the front they were not adequately covered by fire. It was here that the enemy managed to establish a corridor through them, and so open up an alternative supply route. Our mines were thus turned to the enemy's advantage, for they gave him much-needed protection. He formed a sort of bridgehead covering the eastern exit of this funnel and fought with the greatest determination to prevent us breaking through.

By forcing the enemy to change his plan it really looked as if he had suffered a severe defeat — he had certainly suffered a reverse. Everyone was very optimistic, and the reports from Eighth Army were couched in heartening language. There were scenes of great confusion in the area which we all knew as the "Cauldron." Transport was jammed in the "funnel" and the enemy was desperately endeavouring to widen the gap he had made in our minefields. Unfortunately he was succeeding. And in spite of the very great damage inflicted by the Desert Air Force on his vehicles, and by the Army against his retreating tanks and guns, Rommel's trusted soldiers kept their heads and saved an ugly situation from further deterioration.

We were perhaps a bit too optimistic, and because of this it looked as if insufficient care and preparations were taken in staging an attack to eliminate this enemy "bridgehead." I was told afterwards by several units who had taken part how they had been ordered forward to the attack at a moment's notice, and had just "driven into battle." The result was unfortunate for they were badly mauled by the enemy's guns and tanks. This initial success seemed to go to people's heads, and the troops suffered accordingly. It is also open to question whether we should not have risked using sooner some of the resources held down in the static defence area. These might have just turned the scale. But there are always "might-have-beens" after a battle is over, when we know exactly what the enemy was really up to.

In spite of this early advantage, we were not able to exploit the situation. All sorts of plans were being put in motion, and eventually I think a "left hook" by our forces was commenced. We hoped to cut in behind the enemy and interfere with his supply. Rommel was, however, too quick for us, and he managed to stage a comeback in a shorter time than most of us thought possible. This led to the gradual disintegration of our whole defensive system. He debouched from the "Cauldron" area and another series of armoured battles took place. In spite of the bravery of our tank crews, who were mostly out-tanked, of the magnificent work of the gunners, who were frequently firing at enemy armour over open sights, and of the unceasing attacks by our fighter-bombers, the strain began to tell and our tank strengths reached a dangerously low level.

I paid a visit to Eighth Army with Auchinleck about this time and stayed there two days. It was now obvious that we had missed any chance of a counter-stroke, and a far more disturbing problem had raised its head. Could we, or could we not, hold the Gazala position? And if not, what were we to do? It was a nasty situation with such questions as these to be settled. What could we save from the static area? What should we do about Tobruk? Where was the next suitable line to make a stand? Would we be able to control a general withdrawal or retreat? Few commanders have been faced with more complicated or difficult decisions. Ritchie, the Army Commander who had been appointed from out of an office in Cairo, and who had not had the advantages of previous experience of high command, was now faced with this unpleasant situation. During the next week or two he stood the strain well, and it should be remembered he was not entirely master in his own house, unlike Montgomery when he eventually assumed command of this much-tried Army.

III

Because of this last remark I will take the reader back to the Cairo end of affairs. I have always found that in bad days the further away you are from the scene of the fighting the more difficult things appear. There was no exception to this rule just about then. To say the least of it, there was a certain apprehension as to the security of this great Middle East base, and there were some who began to think that with Rommel all things were possible.

During this difficult period Auchinleck had a lot to say regarding the major decisions within Eighth Army. If he was not up there himself, frequent signals would be exchanged. In addition he would send up one of his principal staff officers every day or two to convey his view's to the Army Commander. I find it difficult to make up my mind as to how right or wrong the Commander-in-Chief was in this respect. One can easily say an Army Commander should be given his task and then be allowed to get on with it without interference. I have heard it said that Montgomery would never have stood it for a day. Auchinleck was, I know, disturbed over this matter, and once talked to me about it. I am sure at the time I felt there were some very good reasons why Ritchie could not be given a completely free hand. It is only fair to say, however, that this having to wait for agreement to some plan or other did increase the Army Commander's difficulties, and this was brought out particularly in the Tobruk disaster. For those who might criticise Auchinleck for undue interference, it should be remembered that this was the one and only active campaign, and upon its outcome the result of the war might well rest. Could the Commander-in-Chief stand aside and leave Ritchie to shoulder the full responsibility? Then, because of the sensitiveness of the base organisation, questions affecting the other Services, and certain political factors, some decisions could not be made from the Army viewpoint alone. Once the above is accepted, it is easy to realise the dilemma in which the Commander-in-Chief found himself. And as I have already said, he was very worried that by his control he was making Ritchie's task more difficult.

During this period the Commander-in-Chief used to hold meetings in the war room after dinner each evening. They used to go on sometimes for hours. They were normally attended by the C.G.S., the Brigadier Operations, the Lieutenant-General in charge of Administration (General Riddell-Webster, who later became Quartermaster-General) and myself. Reports from liaison officers would be heard, and the latest signals from Ritchie discussed. At the end of the meeting Auchinleck would normally draft out a signal to his Army Commander giving him guidance as to future action. At some stages events outran these signals and Ritchie had to act entirely on his own.

Once we had lost the initiative and had suffered heavy tank losses, it is difficult to see how Rommel could have been held up until the Alamein position was reached, for this was the only area where both flanks had natural protection. On the northern flank was the sea, and on the southern the impassable Qattara Depression. Through, I think, Auchinleck's foresight a great deal of work had been carried out to make this a strongly defended area. With an open flank it was essential to have a strong armoured force in reserve so as to defeat an enemy attempt at carrying out a "right hook." This fact was brought out time and time again by Montgomery when he in turn "left hooked" Rommel back to Northern Tunisia. We had no strong armoured force available, and therefore when once the decision to withdraw from the Gazala line was made, Eighth Army was faced with a critical situation. With this decision to withdraw went the problem of Tobruk. To give this port to the enemy would help him in his supply problems, and it would also be a very great political disaster. Because of the epic siege of 1941 Tobruk had gained a far greater importance in public eyes than its military value in 1942 warranted.

Withdrawal had not to be too rapid; for not only would there be a risk of loss of control, but it was most necessary that time should be available for moving back, or at least destroying stores, so as not to assist the enemy. At a first glance, the frontier appeared to be the right place to make a stand. Here there were some prepared positions and there was a pronounced escarpment. But unfortunately these were considerable assets if the defence expected an attack from the east, but when facing the other direction the escarpment became a disadvantage. Further, there was an open flank and so without considerable armour the position could be turned with reasonable ease.

We were lucky to get back the major portion of the 50th Division; the last formation to hold the Gazala defences. They were virtually cut off and brilliantly fought their way out under their stout-hearted commander, General Ramsden. It is an epic which deserves a story all its own.

Ritchie did not have sufficient troops to settle into Tobruk and get the defences fully organised before withdrawal from Gazala commenced. The South African Division was moved back to take up its stand in the fortress. They were supported by a Guards' Brigade and a very mixed bag of supporting arms and administrative troops. It must be remembered that within the Tobruk perimeter there was a tremendous amount of supplies, petrol, ammunition and transport. Therefore to hand over all this to Rommel would be a disaster, whilst to destroy it all would take time. If Tobruk was to be held, then it would be isolated in the fullest sense of the word. The nearest friendly troops, other than light forces would be in the area of the frontier, some eighty miles away. What little armour we had left would be required to co-operate with our main forces. Owing to the airfield situation, no adequate air support could be given, Tobruk being out of close fighter range. To have a real chance of successfully defending the fortress for a prolonged period, the garrison would have had to be considerably larger than that which was ordered there. So it can be seen that to deny this port to the enemy would be a very costly affair. Experience has shown that a commander must beware of locking up his forces in a fortress, unless an early relief appears possible, I doubt whether many felt such a relief operation was just round the corner in June, 1942.

A number of signals passed between Ritchie and his Commander-in-Chief concerning the policy as regards Tobruk. Auchinleck, in his turn, received signals on the same subject from home. In my recollection these signals were correct and helpful. I am sure the decision was left to the Commander on the spot, although quite naturally the political significance of giving up the fortress without a fight was mentioned once or twice. How far such remarks influenced Auchinleck's ultimate decision I do not know; I guess, however, they did. It is easy to say so now, but many of us felt it at the time, if the decision was to hold Tobruk, then it should have been made earlier than it was. I will describe the fateful meeting on the subject held in the War Room at G.H.Q., Cairo.

Ritchie had to receive a definite instruction one way or the other by the next morning. The meeting took place about 9.30 p.m. with the usual officers attending. The Army Commander's latest appreciation was read out and discussed, as well as a signal from London. We were all asked our views. I had to get up and give the enemy reactions. I said I considered that, if not interfered with by strong Allied armour and air, I felt the enemy could punch a hole through the Tobruk defences. Auchinleck thanked me for my views and said that although he appreciated the dangers he felt an attempt should be made to hold it. The evening meeting did not break up until past midnight and the Commander-in-Chief drafted his instruction to Ritchie himself. I think the latter was given some latitude, but I am not sure. Although not happy, I remember going to bed with a certain relief — at last a definite decision had been made; and firm decisions at critical moments are like gusts of fresh air in the fog of war. I didn't suffer from any stuffiness under my eventual Chief, Montgomery — he found no difficulty in making such decisions!

As things turned out, I don't think the scratch garrison of Tobruk had a hope of survival. The garrison was not strong enough, and insufficient time was available to sort things out and get the defence organised properly. Air support, through no fault of the gallant Desert Air Force, was quite inadequate, and the enemy were in a position to form up and lay on their attack without interference. There were some hard things said about the South Africans after the capitulation, but I could never myself blame that division; they never had a chance. Under Montgomery at Alamein and before, the South Africans conducted themselves magnificently.

Rommel was not slow in staging his attack. He appreciated the fact that time was on our side. We wanted time to organise the defence. He wanted the petrol, the supplies and the port. He launched his attack in two or three days, and carried it out on a narrow front from the south-east of the perimeter. The ground was prepared by repeated Stuka dive bombing attacks against the defences without interference. The end came very soon. Command arrangements broke down, and unfortunately the demolitions were not all completed. Much petrol, transport and supplies fell into Rommel's hands, and it was this that no doubt persuaded the German Commander, and eventually Hitler, that the capture of the Nile Valley was now a practical proposition.

We deduced in the Intelligence Directorate that the enemy would adopt the same plan that they had prepared but never carried out the year before. We were fortunate in having captured a complete copy of the orders. We therefore flew these up to Eighth Army. I believe it was subsequently dropped on the Fortress. The Germans followed this plan exactly, but being forewarned didn't help us. The garrison capitulated on June 21st and most of them were captured. There were, however, some stout-hearted dashes to safety by isolated units.

I was up visiting Eighth Army Headquarters when the news of Tobruk's fall came in. It was a heavy blow, for no one had expected it quite so early. However, that resilient force kept going, and morale was still surprisingly good. Reinforcements were on their way from all over the Middle East, most welcome amongst them being that great fighting machine, the New Zealand Division with Freyberg at its head.

Incredible scenes occurred along the long desert road from Solium eastwards. Transport was to be seen nose to tail crawling along four deep. Everything appeared mixed up. You saw a tank followed by a truck, then a bulldozer, an R.A.F. vehicle, several guns, and so on. How all this mess got sorted out I could never tell. It was a great achievement, and the Army's thanks are due in no small way to the Desert Air Force who, by their efforts, prevented the German Air Force from turning this retreat into an uncontrollable rout. They worked unceasingly and with a great spirit of sacrifice.

After an unsuccessful attempt to hold the small port of Mersa Matruh, the Army arrived back at Alamein very exhausted, but still very ready to fight. The New Zealand Division had come straight up against the crack German Panzer 15 and 21 divisions, south of Matruh. Here a memorable engagement took place, and I believe this mauling of the enemy's spearhead probably went a long way to saving the situation. It is said that Frey berg was seen directing the operations with one foot on a pile of German dead when he was wounded through the neck.

For some time past several people had been pressing Auchinleck to take over command of Eighth Army himself. Tedder, who was then Air Commander-in-Chief, was one of these. As the Army was arriving back at Alamein, the Commander-in-Chief decided to take over from Ritchie. He left his C.G.S., Corbett, behind to act in his absence and took with him the Deputy Chief of General Staff, Dorman Smith.

Gradually the Army sorted itself out into the defensive position of El Alamein. Gradually the enemy attacks grew weaker and Rommel became short of ammunition and supplies. They were most anxious days, but great days. Neither side had fresh reserves sufficient to alter the stalemate. An extra fresh corps on either side might have meant a great victory. One began to see that the enemy were at least as exhausted as ourselves. The 90th Light Division attacked time and time again on the vital coastal road sector, but each time the operation petered out shortly after our artillery and the R.A.F. got at them. It was now pretty certain the Axis forces, in soldier's slang, had for the time being "had it."

Auchinleck asked me to come up and stay with him for ten days in July. We were now firmly dug in, were strengthening our position daily, and undertaking some offensive operations. These latter were a mistake. The troops and formations were either too tired or too green and untrained to the desert. It was difficult to see the object, as I am sure, whatever local and initial success might have been obtained, no large scale exploitation was possible. It would have been better to conserve all our resources and wait until ready to do an "Alamein." In one operation a newly-arrived armoured division from England, equipped with slow-moving and obsolete infantry tanks, was thrown into battle with little time for preparation and training. These poorly-trained but gallant troops dashed on, and eventually ran into the usual German gun screen of 88 mm., with the result that they lost a large proportion of their machines. In spite of these setbacks, we were beginning to breathe again, and hopes were rising. A lot depended upon whether Rommel could accumulate supplies and equipment for another strong thrust. There was, therefore, an intensification in the efforts to sink ships, damage ports and write off transport. The Royal Navy and R.A.F. suffered very heavily from these operations as they pressed home their attacks with the greatest gallantry. This intensive period lasted until after the battle of El Alamein, and the Army's success here was in no small measure due to the success of these operations.

IV

I must jump back a bit to the critical days in order that I may give you some impression of how things were going in Cairo.

To start with, I should say that throughout this period the Egyptians and their officials behaved extremely well. They seemed to appreciate our difficulties and certainly did nothing to increase them, and as far as I know, we got very willing co-operation and help. There was no sign of panic as many had expected. There was a run on the banks, which was only natural. It was a severe test with the enemy within fighter range of Cairo, whilst his guns could be heard distinctly from Alexandria. I was a member of the Mohamed Ali Club, and I made a point of visiting the clubhouse as much as I could just then. I shall always recall, with very few exceptions, the extreme friendliness and the genuine sympathy which I encountered.

The Navy, owing to the nearness of the enemy, were forced to abandon Alexandria as their naval base, only light forces being retained there.

At G.H.Q. I'm afraid a pretty good "flap" did occur for a few days. Risks could not be taken with certain installations, organisations and documents. And so various moves into Palestine and elsewhere were started. In addition, documents were sent away, and departments were told to burn all unimportant papers, in order to make a move easier, if such a contingency ever occurred. It was inevitable that there was a certain amount of alarm and despondency, and the smoke from the various chimneys of the G.H.Q. buildings was an amazing sight. Wherever one walked bits of charred paper came floating past. Later, special incinerators were provided to help with the cremation of these relics. It was extraordinary how much was burnt, and more extraordinary how little any of these papers were missed. Afterwards we all blessed Rommel for making our lives that much the easier! Plans were of course prepared for a move of G.H.Q., but luckily the necessity never arose.

The whole of the Delta was re-organised into Commands, and intensive preparations made for its defence. The system of canals favoured defence, and delaying action. We planned to fight for every yard, but I shudder to think how the practicable application of such a plan would have turned out when the German Air Force started strafing Cairo, with its vulnerable and inflammable buildings, and its enormous population.

The roads through Cairo and from Mena and Alexandria to the Western Desert were always packed with transport. It was a heartening sight when one drove or flew along, for most of these were reinforcements.

I came in contact with most of the "Great" at this time. Admiral Cunningham was, as always, entirely unmoved. The Navy would do anything to help.

Many of us considered Tedder was a fine example to everyone. He was cool, quiet, confident, and always ready to have a chat or give advice. He certainly was a fine influence in many places. I often made excuses to see him, so that I could have a talk about things and hear his views.

Then there was the new Minister of State, Casey. I took a great liking to him. He was wise and very accessible. I used to dine with him on occasions, and we would discuss the situation at length. He was always full of fight, but on the other hand, appreciated the difficulties that confronted us. It is no surprise to me that he made such a success as Governor of Bengal. I felt that Auchinleck did not make the best use of the Minister of State. I believe he thought, possibly unconsciously, that the politician was critical of his handling of the situation. It was a pity, because Casey was out to help, and would have responded wholeheartedly to the full confidence of the Commander-in-Chief.

At the beginning of the second half of July I returned to Cairo from the ten-day visit that I had paid to Eighth Army. I had not been back for more than two days before a signal arrived from Auchinleck ordering me up as B.G.S. I was to come at once. I was considerably shaken, for I had no previous experience as a General Staff Officer in the field, other than in the capacity of a visitor. To take over the chief staff appointment in the Army at this crucial time appeared to me a risky business. It seemed hardly fair to the troops, or to myself. I was so worried that I went and discussed the matter with the Military Secretary. He agreed with my views, and said he would fly up the next day and talk to the Commander-in-Chief about it. In the meantime I went on with my work as D.M.I.

The next day I received a sharp signal telling me to hand over my present job, and to report at Eighth Army Headquarters forthwith. Auchinleck had seen the Military Secretary, so there was no more to be done about it. My handing over took about an hour, and it took little longer to pack my kit. I spent the rest of the morning saying "good-byes." I went and had a talk with Tedder, who was very encouraging. He kindly lent me an aircraft to fly me up, and so in a few hours of receiving my orders I arrived at the headquarters of the Army with which I was to witness history in the making, and with which I was to spend so happy a year and a half.

V
TAIL-PIECE (A TRUE STORY)

The scene is a busy airfield just outside Derna in Cyrenaica, and the time is early morning of a hot June day in 1942. All is excitement. Perspiring and lavishly dressed officials are lined up, obviously awaiting the arrival of some distinguished person. They have not long to wait, for the northern sky is smattered with many aircraft, and their noise engulfs the scene. As they approach it is possible to gather details of this circus. Many fighters — probably some three squadrons — are busily swarming around a large and slower moving plane, fussing around her as do drones around their queen. There is something about it that catches the eye. It has large red Geneva crosses painted all over it. Are we then to witness the arrival of some wounded hero, or perhaps the last earthly remains of some soldier who has deserved this special salutation? But no, we are wrong with our guesses. For after the great machine has taxied across the airfield and stopped in front of the impressive array of officers, the doors open and out steps a small, rather fat and pompous figure. He is magnificently turned out in uniform and his hand is raised in the Fascist salute. It is, of course, the Duce, the "Protector of Islam." A little additional insurance has been taken out at the expense of Geneva, for the Italian air force don't quite trust the R.A.F.!

After the roar of "Duce, Duce, Duce" had died down, the Dictator heard the news. It is good, it is excellent. Rommel expects to be in Alexandria any day. His German soldiers will see to that. There is a lot of spit and polish going on in the Italian ranks — they've got the time, for they're rather far behind. This is very necessary, for they are preparing to escort their Chief through the streets of Cairo when the triumphant march takes place. He is going to be most generous on this occasion, and has brought over with him many boxes of Egyptian pounds — made in Italy of course — to scatter to the multitudes.

A day or two elapses, but no summons from the front has yet arrived. However, what does a day or so matter, life is very pleasant here. The food is good, the climate warm. And then, of course, there is such pleasant company with whom to pass the time. This hot sun will make her hair all the blonder. And as we well know, Duces prefer blondes! He finds it so satisfying to spend a short time each day strutting round the prisoner of war cages where soldiers of the British Empire are being held. He can feel really sorry for them all. Empires must end sooner or later, and how stupid these men must feel for having backed the wrong horse, and for attempting to pit themselves against the rejuvenated Empire of Rome. One can afford to be generous and understanding, and pass the time of day.

But time passes by, and this defeated army of the fallen Empire still bars the way to the Nile. Over two weeks have elapsed, and the entertainment of Derna begins to pall. No more visits to the P.O.W. cages, and even blondes have their limitations.

Northward flies the Duce. His journey has been in vain. There is, of course, the same cavalcade. The fighters and the same large hospital plane. The Italian Air Force still can't quite trust the R.A.F.

CHAPTER VI: WITH EIGHTH ARMY UNTIL THE BATTLE OF EL ALAMEIN

I

FLYING up to the Desert that hot July afternoon, I tried to determine my true reactions to this sudden upheaval. After much labour, I thought I had at last got a grip of Intelligence work, and now I was starting all over again to learn another "trade." I frankly shuddered at the prospect, but nothing that I could do would alter things. In the bottom of my heart there was a longing to make the grade, and I could not help feeling a certain excitement.

Late in the afternoon I arrived at Auchinleck's H.Q. It was located in a rather unpleasant spot on the Ruweisat ridge. It was a sort of compromise between a Main Headquarters and a Montgomery Tactical Headquarters. And I'm afraid, like many compromises, it was a most unsatisfactory arrangement, certainly as far as the staff were concerned. Every section or branch had to split their resources, and this spelt inefficiency, for the two echelons were many miles apart. It was also a bad piece of desert with much soft sand, and very inaccessible. The flies were frightful, and the messes most primitive. Eventually the Chief Engineer built a cage of wire to keep the flies out whilst we ate. Something must have gone wrong, for it merely kept them in, and acted as a fly-trap. It was like feeding in an aviary, with thousands of flies instead of birds. The Headquarters of the Desert Air Force and their Commander, Coningham, were back at Burg-el-Arab, over forty miles away. This alone produced great difficulties in the laying on of the best air support.

I reported to Auchinleck, and then to my old friend, Jock Whiteley, whom I was to succeed. He was off to another job, and was shortly to do great work as Assistant Chief of Staff Operations to Eisenhower in North Africa. He agreed to give me three days of his advice and help before I took over, and I must say I did not waste my time. There was so much to learn.

The general situation was as I have already described in the last chapter. Both sides were exhausted. We had carried out one or two unsuccessful local attacks. Rommel was short of munitions and supplies, and was endeavouring to build up for another blow. The R.A.F. were daily pounding any target that presented itself. As we were so close to our own base we had no administrative troubles, and could afford to use far larger quantities of ammunition, petrol and bombs than could our enemy. Auchinleck had decided that we must have time to re-organise, train and re-equip and so prepare for an offensive.

Great activity was going on to increase our defensive strength. More minefields were being laid and strong points constructed. The plans in the event of an Axis attack were many and varied. In one, a network of O.P.'s (observation posts) were being established on prominent features. Each was being turned into a strong point, with concrete, wire and mines. They were laid out in considerable depth, and the theory was that, in the event of enemy attack and penetration, these strong points would be occupied in accordance with the situation, and from them would be directed powerful artillery fire. I never quite understood how it was to be done, but the artillery was to be concentrated in support of the threatened sector or sectors, and then be linked up and controlled from these O.P.s. It was all too uncertain and fluid a plan for a sound defence. There was a great danger of the guns being driven hither and thither, and confusion setting in. Even if they all organised themselves into a fresh command there were many things which could go wrong with these "Master O.P.'s" and so render the plan abortive. Dust, smoke, or air attack might well achieve such a result.

The various plans being worked out represented the state of mind of Eighth Army, or at least their High Command, at that moment. They were still looking over their shoulder. Other defensive positions far to the rear were being reconnoitred, and in some cases work was being done on them. A new site for the Headquarters had been selected on the Nile, sixty miles south of Cairo. I don't say that it is not prudent to be prepared for the worst, but on the other hand, if there is too much of this sort of thing it is most unlikely that the troops will fight their best in their existing positions. The wrong outlook is likely to be encouraged — one of hesitation. Another result of this looking over the shoulder was that considerable reserves were being held back for the defence of the Delta.

I very soon found I was becoming overwhelmed by having to examine a number of such plans and schemes, both defensive and offensive. There was a fundamental weakness in the staff set-up. The Commander-in-Chief had, as I have already related, taken up with him the D.C.G.S. from Cairo. He was now designated "D.C.G.S. in the Field," and acted as a sort of personal adviser to Auchinleck, but carried no responsibility in Eighth Army. His quick brain and fertile mind produced appreciations and plans at a quicker rate than anyone I have ever met; he was perhaps too clever to be wise. The usual procedure was for these papers to be marked by the C.-in-C.: "B.G.S., please examine this idea." At first I sat up all night conscientiously working on these projects, but soon I found they took up too much of my time and. I regret to say, wasted a lot of it as well. Some had merit and might have been of use when we became strong enough, but a lot were somewhat impracticable. I liked the D.C.G.S. a great deal and he had no doubt helped to stabilise the front at Alamein, but I felt he would be better employed at his normal job in Cairo. We had a talk about it, and he agreed with me. The Commander-in-Chief allowed this move to take place when I had more or less got into the saddle, and then I found my work became quite a lot easier.

For the first two or three weeks I felt just like a new boy at a public school. I was surrounded by the old hands, many of whom were pretty deeply dyed in the old methods. I can't say I was very happy, and trod carefully. I could see that I must watch my step, and not throw my weight about until I was sure of my ground.

It said a lot for the British, Dominion and Indian soldiers that, in spite of the many defeats and the long retreat — and in many cases this was the second time they had been thrust back after a successful offensive — their morale had not been broken. There was, however, what can be described as a state of bewilderment. Everyone was wanting to know why this great Army had, after so promising a start, failed to hold the enemy. There appeared to be a sort of craving for guidance and inspiration. There was no stability of outlook, and no great confidence in the outcome of a fresh encounter.

As the days went by, however, optimism returned and my Commander-in-Chief was busy examining plans for the offensive that must eventually take place. A lot of time was spent in planning reinforcements, training and re-equipment. Early in August he had a conference with his Corps Commanders, at which it was decided that a considerable pause was necessary before such an operation could be launched. Auchinleck was even considering returning to Cairo to reassume his appointment as Commander-in-Chief. The difficulty was to find a suitable successor.

One night we were going for a stroll and he asked me whom I should nominate if I had to make the choice. My reply was interesting in the light of events. "I am sure you want a new man altogether, someone who hasn't any sand in his hair. The only ones I knew in the old days who very obviously had the necessary qualities were Montgomery and Slim." My previous contacts with Montgomery I will shortly describe, and Slim had taught me at the Staff College and was to my mind the outstanding teacher there.

I believe it was in the second week in August that we were visited by the Prime Minister, the C.I.G.S.[14] and others. I think they only spent one day in the Desert, but it was a very full one. They saw and spoke with the senior commanders and saw a number of troops. They no doubt obtained a pretty accurate "feel" of the state of Eighth Army. Auchinleck had a long discussion with them, and went over the maps and future plans in his map lorry. Churchill was naturally eager for another offensive and wanted it soon. He was off to Moscow, and so this was important. The Commander-in-Chief would not promise anything very quickly — and how right he was. I thought perhaps he was a bit abrupt in the way he refused to be drawn over this matter. I remember noticing that the Prime Minister did not like this attitude, but he was an admirer of the "Auk" and had been lavish in his praise for the way he had pulled the November offensive out of the fire.

Either the next day or the day after Auchinleck was summoned to Cairo. He appeared, I thought, a little worried before he left, but returned full of hope and heart. We went for our usual stroll that evening, and he discussed with the greatest

---

[14] Now Lord Alanbrooke.

enthusiasm our plans. Considerable reinforcements and new equipment were promised, and it now looked as if before many weeks were over we would be in a position to assume the offensive.

The next day one of the Prime Minister's staff came up during the afternoon with a letter. I guessed what it might contain. The Commander-in-Chief was very quiet at dinner, and afterwards asked me to come for a walk. He put his arm in mine and said: "Freddie, I'm to go." He had been offered another appointment which he refused to accept. I felt intensely sorry for my Chief, for I had become very fond of him. It must have hurt to have to leave on the threshold of a new era. He was a great lover of India, and was unsurpassed in his knowledge and understanding of Indians and the Indian Army. He had during his brief period as C.-in-C. India done remarkably well; how at this moment must he have regretted the day that he had been moved from that post to the Middle East. There was no one more pleased than myself when I heard that he had once again assumed that important role. On balance, however, I'm sure the decision was right. Fresh minds were required, and in war both men and machines require periods of rest.

I saw him off early the next morning, and left in his hand a letter in which I had tried to say what I felt.

About this time that fine desert soldier "Strafer" Gott was killed in an air crash on the way to Cairo. Ramsden, the senior Corps Commander, was acting Army Commander, and I waited to hear who my next "Master" would be. I soon heard Montgomery had been chosen, and that Alexander was coming out as Commander-in-Chief Middle East. I knew no better choice could have been made, and it was certain they would make an excellent team. They had left Dunkirk together in 1940.

II

On August 12th I received a signal telling me to meet the new Army Commander at the crossroads outside Alexandria at 7 a.m. the next morning. I spent the day in writing a paper giving my views on the present position in Eighth Army, and drawing attention to certain matters which I thought required urgent attention. I will only mention one or two of them:

> (a) The dangerous "looking over the shoulder" defensive policy.
> (b) The unsound fashion that prevailed of fighting in battle groups or "Jock Columns" as they were called, and not in divisions as the Army had been trained to fight. Only in this way could the Army develop its full strength.
> (c) The unsatisfactory headquarters set-up.
> (d) The fact that the Army and the Air Headquarters were not together.

It was a hot and sultry morning, and as I drove towards Alexandria I experienced considerable excitement. I was, of course, delighted that Montgomery had been selected, but I did not expect I should remain long in office. It was only natural that he would bring out his own Chief of Staff. I was looking forward to the meeting, for I knew at the very least it would be exhilarating.

I arrived at the crossroads, and had only been there five minutes when his car turned up, and after a characteristic greeting with a wave of the hand, he asked me to jump in beside him, and off we started for the Ruweisat Ridge.

Montgomery was full of spirit and looking very fit. He said, "Well Freddie, you chaps seem to have been making a bit of a mess of things. Now what's the form?" I rather nervously tendered my paper, but he thrust it back, saying: "I don't like reading papers, tell me about it." I spent some time running through the various points, and then answered numerous questions. He then said: "I was only told I was coming out here in London forty-eight hours ago, but I have been doing a lot of thinking since. Yesterday I spent at G.H.Q., Cairo, and worked out with Harding[15] how I want this Army organised. You'll never win a campaign as it is at the moment."

He then went through his proposals for the future. It was extraordinary how he had spotted most of the weaknesses even before his arrival. And he gave out his ideas to a gathering of all the Headquarters Staff officers that very evening as the sun was setting below the Ruweisat Ridge. On arrival at the Headquarters — I saw at once that he didn't like the look of it — he said: "I want to speak to all the staff." I asked "When sir?" "Why this evening of course," was his reply. I had to get busy, as they had to be summoned from far and wide, but we just got them there in time.

That address by Montgomery will remain one of my most vivid recollections. It was one of his greatest efforts. We all felt that a cool and refreshing breeze had come to relieve the oppressive and stagnant atmosphere. The effect of the address was electric — it was terrific! And we all went to bed that night with a new hope in our hearts, and a great confidence in the future of our Army.

I wish someone had taken it down in shorthand, for it would have become a classic of its kind. I will attempt to describe what he said.

---

[15] Now Lt.-Gen. Sir John Harding, who was then a D.C.G.S. at Cairo, dealing with organization, training and equipment.

He was going to create a new atmosphere. This question of atmosphere was very important, and he wasn't satisfied with the one had he found. The bad old days were over, and nothing but good was in store for us. A new era had dawned. He then went on to explain the mandate which General Alexander and himself had been given by the Prime Minister. This was to destroy the Axis forces in North Africa. It was written on a half-sheet of notepaper. If anyone didn't think we could do this, then he must go, for there were to be no doubters. "No, I won't have any doubters."

Any further retreat or withdrawal was quite out of the question. Forget about it. We must stand and fight where we were. There was to be no question of going back. He had ordered all plans dealing with withdrawal to be burnt. He hoped that signal had already gone out. It had! The defence of the Delta meant nothing to him, and so all resources earmarked to that end were to be used to strengthen Eighth Army.

The Prime Minister was going to see that we had a sufficiency of reinforcements and material.

He then turned to Rommel and the attack we were expecting him to make. He would not be very happy if it came within two weeks. If it came after that, he would welcome it — "It would be excellent."

He would start immediately with the planning of a great offensive. For this he must have a reserve which could train out of the line. A "Corps d'Elite." It would consist of two armoured divisions and one motorised (New Zealand) Division. This was, of course, producing a counterpart of the Africa Korps.

As to the date of the offensive, we would not attack until he was ready. We could rest assured of that — whatever the pressure, from whatever quarter.

Then he turned to Battle Groups, and he said from that moment onwards the expression ceased to exist. Divisions would fight as divisions, and be allowed to develop their great strength. Tip and run tactics were over.

He condemned our Headquarters arrangements and ordered that immediate steps would be taken to find a healthier spot where we could all be together. And we must join up with the R.A.F. It was essential that the planning for the offensive should be a joint one from the start.

His views on a Chief of Staff were then given. He said that he always worked the Chief of Staff system, and that he issued *all* orders through him. His Chief of Staff had considerable power and responsibility, and that he could issue orders in his name — within of course the framework of his policy. His Chief of Staff would have his entire confidence.

It was possible he said that he would be obliged to make some changes in commanders and staff, but this would only be done where necessary.

He finished by saying he would tolerate no "bellyaching." This is a grand word, and so aptly describes the type of indiscipline that prevailed amongst commanders in the Army at this time. It had gradually crept in, starting from too much of the "old boy" system. It was rare that an order would not be queried by the recipient, and an endless argument started. All this was to stop, and it did stop, and the change in atmosphere, and lightening of staff work was very great. One or two who were too steeped in this attitude were rapidly disposed of!

That is about all I can remember, but I think it is enough to convey the strength and character of the new commander.

The gist of this address and some additional points were circulated to Corps Commanders. They were told how the Army Commander worked, and some details of his methods.

III

Montgomery spent the next day or two in touring the whole Army and meeting everyone. He spoke to officers wherever he could, and got across his points. The result was tremendous, for everyone realised that at long last here was something definite. They knew what they had to do.

We found a very pleasant site for the Headquarters at Burgh-el-Arab, some twenty miles from Alexandria, and right on the coast. We could walk out of our caravans into the sea. This made a great difference to everyone's morale, health and capacity for work, and was important, for we had a lot to do in a very short time.

I laughed when Montgomery first saw our mess on the Ruweisat Ridge, the mosquito wire cage, with the table and flies within.

"What's this, a meat safe?" he said. "You don't expect me to live in a meat safe, do you? Take it down at once, and let the poor flies out!"

Down it came, and we were finished with meat safes.

He was very particular about messes and one's personal well being. I'm afraid we had all become rather shoddy in our habits. This was to stop. A good large mess tent was to be found, with a good cook, white tablecloths and shining cutlery. Meals were to be at fixed times and some reasonably comfortable furniture was to be provided. This was all in keeping with Montgomery's number one factor in war — *morale*. It certainly made a great difference, and the example was followed downwards to everyone's advantage.

He was equally particular about servants and told me to signal G.H.Q. for "the best available batman in the Middle East." I did so, and lent him mine in the meantime. By the time this "Jeeves" arrived my Chief had decided to keep mine, and so I had the "best available batman in the Middle East"! I think I lost on the deal, although I can't complain, for Lawrence remained with me throughout the war, and served me most faithfully.

About two days after the new Commander's arrival, he asked me to come along to his caravan, and in his direct way said: "Well Freddie, as you know I will be making some changes shortly. If you happen to be one of them I will see that you get something good."

As I expected this I didn't mind, and in one way I was rather relieved. However that was the last I heard of the subject, and we remained together until the end of the war.

IV

The preparations for an offensive and dealing with Rommel's attack when it came went on concurrently at a terrific speed.

The Army Commander carried out a very detailed examination of the whole front to decide how he would fight the defensive battle. The new policy meant that a great deal of ammunition and supplies had to be moved to the forward area, so that the troops there could fight in their present positions for a long period. He appreciated at once that the Alam Halfa ridge was of vital importance, but was virtually undefended. The ridge was in rear of the Alamein line and commanded a large area of desert, and was undoubtedly a key to the whole defensive system. Any "right-hook" by Rommel must capture this feature to be successful. No troops were available within the Army, and so he asked that the 44th Division, which had recently arrived in Egypt, should be sent up. The story of the move of this division will give an idea of the change of tempo.

Before Montgomery's arrival G.H.Q. had said that 44th Division would not be available until the end of August at the earliest. Montgomery told me one evening at 5 or 6 p.m. to phone up Cairo and say he required the Division *at once*. I got on to the staff at G.H.Q. and was told that this was quite impossible, but that they would try and get elements of the Division moving in a few days' time. I reported this to the Army Commander. He seized the phone and had a few minutes' talk to Alexander. Later that night I was rung up and told that the division would start moving that night, and it arrived up complete, I believe, in a couple of days. This insistence probably helped considerably in repelling Rommel's attack at the end of the month.

A considerable strengthening of the existing positions took place. More minefields were laid, and all work on positions in rear was stopped, in order to release additional labour and resources.

As he considered some of the armoured units were far from trained, steps were taken so that the tanks could be fought from dug-in positions, supported by a great weight of artillery from behind. This measure proved invaluable during Rommel's attack.

In the area to the south of our main defences, light forces were positioned with the object of carrying out harassing tasks in the event of an enemy attack around our left flank.

The days crept by and the dangerous two-week period was nearly over. A clear-cut defensive plan had been laid down, and the various moves rehearsed. In addition we worked out exactly how the air should co-operate. So, by August 28th, we were all breathing easily and quite happy to take on Rommel when he attacked. We expected this during the full moon at the end of the month.

Two fresh Corps Commanders arrived out, Leese and Horrocks. They were Montgomery's choice, and I'm sure he never regretted it. They were both great Commanders, possessing drive and enthusiasm — in fact all the right qualities. Leese was more methodical and thorough, whilst Horrocks was more spectacular and colourful. I always used to think of him as a Marshal Ney. We all got on well together and this cemented the happy family that Eighth Army became. Their two Bs.G.S. were excellent staff officers. I venture to say there was complete mutual trust between us all. Stickiness or pomposity did not exist.

Besides all these activities in connection with defence, the offensive arrangements were going ahead without hindrance. The new Corps was in process of forming. We were receiving the new Sherman tank — a great step forward — and crews had to be trained in its use. Self-propelled artillery was also arriving. In addition, more transport and guns were forthcoming. So there was a great deal to do with regard to the equipping of formations; besides this, intensive training must go on to fit them for offensive action. Efforts were being made to prepare the troops in the technique for the break-in battle. In this the problem of the mine was paramount. We knew that the enemy had laid very deep and extensive minefields, and so all brains got to work to devise rapid means for dealing with them. Our own engineers developed several machines which proved the forerunners of the most modern devices. Methods for dealing with wire were another preoccupation. We set aside a large training area in the south where formations and units could practice these latest methods. We called it the "Break-in" course. Then a great deal of night training took place, as the

Army Commander had decided that the attack would start at night, so as to help in the minefield problem.

The Army Commander made up his mind as to the general plan very early on. He asked, as was his custom, for staff studies to be prepared, and after hearing the factors affecting the problem, decided that the main attack should take place on the northern sector. There were many snags, such as soft sand, minefields, and difficulty of concealment, to be contended with, but he considered this would have the best results, and would when successful strike right at the enemy's heart, i.e. his L. of C. and administrative areas. The Navy would also be able to help.

I will now break off from the preparations for the battle of El Alamein, and deal with the battle which is now called Alam Halfa. This is in keeping with events, for Rommel's attack did in fact hold up our offensive preparations.

V

This attack, which started on August 31st, proved a heaven sent event. It gave the whole Army, its Commander, staff, and the fighting troops, a great opportunity of running themselves in. In particular: —

(a) It gave the troops confidence in themselves and in their new commander, for the battle was fought exactly as he predicted. The forces under him merely carried out his orders, and the battle virtually won itself.

(b) Rommel's Army was weakened in morale and material, and so our task at Alamein was made that much the easier.

(c) The Army and R.A.F. staffs got excellent practice in wielding the very formidable air power that was now available for the support of Eighth Army.

(d) The new system of speeding up information from the battle front to the Army H.Q. was tried out. This was developed by my G.S.O. 1 Operations, Mainwaring, to whom must go the credit. We had found that information took too long to reach us, and this was of particular disadvantage in connection with the laying on of air support. We, therefore, established a network of reporting centres which were echeloned down from the most forward points of interest to Corps H.Q. They gathered and relayed information by wireless direct to Army H.Q., and so a great deal of time was saved. The system has now been accepted throughout our Army, but at that time it was a great innovation. A special section at our H.Q. sifted and passed on all the information received. It had some growing pains at first, but from the battle of El Alamein onwards it worked to our great advantage. Later it was further developed, and roving units with specially trained and experienced officers in command, were despatched to vital points to send back their impressions as to how things were going. We called it the "J" Service. A more or less similar system had been developed at home, and went by the name of "Phantom." Shortly after midnight on August 31st I was wakened up in my caravan with phone calls from both Corps. It appeared that the attack had begun. There were thrusts in the north, centre and south, but the southerly one was the attack that mattered. It came in between the left flank of the New Zealand Division and an isolated hill called Himeimat. Here Rommel employed his 15th and 21st Panzer Divisions, the 90th Light Division, and the 20th Italian Corps, which included the Ariete and Littorio Armoured Divisions. It will be seen, therefore, that it was a pretty formidable affair.

I felt very "hit up" on hearing this news, for I realised the importance of the issue, and in addition it was the first big battle that Eighth Army had fought since I had become its Chief of Staff. I felt I had better go and wake up the Army

Commander and tell him the news, and so walked over to his caravan. I told him what was happening, and all he said was "Excellent, excellent," and then turned over and went to sleep, breakfasting at his usual hour in the morning!

We were not quite certain at first whether the main thrust was around our southern flank, but by the morning of September 1st we were satisfied. The Army Commander did not want the enemy to make a wide turning movement towards El Hammam, but to move northwards towards the Alam-Haifa ridge, where we had appreciated he would make for, and where we were well prepared to receive him.

I will break off here to describe a ruse which we afterwards learnt had helped to defeat Rommel. We always produced "going" maps which were layered in colours to show the type of desert in so far as it affected movement. We knew the enemy had captured many of our maps and was making use of them. At the time of the retreat to Alamein no "going" maps existed of the area to the rear of our positions. These we produced after we had settled in. I, therefore, decided to have made a false "going" map which would link up quite correctly with the maps already in enemy hands, and then to falsify a particular area to suit our plans. The area I selected, in consultation with our Intelligence staff, was one south of Alam Halfa. Due south of the highest point was an area of very soft sand. As we appreciated the enemy would make for this ridge I thought that by showing this bad area as good going, the enemy might be tempted to send his tanks around that way. It would also give him a shock if he were making for El Hamman, for instead of a "good gallop," he would find himself wallowing in deep sand. We had this map secretly printed in very quick time by the energy of an old associate of mine in the M.I. Directorate in Cairo — Stuart-Menteith. Then we plotted with 13th Corps to have it "captured" by the enemy. In the south, light forces were continually patrolling around the enemy's minefields, and so it was arranged that a scout car should get blown up on a mine, and that the crew would be taken off in another truck. Left in the scout car were soldiers' kits and the usual junk, whilst stuffed away in a haversack was an old and dirty "going map" (the fake) covered in tea stains, but quite readable. The car had been ransacked by the next morning, and the map had disappeared.

The enemy certainly got badly "bogged down" in this particular area, but how much the map was to blame I don't quite know. From interrogation of prisoners, however, we did obtain confirmation that a falsified map led the enemy to send their tanks into this sandy terrain, which trebled their fuel consumption. We also knew that Rommel put down the failure of his offensive to petrol shortage. So it looks as if it probably helped.

Back to the battle. Once Montgomery was sure that the main enemy attack was directed against the Alam Halfa ridge, he was able to move the bulk of his armour between the ridge and the New Zealand position in the Alamein defences. This has all been rehearsed, and so went smoothly. By mid-day 400 tanks had been concentrated in this important area.

The enemy attacks against our positions made no progress, and were very costly. We could produce a great weight of artillery fire against him, and the R.A.F. kept up a continuous bombardment of his transport. The light mobile forces of 7th Armoured Division were harassing the enemy columns in the area north and west of Himeimat, and causing him a lot of trouble. That dashing cavalry and later paratroop commander, "Shan" Hackett, was having the time of his life.

Once Montgomery was satisfied that the enemy was well and truly committed, he began to re-group, ready for a counter-stroke. He thinned out 30th Corps (the Northern Corps) to obtain reserves, and brought up a brigade of 50th Division from the rear areas to take the place of the armour he had moved.

Early on September 3rd, the enemy had given up his expensive attack, and withdrawn from contact; in the afternoon three strong enemy columns were seen from the air to be moving westwards.

On the night of September 3rd/4th the New Zealand Division began its attack southwards from the Alamein line proper. This threatened to close the gap by which Rommel had entered our positions. He, therefore, reacted very strongly, and this no doubt decided him to accelerate his departure. He was also in a very bad way administratively, and had left the battlefield littered with his burnt out and damaged vehicles and tanks.

Montgomery called the battle off on September 7th, and would not allow our troops to follow up. At the time some criticism was to be heard, because he did not immediately start a counter offensive. How wise he was. From the point of view of both training and equipment, he realised that his troops were not in a position to undertake an operation of this sort. He had made his plan for his offensive, and he would stick to it. Also he saw that it would be to his advantage to keep the enemy in this southern sector, for it would help the major attack in the north which he had planned.

So ended Montgomery's first battle as Commander of Eighth Army; the result heralded well for the future.

Towards the end of the battle Wendell Wilkie came out to stay with the Army Commander. We all took a liking to him.

He had much charm, and we thought, great vision. He was taken up to see the front — at very close quarters — and thoroughly enjoyed it. There was a particularly good air fight fought over his head. He was for ever impressed with the importance of this battle, and he has given it prominence in his writings. He saw in it the turning point. It is hardly ever spoken of nowadays, and comparatively few knew it took place. It deserves study and a prominent position in our military history.

Before turning back to the preparations for Alamein, I will quote messages that went between Montgomery and Coningham, A.O.C. of the Desert Air Force, which I think shows so well how we were all feeling after Rommel's set-back.

> From Coningham to Montgomery 5/9/42: —
> "Do allow me on behalf of the R.A.F. in the Western Desert to congratulate you and the Army in winning the battle in such a flawless manner (.) We are delighted and all are enthusiastic (.) Please give 13th Corps a special cheer on our behalf (.) We want some more please (.)"

> From Montgomery to Coningham 5/9/42: —
> "Thank you for your message (.) We in the Eighth Army realise very fully that without the magnificent cooperation of the R.A.F. the battle could not have been won (.) I would be grateful if you will convey to all ranks under your command the sincere thanks of the Eighth Army for the gallant way in which the R.A.F. supported the land operations (.)"

And here is an extract from a letter sent by Coningham about the same time: —

> *"In all my force there is an atmosphere of enthusiasm and expectancy at the prospect of going on to greater things as part of the Eighth Army. United we conquer!"*

VI

Shortly before Rommel had been defeated, the Prime Minister came and paid us a visit on his way back from Moscow. He stayed in the mess at Burgh-el-Arab. There is no doubt that he enjoyed his trip a lot. In the first place after a poor beginning, his talks with Stalin had been satisfactory. Then the new atmosphere which he found in the Eighth Army gave him great confidence in the future. And overall, Churchill was never so happy as when staying with the Services, and the nearer the firing line the better.

Montgomery took special care to see that the Prime Minister and his party would be comfortable. He gave up his own caravan and sited it within a few yards of the sea, so that our guest could bathe when he felt so inclined. The weather was hot, and so the opportunity was taken several times. The troops were delighted to see their Prime Minister wading into the water in the untanned nude. He paid visits to the troops and met with the usual demonstrations of affection. There is no doubt how he inspired us all.

It was found that there was no brandy in the mess, and so an A.D.C. was sent into Alexandria to buy some. A local product was found, and to drink this, one had to have a cast-iron stomach, and a very good head. I'm afraid a little deception was tried out — we were very "deception minded" in those days — and the liquor was poured into an empty bottle bearing the labels of a well-known French brand!

The dinner party was a great success, and I don't think we got to bed before 1 a.m. As usual the Prime Minister did all the talking, but no one ever complains at this, for it is a rich entertainment. I have been present when he has been Montgomery's guest in many places, twice in North Africa,

Italy, at home before the invasion, and two or three times on the Continent. I never ceased to be attracted by his conversation and his knowledge of the world, and its history. These occasions are all delightful memories.

He gave us that evening the most vivid description of his visit to Moscow. How he had to talk "cold turkey" before it was accepted that we were doing something to win the war. He had come away with a very deep impression of Stalin's leadership. He enthralled us with details of our gathering war effort, and what we were preparing for the enemy. I well remember him saying: "Germany has asked for this bombing warfare, she will rue the day she started it, for her country will be laid in ruins." Then this was the day of the Dieppe raid, and reports were arriving from London throughout the evening. So there was plenty to talk about. That night is still vivid in my recollection, for it was rather a new experience for me to hob-nob with the very great. I can still picture the scene, Churchill settling down after dinner, the bottle of doubtful brandy placed in front of him, together with a very large glass borrowed from an hotel in Alexandria. Out of his pocket he produced the largest cigar I have ever seen — it was a present from some Egyptian admirers, and measured 12 inches long. The Prime Minister held it with both hands! The hours passed by, and the level of the brandy sank, but our Prime Minister was up bright and early the next morning bathing in the blue Mediterranean. It was one of the better evenings.

VII

I had left the preparations for an offensive in order to describe Rommel's attack in its correct chronological order. I will go into this period in some detail because of the importance in our war history of this particular battle, and it will serve as an example of what is involved in an operation of this sort.

There was no way round the enemy position, the sea and the Quattara Depression seeing to that. So a hole had to be punched through their defences. Montgomery had decided to launch the main attack on the right flank with Leese's 30th Corps, with a secondary attack on the southern flank by Horrocks' 13th Corps. The plan was to pass 10th Corps (General Lumsden) through the gap made by 30th Corps to sit astride the enemy's supply line, and so force him to deploy his armour against us, when it would be destroyed. This was in accordance with the normal teaching. Having destroyed the enemy's armour, his unarmoured troops could be dealt with more or less at leisure.

The Army Commander had laid down three basic fundamentals which would govern the preparatory period. These were: Leadership — equipment — training. He very soon had put the first matter in order. The re-equipment of the Army was going well and smoothly. But early in October he realised that the training of the Army was still below what was required. He then decided that the troops must not be given too ambitious tasks. In view of this weakness, Montgomery made one of his rapid decisions. He would alter the conception of the plan so that instead of first going out to destroy the enemy's armour, he would eat away the enemy's holding troops — who were for the most part unarmoured — and would hold off with our armour that of the enemy, to stop them interfering. Without their infantry divisions to hold the line and ensure the enemy's mobile forces firm bases, the enemy's armour would be at a grave disadvantage with no outside protection, and their supply routes constantly under our threat. It was unlikely that they would stand idly by whilst this "crumbling" process was going on. It was probable, therefore, that we would force his armour to attack us, which, once we were in a position to receive it, would be to our advantage.

The final plan in outline as given out by the Army Commander on October 6th, was as follows:

(a) Main attack by 30th Corps in the north on a front of four divisions. Two corridors were to be cleared through the minefields, and through these lanes 10th Corps was to pass.

(b) 13th Corps in the south were to stage two attacks. One directed on Himeimat and the Taqa feature. The other into the area of Gebel Kalakh and Qaret El Khadim. These attacks were made with the primary object of misleading the enemy and thereby holding forces that might otherwise be used against 30th Corps.

(c) Both the above Corps were to destroy the enemy holding the forward positions.

(d) 10th Corps was to deploy itself so as to prevent 30th Corps' operations from being interfered with. And its final object was the destruction of the enemy's armour.

(e) The attack was to start at night during the full moon.

The artillery plan was very carefully prepared. We would go into battle with great gun power and excellent supplies of ammunition. The battle was to open with a very heavy counter-battery bombardment, and then all or most of our artillery would concentrate on the enemy defences by barrage and concentrations. In the British Army nothing like it had been witnessed before during the war.

Montgomery was determined not to have a failure, and we collected very formidable totals of guns and tanks by "D" day. I give the figures below: —

Guns.[16]

25 pdr. (Field): 832
4.5 (Medium): 32
5-5 (Medium): 20
6 pdr. (anti-tank): 753
2 pdr. R.A. (anti-tank): 105
2 pdr. Inf. (anti-tank): 416
105 mm. Field: 24

Tanks.
Shermans: 267
Grants: 128
Stewarts: 128
Crusader 6 pdr.: 105
Crusader 2 pdr.: 255
Crusader (Close Support): 35
Valentines: 196

These were riches which Eighth Army had never seen before.

The air plan was a good one. Before the battle Coningham had been wearing down the enemy's air effort. On one or two occasions he had shown brilliant leadership by taking advantage of fleeting opportunities when isolated rain storms had grounded portions of the enemy's air force. Low flying attacks laid on with great rapidity had taken a very heavy toll of the enemy's machines and petrol.

During the first night the air were to undertake attacks against enemy gun positions, and so help our counter-battery plan. Later they were to switch to the areas in which we knew the enemy armoured divisions were located.

I think our available air strength on "D" day was:

Fighters: 500

---

[16] Guns and tanks excluding replacements.

Bombers: 200

Not so many when compared with the later years of the war, but at that time a considerable force.

The "going" was one of the matters which gave us a lot of anxiety. We went to endless trouble to obtain information as to what the ground was like in the area over which we were making our thrusts. Air photos, interrogation of prisoners, interrogation of our own troops who had at one time or another traversed the area, were some of the means employed. It was most important to know where our tanks and transport could go. We had to build — I think it was six — tracks leading up to 30th Corps starting line. This was a tremendous work through very soft sand.

The deception arrangements were particularly interesting. We had decided that strategic surprise was out of the question, for the enemy must know we were going to attack. But tactical surprise was quite possible. We considered we could delude the enemy as to the weight, the date, the time and the direction of our attack. Our plans were all made with this in view, and they proved most successful.

The first problem was to try and conceal the concentration as much as possible from the enemy. The staff worked out the complete layout on the day of the attack, i.e. the number of guns, tanks, vehicles and troops. A very large "operations" map was kept which showed this layout in various denominations. We then arranged to arrive at the eventual density as early as possible, and to maintain this density up to the last moment, so that the enemy's air photography would show no particular change in the last two or three weeks. To achieve this we used spare transport and dummy transport. These were gradually replaced by those belonging to the assault units and formations as they came up to take over their allotted sectors. These changeovers took place at night. We had special dummy vehicles made under which guns could be concealed. And in this way we hoped to get the enemy used to the pattern, and there would be no significant change even on "D" day. All moves forward were of course rigidly controlled. Slit trenches were dug and camouflaged at night in which the assaulting infantry could be concealed.

The next task was to make the enemy think that the main attack would be launched in the southern sector. This, I might say, was not very popular with 13th Corps, but they nobly accepted the plan for the common good. Besides various other methods adopted, we built large dummy dumps away to the south, and also a dummy pipe line and water installations. It was so arranged that the work would appear to the enemy to be aimed at completion a week or two after the actual date of our attack. On the night of the attack the wireless traffic of the Headquarters of an armoured division was so employed as to indicate that a large move of armoured forces was taking place in the southern sector.

On the night of the attack we arranged for a feint landing to take place behind the enemy's lines. About 4 p.m. in the afternoon a convoy was to sail westwards out of Alexandria. After dark all but a few fast craft would put back, but those remaining were to stage a dummy landing. Shelling of the coast, mortar and machine-gun fire and light signals were used. It was timed to take place about three hours after the attack had started, and it was hoped that this would tie down enemy reserves. The loading of the ships had been carried out so that any enemy agent could see. Tanks were shipped and troops marched aboard.

There is no doubt that all these measures helped materially to confuse the enemy and gain us tactical surprise.

On the administrative side there was a great deal to be done. We were fortunate in having as the senior administrative staff officer Sir Brian Robertson, the son of the famous Field Marshal. Behind the army area we were getting magnificent support from the administrative side of G.H.Q. Middle East.

The whole basis of administration had to be altered. Before, when *defence* was paramount, the weight of resources was held back; now that *offence* was our watchword, they had to be placed as far forward as possible. The carrying forward and the camouflaging of the dumps was no small task. Preparations were made to construct the railway forward as rapidly as possible. For the mobile warfare we were expecting, a "road-head" organisation was worked out, and each Corps had a mobile administrative "township" of its own called a F.M.C. (Field Maintenance Centre). Here reserves of all kinds were held — personnel as well as munitions and supplies.

We also formed an "Administrative Assault Force." This consisted of a team of experts who would undertake the organising and opening up of a port immediately after its capture. A shipping programme was prepared so that at the earliest moment after a port was opened we could receive supplies by sea. Shipping was earmarked and loaded ready for use.

Recovery of vehicles, particularly tanks, was another matter which we made a great drive to improve. A revised organisation on a big scale was set up, for in these desert battles tank casualties of one kind or another were very heavy, and it was essential to have a very rapid and efficient system of recovery, repair and delivery. The scheme embraced both machines and crews. The working of this organisation could often win or lose a battle.

I hope some who read this book will not think I have been wasting paper mentioning administrative points which nowadays are well known and well tried. In those days, however, we were pioneering in many directions, and the lessons of the battle of El Alamein formed the pattern for far larger enterprises later on. Our growing pains and problems at that time are therefore not without interest.

VII

The date for the battle was October 23rd, 1942. It was only by Montgomery and Alexander taking a firm stand that this date was accepted, and the troops launched fully prepared for the contest. Owing to the minefield problem it was essential that the attack should take place at night, and that the night should have a moon. The troops must see a certain amount to deal with the mines. Then, as a prolonged dog-fight was envisaged, a waning moon was not acceptable. These considerations, therefore, limited the choice to a certain period each month. Churchill was pressing for the attack to take place in September. Admittedly he had very good reasons for an early offensive, one being the fact that the North African Anglo/U.S. landings were due to take place early in November, and therefore the harder and more prolonged the fighting further east, the easier TORCH's (as the operation was known) task would be.

I remember Alexander discussing the Prime Minister's signal with my chief. Montgomery took a sheet of paper and wrote out very carefully four points on which to base a reply. These were:

(a) Rommel's attack had caused some delay in our preparations.

(b) Moon conditions restricted "D" day to certain periods in September and October.
(c) If the September date were accepted the troops would be insufficiently equipped and trained.
(d) If the September date were taken, failure would probably result, but if the attack took place in October then complete victory was assured.

The reply was sent on those lines. What could a Prime Minister do with this clear-cut military opinion before him? Well, the attack took place on October 23rd.

Between the failure of Rommel's offensive of August 31st and the start of the battle of El Alamein a somewhat "woolly" operation was staged against the ports of Tobruk and Benghazi. It was directed and planned by the Naval and Army staffs in the Delta. Montgomery had nothing to do with it, and he certainly viewed the whole business with disfavour. He once said to me: "You can't run a military operation with a committee of staff officers in command. It will be nonsense!" And it was. I think it was a legacy from that period when we had just arrived back at the Alamein position, and everyone was trying to find a cheap and easy way to "win the war." The idea was to undertake combined operations against the two ports, capture them, or at least cause considerable damage to their installations. The plans were very complicated and success depended upon everything going right. Some magnificent men were used and unfortunately lost in the attempt.

Stirling of the S.A.S.[17] led the attack against Benghazi, basing himself on Kufra for the purpose. This meant a very long journey across the desert. He had orders not to press the attack if the enemy were found to be too strong. This turned out to

---

[17] Special Air Service.

be the case, and he wisely withdrew his force after encountering a very well defended perimeter. On the way back he was attacked resolutely by enemy aircraft. A detachment of the Sudan Defence Force staged a raid against Gialo in order to assist Stirling's return.

The party for Tobruk moved in from Egypt and here a ruse was employed. An entry into the perimeter was effected by driving through the defences in captured enemy lorries, and using certain articles of clothing in order to make the enemy accept them as their own troops. Most of the initial party could speak German fluently. Others, I believe, were to be let in behind them. Attacks were to be made against the coast defence guns, and it was hoped to release any of our prisoners of war from the cages. Another party were to arrive by sea, but things did not turn out as planned and they landed at the wrong places.

The whole operation was a dismal failure and no good resulted from it.

Little has been heard of these attacks, and that is why I think they are worth mentioning. Staff colleges please note: "Combined Operations and how not to run them."

VIII

Large scale rehearsals for the coming battle were carried out, and the lessons learnt gone into very carefully by the Commanders. And by the end of the third week in October we began to realise that all these vast preparations were successfully reaching their conclusion. From the staff point of view there was a healthy slackening in the *tempo* of work, denoting that the stage was set.

Montgomery had been indefatigable, and had satisfied himself that all was in readiness. He very rightly had decided that in order to get the best out of his troops it was necessary for them to know the whole plan so that they would realise how their particular contribution fitted in with the general scheme of things.

On October 19th and 20th he addressed all officers down to lieutenant-colonel level in 30th, 13th and 10th Corps. It was a real *tour de force*. These talks were some of the best he has ever given. Clear and full of confidence. I warrant there were no doubters after he had finished. He touched on the enemy situation, stressed his weaknesses, but was certain a long "dogfight" or "killing match" would take place for several days — "it might be ten." He then gave details of our great strength, our tanks, our guns and the enormous supplies of ammunition available. He drummed in the need never to lose the initiative, and how everyone — *everyone* — must be imbued with the burning desire to "kill Germans." "Even the padres — one per weekday and two on Sundays!" This produced a roar. He explained how the battle was to be fought, and finished by saying that he was entirely and utterly confident of the result.

The men were let into the secret on October 21st and 22nd, from which date no leave was granted. And, as a result of everything, a tremendous state of enthusiasm was produced. I have never felt anything like it. Those soldiers just knew they were going to succeed.

This question of morale, which Montgomery puts as the No. 1 factor in war, is well brought out in the following extracts from his instructions for operation "Lightfoot" (code name for battle of El Alamein). They were issued on September 14th and October 6th, and are prophetic as well as excellent stuff to give the troops.

> This battle for which we are preparing will be a real rough house and will involve a very great deal of hard fighting. If we

are successful it will mean the end of the war in North Africa, apart from general "clearing up" operations; it will be the turning point of the whole war. Therefore we can take no chances.

Morale is the big thing in war. We must raise the morale of our soldiery to the highest pitch; they must be made enthusiastic, and must enter this battle with their tails high in the air and with the will to win.

There must in fact be no weak links in our mental fitness.

But mental fitness will not stand up to the stress and strain of battle unless troops are also physically fit.

This battle may go on for many days, and the final issue may well depend on which side can best last out and stand up to the buffeting, and ups and downs, and the continuous strain, of hard battle fighting.

There will be no tip and run tactics in this battle; it will be a killing match; the German is a good soldier and the only way to beat him is to kill him in battle.

I am not convinced that our soldiery are really tough and hard. They are sunburnt and brown, and look very well; but they seldom move anywhere on foot and they have led a static life for many weeks.

During the next month, therefore, it is essential to make our officers and men really fit; ordinary fitness is not enough, they must be made tough and hard.

This battle will involve hard and prolonged fighting. Our troops must not think that because we have a good tank and very powerful artillery support the enemy will all surrender. The enemy will not surrender, and there will be bitter fighting.

The infantry must be prepared to fight and to kill, and to continue doing so over a prolonged period.

It is essential to impress on all officers that determined leadership will be very vital in this battle, as in any battle. There have been far too many unwounded prisoners taken in this war. We must impress on our officers, N.C.O.'s and men that when they are cut off or surrounded, and there appears to be no hope of survival, they must organise themselves into a defensive locality and hold out where they are. By so doing they will add enormously to the enemy's difficulties; they will greatly assist the development of our own operations; and they will save themselves from spending the rest of the war in a prison camp.

Nothing is ever hopeless so long as troops have stout hearts, and have weapons and ammunition.

These points must be got across *now* at once to all officers and men, as being applicable to any fighting.

Two or three days before the battle, I spent a couple of nights in Alexandria as I was feeling a little under the weather. It was an odd paradox, this peace-time existence in "Alex" with a battlefield at its very gates. I had visited formations in the forward area in the morning, drove back to my headquarters and changed, and then on to Alexandria. Here we had a very good lunch at the club with orchestra playing and well-dressed women everywhere to be seen. You could hear the guns if you cared to stop to listen. An afternoon at the races and then whatever other form of entertainment you wanted. It didn't feel real, and dining with some friends in their charming house, one might have been at Deauville or Cannes. No one seemed to know that great things were afoot, and that the blood of many thousands of soldiers would be shed before the week was out.

Admiral Harwood kindly put me up. I was allowed breakfast in bed, and slept better than I had done for many weeks. That thirty-six hours' break did a lot to fortify me for the strenuous time ahead.

On the morning of October 22nd, Montgomery held a press conference. He explained the plan, his intentions, and his firm conviction of success. Many of the war correspondents were rather shaken by the confidence — this bombastic confidence — he displayed. They felt there must be a catch in it — how can he be so sure? Some, I think, thought the maze of minefields and deep defences that the enemy had constructed would prove too difficult a problem to justify such a sanguine attitude.

In the afternoon we drove up to our battle Headquarters. This we had very carefully prepared. It was tucked away on the coast within a few minutes of 30th and 10th Corps Headquarters. We had well protected buried cables back to our Main Headquarters and the Corps, and so communications were assured. Vehicles were dug in as we were rather far forward and near the desert road, which would undoubtedly become — as it did — a target for the enemy air. At that time I decided to make this Tactical Headquarters my base, and it worked very well. My people could talk to me on direct lines and come up for conferences within the hour. We had a small mess, and we felt very snug.

It was a lovely evening, and I drove out after dark to see by the light of the moon the move forward of some of the troops. All was going well, and everyone looked cheerful. This was the day so many of us had been for so long preparing and waiting for. I felt really thrilled.

I returned later and paid a call on George Walsh, Leese's B.G.S. We had a drink and then I had some food with 30th Corps Commander and his staff. I don't know what we talked about, but we were all trying to conceal our excitement, and kept looking at our watches to see how far off was "H" hour. I went back to my office and rang up Mainwaring, my G.S.O. 1 Operations, at Main Headquarters, and had a chat to find out how things were going. I couldn't, of course, do anything now, it was too late. Then a chat with George Beamish, my opposite number in Desert Air Force, and others with 10th and 13th Corps. The usual thing — "How's it going — best of luck — anything you want?" Coningham of the R.A.F. came up and spent the night — he had a caravan permanently at Tactical Headquarters, so that he could stay when he so desired.

As the time drew near we got into our cars and drove to a good view point to see the opening of the battle. We passed the never-ending stream of tanks and transport. All moving with clockwork precision. This was 10 Corps moving up to its starting line. The moon provided sufficient light to drive by, but the night protected them from the prying eyes of enemy aircraft. We had some of our own aircraft up over the enemy's forward positions making distracting noises. Otherwise all seemed fairly quiet and normal. An occasional Verey light and burst of machine-gun fire, a gun firing here and there, as would happen any night. We looked at our watches, 21.30 hours — ten minutes to go. I could hardly wait. The minutes ticked by, and then the whole sky was lit up, and a roar rent the air. Over a thousand of our guns had opened up. It was a great and heartening sight. I tried to picture what the enemy must be thinking, did he know what was coming? He must do now. How ready was he? Up and down the desert, from north to south, the twinkling of the guns could be seen in an unceasing sequence. Within the enemy's lines we could see an occasional deep red glow light up the western sky. Each time this happened the 30 Corps C.C.R.A.[18] — Dennis — let out a grunt of satisfaction. Another Axis gun position had gone up. We checked each change in the artillery plan; the pause whilst the guns switched to new targets. It was gun drill at its best. Now the infantry had started forward. We could see the periodic bursts of Bofors guns which, with their tracer shell,

---

[18] Commander Corps Royal Artillery.

demarcated the direction of advance. Behind us great searchlight beams were directed towards the sky. These beacons were used to help the forward troops resect their positions, and so find out when they had reached their objectives, for few landmarks existed in this part of the desert.

About eleven o'clock I crept away and drove back to our Headquarters. I knew we could expect to hear little of interest for some time yet, and so I snatched an hour or two's rest before being wakened up to hear the first reports.

As I closed my eyes I felt full of confidence and hope, but never did I think that this was the opening of a campaign that would bring us to the very gates of Carthage in so short a time.

CHAPTER VII: MONTGOMERY

I

BEFORE I turn to tell the story of the battle of El Alamein and of my three years association with Field-Marshal Montgomery, I propose to devote a chapter to a description of this remarkable man. It will, I hope, help readers in their understanding and their appreciation of a very great soldier. It is obvious, having been in close contact with him during such a momentous period, that I should be one of his greatest admirers. On the other hand I am not so biased or bigoted as not to realise he had some weaknesses, as have all men. But these, when set against his achievements and his genius, are soon lost in the overwhelming strength of the credit side of the balance sheet. Montgomery has, in spite of his many successes, been subject to a considerable amount of criticism, some of it possibly deserved, but much of it ill-informed and unfair. To do justice to this subject, a book not a chapter is required. And Alan Moorehead is, as I write this, engaged on such a work. My study must, therefore, be a potted version. But I hope, one that will help in dispelling "false rumours," and one that will assist in bringing out the whys and wherefores of many of the events described in these pages.

I will start with my contacts with the Field-Marshal before I met him on that hot and sultry morning at the crossroads outside Alexandria: the newly appointed Commander of Eighth Army; myself as the rather new and inexperienced B.G.S. of that "Desert Force."

It was in Southern Ireland in 1921, as a second lieutenant, that I first heard of him. He was Brigade Major of the Brigade to which my battalion belonged. I doubt whether he remembers me, but I still remember him well in that capacity. He always possessed that ability to get himself across. We certainly all thought he was a most efficient and experienced staff officer.

My next contact was more intimate and for a longer time. Montgomery was appointed G.S.O. 2 of the 49th Division. He decided to live at my regimental depot mess in York. I was posted there myself in late 1922.

Many who have met Montgomery for the first time during the late war might not realise that throughout his career he has always had a very warm spot in his heart for the young officer. There are so many of us who have him to thank for knowledge imparted and inspiration. There are various reasons for his interest in the young. First I think he has always been imbued with the need to do all in his power to increase the efficiency of the Army. He had taken soldiering seriously from his earliest days, and he spared no pains to increase the young officer's interest in his profession. Then I am sure he felt that one of the best ways to keep young was to mix frequently with those younger than himself. I have seen him so often after an exhausting and worrying day in the field dining at his small Tactical Headquarters with his A.D.C.'s around him. Every now and then he throws a "bone" to be worried by them, and whilst the argument goes on, he leans back and relaxes. By the end of dinner he has been visibly refreshed and is ready for a good night's rest. Finally, I think throughout his service he has looked upon the older generation in the Army with suspicion, and as the result of all this he still retains the critical enthusiasm normally associated with youth.

At my Depot his presence in the Mess proved a great asset. I am sure all those who came in contact with him in those days were quite certain that he was destined for great things. To start with he was so obviously sincere with regard to his efforts to inspire and teach the younger generation. He was also looked upon as rather a novelty, in that he unblushingly proclaimed that soldiering was his one and only love. I'm afraid at that time such an attitude was somewhat rare, or at least unfashionable. One of his maxims was that "You cannot make a good soldier and a good husband." Some years later when serving in East Africa with another officer in my regiment who was at our Depot during Montgomery's stay, we were shaken to read in *The Times* the announcement of his engagement. We then and there sent him a cable saying: "Which is it to be, the soldier or the husband?" We received no answer, but time showed that he excelled at both.

He created a wonderfully refreshing atmosphere in the Mess. As always, he was extremely outspoken and provocative, and had that happy knack of making us young officers think about our profession and become interested in the military art. In my small way I had a certain amount to do with the training of Territorials. With Montgomery's help I was allowed to start some new methods. For instance, he produced the financial backing to allow me to tour our Territorial Battalions with a team of instructors, so that we could hold courses in the evenings and week-ends in their own areas. This was quite an innovation in those days, and I enjoyed the experience enormously.

Montgomery rarely went out in the evenings. He did, however, play bridge — very well indeed. He also played golf to about a 9 handicap, and I had many a game with him. One year he asked me to partner him at the Army Golf Meeting at Hoylake. I was a very erratic player and my temper did not behave itself very well when playing badly. He overlooked these human failings and we enjoyed ourselves. During the competition I recollect my partner playing an unusually good brassie shot which dropped on the green whilst two senior officers were putting. One of them — a very pompous Brigadier at the time — came across and said some very rude things and was generally offensive. I could see that the future Field-Marshal did not like it, and as the great one sailed away he turned to me and said: "Silly old ——, he's no use anyway." Always outspoken and generally right. He certainly was in this case!

I think it was Montgomery who started what were termed in the Army "Backward Boy Courses." These were courses held each year to assist those officers who were studying for the Staff College. They lasted between a week and a fortnight, and dealt with the various subjects that were included in the Staff College Exam. This first effort of its kind was an astonishing "one-man" performance. Montgomery lectured on all the subjects, set papers and corrected them. He can have had little sleep during this period. I was allowed to attend in spite of my tender years, and there was no doubt about the success of the venture. Everyone was enthusiastic and full of gratitude, for previously, those officers wishing to study for the Staff College received little or no assistance. Montgomery realised the need for this, and recognised the fact that this duty fell upon those who had already been trained for the staff. It is just one example of his many efforts throughout his service to spread military knowledge.

As far as I can recollect, not so long after this, Montgomery became sick and had to take some leave. It was generally accepted by us all as being the result of too much hard work.

In 1925 my tour at the Depot was coming to an end. I could not face the rather narrow life of regimental soldiering after the comparative freedom of my Depot life. I felt the call of Africa, and applied for a post with the King's African Rifles. I consulted Montgomery about it, and was rather surprised when he agreed. "But don't stay too long — not too long," was his comment. How right he was, for there was no better training ground for the young officer than Africa, serving in His Majesty's Colonial Forces.

It was several years before we met again. I had returned from Africa and was Adjutant of my battalion in Egypt. We were stationed at Ismailia, as part of the Canal Brigade. It turned out to be rather an exceptional formation, as far as the eventual destiny of some of its commanders were concerned. We were lucky enough to have "Tim" Pile as our Brigade Commander. It surprised none of us that later he was given the important post of Commander-in-Chief A.A. Command of Great Britain. Our battalion was commanded by Franklyn who had a division in the British Expeditionary Force in 1939-40, and later became Commander-in-Chief of Home Forces. The battalion which was somewhat isolated in Alexandria was commanded by Montgomery. There are some delicious tales told of his rule in Alexandria. Already he was known as a rather difficult and peculiar character, and his command of the soldiers in that area was original and autocratic, but I mustn't attempt to repeat some of the stories told — this is better done by those who were present at the time.

During the annual collective training period — when the Brigade camped in the Desert — the various battalion commanders were tested for future advancement. Each in turn was put in command of the brigade for one of the exercises. In addition to this substitution of commanders, our Brigadier gave other officers a chance of acting for the Brigade Major. Galloway, Pile's Brigade Major, was very popular and first class. Our paths crossed frequently during the war, and eventually he took over from me as Chief of Staff 21st Army Group in June, 1945, when I had to leave through sickness.

Montgomery's turn came along and by some twist of the wheel, I was made his "Brigade Major" for the exercise. It was an amusing one, as were all those directed by "Tim" Pile. The enemy had, for those days, a considerable amount of motor transport. Their aim was to raid one of our two camps and also to hamper our movement in that particular area. Our task was to destroy this force.

Montgomery organised the defence of the two camps, and then formed a mobile striking force for offensive action. Our difficulties were first to locate the enemy — not easy with our limited resources — and then to bring him to battle. Up to nightfall we had received no firm news. The enemy rightly had decided to keep hidden by day. The type of armoured car we then had was not very efficient in the dark, and so I arranged for some night sorties by aircraft. They agreed to use flares which were quite new at that time. Up to about 11 p.m. nothing had been seen or heard of the enemy, and Montgomery showed some signs of wanting to move out with the striking force without knowledge of the enemy's exact whereabouts. I asked him to let me have one more chance of locating them with an aircraft. This he agreed to do. About 1 a.m. the next day I received a most welcome message from the airfield at Heliopolis, saying that a concentration of transport had been seen in a particular wadi some few miles away. This was just what we wanted. By seizing his transport we could hamstring the enemy's activities. And to cut a long story short, this is what we proceeded to do, and success fell to our side.

Montgomery left Egypt to take up an appointment at the Staff College in Quetta. A year later, our battalion followed him to that station. Before arriving I had sat for the Staff College Exam., and as I had left it very late in life, it was to be my one and only attempt, as the following year I would be over age. The results came out in June, 1934, and I found that I had "qualified." But to get in, one had to be "nominated" as well — and the competition was very great. I saw Montgomery a few days later, and he said he would use any influence he had on my behalf. I thanked him, but did not feel very hopeful.

Towards the end of July the nominations came out, and I was amongst the lucky ones. I was up at a rest camp called Ziarat at the time, and the first news I received was from my future Chief. This was followed by a letter from which I quote this extract:

> I am not used to backing the wrong horse when it comes to asking favours of people in high places; it would result only in one's own undoing! You ought to do very well at Camberley. I know many of the instructors there, and some of them very well, one of them — Nye[19] — is in my Regiment. I will write and commend you to them in due course.
>
> We are coming to your dance on August 14th, and are dining first with the Army Commander.
>
> Yours ever,
> B. L. Montgomery.

This letter is interesting for three reasons. First it was obvious that I had been accepted by him as a "proper chap" — Montgomery's classification for one who is of use to the Army. Then it shows to what pains Montgomery goes to help those junior to himself. He took the trouble to write letters to several of the instructors. Even to-day, with his load of responsibilities, this helpfulness still persists. Finally, perhaps

---

[19] Later Lieut.-General Sir A. Nye, V.C.I.G.S.

some will be surprised at the last paragraph. It may be difficult for some to picture the austere Field-Marshal in his dancing days!

I will give just one more example of the pains Montgomery took to help those he considered would be of use to the Army. A brother officer of mine failed in the Exam, which I took. He had "qualified" before, but did not receive a nomination. Now he was too old to sit again. Montgomery knew and liked this officer and so I asked him if he could help. I give in full the letter he sent me in answer to my request. It speaks for itself.

Staff College,
Quetta.
17/10/34.

My dear Freddie,

The numbers going up in India next February for the Staff College Entrance Exam, are very few, only sixty from Indian Army and less from the British Service. The reasons are the war block, reduction of age limit, etc., etc. I discussed the subject with the C. G. S. last week and suggested they should cast back and nominate officers who have qualified before and who are now over age. He is going to consider this and will I think do it, if the case is a good one.

I think we might possibly get a vacancy for ———; at any rate I would like to have a try. The C.G.S. out here does the nominations for Quetta, and not the War Office, and I would write personally to him and put the case before him.

But I would like to be certain of my facts, and be clear as to ———'s record. Could I have a look at his Record of Service, as that would give me the necessary information.

We must dine on Saturday at 8.15 p.m. as the cinema begins at 9.30. Will you communicate with ———, and both come along at 8.15.

Yours ever,
B. L. Montgomery.

I presume your C.O. would have no objection if I try to pull a few strings on ——'s behalf.

Montgomery's dinner parties at Quetta were great fun. He would invite a mixed bag, Indian and British Service — Cavalry and the other arms. His wife was a delightful and amusing hostess, and very artistic. The dinner being finished, we would sit over our port and coffee and talk. He would put forward various problems for discussion, and these were interposed with provocative statements that were certain to produce considerable argument. I enjoyed those evenings a great deal.

I don't think I saw Montgomery again until one day at Catterick in the autumn of 1937. I was asked to dine with the G.O.C., General Williams. Montgomery, I was told, would be there. A tragedy had occurred in his life; for his wife had died a short time before. Williams had been the Commandant of the Quetta Staff College during his time as Chief Instructor, and I suppose Montgomery came up knowing he would find a sympathetic atmosphere.

At dinner I found him rather quiet, but still intensely interested in the Army's problems. After dinner I was put in a chair and made to answer a number of questions relating to the present Staff College course; the system of entry; the regimental officer's opinion on dress, leave, training, messes, quarters, etc. Before bidding good night, I fixed up to go for a walk over the moors the next day.

I think during that walk Montgomery slightly relaxed that iron self-control of his. He talked just a little about his wife — I raised the subject — and I could see what the loss had meant to him. There was a sort of lonely feeling around him, something that I have met on several occasions in the last few years. It was obvious he was going to force himself to get over his grief as soon as possible; and, of course, intensive soldiering provided the best means of achieving this end.

Montgomery was now a Brigade Commander down at Portsmouth, and I only saw him for a few brief moments at a Salisbury Plain demonstration in 1938. In 1939 he was commanding a division in France when I visited the B.E.F. with Hore-Belisha, the Secretary of State for War. We agreed that his division gave us the best "feel" as far as efficiency was concerned. The stage management of the visit was excellent, and one Brigade was lined up along a road facing inwards so that the Secretary of State could talk to anyone he wished.

Our next meeting took place in the Western Desert of Egypt.

II

I will now attempt to analyse Montgomery's character.

The Field-Marshal has the ideal temperament for a soldier. Nothing appears to worry him. He accepts responsibility with complete ease. He is, to use his own expression, the perfect example of the "non-bellyacher." It is a great gift — that of being able to prevent unpleasant things worrying one: not to allow awkward situations or incidents to interfere with the even rhythm of one's life. I have met so many soldiers who either get bothered by big or by little things. Montgomery is not visibly affected by either. I think this is the basis of his success; for not only does it allow him to get on with the important issues, but it also provides the reason for the supreme confidence that he invariably radiates. This is a priceless gift for any Commander to possess, and provides inspiration for his staff. There will be plenty of examples in this story that will help to explain this point more fully.

Next in importance comes the clarity of his mind. When tackling a problem he likes time to think it out. He cuts away all the frills and gets down to those factors that really matter. He simplifies everything to an extent I have not met elsewhere. Some say he over-simplifies — this to some extent is true, but the resultant dividend is enormous. How many times have I scratched my head and said, "How stupid of me — fancy not thinking of that — it's just too easy."

He is a great "de-bunker" of persons as well as of things. Before this war, officers were often helped in advancement because of social attainments, ability at games, money, or the gift of the gab. Montgomery sweeps all such frills aside and assesses a man's true worth. He is not influenced by such matters. But then, of course, he knows so much better than many others what true worth really is. His knowledge of the military art, in all its spheres at the outbreak of war, was, I think, quite unique. This made his task the easier. He had studied the art of command, the psychology of war, and the tasks of the various arms of the service. He could talk with exact and technical knowledge of either the sappers' or the gunners' work; as easily as he could discuss that of his own arm's role in battle — i.e. the infantry.

Whether on paper or in speech he is always crystal clear. There is never any doubt about what he really means. He has consistently practised speaking to officers and men, and has developed a technique that is arresting and most effective. His addresses to troops before battle proved of tremendous value, and will not be forgotten by those who listened to them.

His directness sometimes takes the breath away of those not used to it. I doubt whether he would have excelled as a pre-war diplomat, but with changing fashions in this field, he would be very much more successful to-day.

Dogged persistence is another quality. When once he has made up his mind that some measure or other is right, he will go to all sorts of manoeuvres to get it accepted. Sometimes when I have not agreed with him, I have called it obstinacy! But one can't be always right. If the resistance is too great at first, he lets the matter lie fallow for a while, and then at the tactical moment when one least expects it, the fight is on again, generally to the disadvantage of the opposition. But he never fights about small things. His declared philosophy has always been: "I will fight for the big things — for the things that really matter. I am not prepared to cause irritation and bad blood over the small ones — they are not worth fighting about."

In his treatment of individuals, within my knowledge he has always been most fair. I realise there are some who might not agree with this statement. I have so often seen him give a basically good man another chance, or accept staleness or over-strain as a reason for failure. Often he has said to me, when some Commander has taken a dislike to a newcomer's face, "I will not have So-and-so savaged. He must be given a chance." His critics have been usually those with most to fear, the inefficient, those who have not made, or who will not make, the grade.

The legend of austerity requires some explanation. Like most people I am sure he doesn't adopt austerity for choice. During the war it was a means to an end. He realised that unless he lived reasonably "hard," he would not keep himself in the condition necessary for the ordeal. He was also determined to prevent stories of the Headquarters and Staff living in luxury from circulating amongst the troops, as they had occurred in the previous war. I'm sure a lot of good came of the publicity given to the Field-Marshal's tent and caravan headquarters. No luxurious château, but living in the open like the troops. But don't let it be imagined that his headquarters was a rough-and-ready affair; that one ate out of tins and billy-cans. Nothing could be further from the truth. It was highly organised and comfortable. The Mess was very well served. It had an excellent cook and waiters — white tablecloths and bright cutlery; and the meals served at precisely the normal hours.

Drink was there for the asking, and the smoke of cigarettes could be seen floating up the tent poles after lunch and dinner. But smoking at breakfast-time was a serious offence! The Field-Marshal's appetite is small, and like most of us he is far better for not guzzling. Away from the "Field" Montgomery likes comfort and nice things. When in London he stays at Claridge's.

He is tough and sometimes hard; but I probably know his human side more than anyone else. Unless you have been in daily touch with him, and are able to notice the little tell-tale signs that mean so much, this side of the stern soldier is difficult to detect. He had learnt to conceal his emotion. I know how often some kindly act has been done, and how often these have gone unrecognised. A handful of us know how deeply affected he was when that brave and happy warrior, John Poston, once his A.D.C. and then his Liaison Officer, met his death; and I remember with gratitude how I was ordered on two occasions to go back to Cairo — once from Tripoli and once from Italy — on some trivial pretext. It gave me a few halcyon days with my wife. I remember his kindness to me when I had a patch of ill-health — even to sending little presents of Ovaltine, with instructions in his own hand telling me when to take it.

He is, of course, as any really great soldier must be, physically brave. He was always to be seen in the danger area of the battle-field, being quite unmoved by any unpleasant incident. I rarely accompanied him on these expeditions, as I had to hold the fort at the Headquarters in his absence, and I cannot therefore tell you many tales. I do not profess to be a brave man. I did not have to go through the gruelling novitiate of the battlefield. The bomb, the low-flying aircraft, mines, and the occasional shell were the sum of my experience, and I admit finding them quite unpleasant enough! I am therefore not in a position to describe anything very spectacular. Within my ken, however, I recall these few incidents.

Shortly after the new Army Commander's arrival at Eighth Army, I was talking to him outside my caravan early on the morning that Rommel attacked at Alam Halfa. Suddenly the air became alive with enemy planes. They were bombing and strafing a near-by airfield, and shooting up anything they could see. We were getting a little attention. I'm afraid we had become a little "bomb-happy" at that time. When I joined the Headquarters a few weeks before I found that after each low-flying attack, the whole Headquarters used to be ordered to up sticks and move a mile or two this way or that. Slit trenches were used frequently — I don't say they shouldn't be, but too much of this sort of thing is not only disrupting to the work of a Headquarters, but bad for morale. When the attack commenced, I immediately pressed Montgomery to take cover — feeling the urge pretty strongly myself! He took not the slightest notice and merely went on talking, quite unmoved. I remember the feeling of self-confidence this small incident gave. It set an example for the future; we never again moved our Headquarters because of such attacks, and we took things far more in our stride.

I remember well a conference during the Battle of Alamein — a fateful conference which I will describe in the next chapter — attended by Corps Commanders and myself in the Army Commander's caravan. Without any outside interference it must have been difficult for him to keep cool and calm. It was at 3.30 a.m., and the situation was most difficult. A positive inferno caused by enemy aircraft was taking place outside. But inside all was peaceful. The problems were quietly and carefully examined, orders clearly and firmly issued. I don't really believe Montgomery knew that such unpleasant things were taking place. It was all very reassuring.

Another occasion — before the Battle of Mareth — Montgomery, Leese and several others had one afternoon climbed to the top of a prominent hill north of Medenine in order that plans for the coming battle could be checked up. The enemy had several heavy batteries located on the escarpment to the west of us. I'm afraid all the usual rules of reconnaissance were being disregarded and maps were spread out, flashing in the bright sunlight. Our task completed we started to descend. The Army Commander was in the middle of a discussion with Leese when a shell landed very close to our path. It had no visible effect upon him whatsoever; there was not even a pause in his conversation. He undoubtedly has the ability to ignore everything irrelevant to the matter in hand.

In Normandy one morning I was sitting in Montgomery's caravan discussing future plans with him when an enemy battery started ranging. The area we then occupied was so shallow that no place was out of range of the enemy's guns, and with modern wireless direction finding it was a comparatively easy matter to locate headquarters. A shell burst about one hundred yards short, followed by another about two hundred yards over. Being rather imaginative I was finding it very hard to concentrate, expecting the result of this "straddle" at any moment. Before long, one landed sufficiently near to scatter mud against the caravan. The only remark my Chief made was: "That must have been quite near." But other than that it had no effect upon him.

I'm afraid these examples are but small fry, but others will no doubt in time describe more spectacular occasions demonstrating Montgomery's imperturbable temperament.

I now come to a matter about which there has been a great deal of misplaced criticism. And that is the "Monty publicity."

Montgomery had, before he ever took over Eighth Army, made up his mind how High Command should be exercised. Undoubtedly he was impressed by the teachings of history as to the methods adopted by the really successful soldiers. As far as the soldier is concerned, he is a pretty good psychologist, and I am sure he was determined that the troops under him must know him by reputation and story, as well as recognise him in person. Once this was achieved he had gained a great deal. I am equally sure that he saw the importance of becoming a national figure. This would come naturally by the production of victories; it could be assisted by other means. Whether the Field-Marshal would agree with this or not, I don't know. But I am certain the results were of unusual value; for it helped him to obtain his requirements and assisted him in his dealings with the Great. If one accepts these motives, then many of the criticisms one has heard fade rapidly away.

Many of the things which have gained him special publicity — of which the black beret, the dogs, the canaries, the unusual kit, are examples — came quite naturally into being. I don't say, however, that Montgomery did not subsequently see and exploit their value, in order to further his aims. For instance, the story of the black beret is a typical example. I remember the Army Commander discussing with me the question of headgear in the desert, soon after his arrival. He found the sun rather hot at first, and so very sensibly decided to wear an Australian hat. These are first-class and similar to those we wore in East Africa. They were, however, a bit on the heavy side, and so a little later he chose the beret as his cold weather headgear. As he intended to use a tank for exercising command, the Royal Tank Regiment's black beret was the obvious choice. He was asked by a particular unit to wear their badge on it. Later he added the General's badge, and so the black beret with the two badges became known far and wide, and was wonderfully effective in furthering the two aims of which I have referred. Once Montgomery had made his mark as a successful commander, the appearance of that beret on the battlefield at a critical stage was of immense value. The news soon spread around, and the fighting troops knew all would be well. We used to say it was worth a Division when produced at the right moment.

The various pets arrived quite naturally. They were sent by admirers, or at some moment or other the Field-Marshal would see a particular animal that he took a liking for. Some of the pets were of use. In this category came the hens, the turkeys, ducks, geese and pigs. Some were fun to have about, like the dogs. But some were a great nuisance, particularly to his personal staff! The production of ants' eggs and bird seed in odd corners of Europe was often a difficult matter! There were some great characters. The little bantam cock we had in Sicily and Italy would take on any sized opponent, and many valiant fights took place in our mess tent. Then "Lucy" the turkey. A remarkable bird with great character, and possessing some very low habits! She was really a cock. He escaped the pot up to the time we left Italy, and then was handed over with other important items to General Leese. I don't know how long he lived. There was a beautiful peacock found in Sicily. A very long and thick piece of cord was attached to its leg to prevent it flying away. The A.D.C.'s hated this bird, for it took a lot of looking after, and required a highly organised hunt to catch it every time the Headquarters moved. It was not so well trained as some hens I remember belonging to a Cavalry regiment in the Western Desert. This was in the days when movement was frequent and rapid. Each morning when this particular Headquarters was due to move, the hens, on hearing the engines start up, would race from wherever they were feeding to their particular truck and wait to be lifted up. They were terrified of being left behind — instinct told them what this would mean, with no water or food in the barren sand. The peacock was written off the strength of Montgomery's Tactical Headquarters at Taormina. Here we had a villa perched on the side of the escarpment. When packing up to leave for the next site, the bird could not be found. The relief on the faces of Johnny Henderson and John Poston, the two A.D.C.'s, once the matter had been accepted by their Chief was great: I was somewhat suspicious myself and made certain enquiries. I found a witness who had seen this beautiful bird gliding gracefully away to freedom down from the escarpment with the length of rope behind it. Was it possible that John and Johnny had understood enough aerodynamics to have organised the round-up towards the cliff's edge and so give the peacock the first chance of making a get-away under its own steam since its arrival at our Headquarters — I wonder?

One of the factors that helped to give Montgomery publicity in the early days was the handling of the replies sent to various messages of congratulation and esteem that he received from individuals, associations, factories, etc. Starting with a trickle after his victory over Rommel at Alam Halfa early in September 1942, and rapidly reaching a torrent after El Alamein, this fan mail became quite a problem. I realised the value to be derived from carefully worded replies, and for some time used to handle the matter myself, drafting the messages and submitting them to my chief for approval. I am convinced that these messages did an immense amount of good, not only to the Army as a whole, but also as an encouragement to the sorely-tried war workers and relatives at home. It was an inspiration to read some of those we received. The gratitude they expressed for the turn of the tide, and the determination to work harder for victory. For some time Montgomery answered most personal letters himself. Everyone got a reply. It was astonishing how he found the time to carry out this task. As for the messages, ultimately I found the commitment became too big for me, and I only dealt with the very important ones. By this time, however, this valuable link between the Military Commander in the Field and the people at home was well and truly established.

III

I have dealt very briefly with some of the ingredients of Montgomery's success. I have tried to bring out the strength of his character. I will now deal with some of the matters which might be called "weaknesses." I can show that in most cases there were very good reasons for the actions which have gained him some criticism in certain circles.

First, one must remember that Montgomery has supreme confidence in himself. He thinks things out carefully, and once having made up his mind, he is very loth to change his opinion. Like some of us, he is sometimes wrong, but this is rare compared with the times he is right. This firmness of decision is an invaluable asset for a great leader and a commander in the field to have. Nothing is worse than one who is influenced by the last man he speaks to. Often it is better to make a second-best plan and stick to it throughout, than to reach the best plan by a process of oscillation and hesitation. Then, he has always been very outspoken and sometimes somewhat indiscreet. The combination of this confidence in himself, the power of decision and outspokenness, have at times led to friction. He is rather intolerant of opinions which run counter to his own, and this inflexibility has sometimes served him ill. But I would stress that this attitude is dominated by the conviction that he is doing the right thing. A streak of boyish devilment, however, is at times apt to add a little oil to a smouldering fire. He was sometimes apt to air his opinions concerning events and persons in circles liable to take a delight in spreading his remarks outside, and so causing harm. Such indiscretion shows at least some essential honesty. He will never give an opinion which he feels is untrue. How often have I heard him refer to someone as "useless." If you are in daily touch with Montgomery, you know that this term merely implies a mild rebuke. He referred once to a British Commander, when asked his opinion of his ability, as a "good plain cook"! This sounded very bad when it was repeated outside, but in point of fact he had considerable regard for the officer in question.

Montgomery is essentially a field commander. Here he is in his element, for he lives and thrives on the "smell of powder." He also must be amongst his troops. He is rather intolerant of those who have not had such a fortunate upbringing and experience; and attributes any of their shortcomings to this omission. I think that whilst he was in command of armies in the field, he did not at times appreciate sufficiently the importance of the political and international factors. He would argue that such and such a solution was the soldier's obvious and simple answer to a problem. Why, therefore, should these influences be allowed to interfere?

I have discussed these aspects with Montgomery on occasions, and he contends that the Commander in charge of the actual battle must dominate the situation around him, and when he has formed his opinion that a certain course of action is right, should only upon rare occasions give way. He does, however, fully recognise the difference between this sphere and that of the higher commander such as a "Supreme Commander." Here persuasion and compromise are often necessary.

He has sometimes been criticised for not allowing subordinates sufficient initiative; when an Army Commander — for commanding Corps; and as an Army Group Commander — for commanding Armies. This is to some extent true. On occasions a Commander has been irritated by this, but on the whole it worked excellently. He chose his higher commanders from those he knew, from those who were in many cases brought up under him. They therefore knew the form and accepted it. They knew he was always there to be leant on, and he took infinite pains to nurse them into their commands, and give them the benefit of his experience. He was very careful the way he handled different commanders in this respect. For instance his treatment of Dempsey[20] and Crerar[21] differed, as did the way he dealt with American Armies when they were under his operational command. In the latter case the method was not so forceful or intimate.

All, I am sure, are agreed that for the big set-piece battle Montgomery has few, if any equals. There is not that unanimity of view regarding the more fluid type of operation. Some say he does not take sufficient risks. It is true that he has invariably endeavoured to make certain that an operation would succeed. Surely a Commander cannot be blamed for this. This generally means a smaller casualty bill. I know that Americans have

---

[20] Commanding 2nd British Army.
[21] Commanding 1st Canadian Army.

often stressed this alleged weakness, and have quoted Patton's exploits by way of comparison. I would not deny that Patton was superb at the fluid exploitation battle; that he took risks that other Commanders would have turned down. We should remember, however, the advance by 21st Army Group from the Seine to Holland; here was a phase of the campaign where boldness and speed were seldom if ever excelled. There were two other factors which influenced Montgomery in assessing the risks he was prepared to take. The first was the fact that he had set himself the task of never again allowing his troops to suffer a major defeat. He had made this vow when he saw the results of such misfortunes, on taking over command of Eighth Army. The second was the dwindling British manpower problem. He dare not risk a major reverse. On balance, I would agree that on occasions my Chief was over cautious, but it is so easy to be wise afterward.

Montgomery is a showman — most really great soldiers have been. He likes to be the principal figure on the stage. He dislikes conferences which meant a lot of argument across the table. He preferred to be the only speaker, and the object of the conference to be the giving out of policy or orders. He preferred to discuss the particular problem quietly in his caravan or office with his staff and commanders, and then spend a period by himself making up his mind as to the right action to be pursued. He seldom attended big conferences in England before we landed in Normandy, nor later on the continent. I more often than not represented him at these big meetings. I only remember him turning up at one of Eisenhower's big conferences after Normandy. His absence sometimes took a bit of explaining away, but later on it was accepted without comment. He felt, I think, that these meetings should be held in the forward area. Here, I think, he was wrong, as he did not sufficiently appreciate the problems with which the Supreme Commander was continually being faced, as well as the number of commanders and others that had to be consulted. His answer to this would be that such conferences were for the staff, that his Chief of Staff knew his views, and that if his personal opinion was required on any particular point, then he was always available *at his Tactical Headquarters*! It was a pity to my mind that he did not give way on this point. I could not make him change his views.

Montgomery's handling of visitors was another thing which was responsible for adverse comment about his methods. In this matter I am convinced that he was right. Half the visitors who came to our headquarters were "rubber-neckers" pure and simple. I don't say one has not got to accept this sort of traffic in war, but I do say the *Commander* should not be worried by them. My Chief decided that if he entertained anyone other than those with whom it was important that he should do business, his life would not have been his own, and that the extra strain would have become unbearable. The mere fact of having a strange face at the mess table in his small headquarters meant that he could not relax. He therefore made it perfectly clear on his arrival to command Eighth Army that visitors other than his own nominees would not be allowed in his mess. There were some awkward moments at first as various individuals turned up as a matter of course to have a meal and were politely told that there was nothing doing. To solve the problem we started a "Visitors' Mess," where all but the "very great" were housed. This worked well. Later, particularly in 21st Army Group, when the Field-Marshal lived permanently at his Tactical Headquarters and I lived for the most part at Main Headquarters, I had to deal with a great number of visitors myself. In difficult times it did put an extra strain on one, but I felt it was a legitimate responsibility which a Chief of Staff must accept. In the majority of cases they were most welcome, and one enjoyed having them. I hope that they all felt they had been well looked after.

Besides tackling the problem of visitors to his own headquarters, Montgomery was careful to ensure that his Commanders were not worried either. I will quote two incidents that occurred in the Sicilian campaign that had dangerous repercussions. General McNaughton, the Commander of the Canadian Army at home, arrived out in North Africa unannounced, and expressed a wish to visit the Canadian division which had just landed. Montgomery's reaction to this request was very definite, and perhaps a little brusque. On no account would he allow the visit. The visit did not take place, and the result was a mild Dominion—U.K. crisis. Naturally the Canadians felt that their own senior commander was entitled to obtain first-hand information concerning their own troops. On the face of it, the Army Commander's action seems hard to justify. There is, however, another side to the question. This was the Canadian division's first campaign. Their Commander was young and hoping to win his spurs. Montgomery felt that it was unfair to let this Commander be subjected to the extra strain such a visit must impose. This is no reflection upon General McNaughton, and I am sure he would have done his best not to embarrass the divisional commander. But the fact remains that the visit might have worried him, and so as to protect his subordinate Montgomery shouldered a certain amount of criticism. He did offer to inform McNaughton when the time for a visit was ripe. I must finish this incident by saying that I have every sympathy with McNaughton's feelings, and I blame to some extent the machinery at home which faced the Army

Commander with a *fait accompli*. A warning order regarding the visit would no doubt have led to a request for a postponement until the situation was sufficiently assured.

Another visitor who received firm handling was my friend Drummond Inglis, who became Chief Engineer of 21st Army Group. He arrived out with several others just before we landed in order to gain first-hand knowledge. Very strict orders were issued that no one was to land in Sicily until the Army Commander said "Go." Inglis tried to beat the gun and sailed on a landing craft from Malta. The news leaked out and he was faced with a message on the shores of Sicily saying that if he landed he would be placed under arrest! The reasons for these restrictions were again to ensure that no unavoidable worries were placed upon commanders until we knew things were properly launched. Inglis took it very well, and served Montgomery with great ability in north-west Europe, receiving the K.B.E. shortly after the war ended.

IV

I am always being asked about Montgomery's personal relations with the "Great" — Eisenhower, Churchill, Tedder, Alexander and others. In this book I will mention such men from time to time, but I do not intend to produce any sensational stories about them. For someone who was in my position, nothing would be easier than to bring up odd remarks made, fragments of conversations, and even selected documents to suggest strained and difficult relationships. It is obvious that there are times when men in high appointments possessing great strength of character will not see eye to eye. It is a healthy sign that they do not. Again, when the situation is difficult and nerves are strained, things are sometimes said that do not sound too good when repeated afterwards. They are forgotten unless people in my position wish to remember them merely for personal gain and sensation. If I tried I could no doubt record things said by Montgomery about some of his colleagues that would sound bad. I could just as easily produce the most flattering and generous remarks he has made. One must look at the general over-all picture, and not select odd fragments. No one will imagine that Montgomery always saw eye to eye with the other Commanders and high personalities, but proof that the combination was a success is that together they won victory.

Montgomery can at times be difficult, particularly when he can't get his own way, and as I have said before, he is prepared to fight to get it. Consequently at times there were pretty good "battles." With his own "captains" there was always the greatest possible mutual confidence and esteem. They knew that they would get one hundred per cent, support for their answering obedience.

He has the profoundest respect for that truly great soldier, Field-Marshal Lord Alanbrooke, and never to my knowledge has he questioned his instructions or advice. There was a great friendship between the two. He was always most respectful to Churchill, but once he had won his spurs he would fight when he was convinced he was right — but only on the big issues. Of the top commanders of the other Services, I think he got on best with that lovable sailor Admiral Ramsay and with Air Chief Marshal Leigh Mallory. It was a pleasure to see them work together. Eisenhower's handling of Montgomery was a fine achievement, and although at times there was a measure of disagreement, such difficulties were resolved, and the combination stood the stress and strain of war.

The relationship between my Chief and Field-Marshal Alexander was most interesting. They always worked well together — a good team — but there seemed to be perhaps a falling off towards the end of their time together. Each had different qualities. Alexander excelled at sitting back and getting the best out of Allies and the different Services. He was self-effacing and always generous in allowing his subordinates their full measure of reward and praise. He showed himself most able at dealing with the complex political problems that came his way. Montgomery concentrated all his energies on the battle and those things that went to win them. I know that both recognised each other's assets. I was very impressed with the way Alexander worked with Montgomery in the North African campaign when the former was Commander-in-Chief Middle East. He knew the new Army Commander's ability and decided to let him have his head. This Montgomery took, and to him must go the major credit for the plans, the training, the inspiration and morale of Eighth Army, and its long series of victories. But in achieving these results I am sure Montgomery will not deny that he received magnificent support from behind. I often used to sit in the Army Commander's caravan when Alexander paid his visits to Eighth Army before the battle of Alamein. Montgomery would rattle out his requests — troops, commanders, equipment, whatever it might be. His Commander-in-Chief took short notes and with the greatest rapidity these requests became accomplished facts. It must have been a satisfying feeling for an Army Commander to know that he could count on such unstinted and generous support.

Between Grigg, the Secretary of State for War, and Montgomery there sprang up a great mutual regard and friendship. This was interesting, for to start with, the War Minister was somewhat critical of the new Commander of Eighth Army. He came out to the Middle East, ready if necessary to put this much publicised and dictatorial Commander in his place. Montgomery completely sold himself to his political chief, and this excellent and intimate relationship stood us in good stead until the end of the war. I will describe Grigg's visit in more detail later on in the book. He was as always most outspoken if he thought Montgomery was taking a wrong course, and would send him a letter couched in terms that few but Grigg can muster: very much to the point, witty, and sometimes hardly polite. Montgomery used to show me such letters with an odd little smile on his face — rather "naughty boyish." He really enjoyed receiving them. Grigg liked the clarity of Montgomery's mind and found doing business with him a simple matter. I remember one day towards the end of the campaign in Europe having a long chat with the Secretary of State at the War Office. We were discussing Montgomery. Grigg said that in his opinion he was the only man of real genius that any of our Services had produced during the war, and stressed how from him he had always received one hundred per cent, support.

V

I now come to my personal relationship and method of working with Montgomery. Here I will deal only with some general points. I hope the detail will come out naturally in this book.

To start with I cannot claim that there was anything in the nature of a Foch and Weygand or a Plumer and Tim Harington about us. I hope I shall not be misunderstood in this, for I am very conscious that I could never have fulfilled such a role. On the other hand, I do think we were well suited to each other, and the combination proved a happy as well as a successful one. We both held identical views as to the relative spheres concerning a Commander and that of his Chief of Staff.

Before leaving my appointment in 21st Army Group, I was asked by Montgomery to write a section dealing with the Chief of Staff for his pamphlet "High Command in War." I have extracted a few paragraphs which I give below, and they concisely describe my views. I only hope I practised what I preached.

> The various comments and suggestions are based upon a considerable period of practical experience in the field, and, it should be added, under one particular C.-in-C. It is realised that commanders' methods of exercising command differ widely.
>
> A Chief of Staff cannot be said to have accomplished his task successfully unless:
>
> (a) He takes all detail and sufficient other work off his C.-in-C.'s shoulders, and thus allows his Chief to devote the maximum time to exercise personal command, and for undisturbed reflection and thought.
>
> (b) He ensures that the various echelons of the Army Group H.Q. work as an efficient team, and that a good *esprit de corps* is developed.
>
> (c) The relationship between the Army Group H.Q. and Supreme Headquarters and the War Office is harmonious, and is based on mutual confidence.
>
> (d) He ensures that the Armies recognise that the Army Group H.Q. exists to serve them.
>
> There must be complete mutual confidence and trust between the C.-in-C. and his Chief of Staff. In their discussions no subject should be banned, and the Chief of Staff must at all times be open and frank. Unpleasant facts must never be hidden from the Chief, although there are the right and wrong times to present them.

The Chief of Staff must be able to adjust himself to his commander's habits, his likes and his dislikes. He should watch out for even little things that irritate his commander.

The C.-in-C. shoulders great responsibility and is the man who matters in the eyes of the fighting troops. The Chief of Staff therefore must be careful to do nothing which will detract from his Chief's position. Experience suggests that the following are useful tips:

(a) Avoid all publicity, and never give press interviews or conferences which appear in the name of the Chief of Staff, e.g. use "a staff officer from —— H.Q."

(b) As far as possible, do not accompany the C.-in-C. on his visits to troops. In any case, to do the job properly there isn't the time. Attendance at conferences is, of course, a very different matter.

(c) Don't make a habit of appearing at ceremonials with the C.-in-C. The honour is meant for him alone.

To sum up, the Chief of Staff should keep in the background and get on with his work.

I don't think I remember having had one "row" with my Chief. He was a magnificent master to work for. He never got excited, never lost his temper, gave you the task and then left you to carry it out without interference. Many soldiers I have served under spent their time fussing about details; wanted to see the letter you had written — in fact would not let you get on with the job. Having made his decision, or laid down a policy, he seemed to cast it from his mind — a wonderful gift. His staff always felt they had a hundred per cent, support, and that is a nice cosy feeling. There was often a lot of smoothing out to be done when my Chief had been on the war-path, or explanations in more silky phrases after a "Monty-gram" had gone forth. A "Monty-gram" was the name given to a signal written by Montgomery himself when he was making his views "quite clear — with no room for doubt"!

I very soon learnt how to get what I wanted and even on occasion to make him change his mind. One had to wait for the right mood; it was no good tackling him with anyone else there. An audience was not a help. When my great friend Miles Graham,[22] who was head of 21st Army Group Administration, and I used to go to see the Commander-in-Chief, I had a secret sign to ask him to leave the caravan when I knew that a talk *à deux* would prove more successful!

It will, I think, be of interest if I explain briefly how Montgomery worked. How he dealt with his staff, examined plans, and controlled the battle.

He always worked the Chief of Staff system. That is he dealt with me on all matters and gave me power to make decisions in his name. Naturally he laid down the general policy, and I knew his views on most subjects. This did not mean that he never saw any others on his staff. Every now and then he would get one of his principal staff officers up to have a talk with him; they in turn could always ask for an interview.

It has often been said that Montgomery never issued paper or read documents. This of course is not strictly true. He certainly only resorted to paper on very rare and important occasions, such as for "Personal Messages" to the troops, directives and personal letters to commanders. He did read papers, but I reduced these to the very minimum and normally had the meat produced out of them. As a general rule, however, we conducted all our business verbally. It was a joy to do so, for one could sit there in his caravan and reel off the particular problems and the matters of interest. He could, without effort, rattle off his decisions and give his views in an

---

[22] Major-General Sir Miles Graham, K.B.E., C.B., M.C.

incredibly short space of time. This saved an immense amount of work; for him, for me, and for the staff and clerks under me. Few commanders have this ability to work as he did. It should be, however, the pattern to which all should strive.

We, the staff, used to carry out staff studies dealing with all possible eventualities. It might be the plan for the next phase of operations, the suggested use of airborne forces, proposals for the regrouping of supporting arms, or one of a host of other subjects. I would normally have discussed the matter generally with my Commander in the first place, so that we would not be wasting our time by starting on the wrong leg. I would then either go myself, or more usually when dealing with future plans, take a team with me, and give him a presentation. All maps would be produced and the particular experts in the "Plans," "Operations" or "Intelligence" branches would say their piece. I was particularly fortunate in the men I had under me. Most of us had been together from before the battle of El Alamein: I will mention a few. Miles Graham, Major-General in charge of Administration; David Belchem, a brilliant young officer who alternated between "Plans" and "Operations." There was Charles Richardson, who was my G.S.O. 1 Operations in North Africa and head of the Plans Section in 21st Army Group. Bill Williams, once an Intelligence officer under me when I was Director of Military Intelligence in Cairo in 1942, and who finished up as head of Intelligence in Eighth Army and in 21st Army Group. It was a grand team and we all understood each other perfectly.

After hearing the *exposé* of the particular problem, Montgomery would give his views and his decision, or order another line of investigation. The drill worked well, and everything went along quite smoothly.

When a battle was on my Chief would visit the commanders concerned each day. This sometimes meant hours of driving through all sorts of weather, often in an open car. He would hold any conferences at such times well forward, so as to interfere as little as possible with those fighting the battle. On his return, often very late in the afternoon — but practically without exception in time for dinner — he would deal with other matters requiring his attention. There might be a period with me, his Chief of Staff. A check up on the administrative position with Graham, or talks with one or other of his advisers. He also kept up a very large personal correspondence, writing all such letters himself and never to my knowledge employing a shorthand typist. He writes rather slowly, but very clearly, and it has often amazed me how quickly he seems to get through the paper. It is because he writes straight on without having to make alterations, and there are no long pauses for thought. He knows what he wants to say before he starts.

Even in times of heavy fighting he always kept a keen eye on M.S.[23] matters, appointments, decorations, etc. He was in daily touch by visit or telephone with his Deputy Military Secretary. In 21st Army Group days this appointment was held by that fine old warrior Jack Gannon — who was loved and trusted by everyone. He was a "wise old bird." Montgomery took the most meticulous care over appointments. He had an amazing knowledge of his commanders, right down to the battalion level. He attributes much of his success to his ability to choose the "right chap" for the right job. He made few mistakes. This power over appointments was one of the principles he would always fight for.

---

[23] Military Secretary.

The evolution of his headquarters set-up is interesting. In Eighth Army he took a leaf from Rommel's book and fought his battles from a Tactical or Battle Headquarters. During periods when the fighting was not intense he would usually join up with Main Headquarters. At his "Tac" H.Q. the members consisted of the A.D.C.'s, the Military Assistant, and sometimes an Operations Staff Officer. I was also a member, but spent my time between "Tac" and "Main" H.Q.'s. At the Main H.Q. mess in Eighth Army we were about a dozen strong. The Brigadiers on the staff and the Commander of the Desert Force were all members. This joining up between "Tac" and "Main" H.Q.'s became less frequent as the campaign went on, and in Sicily and Italy rarely took place. In 21st Army Group "Tac" H.Q. always remained a separate entity.

This splitting of headquarters increased my work a lot. Early on, I decided that "Main" Headquarters must be my base, the place where I must live. In Africa I used to spend a considerable time at "Tac," staying there for days and nights on end, but as distances became greater and the Headquarters larger, the bulk of my time was spent at "Main." We had the best possible telephone service between the two H.Q. echelons, and so I could speak to my Chief several times a day. We always had landing strips at both places, and so with the use of a "puddle-jumper" visits were easy.

I admit having been rather critical of the gradual introduction of the policy of isolationism by the Commander. It made things rather awkward at times, and gave all his staff a great deal of extra work. He realised the difficulties it caused, and used to say that he expected his staff to go mad, but he would take jolly good care that he didn't go that way himself! I gradually realised that once again Montgomery was absolutely right. He would certainly have gone mad if he had been surrounded by the activities of a "Main" headquarters. He would never have been able to exercise such intimate tactical command over his forces. At "Tac" H.Q. he was far less accessible and so avoided some visitors who would have otherwise imposed an extra strain on him.

Although I am convinced Montgomery was right about his Tactical H.Q., I believe he lost something by living on his own with his small personal staff. Admittedly, myself and others were constantly visiting him, but it was not quite the same thing. Many of us noticed he became more dictatorial and more uncompromising as time went on; and we felt that this was not only due to the strain of war, but also because he did not live with officers nearer to his own age. I may be wrong; but I think I am right.

In order to keep in touch with the many officers at "Main" Headquarters, Montgomery used to give periodical addresses to them. He usually spoke quite simply, often giving the reasons why he adopted a certain plan, or how he fought a particular battle. Sometimes we heard his views on such subjects as leadership, training, or the general war situation. Once in Brussels he began to speak about the influence of the Army, and those who fought in it, being used to help the country in times of peace. Some interpreted this as an indication that the Field-Marshal was thinking of adopting a political career after the war, and hoped to get the backing of the soldier to carry out his plans — a sort of second Hitler was visualised! It caused quite a stir and my poor Chief was quite embarrassed by the unintentional interpretation placed on his words. He was very careful in future!

I cannot finish a description of Montgomery's methods of command without mentioning his use of Liaison Officers. He was a second Wellington in this respect. He selected these young men most carefully, and they were exceptional officers. They had drive and courage, and developed considerable judgment and a sense of responsibility. They would go anywhere and find out everything. To hear them giving their report to the Commander-in-Chief after dinner each evening was something not to be forgotten. One got a clear and vivid picture of the battle. One could sense the state of commanders, and the morale of their men. After each had said his piece, Montgomery would snap out a few crisp questions and receive equally sharp and crisp replies. He would then go to bed and chew things over. In the morning he was clear as to what the next step should be.

The world has read many of Montgomery's "Personal Messages." They were one of the means he adopted for getting himself over to his troops. *The Times Literary Supplement* once published a Leader on these messages, extolling the fineness and clarity of the style. They were very much sought after by the troops, and were most carefully prepared by the Commander himself. Some who had been with him for two or three years used to think they appeared rather too often towards the end. Familiar phrases such as "you and I together will see this thing through to the end" were smiled at. It must be remembered, however, that the forces under Montgomery were continually changing, and that these personal messages were still welcomed by the majority, and did a lot of good.

VI

I don't know whether the War Correspondents would say Montgomery was good *with* the Press. I think they would certainly say he was good *for* the Press; as he gave them plenty to write about, and lots of stories.

When he first came to Eighth Army his press talks were excellent. There was the one he gave before the battle of El Alamein, when he told the correspondents exactly what he was going to do. How this was to be the turning point in the war, and how victory in the coming battle was certain, in spite of the "killing match" he foresaw. Many of them were surprised, and a little alarmed at his confidence. They were soon to realise the truth of his words.

I shall at a later stage discuss War Correspondents. I am sure Montgomery will be the first to express his appreciation of the way this fine band of men fulfilled their task. I never remember a confidence betrayed.

It is my impression that in a later stage of the war, Montgomery did not go down with the correspondent quite as well as at first. He was on occasions inclined to talk down to them — quite unintentionally I know. At other times, particularly during the Normandy bridgehead period, they gained the impression that he might be concealing something from them: that things were not as good as he pretended. When once one loses grip of the Press it is not easy to reinstate oneself. Montgomery, however, seemed to end up on a high note in this respect.

VII

I hope this chapter will be instrumental in giving the reader a picture of Field-Marshal Montgomery, one that is not too lyrically biased in his favour, but one that will make the stories of his memorable campaign the more enjoyable. For you must know the man if you are to appreciate to the full the job he has done.

So now on to these campaigns — to these golden pages of the history of British arms.

CHAPTER VIII: THE BATTLE OF EL ALAMEIN

I

I DO not intend to give a very detailed description of the Battle of El Alamein, but merely to confine myself to the broad outline, bringing out what I consider to be the stepping stones to victory.

On that night of 23rd/24th October, 30th Corps attacked with the following divisions, working from north to south: —

9th Australian Division;
51st Highland Division;
2nd New Zealand Division;
9th Armoured Brigade;
1st South African Division.

This attack was on the fairly narrow front of 6 to 7 miles, with the northern flank tied to the Tel Eisa feature, and the Miteiriya Ridge forming the limit on the south. There were two corridors which we had planned to clear through the minefield; and echeloned behind 30th Corps assault formations were the two armoured divisions of 10th Corps, ready to move forward.

The enemy's and our own dispositions at the commencement of the battle is interesting for three reasons: —

> (a) The greater part of the enemy static defences are manned by Italians, held in place by being sandwiched between German troops. (Williams used to refer to this as the "corset" policy.)

(b) The German infantry divisions, 164th Division and 90th Light Division, are echeloned in depth, protecting the vital coastal road sector.
(c) The German Armour (Africa Korps) is held in reserve and distributed equally between the northern and southern sectors.

Besides 30th Corps' main attack a brigade of the 9th Australian Division carried out a feint between Tel El Eisa and the sea. This, together with the feint seaborne operation had a worrying effect on the enemy.

Further south the 4th Indian Division launched a strong raid from the area of the Ruweisat Ridge.

At 0200 hours on October 24th, the leading elements of the 1st and 10th Armoured Division crossed their start lines. Although they were a bit behind schedule, this news when we received it at our headquarters was very welcome.

Progress was good, and the task of clearing the lanes through the minefields went on well, but by the morning the armour had not managed to get out into the open. Throughout the night, the Miteiriya Ridge was a very unpleasant place to be, and very fierce fighting took place. The enemy, once he had recovered from the shock, concentrated his artillery and mortar fire on the corridors, and 15th Panzer Division carried out a counter-attack. The Army Commander assessed the situation on the morning of the 24th, and decided that although a very good start had been made, it was important that there must be no slackening in the efforts to get the armour through, and that the "crumbling" operations by the New Zealand Division must start at once.

In the south, 13th Corps had started to schedule. The French had successfully assaulted the high ground about Himeimat, but the soft sand had prevented their supporting weapons reaching them in time, and they were driven off again by a German counter-attack. The other 13th Corps attack after making initial gains was held up between the belts of minefields. The 24th was, therefore, spent in "crumbling" operations in this area. These were secondary to the main attack by 30th Corps, and in spite of these small set-backs their object was achieved, for the 21st Panzer Division was still retained in the southern sector.

Now started a week of terrific fighting. By the evening of the 24th, the 1st Armoured Division had managed to get some elements out of the minefields in positions beyond. Tenth Armoured Division was not so fortunate, and was having a very difficult time. An attack they made at 2200 hours that night, supported by the Corps artillery, made little progress.

The Army Commander went to bed in his caravan that night at his usual time — between 9.30 and 10.0 p.m. As things appeared rather uncertain, I decided to stay up and keep in close touch with the Corps. Towards 2 a.m. on the 25th it was obvious that the situation in the southern corridor about the Miteiriya Ridge was not satisfactory. Various reports were coming in. Congestion was considerable in the cleared lane through the minefields, with a lot of damage being done by enemy shelling and mortar fire. Freyberg was personally directing operations from his tank in this critical zone. Altogether I gained the impression from these reports and those from liaison officers just back, that a feeling in some quarters was creeping in which favoured suspending the forward move, and pulling back under cover of the ridge. I decided, therefore, that this was an occasion when the Army Commander must intervene, and so I called a conference for 3.30 a.m. at our Tactical Headquarters, asking Leese (30th Corps) and Lumsden (10th Corps) to attend. In my long association with Montgomery I think I could count the times I have awakened him at night on my two hands. I went along to his caravan and woke him up. He appeared to be sleeping peacefully — in spite of a lot of attention from the enemy air force outside. He agreed to the action I had taken, and told me to bring the two Corps Commanders along to his map lorry when they arrived. To my mind, this conference should be classed as the "first stepping stone."

II

First Stepping Stone.

Under the best circumstances, 3.30 a.m. is not a good time to hold a conference. The conditions surrounding this one called for the best qualities the Army Commander could produce. I led the generals along the little path to the lorry. Inside, Montgomery was seated on a stool carefully examining a map fixed to the wall. He greeted us all most cheerfully, motioned us to sit down, and then asked each Corps Commander to tell his story. He listened very quietly, only occasionally interrupting with a question. There was a certain "atmosphere" present, and careful handling was required. Lumsden was obviously not very happy about the role his armour had been given. As the situation was being described, I looked out of the lorry door and saw the placid Mediterranean at our feet twinkling in the moonlight. In contrast to this peaceful scene was the constant fire of A.A. guns, the droning of aircraft overhead, and every now and again the vicious whistle and crump of a bomb nearby. A little later Montgomery spoke to the commander of the 10th Armoured Division on the telephone. He heard his version of the situation, and then clearly and quickly made it very plain that there would be no alteration to his orders. The armour could and must get through. He also ordered the Headquarters of this division to be moved further forward.

Before this call had been put through, there had been some discussion in the map lorry, in which the Army Commander, speaking very quietly, gave his views. I remember the reaction his words had on me. They were a tonic, and we felt not only that these orders would stand, but that there was no possible question that the plan could fail. The firm decision to make no change in the plan at that moment was a brave one, for it meant accepting considerable risks and casualties. Unless it had been made I am firmly convinced that the attack might well have fizzled out, and the full measure of success we achieved might never have been possible. The meeting broke up with no one in any doubt as to what was in the Commander's mind.

By 0800 hours that morning the leading armoured brigade of the 10th Armoured Division was reported to be 2,000 yards west of the minefield area, and in touch with the 1st Armoured Division to the North. In addition, we heard that the New Zealand Division and the 8th Armoured Brigade were clear of the main minefields, and were advancing south-westwards in accordance with the plan. This was all very encouraging, and justified the Army Commander's confidence.

During the 25th, the 15th Panzer Division carried out several counter-attacks against us, but they were all repulsed with heavy loss to the enemy. From now onwards fierce fighting took place around a feature we named "Kidney Hill." It was a small kidney-shaped contour on the map, and we had a great deal of difficulty in locating it exactly. Everyone gave it a different map reference. Eventually I believe it was established that the ring contour denoted a depression and not a hill! I was so exercised about this at one period, in connection with laying on very close air support, that I sent out a special survey party to establish its position once and for all.

III

Second Stepping Stone.

By about mid-day Montgomery realised that the "crumbling" operations by the New Zealand Division would prove very expensive and made a decision to switch the axis to an operation by the 9th Australian Division — northwards. The object was to destroy the Germans in the salient, and it might also reduce the strength facing the main drive. This movement proved so successful that I have always considered it "Stepping Stone to Victory No. 2."

The 1st Armoured Division were ordered to fight their way westwards with the object of threatening the enemy's supply routes in the Rahman track area. They would also threaten the rear of the enemy holding the coastal salient. This attack made no appreciable progress until the night of the 26th/27th, when a brigade of the division established themselves about Kidney Hill.

The Australian attack went very well, ground being gained and very heavy casualties being inflicted on the enemy. In this area the enemy's defences were very strong, and their garrison preponderantly German. I think this area saw the most determined and savage fighting of the campaign. No quarter was given, and the Australians fought some of the finest German troops in well prepared positions to a standstill, and by their action did a great deal to win the battle of El Alamein. This division fought continuously for nine days under their fine commander, Moreshead; and at the end of this period they were ready for a well-earned rest.

On the 26th the New Zealand and South African Divisions made slow progress. On the same day the Army Commander decided to re-group. 30th Corps required a pause to re-organise, and although we had forced our way through the main minefields, the enemy had still well organised anti-tank defences facing us.

IV

Third Stepping Stone.
Montgomery has always been most careful to husband his forces, in fact ensures that he has fresh troops available for the decisive moment. This re-grouping now produced the nucleus of reserves for the decisive phase of the battle. I would, therefore, call it the "Third Stepping Stone to Victory."

The 2nd New Zealand Division was pulled out of the line into reserve. Their place was taken by a side stepping north wards of 1st South African and 4th Indian Divisions. The New Zealanders were made first priority for all tank replacements, and they spent a day or so resting and bathing. We could see this cheerful body of men spread out along the beach from our Headquarters, the horrors of the Miteiriya Ridge forgotten, preparing themselves for the ordeal ahead.

October 27th was a good day on the sea, in the air, and on land. News came in that two tankers and a merchantman had been sunk near the entrance to Tobruk harbour. The loss of these much needed supplies to the enemy, including vital petrol, no doubt had a great influence on the battle. The R.A.F. attacked with great gallantry, and their losses were very heavy. The Desert Air Force shot down at least eighteen enemy fighters during the day. On land the regrouping went smoothly ahead, and at 2 p.m. the Army Commander held a conference at his Tactical Headquarters. At this meeting the re-grouping plan was given out, and also plans for the continuance of the Australian attack. 13th Corps were ordered to make final arrangements for moving the 7th Armoured Division and other troops to the northern sector. During the night of the 26th/27th the 21st Panzer Division moved northwards, and so these forces could be spared. In the morning we had located, by wireless direction finding, the Headquarters of this German Armoured Division opposite Kidney Hill.

For most of the day, the two German Panzer divisions launched attacks against our Kidney Hill positions. This suited us well, and the 1st Armoured Division excelled themselves. They claimed fifty enemy tanks knocked out, as well as others damaged. In addition, the R.A.F. was doing good work bombing these attacks as they formed up. Good claims of transport destroyed were made. It was an exciting day, and during the afternoon I stood by our Command vehicle listening to the loud speaker which was tuned to the wireless "net" which served the forward tanks. We heard a running commentary on the fight. One could hear the fire orders being given to the tank crews, and the results of their shooting. This sort of thing: —

"Look out, Bob, a couple sneaking up your right flank — you should see them any moment now."

You would then hear the fire order given by the tank commander as the enemy came into view. Then: —

"Well done — good shooting — another brew up."

We ticked off the numbers claimed and felt very pleased. Looking westwards there were visible signs of success. Pillars of black smoke towering into the sky showed the truth of the reports we were hearing on the radio. Then every three-quarters of an hour, the fleet of medium bombers would fly overhead, and drop their load with a terrific crump on the enemy concentrations. A great cloud of dust would rise up, interposed with black smoke which came from vehicles hit.

After this Montgomery decided that the 1st Armoured Division needed a rest, and withdrew it into reserve. This particular sector would, for the moment, remain a defensive one. In order to strengthen the New Zealand attack when it came, infantry brigades moved up from 13th Corps were made available for this task.

On the night of the 28th/29th the Australian Division attacked again, and drove a wedge into the enemy positions which almost reached the road between Sidi Abd El Rahman and Tel El Eisa. On the 29th the enemy did all in their power to destroy this wedge, but all these attacks made with both tanks and infantry failed.

V

October 29th was a very interesting day. Plans and preparations were going ahead for the launching of the breakout attack. We had given it the code-name "Supercharge," a name with which we christened other decisive attacks during the next two or three years.

The Army Commander's intention was to launch this attack as far North as possible. Some of us felt, however, that better results would be gained by adopting a more southerly axis. The further north we went, the more Germans, mines and prepared defences would we meet.

During the morning we were paid a visit by the Commander-in-Chief — Alexander, the Minister of State — Casey, and Alexander's Chief of Staff, McCreery. The Army Commander described the situation and his plans, and radiated confidence. There had been a signal or two which suggested that some people were a bit worried that things had not gone faster.

Montgomery's reply to such suggestions was that he had always predicted a ten-day "dog fight" and he was perfectly confident that he would win the battle. I was taken aside by Casey, who asked me whether I was quite happy about the way things were going. I feel he had been asked for a personal report on the political level, but I don't know. I replied as I felt: "We are certain of success."

Williams tells me that he remembers a conversation I had with Casey at which the Minister of State mentioned the need for sending off a signal to Churchill preparing him against the possibility of a reverse. Apparently I replied: "If you send that signal I will see that you are hounded out of political life!"

McCreery also felt that "Supercharge" might work better further south, and we discussed this matter together. The party left, I think, reassured.

VI

Fourth Stepping Stone.

Later on that morning our Intelligence obtained good information which showed that 90th Light Division had moved north. No doubt the Australian attack was the cause. I took this news in to the Army Commander, who instantly decided to change the axis of the attack further south. The sector chosen would mean that our thrust would strike the junction point between the Italians and Germans, and would also include a good chunk of Italians in the frontage selected. I rang up McCreery who was delighted to hear of the new direction. This decision was, I am certain, a decisive contribution towards the victory.

The Australians continued their attack on the night of 30th/31st and crossed the coast road. At one time it looked as if the bulk of the Germans inside the salient would be cut off and destroyed. They managed, however, to get away with the help of tank reinforcements. Our attack to the North paid a big dividend. It kept the enemy's attention focused on the coastal area, besides causing great damage amongst the Germans themselves.

On November 1st we heard that 21st Panzer Division had moved to the North, and so everything was set for the next phase. After a delay of twenty-four hours "Supercharge" went in with a creeping barrage at 01.00 hours on the morning of November 2nd. Three hundred 25-pounders and the Corps medium artillery supported the attack.

The frontage of attack was 4,000 yards, and the depth of the advance 6,000 yards. The infantry attacked (151st and 152nd Infantry Brigades) and everything went wonderfully well. On reaching their objective the armour moved through and formed a bridgehead, through which it was proposed to pass the armoured divisions of 10th Corps. The objectives were reached, but the 9th Armoured Brigade suffered heavy casualties from enemy anti-tank weapons. Soon the 1st Armoured Division came through to assist, and a large armoured battle was fought.

Steps were immediately taken to extend the width of the salient. The Māoris on the North performed great work, whilst on the southern side the 51st Division gained ground. On November 3rd we knew that the enemy was beaten. Welcome air reports came in showing that the retreat had started. We knew that Rommel had insufficient transport or petrol to get back more than a portion of his force, and knowing the Germans, we appreciated who would be left behind — the Italians of course!

The 3rd did not, however, see us right out into the open country, for the enemy were still plugging the hole with antitank guns. On the night of the 3rd/4th, however, a clean break through was made by the 51st and 4th Indian Divisions, after mounting a speedily prepared attack with the greatest success.

The battle had been won in eleven days, which was just about the Army's Commander's estimate of how long the heavy fighting would last. The enemy was defeated and in full retreat, and our armour and armoured cars were now operating in the open country. We were all exhilarated by the success, and there was great enthusiasm amongst all ranks in the Army.

On November 3rd or 4th von Thoma, the Commander of the Afrika Korps, was captured. Montgomery's treatment of this German general was the subject of some criticism. Here is the story.

When "Supercharge" was achieving success, von Thoma got on the phone to Rommel and told him that we had broken through to the South of his sector. This was of course perfectly true, but Rommel became very angry and said that there was no truth in the report, and the Italians had said nothing whatever about it. The Italians presumably were in far too great a state of "flap" to think of letting anyone know what was happening. On receiving this reply from his chief, von Thoma got into a tank and drove up to the threatened area to see for himself. His tank was hit by our guns and was burnt out, von Thoma just managing to escape with a burn or two on his legs. Within an hour of capture he was brought back to our headquarters, where as the day was well on, we decided to keep him for the night. He was given a small tent, some water to wash in, and an officer who spoke German to watch over him. I brought him along to see the Army Commander, who received him formally, and then invited him to dinner in our mess.

It was an interesting meal, for the German described the recent operations and their reactions to our moves. He was very careful not to give away any future plans. He paid a tribute to our dogged fighting, and said that our bombing had been terrific, and had had a serious effect upon the morale of their troops. Our guns, he said, had knocked out most of his anti-tank guns, and so there was little to stop our armour. He was depressed about the present battle but hoped that Rommel would be able to stage a comeback from Agheila. Montgomery drew on the tablecloth the latest situation, and when he told von Thoma that our armoured cars were at that moment racing towards Fuka, the latter looked very upset and said: "If that is so, sir, then our forces are indeed in a difficult situation." On leaving the headquarters for Cairo the next morning, he asked to take his leave of the Army Commander. On being brought before him von Thoma clicked his heels and made a little speech, the gist of which was that he was grateful for his treatment, which had been most chivalrous. He had been led to believe that such things were not possible amongst the English. He would make it his business to see that "his friends" in Germany knew of this. He finished by saying that he hoped the Army Commander would come and stay with him at his estate in Germany when the war was over. Von Thoma was still a prisoner when the war finished, but I doubt very much whether he will ever see his estates again.

VII

When on the 3rd all information showed that the enemy was in full retreat, it was decided to switch the full weight of air power to strafing the columns of transport. Reports described a scene of vehicles, head to tail, four and sometimes eight deep, either on, or just off the road wending their weary way back westwards. With such "juicy" targets available, we had visions of the retreat being turned into a complete rout. With the virtual air superiority we possessed, and the state of disorganisation of the enemy, it looked to us in the Army that here was the "dream target" for the R.A.F. In the event, the results appeared very disappointing. When setting out along the road between the Alamein battlefield and Daba, I had expected to see a trail of devastation, but the visible signs of destroyed vehicles were few and far between. After Daba much better results had been obtained, but even here a lot of the vehicles we found had stopped through shortage of petrol. These remarks are not intended to be a dig at that wonderful team, the Desert Air Force. I am merely trying to analyse the facts and find the lessons. At that period of the war we had not learnt the technique of low strafing. The fighter bombers had been employed in air fighting and bombing, and this is where we were at a disadvantage. I believe the attacks on the retreating columns were made mostly with bombs, and that the aircraft were not allowed to come down low. I took this up with my opposite number, Beamish, in the R.A.F., but the orders were very clear. I realise that, just as in the Army at that time, so in the R.A.F., we were not strong enough to take undue risks. Again the pilots, in view of their other activities, had not had the training in the low flying type of attack with cannon. The Desert Air Forces' primary role was to keep the enemy's air force under control, and if this failed, the Army would have been the first to shout. I do feel, however, that an opportunity was lost, and that it might have been possible to have produced a form of paralysis in the enemy's rearward movement. After we arrived at Tripoli Air Vice-Marshal Harry Broadhurst, a famous "Battle of Britain" pilot, took the matter in hand and carried out intensive trials and practice to get his force proficient at this low flying technique. We were to reap the reward of all this during the battle of Mareth.

VIII

During the battle of El Alamein I held various planning conferences to discuss ways and means of having a self-contained pursuit force ready when the enemy cracked. We had all the detail worked out — the selection of units, the R.A.F. component, the airfield parties, supply echelons, etc. But when the time came the battle itself merged gradually into pursuit without this special organisation being required. Montgomery decided to give the task of following up the beaten enemy to 10th Corps, whilst 13th Corps was to have the dubious task of clearing up the battlefield. 30th Corps was to follow up behind. Horrocks did not think much of his "Mrs. Mop" role, but set to with a will, realising that later on he would be employed more actively. This turned out to be the case, for he succeeded Lumsden in command of 10th Corps in a few weeks' time. 13th Corps Headquarters left Eighth Army to rest and train for the Sicilian campaign.

This task of clearing up the mess was a big one. Thousands of Italians were wandering forlornly about the desert, short of food and water. All their serviceable transport had been taken for the Germans and the few Italian formations that might be of use to Rommel. They had to be rounded up, disarmed and fed, and then evacuated to the Delta. There were also enormous quantities of stores and weapons to be disposed of.

I doubt whether many people realise how near Montgomery was to destroying the retreating remnants of Rommel's forces, and that only a most unlucky break in the weather deprived him of this prize. A great deal of the rear administrative troops and installations would have got away in any case, but there was every hope that the fighting troops and a good slice of the forward administrative units would have been rounded up.

The Army Commander decided to cut the coast road at the bottlenecks of Fuka and Matruh. The 2nd New Zealand Division was ordered to Fuka and the 1st and 7th Armoured Divisions to Matruh. On November 5th these three divisions were grouped together under 10th Corps. The enemy desperately defended his rearguard positions covering Fuka, but by the afternoon of the 5th we had broken through. Now everything depended upon our reaching the area of Charing Cross, which was the bottleneck in some hilly country southwest of Matruh. By the evening of November 6th, 1st Armoured Division was nearing this locality, and it looked as if Rommel's fate was sealed. As luck would have it one of those very heavy rain storms occurred which for a short period flood the desert. By the morning of November 7th this division, as well as the New Zealand Division, were completely bogged down. They could not move and neither could the petrol and supplies which were on their way to them. It must have been extremely annoying for the 1st Armoured Division to be virtually in earshot of Rommel's troops as they slowly made their way along the coast road; the only navigable highway in that part of the Desert. The pursuit continued on the 9th, but the enemy had escaped.

There was yet another occasion when rain deprived Montgomery of the full fruits of victory. This happened a few days later when the 7th Armoured Division had been sent round over the desert to cross the frontier between Solium and Fort Maddalena with a view to cutting off the enemy's retreat by holding the escarpment bottleneck at Solium. Everything was going well, and the division was within a few miles of their goal. They were, however, held up awaiting further supplies of petrol. Supply columns were following them up along the same route. Just at this very moment the rain came, and the delay so caused prevented our armour from reaching a position which would have cut off the enemy's forces. In war, however, you can't have it all your own way, and the weather had behaved itself admirably during the decisive period of the big battle itself.

Montgomery decided to give the enemy no rest. It was important that the port of Tobruk should be in our hands at the earliest moment, in order to ease the administrative situation. The port was in fact entered on November 13th. There was also another reason for speeding up our advance, and that was to gain possession of the important airfields in the Derna-Tmini-Mekili triangle. They were called the Martuba group. With these in our possession we could assist convoys to Malta, and also attack Rommel's supply routes, as well as allow the Desert Air Force to provide support to our further advance. This question of the Malta convoys had become a vital matter. Unless supplies could reach the island within a week or two, the end of the fortress's gallant resistance was in sight. Terrible losses had been suffered by the Royal and Merchant Navies in their endeavour to get through during the period that the Axis air forces dominated the Central Mediterranean. The vital convoy was to leave Alexandria on November 16th for Malta. Martuba was occupied on the 15th and so the R.A.F. were just in time to give the necessary protection to see the ships through to their destination. It was a near thing.

It was, I believe, at Mersa Matruh that we received the news that our Army Commander had been promoted to the rank of General, and that he had been appointed a K.C.B. The genuine delight with which this news was received throughout the

Army was very marked. At Matruh I suffered a severe blow. I heard the news that my G.S.O. 1 Operations, Hugh Mainwaring, had been captured. It was an unfortunate story, and I feel I was in part to blame. We were at Daba waiting to move the headquarters forward to the Matruh area. One morning very early we received reports that Matruh had been captured. On hearing this Mainwaring requested permission to send the headquarters reconnaissance party off, and he asked if he could go with it. I readily agreed.

I set off myself later in the day. The weather was horrible, it was raining hard, and the roads were congested with traffic. Not far from Matruh we came across a raging torrent which the Sappers had negotiated by a long diversion. It was getting dark and I missed the track, my car sinking up to its axles in mud. I was very cold and rather miserable, as I had no idea where the headquarters site was exactly, and I saw little prospect of getting my car out that night. I wandered around in the dark, and by chance bumped into a tank which appeared to be doing nothing in particular, so I asked for help which was readily given, my car being dragged out and placed on the proper track again within half an hour. It was a real bit of luck, and this was followed by another break, for just as I was starting off I spotted one of my officers who told me the exact location of the headquarters. I arrived there about 7.30 p.m. and was greeted with the news that Mainwaring and the Army Commander's stepson had both run into an ambush and had been captured. They had been most unlucky for although the main road and town of Matruh had been cleared, a party of the enemy were still holding out in a small area near the sea, and it was here that these officers had gone to see how it would do for a headquarters area. It was a bitter blow, for Mainwaring was a first-class officer. He had great character and experience, and after an initial set-to following my first arrival in Eighth Army in which he gave me some very good advice, we got along famously together. In his place I put in Richardson, who up till then had held the appointment of G.S.O. 1 Plans.

From scanty information we gathered that the two officers had driven straight into a German post, and so I was rather worried about what papers the enemy might have captured. Mainwaring was certain to have had with him a little notebook full of information that he used to carry. We all hoped that we should see both these officers again before long, for they were the type that would not miss an opportunity to escape. But time wore on and it became obvious that they were either dead or had been evacuated from Africa. Later we heard that they were in a prisoner of war camp in Italy. They both made their escape when Italy tried to get out of the war and managed to come through our lines in Eighth Army when we were advancing towards the Sangro river. We had great foregatherings and after we had heard all their news, and they had been given some new clothes, they went back to England for some leave. Mainwaring told us that he did have his notebook on him, and had no time to get rid of it before he was caught. For some reason or other, however, he was not searched, and on his way back in a lorry he managed, by careful manipulation, to tear the pages out one by one and scatter them over the desert.

IX

About the time that we had reached Tobruk there was a certain amount of talk about sending a force across the Cyrenaican Bulge to cut off Rommel's forces as they withdrew south from Benghazi. The idea sounded an excellent one, and a very reasonable proposition when studied back at Cairo on a small scale map. But Montgomery would not agree to such a course. His reasons for not doing so were very sound:

(a) He was determined that he would not repeat the mistakes of the past, and place himself in a weak position south of Benghazi which might give Rommel a chance to launch a counter stroke. I realise it can be argued that this time Rommel, after his heavy defeat, would never be in a position to stage a comeback so soon. The Army Commander, however, was perfectly confident that by keeping his balance and taking no spectacular risks he would be able to deal with the enemy forces.

(b) Administration was becoming very stretched, and he could not afford to embark upon ventures of this sort which might overstrain his resources. In any case, only a comparatively small force could have been maintained.

(c) The weather was uncertain at this time of the year, and rain might well have strangled such a move, as it had done near Matruh. Some heavy rainstorms did in fact take place about this time.

(d) Even provided a force could have been despatched and maintained across the Bulge to the Benghazi-Tripoli road, it is very open to doubt whether it could have achieved its object. With no particularly good tactical bottleneck to hold, Rommel, if beaten to it, might well have been able to manoeuvre around our positions.

(e) Any force we sent would have to be content with very meagre air support.

In view of the above arguments, Montgomery decided to continue with his original plans and stated that he felt that this was a job for the R.A.F., i.e. a long-range harassing role. He did not entirely turn down a move across the desert, for besides advancing on the road axis through the Jebel El Akdar, he later sent a force of armoured cars and tanks directed on the Msus and Ahtelat axes. Although the Army Commander saw the importance of reaching Benghazi as early as possible and so giving the enemy as short a time as possible for demolitions, the administrative situation would only allow light forces to be used to this end. Those that were despatched to Msus and Antelat met heavy rain and were delayed considerably.

Coningham rose to the occasion and operated his aircraft from a secret airfield deep down in the Cyrenaica Bulge. This was sufficiently far West to allow the aircraft, by the use of long-range tanks, to carry out harassing attacks against enemy transport using the road running south of Benghazi. The weight of air attack was, however, not very great.

I will now mention an example of how careful those in high places must be when dealing with each other. How quite innocent intentions are often not received as they are intended. When some discussion was taking place on the subject of sending a force across the Bulge to cut off Rommel, Tedder, the Air Commander-in-Chief in Cairo, sent Montgomery a signal in which he expressed the hope that such an operation would take place. As far as I remember it stressed this great opportunity as one that should not be missed. I'm afraid this signal did not go down "with a swing." The Air C.-in-C. no doubt had a joint responsibility as to what strategy should be adopted, but whether it was wise to commit himself to paper on a tactical issue when sitting back in Cairo and not in possession of all the facts is another matter. In view of this, and the fact that he was dealing with a general who had just achieved the greatest victory the British Army had yet won in the war, I venture to say it might have been better if Tedder had first flown up for a friendly chat if he had wished to express his views. Knowing Tedder, I am sure he only meant good, but I have mentioned this incident as one that should be studied by future commanders. Little things like this often have an influence far in excess of their real importance.

X

Benghazi was captured on November 20th and on the 23rd the 7th Armoured Division had forced the enemy out of his positions about Agedabia. He withdrew to hold the Agheila defences.

Montgomery brought up the 30th Corps Headquarters to plan and carry out the Agheila attack, 10th Corps remaining back in Cyrenaica.

The Desert Air Force were at this time suffering from weather and maintenance troubles, and so for a short period our advanced forces in the Agedabia area had a rather unpleasant time from the enemy's air. The position, however, soon got better and by November 26th two fighter wings had been established at Msus.

At the end of November I went forward with the Army Commander to see Benghazi and to stay with General Leese. It was good to drive through the first big city we had captured since I had been in Eighth Army. The port was badly damaged, but the Navy and our Sappers were working feverishly to clear the mines, remove wrecks, repair unloading berths, etc. There was real drive behind it all. We visited the cathedral and then ate lunch beside the water, before driving southwards to where Leese had established his headquarters about 20 miles south of the city.

That night I was taken ill and after a couple of days was flown back to Cairo and admitted to hospital. It was a bitter blow, but it had its compensations, for during the five weeks I was away I got married. During my absence Erskine, the B.C.S. of 13th Corps, came and answered for me.

I shall end this chapter by tabulating the dates and distances of our advance from El Alamein. We had shown ourselves as capable as Rommel in this matter of desert mobility.

Date: November 5th, Places: El Alamein, Miles from El Alamein: ——
Date: November 11th, Places: Sollum, Miles from El Alamein: 270 miles
Date: November 12th, Places: Tobruk, Miles from El Alamein: 360 miles
Date: November 17th, Places: Msus, Miles from El Alamein: 560 miles
Date: November 20th, Places: Benghazi, Miles from El Alamein: 700 miles
A distance of 700 miles in 15 days.

CHAPTER IX: THE PURSUIT FROM AGHEILA TO TRIPOLI, AND THE BATTLE OF MEDENINE

I

MONTGOMERY was determined that no time should be lost in driving the enemy out of the Agheila position. Twice before we had been defeated after reaching this point, and so it was now considered a place of ill-repute. Better in our hands than in Rommel's.

After our long advance it was necessary to get our administration in proper order. Until the port of Benghazi was working well, most of our supplies had to be carried from the Tobruk area. These in turn came by sea to the port or by road and rail to depots in that locality. The joint Army/R.A.F. tonnages were great, and it looked as if December 14th would be the earliest date by which the attack could be launched. The enemy's positions were very strong as the difficult going and salt-pan area restricted our advance to certain narrow channels. With information we obtained from the Long Range Desert Group it appeared possible to outflank the enemy positions by a very wide movement round the south. The Army Commander decided to send the strong New Zealand Division by this southern route, with the object of cutting the enemy's communications to the west of the Agheila defences. The Highland Division (51st) was to attack astride the road axis, and the 7th Armoured Division would move in the centre between the 51st and the 2nd New Zealand Divisions. The aim was annihilation, but unfortunately Rommel was not prepared to risk a major battle and withdrew the greater part of his forces, though not without heavy losses. This is briefly how things went.

Early in December information showed that Rommel was pulling back most of his remaining Italian troops. Leaving the Italians to their fate at El Alamein had probably not been very popular in Rome, and so this time he decided to remove them before the battle! In order to reduce our casualties to a minimum, a big artillery and bombing programme was laid on to start on December 12th, and this was to coincide with a policy of large-scale raids. These activities would also draw attention away from the outflanking movement. The enemy must have thought this was the big attack, for on the 13th he began to withdraw. He was rapidly followed up by the 51st Division and the 7th Armoured Division.

Freyberg, with his New Zealanders, were doing well. The El Agheila — Marada track was crossed some 45 miles from the coast, and moving very rapidly the division reached the area of Merduma on December 15th. It was an exciting moment as most of the remaining German tanks and the 90th Light Division were still to the east. With the pressure from the 51st and 7th Armoured Divisions, the enemy's position was most unpleasant. Some very fierce fighting took place on December 16th, the enemy having broken up into small bodies which desperately fought their way back. In the process they suffered heavy losses from both ground and air attack. If administrative considerations had not limited the size of the force we could send round the southern flank, the result might have been decisive.

In view of the same administrative factor, only light forces could follow up the retreating enemy after Nofilia had been reached by the New Zealand Division. The situation was, however, very satisfactory, for with little loss we now held the gateway into Cyrenaica, and Rommel's forces had been further weakened. In exactly a month we had advanced 1,000 miles, and time was now required to build up our administrative position before the next major operation could take place.

On November 8th the Allied Expeditionary Force, which included the British First Army, had landed successfully in North Africa. Prior to having forced Rommel out of the El Agheila defences, we had been told that Tripoli would be a First Army objective. But now it looked as if we were more favourably placed to undertake its capture, and planning for this purpose was now well under way.

All information pointed to the enemy making his next proper stand in the area of Buerat. There was a naturally strong position here, but it suffered from the usual fundamental weakness of being susceptible to a "left hook." Work was observed to be going on to strengthen the defences, and an armoured force had been positioned at Sirte, in order to delay as long as possible our contact with the Buerat position.

Before we could undertake a general advance, it was necessary to build up stocks of all natures of supplies in the forward areas. The tonnage figures were great, and were swelled by the additional requirement of providing all the material for rendering the airfields in the Benghazi area suitable for all-weather use by our heavier type bombers. We were still transporting nearly 1,000 tons per day by road from Tobruk, but as a result of the work done at Benghazi, about 3,000 tons per day were passing through that port by early January.

In addition to putting our administrative house in order, considerable work had to be undertaken to construct airfields in the Marble Arch-Nofilia area. As fighting had never yet taken place in Tripolitania, few airfields existed. It was not like the old days when the various groups of airfields were used alternately by the enemy and ourselves in accordance with the swing of the operations.

Montgomery decided that he would base his preparations for tackling the Buerat battle upon a ten day fight by four divisions. The administrative staff worked out that this would require a three week period for dumping the necessary commodities in the forward area. He, therefore, fixed January 15th as the provisional date for the operation. These calculations were, of course, based upon the existing forecasts concerning Benghazi's port capacity. In the meantime the formations were positioned for tactical and administrative considerations as under: —

(a) 2nd New Zealand Division — Nofilia area.
(b) 4th Light Armoured Brigade — Sirte in contact with enemy.
(c) 7th Armoured Division — Marble Arch.
(d) 51st Highland Division — El Agheila.

Sirte was entered on Christmas Day, and by December 29th our patrols were in touch with the enemy's main defences of the Buerat position.

The Army Commander had decided that once 30th Corps moved forward he would bring up 10th Corps to occupy the El Agheila area, in order to maintain balance. I think the provisional forecast date for the move of this Corps was January 20th. The grouping of the divisions would then be:

30th Corps.
7th Armoured Division.
51st Highland Division.
2nd New Zealand Division.

10th Corps.

1st Armoured Division.
50th Division.
4th Indian Division.

II

The governing factor in the Army Commander's plan for the next operations, was that once he attacked the Buerat position, the forces must go right through to Tripoli. He assessed that up to three days would be required to roll up the defences; and up to a total of ten days to reach Tripoli. If he failed by anything but a small margin, the situation would not be good, for without the use of Tripoli as a supply port, strong forces could not be maintained so far forward. If, therefore, Rommel prevented us capturing the port for, say, two weeks, it might well prove necessary to withdraw the bulk of our forces. The enemy had available an excellent natural defensive position from Homs to Tarhuna, and therefore if we started the drive with an accumulation of supplies necessary for only ten days fighting, there was a considerable risk involved. Montgomery decided, however, to accept this risk. He would attack with four divisions when ten days maintenance had been brought forward, and he would drive these formations with the greatest determination. In retrospect many may not consider Montgomery took much risk, but at the time it was a brave decision.

The outline plan was as follows; 30th Corps would carry out the attack with the following formations under command:

7th Armoured Division.
2nd New Zealand Division.
50th Division.
51st Highland Division.

22nd Armoured Brigade.

The 50th and 51st Divisions would attack astride the coast road, whilst the remaining two divisions would carry out a "left hook." Rommel we knew was most susceptible to such treatment.

The 22nd Armoured Brigade would be kept in Army Reserve in the first instance. 10th Corps would be brought up to the Buerat area when the maintenance position allowed.

I give the following little story to bring out the necessity to change continually the personnel of planning staffs with those possessing up-to-date experience. After the capture of the El Agheila position, a staff officer from Eighth Army Headquarters was visiting Benghazi. Here he met a high personage from Cairo. They started talking about the future. The staff officer said, "The Army Commander hopes to be in Tripoli in five weeks time." The reply he got was: "Oh! that's impossible, we have just approved a Joint Planners paper which says that a two or three months' pause is required to ensure a safe maintenance situation." He wasn't a soldier!

Early in January reports were received that the Italians were moving back from the Buerat position, but it appeared likely that Rommel was prepared to fight with his German troops.

As all these preparations were in full swing, a disaster occurred. Between January 4th and 6th a gale took place at Benghazi which caused untold damage to the port and shipping. The outer breakwater was smashed, and this allowed the heavy seas to enter the inner harbour. Four ships were sunk, including one carrying 2,000 tons of ammunition. In addition, many of the lighters and tugs were sunk or damaged, and the sum total of these misfortunes spelt a serious drop in our intake through the port. The tonnage dropped from 3,000 tons to under 1,000 tons per day. In view of our future plans and the small margin of safety we were working on, the repercussions of this set-back are easy to understand.

Montgomery's reaction to all this was characteristic. I think it was Erskine (answering Chief of Staff for me) and Graham who went to his caravan to break the news. There was no excitement and no despondency. He just laughed on hearing this tale of woe, and of the ships careering about the harbour out of control. "We can't have that, you'd better tell the Navy to catch 'em — they'll do some damage if we're not careful!" He then went on to say, "I've no intention of changing the date of my attack — so we had better modify our plans. You must work out how we can get over the administrative problem, and let me know."

After the matter had been examined in detail, and the administrative implications worked out, the following modifications to the original plan were decided upon: —

(a) To accept a weaker force for the attack. 50th Division would now be left at El Agheila, and to compensate for this, the Army Commander ordered that the coastal thrust should not be pressed if the opposition was heavy. This attack, therefore, became a containing type.

(b) The move forward of 10th Corps was for the time being abandoned. All its transport resources were to be used to run a carrying service forward from the port and railhead at Tobruk.

Naturally, 10th Corps and their new Commander, Horrocks, were terribly disappointed, but without grumbling they got down to the task and played their part magnificently, and the situation was saved. The Royal Navy also did wonders in repairing the damage done to Benghazi port, and by the date of the attack we were back again to the old tonnages. As the 1st Armoured Division was to stay behind, all its tanks were taken for the coming battle. This now gave us 450 tanks, which would more than offset the loss of a division, and the move forward of 10th Corps.

III

Unfortunately during this period of preparation I had been away from Eighth Army, and so before describing the move to Tripoli, I will take you back to Cairo.

After about a week in hospital the doctors told me that they considered I should have a month or two's rest, and suggested a trip to South Africa. Three days later Montgomery arrived for a visit, and appeared to have a remarkable effect upon the doctors and myself. He said he wanted me back soon, and if not quite fit, he would see that I was worked gently! For my part the visit seemed to put new strength in me. The result was that I was given just over three weeks leave, and got married on December 17th. I spent my honeymoon in Jerusalem, and put myself under a very clever Jewish doctor called Freund. I am sure that without his care and attention, I would never have been able to arrive back in Eighth Army just in time for the advance to Tripoli on January 15th.

From time to time I had a letter from the Army Commander, but other than that I kept clear of all work. The nearest I got to it was discussing the Battle of El Alamein with all and sundry. One day in the lounge of the King David Hotel, the Emir Abdullah was sitting surrounded by some friends, apparently having a heated argument. I was later taken over by a mutual friend to be presented to His Highness. On hearing of my appointment the Emir asked me to give my opinion as to what had been the biggest factor in the winning of the recent big battle. I replied that leaving out the fighting quality of the troops, perhaps our massive use of artillery was the most important factor. Upon this His Highness showed excitement and delight. I had said the right thing, for just before I arrived, El Alamein had been the topic that had led to such argument, and the Emir's views had been reinforced by mine. He is a charming person and he invited both my wife and me down to spend a day with him at his camp in the Jordan Valley. It was a delightful experience.

During the comparatively slack period of the pursuit, Montgomery had written his first pamphlet whilst with Eighth Army. It was called "Some brief notes for senior officers on the conduct of battle." It was in keeping with his make-up, i.e. that burning desire to impart knowledge to others. We had learnt a lot of lessons and gained a great deal of experience, and he felt there was no time to be lost in the process of passing this on. About this time also he put forward a proposition to the War Office, suggesting that there should be an exchange of some senior commanders at home with some in Eighth Army. If necessary those officers who had reached high command without any practical experience, might be asked to drop a rank and so prove themselves capable commanders in the field. As a result, exchanges took place greatly to the advantage of the Army as a whole. There were at least two keen and excellent soldiers who willingly and wholeheartedly gave up the rank of Lieutenant-General at home in order to have the chance of commanding a division in battle.

On January 14th, Sholto Douglas, the new Air Commander-in-Chief in Cairo very kindly gave me a lift up to Eighth Army in his Boston, and so I managed to arrive just in time for the next move forward.

IV

Our Headquarters were situated on either side of the coast road near the Wadi Tamet. Here I found everything ready for the advance which was to start the next day. The Army Commander decided very rightly to keep Erskine with him until Tripoli, partly because I was not in the picture, partly to give me an easy time, and finally because he foresaw in view of the great distance involved, he would require a second "Chief of Staff" back with Main Headquarters.

Montgomery planned to combine his task of Army Commander with that of Corps Commander. He considered that in view of the distance between the coastal and the "left hook" thrusts, it would be impossible for 30th Corps Headquarters to exercise sufficient control without some help. He therefore decided to command the coastal punch himself, retaining also the 22nd Armoured Brigade.

This move was not popular either with Main Army Headquarters or with the Desert Air Force. It meant that soon the Tactical Headquarters was "swanning" about in all directions, and this made communication between the two echelons of the headquarters most difficult. In the event, I think the arrangement was fully justified, for some pretty forceful commanding on the Corps as well as on the Army level was required to ensure success.

It was, therefore, arranged that Erskine should go with Tactical Headquarters, and that I should be based at Main.

The story of the advance can be told quite briefly. At 0715 hours on January 15th the outflanking move by 30th Corps started off. And at 2230 hours on the same day the Highland Division attacked. This latter attack was held up primarily by mines, as the enemy had started to withdraw just before it commenced.

Within twenty-four hours the "left hook" had crossed the Wadi Zem Zem, having broken through the enemy's main defences. The Army Commander directed the southern column to advance on the axis Beni Ulid-Tarhuna, and the coastal thrust to be continued with renewed vigour. Tactical Headquarters and the 22nd Armoured Brigade moved via Bir Dufan. By the evening of January 17th the 51st Division was within a dozen miles of Misurata, whilst 30th Corps had reached Beni Ulid. By the skilful use of mines and demolitions, the enemy made it difficult for us to maintain contact with his withdrawal on the 18th. He now tried to hold us up on the general line Homs-Tarhuna, and Montgomery admits to experiencing certain anxieties at this stage. He realised the value of this good tactical defensive position, and he was not satisfied at the rate of advance of the coastal thrust. Unless a firm grip were taken he felt there was a danger of not reaching Tripoli within the ten day period which he had set himself.

As a result of vigorous action the rate of our advance improved, and on the evening of the 19th the 51st Division entered Homs, and on the 21st they had reached the hills about Corra Dim and could see the plain of Tripoli ahead. It was now that Montgomery decided to change the weight of his main thrust to the right flank, and ordered on January 22nd the 22nd Armoured Brigade — which was still in Army Reserve — to pass through the 51st Division and to advance to Tripoli itself. The Army Commander was forward at the time "cracking the whip." Demolitions had caused great congestion. I was in the vicinity myself, and it looked a ghastly picture, and one wondered whether it could ever be sorted out in time. I sent back for extra traffic control resources, but there was nothing much one could do. The great thing was not to "flap," and in all probability it would prove one of the self-adjusting types of trouble. One had to be thankful that the Desert Air Force had gained such supremacy over the enemy air forces, for otherwise here were perfect targets for the asking.

In order to deal with the enemy rearguard which was holding up the advance, the Army Commander ordered a battalion of the 51st Division to ride forward on the tanks, and then to attack the enemy. This was to take place in the moonlight. To the south-east 30th Corps had pressed forward to within under 20 miles of Tripoli.

In the early hours of January 23rd, Tripoli was entered by our troops. Rommel had evacuated the city without a fight, and his troops had withdrawn twenty or thirty miles to the westward.

It is very odd that Rommel stayed defending the Buerat defences when he had available the naturally strong positions in the hills from Homs to Tarhuna. Here it would have been difficult for us to have turned his flank, and there is no doubt that the final advance to Tripoli would have taken a great deal longer. I think by this time Rommel had realised that his only chance was to get within supporting distance of the other Axis forces in Tunisia, when it might then be possible to stage a counter-stroke. By that time he might well expect our maintenance to have become very difficult, whilst his might have improved. This was always one of the questions we hoped to ask him when the war was over.

The laying on of air support during this advance was not easy. Back at Main Headquarters where such matters were controlled jointly with the Headquarters of the Desert Air Force, information was difficult to obtain. The distances had reached a stage when our wireless sets were not up to the job. We did our best with relay stations, but once or twice we got complaints from the forward troops. It is a question of not being able to have it both ways. If the Army rush forward too fast, then they must accept a slackening in the air support. Nowadays it is easy for the air to keep up, owing to longer range aircraft and speedier methods of constructing airstrips. But then it was asking too much. Coningham was a bit worried about the matter at the time, but Montgomery had realised what such a rapid advance would mean, and had accepted the risk of restricted air support.

During the morning of the 23rd Montgomery received the official surrender of the city from the civic heads. He then took a drive around and ate his sandwiches by the harbour. It was a pity that he did not wait for, or invite, his co-commander Coningham to take part in this small ceremony. I know the commander of the Desert Air Force felt it, for he had naturally hoped that after all these months of desert fighting he would have the satisfaction of taking part. On the other hand, I doubt whether the Army Commander thought of it at the time. He was very busy, had a lot to do, and the Air Headquarters unavoidably was far behind. The longer the war went on, the more I realised how such small things as this influence the relationships between commanders.

There is no doubt that Montgomery enjoyed this battle. It was full of excitements and variety. It presented great scope for his powers of command, and I'm sure he was delighted at the opportunity of acting as a Corps Commander! I found it very difficult back at Main Headquarters trying to keep in touch and anticipate his wishes. I stayed only one night with him during the battle, and it wasn't until I think the 26th, that the Headquarters once again got together.

V

It was a tremendous relief to us all that Tripoli had been won.

This was indeed a prize worth having — something tangible to show for our labours — a big city of many thousands of inhabitants. But what was more welcome than anything else were the green trees and pastures which greeted us. Nothing spectacular by European standards, but a great and satisfying contrast to the arid desert in which we had lived so long.

The Army felt it needed a rest and time to check up on things.

It was obvious that there would have to be a considerable pause before we were in a position to tackle the Mareth line. This we all realised would prove a formidable business, for reports suggested that there was no flank to turn, and that there were many modern concrete defences. Until the port of Tripoli was unblocked and reserves were accumulated, we must live a hand to mouth existence, and nothing but light forces could be sent forward into Tunisia. Again, until the port was working properly, we would be compelled to keep 10th Corps transport working on our L. of C., and it was important to have this Corps available for the Mareth Line attack.

Work went rapidly ahead to repair the extensive demolitions which the enemy had carried out in the harbour. The entrance had been blocked completely, and the quays and installations had been destroyed. Air photos had shown us the progress of the sinking of the blockships, and the R.A.F. did their best to interfere. A formidable task presented itself. The Army Commander arranged that the joint resources of the Royal Navy and the Army should be pooled to tackle the job. As a result of this, the first ship entered the harbour on February 3rd; by the 6th a convoy was accepted, and by the 10th 2,000 tons were being handled in a day.

When asked whether he would take over the Governor's palace, Montgomery's answer was "Certainly not." A pleasant site was chosen a few miles south of the city where the whole Headquarters could work together. Strict orders were issued that all troops must remain on a field basis — there must be no softening up by a comfortable life in this city.

Although it was only possible because of administrative limitations to send the 7th Armoured Division against the retreating enemy, everyone else was kept busy in the Tripoli area. The Army Headquarters remained there for about a month, and some interesting events took place during this period.

The Army Commander decided to hold a review and a march through the city of Tripoli. This would serve some useful purposes. It would give everyone an excellent opportunity to smarten up after many months in the desert. Personal cleanliness had been difficult, whilst the state of clothing and the turn out of equipment was not all that could be desired. It would also have a salutary effect upon the local population. And lastly it would provide a suitable spectacle for the Prime Minister to witness during his coming visit on February 3rd.

30th Corps laid on a big parade which took place during the morning, and the New Zealand Division held a special review of their own during the afternoon. It was astonishing how the troops in so short a time had managed to smarten themselves up. Their personal turn out, drill, and the "spit and polish" of their vehicles and guns were surprisingly good. I shall never forget watching Churchill standing at the saluting base with the tears rolling down his cheeks — it brought a lump to one's throat. He no doubt felt — and justifiably so — that this African campaign was his particular baby. He had backed it up to the hilt and given us all our needs. They were, I think, tears of gratitude. The review acted as a tonic to everyone, and afterwards the difference in the soldiers' deportment in the streets was very noticeable. Some of our soldiers had lived continuously in the desert for three or four years — they needed a change.

With the Prime Minister came the C.I.G.S. (now Viscount Alanbrooke) and Alexander, and talks took place as to the future conduct of the campaign. At the Casablanca Conference in mid-January it had been decided that General Eisenhower be appointed Supreme Commander in North Africa, with Alexander as his Deputy, commanding all the land forces, and Tedder as the Air Commander-in-Chief. It was during this or a later visit by Alexander that the relative roles of First and Eighth Armies were discussed. As a result of these talks the Supreme Commander decided that Eighth Army should have priority as First Army were not ready for a major offensive. Also the weather in Northern Tunisia was very bad at this time of the year.

It was during this visit that the Prime Minister delivered a magnificent oration to the Army Headquarters. He was in his best form, and the subject one to his liking — a victorious campaign. We will always remember his final words, which ran something like this:

"In days to come, when asked by those at home what part you played in this war, it will be with pride in your hearts that you can reply — 'I marched with the Eighth Army'."

I am sure we all felt that "pride in our hearts" on this occasion.

Montgomery decided to make use of this interval in Tripoli to check up on our battle technique, and he considered that this would prove an admirable opportunity for passing on our experience to others. He therefore arranged for a series of lectures, demonstrations and discussions to take place on

February 15th, 16th and 17th. These included addresses by the Army Commander himself on "High Command in War," and by Coningham of the Desert Air Force on the employment of air power in support of armies. Then we had demonstrations on models of the latest methods for the employment of tanks, artillery and infantry. General discussions on these subjects took place afterwards. Outside in the open a lot of time was taken up with the mine problems. Spectators could see all the various types of mines we had met, and the various gadgets we had developed for dealing with them. Then demonstrations were held to show the latest drill we had developed for clearing lanes through minefields. We also demonstrated the latest methods we had evolved for laying on air support. This was a joint Army/R.A.F. item, and I believe it proved most useful. Altogether it was a comprehensive course, which served a very useful purpose.

Several Generals came out from home, from India and elsewhere. Montgomery had also invited some of the American Generals who had recently arrived in North Africa. It was the first time most of us had set eyes on George Patton. At first he did not appear to be very impressed, but later he was enthusiastic in his praises. The story is told of his reply when asked what he thought of Montgomery's address on "How to make war." His reply came slowly with a lovely Southern accent: "I may be old, I may be slow, I may be stoopid, and I know I'm deaf, but it just don't mean a thing to me!" Poor George Patton, what a great man he was, and how we came to respect and admire him during those next three years.

Bedell Smith, Eisenhower's Chief of Staff, came and paid us a visit in Tripoli. I took to him at once, and I can never be sufficiently grateful for all his kindness and help from that time onwards. He was a wonderful colleague, generous, open-hearted and wise. I never appealed to him for help in vain. We got to know each other well enough to say always exactly what we meant. We certainly had some "tricky" times together, but I found, as with all Americans, the best way was to be entirely outspoken and frank. After the war I think it was Liddell Hart who said to me: "They say you and Bedell Smith are the only British and American officers who completely understood each other during the war. The reason suggested is because you both have bad stomachs!"

During dinner the talk centred upon the future plans for Eighth and First Armies. Montgomery, in his usual confident way, said he would have captured Sfax by the middle of April. Bedell Smith, I believe, suggested that this would be pretty good going. The Army Commander then said: "Will General Eisenhower give me a Fortress for my own personal use if I capture Sfax by April 15th?" Eisenhower's poor Chief of Staff, thus cornered, said he was sure he would. We entered Sfax on the morning of April 10th and Montgomery immediately sent the following signal:

"Personal Montgomery to Eisenhower (.) Entered Sfax 0830 this morning (.) Please send Fortress (.)"

It proved of great value to Montgomery, especially during the period we were planning and preparing for the invasion of Sicily. His troops were spread out between Northern Tunisia and the Levant, and he had to spend a lot of time in the air visiting his parish. This aircraft met its fate in Sicily when we had to force land on our way back from a visit to Patton's Headquarters at Palermo. It was replaced by a very nice Dakota machine.

VI

The problem of the Mareth Line was full of interest. The defences had been well sited between the sea and the Matmata Hills. The system had been built by the French in case of Italian aggression from Libya. The Wadi Zigzaou had been developed to make a formidable anti-tank obstacle, and this was followed by concrete and steel emplacements and strong points. They were constructed in depth and had a great deal of wire and mines to strengthen them. Besides the main defences facing more or less east, there was a switchline to the southwest of El Hamma and west of the hills.

After the flat coastal belt stretching for some twenty miles, the Matmata hills rose up and presented a fine natural obstacle. A frontal attack, in view of the well built defences, would obviously prove costly, and so we did everything we could to obtain information as to the possibility of turning the defences from the west. There appeared to be some divergence of opinion as to the feasibility of such an operation. French soldiers whom I interviewed were mostly of the opinion that it would be impossible. They contended that this particular matter had been borne in mind when laying out the defences. One officer I spoke to described how during manoeuvres before the war an exercise was set to see what could be done. He said that out of the large force that was sent round only three vehicles got through. The "going" was *incroyable*! We didn't accept this as final, for we knew the transport used by the French before the war could not compare with the latest types which we were using with their special desert tyres. Apart from air photos and Arab information, we relied to a great extent upon the Long Range Desert Group. They were ordered to carry out special reconnaissances in that area, and by various means managed to produce sufficient information to warrant our accepting as a feasible proposition an advance up the western side of the Matmata Hills along the narrow corridor linking up with the sand sea. I had a project at one time of flying a captured German "Storch" aircraft over a particularly important area to examine the ground. Dick Atcherley, who was commanding the fighter group, volunteered for the job, but later we decided it wasn't worth the risk, as our information was then fairly complete.

A great deal of work was done on the preparation of maps, building of airfields, dumping supplies forward, as well as training the troops for the next phase. A programme was worked out which dealt with all the matters that had to be done before we were in a position to attack, and it looked as if we might launch our offensive about the middle of March. One of the major limiting factors was the date of concentration of the 10th Corps. As I have already explained, their transport was still being employed on the L. of C., and until the port of Tripoli was working well we could not release it from this Carter Paterson commitment.

Montgomery aimed at a methodical advance to gain possession of the principal road centres, and areas in which we could build airfields for the support of our attack. The first stage was to include Ben Gardane, and thence to the line Medinine-Foum Tatahouine.

Rain and the very water-logged country delayed our advance from Tripoli, but on February 16th we captured Ben Gardane. Medenine was captured on February 17th, and Foum Tatahouine fell on the following day. The administrative position had now allowed an increase of strength in the forward zone, and besides the 7th Armoured Division, the 22nd Armoured Brigade and the 51st Division were operating against the enemy.

There was one other formation that was in touch with the enemy — General Leclerc's force. This fine Frenchman had moved his troops from Lake Chad across the desert and gained contact with Eighth Army about the time we arrived at Tripoli. It was a real mixture — a bit of everything. He had Frenchmen and native soldiers, some artillery of various types, an armoured car or two, machine guns, some oddly assorted transport which by some miracle had made the journey, and even some aircraft. They were short of most things, food, clothes and material; but a wonderful spirit went a long way towards surmounting the deficiencies. I remember my first meeting with Leclerc. I was sitting in my caravan outside Tripoli when he arrived to report. At first I thought one of the characters of Wren's "Beau Geste" had come along to pay a call. His appearance personified the hardened French colonial soldier. He was thin and drawn, but intensely alert. His clothes had long since seen their day. Thin drill uniform with threadbare breeches, and old but shapely riding boots. A French *képi* completed the picture. He told me who he was and from whence he came. He said this just as you might say you had dropped over from the next village to tea. I took him along to the Army Commander, who shook hands and looked him up and down. Leclerc said, "I place myself and my troops under your command." Montgomery then said he accepted the offer, and told me to discuss with the French General details of his co-operation and matters affecting material and supplies. Later Montgomery told me, "I can make use of that chap." This was indeed high praise, for he was normally very loath to complicate matters with Allied detachments. He was so right, for Leclerc and his men did great work with Eighth Army.

I would call him an excellent example of the "non-bellyacher." You gave him a job and he got on with it without fuss or bother. He naturally had many wants at that time, and had prepared a list of the items — it was a formidable document. For the time being we could only meet a small portion of his full requirements. We went through the list, and I said what could or could not be done. His answer was the same in either case, "*Entendu*!" I was glad we could soon give him some battledress for the weather was very cold at that time. During the battle of Mareth he came under command of General Freyberg, and the two got along famously. He was given one or two Sherman tanks, and the whole of his force were immensely proud of them. I doubt whether at that time he ever dreamt that one day he would be landing in Normandy in command of an armoured division equipped with the latest model of these tanks.

By the middle of February the Army Commander had decided upon his outline plan for the Mareth battle. A frontal attack would be made by 30th Corps along the coastal axis, whilst the New Zealanders, reinforced so that they were virtually a small Corps, with Leclerc under command, would move round the western side of the Matmata hills and endeavour to strike round their northern limits, and so threaten the rear of the defenders. 10th Corps, consisting of a strong mobile armoured force, would be held in reserve, and ready to exploit success, and if possible "rush" the bottleneck of the Gabes position. We would also have a great weight of air power to assist us in this attack. The staff had worked out that 10th Corps should be concentrated in its selected area by March 16th, when our administration position would be strong enough to start major operations once again. This forecast carried the uncertainty that enemy aircraft attacked Tripoli harbour most nights, and a few lucky hits might have worsened our position considerably. The R.A.F. and our well-handled

A.A. artillery saw us through this vital period. Ben Gardane had been chosen as the forward administrative area, where we were building up our dumps to see us through the coming battle.

In accordance with the decision that Eighth Army would have priority, we asked for certain assistance from our brother Army to the north. We asked for petrol to be stocked for our use at Gafsa and also if it were possible for a thrust from Gafsa towards Gabes to be staged. The first would help us on our way, and the second request would undoubtedly worry the enemy opposing us. Care would, of course, have to be taken to prevent any mix-up between both armies.

As an example of the tonnages we were dealing with at the time, I give those lifted from Tripoli along the one road in preparation for the battle of Mareth between March 1st and 20th:

Ben Gardane area:
 Petrol and oil: 16,000 tons
 Ammunition: 10,000 tons
 Supplies: 4,000 tons
 R.A.F. requirements: 5,000 tons
To another dumping area:
 New Zealand Division's requirements: 6,000 tons
Total: 41,000 tons

VII

One of the results of the unified command under Eisenhower was the setting up of a separate Tactical Air Force Command. To this Coningham was sent as its first Commander. His place in the Desert Air Force was taken by his Senior Air Staff Officer, Broadhurst. He was very young for the job, but we all had great confidence in him. He was a delightful man to work with, and full of initiative and new ideas. He was also prepared to accept risks. A farewell party was given to Coningham to which Tedder came — I was also invited. We were genuinely sorry to see "Mary" go, but we realised it was a good thing to have someone with his experience, and who knew the form so well, in this important appointment. In the speeches there was the good-humoured leg-pulling about our respective alleged little weaknesses. The R.A.F. suggested that we shouldn't be so sensitive of the 88-mm. gun, whilst we told the R.A.F. they would "kill" more vehicles if they got to work low down with their cannons. The answer to both these matters is — "let the other chap go and see what it is like before he airs his views!"

In the middle of this period of preparation the 2nd United States Corps was attacked strongly in the Gafsa area. The attack was launched on February 15th, and by the 20th they had been forced back towards Tebessa, and a somewhat critical situation arose. For it now looked as if the 5th British Corps to the north might as a result have to withdraw from its forward positions. Alexander was very worried by this turn of events, and sent an appeal to Montgomery on the 20th asking him to try and do something to attract the enemy's attention, and so draw pressure away from the Americans. We were at our camp south of Tripoli when this signal arrived. I took it along to the Army Commander and his reaction was immediate and generous. It is at such moments that Montgomery is at his best. He always responds wholeheartedly to an appeal, and he certainly did in this case. Although it meant upsetting his carefully worked out programme leading to the battle of Mareth, he ordered the 7th Armoured and the 51st Divisions to press forward, and so worry the enemy and threaten the weakened garrison of the Mareth Line. Leclerc's force was also instructed to move forward from Ksar Rhilane. Montgomery did not like the manoeuvre for it unbalanced his dispositions, and correct balance was something upon which the Army Commander was normally most insistent. The 10th Corps were still "grounded," and the nearest division with which to reinforce was the New Zealanders who were back at Tripoli. In addition the Ben Gardane area was in the process of being developed as an important administrative area, and so if by sticking out our necks too far we gave Rommel an opportunity to concentrate against these two forward divisions before more troops arrived, the result might have been very serious indeed.

Tactical Headquarters were ordered to move forward into Tunisia the next day, and to be followed the day after by Main.

The Desert Air Force also responded to this call and in spite of many difficulties commenced operating four fighter wings from airfields as far forward as Medenine.

I wish I had a copy of Montgomery's reply to Alexander to reproduce in full. It started by saying what he proposed to do, went on to say that he expected this action to force Rommel to turn against him, and finished with something like this: "... in this way we will get Rommel running about like a wet hen between us." This is just what did happen, and the proposal became known as the "Wet Hen" policy.

Army Headquarters were now established just short of Medenine, and attacks by the two forward divisions in the coastal sector had pushed the enemy back to the Mareth Line, and its outposts. In the hilly sector, however, he held on grimly to the high ground about Halouf. This was a considerable embarrassment to us as it gave him excellent observation over all our positions, and he caused us a lot of inconvenience from the shelling of his long-range guns. The Desert Air Force had a rotten time. When the weather was clear their forward airfields were accurately shelled, and every now and again they were forced to evacuate them temporarily. The enemy gunners must have had a lot of fun, for after a few shells had landed, a large covey of aircraft would be seen to leave, and later back they would come again.

By about February 26th the danger to the 2nd U.S. Corps had passed, and the situation was well in hand. We used to like to think that we had saved First Army from disaster! In retrospect I think we must be more generous. Our pressure no doubt had some influence upon any further exploitation of the situation by Rommel, but it is obvious that things were got under Control after the initial shock had been overcome.

By the end of February, it became apparent that the "Wet Hen" policy was proving a success, for our old friends 15th and 21st Panzer Divisions were in the process of concentrating against us. We also had to expect meeting the new Tiger tank which had already been used against the First Army. Knowing what an opportunist Rommel was, we also had to expect he would send the 10th Panzer Division against us as well.

Montgomery frankly admitted to me that for once, through his action to assist First Army, he now found himself unbalanced. So we worked feverishly to prepare ourselves to meet this attack when it came. It was a very anxious time, but full of interest. The following measures were taken: —

   (a) The New Zealand division, which was preparing for its outflanking move round the Mareth Line, was ordered up by forced marches from Tripoli.
   (b) The tanks of the 2nd Armoured Brigade which were just arriving in the Tripoli area were brought up to Ben Gardane and handed over to the 8th Armoured Brigade, which in turn was ordered forward.
   (c) The 201st Guards Brigade was brought up.

(d) Certain units of the 50th Division were rushed up.
(e) Great efforts were made to increase the forward airfields.

We had only one road — and this was fast breaking up — to carry all this traffic. And in addition to the forward move of formations, there was the very heavy maintenance traffic. For some days there was head to tail transport along its entire length, but the staffs maintained control, and the sappers kept the road in sufficient state of repair. It is a marvel to me that we fulfilled the programme without a major breakdown. The Desert Air Force kept the road practically free from interference by day, but at night it was subjected to constant attack. In spite of this our losses were very small.

By March 5th we were ready for the attack, and a very strong force was ready to receive it. Rommel had missed his opportunity, and we all breathed freely again. On this morning I went to give the Army Commander a report on the way things were going, and I asked him how he had felt during the last few days. He had shown no outward sign of anxiety, but had gone everywhere looking the picture of confidence. He admitted to me then that "he had sweated a bit at times!" Another small thing that added to our discomforts was the fact that the Mareth water possessed the properties of high-powered Epsom Salts! It was no respecter of rank, and one and all suffered accordingly!

VIII

The battle of Medenine was a little classic all of its own. It was the perfectly fought defensive battle. We were prepared to receive the enemy, a clear and definite defensive plan had been issued and rehearsed, and the result was the complete failure by Rommel even to penetrate our positions.

When studying Montgomery's campaigns it is interesting to see how his greatest offensive victories were each preceded by a defensive success. Alam Halfa before El Alamein — Medenine before Mareth — and the failure of the German Ardennes' offensive in Belgium before the advance to and across the Rhine.

During March 4th and 5th, Rommel manoeuvred his forces for the attack. We heard afterwards from prisoners that he had gone round trying to whip up his troops to a high state of enthusiasm, and impressing upon them the importance of the coming battle. But he was not the same Rommel, apparently his health was poor and his face was covered with boils.

As at Alam Halfa the battle fought itself. The enemy attacked in the morning south of the Gabes road with about 140 tanks and infantry. It was directed towards the very important feature just north of Medenine. This attack was held. In the afternoon, further attacks developed, and were dealt with in a very short space of time. Our artillery was so positioned that the majority of our guns could bring down concentrations upon the enemy from whatever sector he attacked. Great havoc was done in this way. Besides many damaged, Rommel lost fifty-two of his tanks, which were counted on the battlefield. Our casualties were 130 all ranks killed and wounded, and no tanks lost. After the battle Rommel left for Germany and took no further part in the African campaign.

There are one or two points of special interest concerning this battle. In the first place the infantry held their positions against strong infantry and tank attacks, with no wire and few mines to protect them. Then the anti-tank guns were sited to kill tanks and not to protect the infantry. There is a great difference between the two. The effect of the concentrated use of our artillery was devastating. And finally, there was the effect of this success upon our own troops, with the opposite effect upon our enemy.

We were now ready to continue with our preparations for dealing with the Mareth Line. A certain amount of dislocation had been caused by the various moves necessary to meet Rommel's attack, but we worked out that the date laid down by the Army Commander could be accepted in spite of it all.

CHAPTER X: THE BATTLE OF MARETH TO THE END IN NORTH AFRICA

I

I HAVE already described the Army Commander's broad plan for dealing with the Mareth Line: the frontal attack along the coastal axis, and the outflanking movement by the New Zealanders. Before the battle proper could commence, however, certain preliminary moves and actions had to take place. And I will describe these as far as possible in their chronological order.

Away to the west Leclerc's force had reached Ksar Rhilane, and here they were fulfilling an important role in preventing enemy reconnaissance further to the south, for behind them the New Zealand division was shortly to concentrate and start their move. During the second week in March it became clear that this infiltration by the French troops was attracting Rommel's attention, and it looked as if special measures might be taken against them. I therefore asked Leclerc to fly in to our Tactical Headquarters to discuss ways and means of strengthening his force. He arrived and expressed himself as perfectly content with his role and the situation. If the enemy attacked him, well they attacked — surely that was what he was there for — to fight. I admit we were rather worried that this small isolated force might take a nasty smack. But after my talk with their Commander, I felt much happier. As a result of this conference we managed to send them some more anti-tank guns, and some A.A. artillery. I think we also helped over some field guns. On March 10th the enemy attacked using aircraft and a mixed force, including armoured cars. Leclerc gave Rommel something he probably did not expect — a "bloody nose," and a pretty clear reminder that France would certainly rise to fight again. The losses to the enemy were twelve armoured cars, twelve guns, and about forty vehicles. The Desert Air Force happily co-operated, and severely mauled the enemy air force in the sky.

About March 14th, the New Zealand Corps — we called the swollen division a corps during this operation — consisting of the 2nd New Zealand Division, the 8th Armoured Brigade, some additional artillery and Leclerc's Force, commenced its move to the assembly zone some 30 miles south of Foum Tatahouine. They laid up in Wilder's Gap, which was a reconnoitred way through the Matmata Hills to the narrow fair going strip of country leading north through Ksar Rhilane and Bir Soultane. This move was completed by the 18th, and Freyberg had gone to great pains to conceal the move and concentration from enemy eyes. On the night of the 19th/20th the advance to the north commenced, but I will break off here in order to deal with other pre-battle activities.

Montgomery had given a great deal of thought to the stage management of this battle. He had several discussions with Leese (30th Corps) over the question of which covering positions it was necessary to capture before the main battle could commence. He spent many hours examining the country from an excellent viewpoint on the top of a prominent hill just north of Medenine called Tadjera. He decided finally on what was required, and amongst them were some defences on the south-western end of the Mareth Line, which we called the "Horseshoe feature." Its capture would not only allow us to command the main road, but would also tend to mislead the enemy as to the direction of our main attack. This operation was undertaken by the 201st Guards Brigade on the night of March 16th/17th. They unfortunately had a bad time of it. Every sort of mine was encountered, including both anti-tank and anti-personnel. These were "sown" in very great numbers, and in spite of the greatest dash and bravery, it was found impossible to bring up their vehicles and supporting arms. The enemy suffered heavily, but our troops had to be withdrawn the next morning. The other operations in connection with the enemy covering positions went well during the night of the 17th/18th.

The 50th and 51st Divisions were gradually moved forward to their allotted sectors, and the former was now all ready for the attack which was to take place across the Wadi Zigzaou, not far from the sea.

We were finding some difficulty in getting all our guns into position. Space was rather restricted, and we were overlooked the whole time from the high hills to the south-west. Although great care was taken to move up batteries in the dark, and all camouflage resources were employed, it was impossible to conceal entirely the whereabouts of our guns from the enemy. The artillery also suffered a certain amount of damage from enemy night flying aircraft which patrolled above the area and swooped down bombing and strafing on seeing a gun flash.

The Ghurkas from the 4th Indian Division were given a sort of roving commission in the hills towards Hallouf. Their main task was to beat up any posts, destroy any large guns which were firing from that area, and generally cause alarm and despondency. They appeared to have had excellent sport. They got busy with their knives very quietly in the dark. I don't think the Germans quite liked it. I remember one particular Ghurka situation report which finished as follows: —

"... Enemy losses 10 killed, ours nil (.) ammunition expenditure nil (.)"

The Desert Air Force were working feverishly to regroup their squadrons, and with the help of our Sappers construct new airfields. For the latter we found that some of the salt pans in the area were now dry enough to allow their use as airstrips.

The Army Commander, as usual before a big battle, attended the model demonstrations run by the formations carrying it out — in this case 30th Corps and 50th Division. He made certain modifications to the plan, and then gave his series of pep talks to all officers down to the Lieutenant-Colonel rank. This was, of course, the most important operation since El Alamein.

On March 17th, the 2nd United States Corps, having recovered from its initial set-back, carried out an attack and captured Gafsa. The operation progressed and reached Maknassy and El Guettar, where it was held up. We were delighted with this American advance, for not only was it in answer to the request we had made when back in Tripoli, but it also contained enemy formations, including the 10th Panzer Division, which might very well otherwise have been used against us. Rommel could obviously not risk his communications with Northern Tunisia being cut.

During the 19th, patrol activity was increased, but the front where the initial attack was to be made was relatively peaceful and quiet. Before the guns for the opening of this important battle blaze out, there are one or two matters of general interest worth recording.

II

Although not quite sure of my dates, I think it was between the battles of Medenine and Mareth that the Army Commander was visited by Admiral Ramsay and General Dempsey. The Admiral had been selected as the Naval Commander for the "Eastern Task Force" for the invasion of Sicily, and Dempsey was now commanding the 13th Corps, a formation already earmarked for the same operation. It was the first time I had met either, and I remember how impressed I was by both — both highly intelligent, human and easy to get on with. They appeared to me to be ideal commanders for such a difficult campaign.

It had already been decided that Eighth Army would command the British forces to be employed for Sicily. It had also been decided that the landings must take place in July. There were, therefore, only about three months left before "D" day. And yet the Commander — Montgomery — and Eighth Army, were still heavily involved in the North African campaign. The Admiral and the General had come up to discuss plans with Montgomery. The plan Ramsay and Dempsey were working on was one produced by a planning staff in Algiers called "Force 141." Things were all topsy-turvy, for the eventual commander should have been in on the planning from the very first. It must be he who decides upon the plan, and his staff which works out the details and implements it. This was the first time Montgomery had even looked at a large-scale map of Sicily, let alone studied a plan. So it was obvious that he could give very little useful guidance to the Admiral with whom he was to work and one of his Corps commanders. Dempsey was in this case doing a lot of work that should rightly have been undertaken by Eighth Army Headquarters. Montgomery's first reaction was that he considered the outline plan involved too much dispersion. He therefore merely instructed Dempsey to keep him informed about how things were going, asked for a copy of the plan, and told him to concentrate upon the training and combined operations side, as well as the collection of intelligence material. He felt that the time was not far off when he would have to have his own representative and staff back at Cairo in close touch with the Naval and Corps Headquarters. It was this last reaction of my Chief which was instrumental in preventing me from seeing the final stages of the Tunisian campaign. But this turn of the wheel had other compensating advantages.

Another visitor who wandered through the Army area at this time was Prince Bernhard of the Netherlands. He came and had a chat with me in my caravan. Little did either of us know that in exactly two years time we would be sitting once again together in Belgium, he as the Commander of the Dutch Forces, and myself as Chief of Staff 21st Army Group, discussing future operations for the liberation of his country.

Our Allies were becoming increasingly interested in what we were doing in North Africa, and during this period both the Russian and Chinese sent missions to visit us. We felt proud of the notice being taken of us.

From Tripoli onwards we had a new problem thrust upon us — that of feeding and looking after the civilian population. In the good old Western Desert days, the few Arabs who existed looked upon this moving warfare as a heaven-sent annual entertainment, especially laid on for their benefit. For in the armies' wake there was loot and food galore, and treasures that they had never dreamed of. But now things were very different. Many thousands of civilians were in need of food and clothing, and other articles. We were responsible for the military government in enemy occupied territories, i.e. Cyrenaica and Tripolitania, but the French, initially under our general supervision, were taking on the task in their own colony, Tunisia. Here the food situation was extremely bad, and Headquarters Middle East were most helpful in doing their best to meet some of their needs.

Montgomery moved his Tactical Headquarters well up to the front for the battle itself, so as to be on the spot, and within easy personal contact with his commanders. Main Headquarters and the Headquarters of the Desert Air Force remained where they were, just east of Medenine. Communications would not permit a further move. With signal telephones and inter-communication aircraft, it was easy to keep in touch. I decided to base myself at Tactical Headquarters for the opening of the battle, but as will be seen, events forced me back to Main on the third day of the operation.

III

The enemy dispositions at the time of the battle were interesting. As usual the Italians were holding the line with German backing where it could be spared for the important places. The 50th Division's attack was to meet the "Young Fascists" — the best of the Italian troops — and 90th Light Division was ready to stop a move down the main road axis. Of the two Panzer divisions, 15th was ready in reserve behind the Mareth Line proper, and 21st had not yet arrived; whilst 164th Division was looking after the El Hamma switch line, and the threat from the New Zealand advance.

The enemy now appeared to be fully alive to the move of the New Zealand Corps around his flank, and so the Army Commander ordered Freyberg to continue his march northwards by daylight on the 20th. It was impossible to conceal completely this huge force, consisting of 27,000 men, 200 tanks and many guns. There was a very difficult wadi north of Ksar Rhilane from which Leclerc had to clear the enemy, in order that the New Zealand sappers could construct crossings over the one hundred yard gap. The French were successful in their mission on the night of the 18th/19th.

In spite of the extreme difficulty of the country the New Zealanders were only a few miles short of the bottleneck which we called "Plum," i.e. between the Djebel Tebaga and Djebel Melab. It was here that the El Hamma switch line was situated. This was great news and augured well for the future, and in an hour or two the coastal attack was due to go in.

At 2230 hours on the 20th, with the help of a great artillery barrage, the 50th Division's attack commenced. The initial objectives were three strong points just north of the Wadi Zigzaou. This wadi was a horrible obstacle. It contained water, and had been registered by the enemy's guns and mortars. It was also subject to intensive enfilade fire from the flanks. There is no doubt that this division did extremely well in taking their objectives, but when dawn came there were still pockets of the enemy holding out in some of the defensive works. The main problem was building a crossing over this wadi in order that supporting arms and supplies could reach the forward troops. The sappers worked like beavers, but suffered heavy casualties. Our gallant Chief Engineer, Kisch, who was always to be found at the most dangerous spot, was to be seen directing operations. But even his inventive brain could not compete with the enemy's fire and the water. Progress was, however made, and a few Valentine tanks were got across, but that was all. The crossing was not good enough for wheeled vehicles, and few if any anti-tank guns were got over. These strong points were formidable affairs. They were built with concrete, with well revetted trenches, and deep dug-outs. Minefields and wire gave them further protection. It is remarkable they fell so easily.

Our forward positions were held all day on the 21st, and that night another heavy artillery barrage allowed the bridgehead to be extended both laterally and in depth, the 50th Division again being employed. By this time the Young Fascists had been backed up by German troops, and there was some very stiff fighting. Even by the 22nd no good crossing had been made over the wadi, but reports from the sappers suggested that some time that morning they hoped to have it fit for wheeled traffic.

From now onwards we had a run of bad luck. The 15th Panzer Division began moving up to counter-attack. The air had seen them forming up. But shortly afterwards we had a cloud burst or two, which not only completely wrecked the crossing place, but also prevented our using the bombers which were just forming up to deliver a powerful blow against 15th Panzer Division. If this attack had been able to go in, I am sure the subsequent counter-attack would have proved a less formidable affair. 50th Division were most unfortunate, for the support that we had hoped to give them was not forthcoming. They had to withstand the full weight of the German counter-attack, with few supporting weapons, and no air support. As a result the second night's objective was lost. They gripped on, however, with the help of a few Valentine tanks to one locality on the north side of the wadi. This was held during the night of the 22nd/23rd and the day of the 23rd, but the Army Commander decided to withdraw them under artillery concentration during the next night. This operation was successfully carried out. So, as far as the Mareth front was concerned, we were now where we had started. Our casualties had not, however, been unduly heavy, and the attack had attracted the enemy's attention and tied down one of the

Panzer Divisions (15th), as well as 164th and 90th Light German infantry divisions.

In the meantime the Army Commander had modified his plans. During the early hours of March 23rd he realised that the coastal attack had for the moment failed, and that to persevere with it at the moment would prove most costly, and might even then achieve no success. He therefore called a conference just after breakfast on the 23rd at which Leese, Horrocks, their B.G.S.'s and myself were present. In his usual unruffled and confident way he gave out his orders.

He would give up the coastal thrust, and the 50th Division would be withdrawn across the Wadi Zigzaou that night. It had forced the enemy to reinforce the sector with German troops. This was excellent, for it would provide a great opportunity for the outflanking of the Mareth Line. Every endeavour must be made to make the enemy think we were just re-organising for another frontal attack, and all steps, deceptive and otherwise, must be taken to this end. The staffs must work out details. Now was his great opportunity; he would reinforce the "left hook" immediately. Headquarters 10th Corps and 1st Armoured Division would move at once to join the New Zealand Corps. They would follow the same route as that taken by Freyberg.

30th Corps would now lay on operations with the object of opening up the road Medenine-Halluf-Bir Soltane through the hills. This would be an important development, for it would facilitate and shorten the maintenance of the "left hook" formations, as well as allow a switch of forces between the two flanks. If good progress were made, it might even be possible to cut in behind the main Mareth Line with a short "left hook." The 4th Indian Division was given this task, and got under way with great speed.

He ended the conference by saying that he had complete confidence in the outcome of the battle.

We broke up and went our various ways. I had a quick talk with both Corps Commanders, and arranged some details and ordered a full-blooded staff conference. I then decided to shift my base back to Main Headquarters. With all these moves taking place, traffic control and movement tables were the first priority, and these we tackled at once. Knowing Horrocks and his enthusiasm, I realised that I had no time to lose, for he was like a dog with six tails. We had, of course, anticipated a move such as this, and an outline staff plan had been prepared, so in the event we had no great difficulty in getting things going. All our tank transporters had to be got up to move the tanks of the 1st Armoured Division, and a complete change in the maintenance centre of gravity had to be laid on. Special A.A. protection for the various road bottlenecks had to be arranged for. These were some of the things that had to be done in a very short time.

I then flew back to Main Headquarters to put them fully into the picture, and I also had to look into the air side of these changes of plan.

IV

During these two or three days the New Zealand Corps had begun to eat their way into the bottleneck to which I have already referred. The Italian troops holding it had been rapidly reinforced by Germans, including troops of 164th and the 21st Panzer Divisions. General Freyberg was confronted by considerable difficulty. The enemy were in possession of excellent observation from the hills on either side of the valley, and it took some very laborious and fierce fighting to establish a foothold on the Tegaba Hill and on the high ground to the east. There were also extensive minefields to be picked up, covered by fire from either side.

The 1st Armoured Division never stopped moving until they got to their destination. It was a classic march of its kind.

Certain things stood out which would influence our plans for breaking through the enemy switch line. These were:

(a) There was no time to be lost as the enemy was bound to go on reinforcing this sector with German troops. Therefore any plan adopted must be simple and easy to lay on.
(b) We would have a great superiority in the air and in in tanks; this must therefore be exploited.
(c) For the first time we would be in Rommel's favourite position for an attack, i.e. with the sun behind in the afternoon.
(d) From the reports received from the New Zealand Corps it looked as if we should very soon be through the enemy's carefully laid minefields.

On my return to Main Headquarters I had a long discussion with Broadhurst, A.O.C. of the Desert Air Force. I explained the situation to him. We in the Army had always wanted to try out what is generally called a "Blitz" attack. The Germans employed it on frequent occasions, and used their dive bombers for that very close and intimate air support which we felt would prove very effective. Hitherto the close support given to the attack had always been by bomb from the light bomber, and the fighter bomber. The R.A.F. had for very good reasons been against the dive bomber, but we felt the cannons from the fighters might prove more deadly and disrupting to the enemy than the fighter bomber with their bombs dropped from comparatively high altitudes. In view of the importance of this attack, and the narrow frontage to which we were confined, this did look to be the right occasion for trying out this type of attack. Using the fighter in this low-flying role over the immediate battle area was a considerable risk, and it was possible that the casualties would prove very severe. On the other hand, we felt that, from our own experiences from low-flying attacks, the defence took some time to recover equilibrium, and that some sort of temporary paralysis often set in.

Broadhurst listened to the arguments, and after a long discussion said, "I will do it, You will have the whole boiling match — bombs and cannon. It will be a real low-flying blitz, and I will talk to all the pilots myself." With his reputation as a fighter pilot, we knew what this would mean — tremendous enthusiasm.

We were delighted, and I rang up the Army Commander to tell him what we could expect.

The 24th and 25th were spent in a maze of planning. There was a tremendous lot to be done between the Air and ourselves. We wanted to let every pilot know what to go for and what to expect, so we prepared detailed maps showing the exact locations of the enemy guns, transport and defences. These were reproduced from air photos and other intelligence. The squadron leaders were sent to fly over the battle area and so get to know their way about. An experienced squadron leader was to direct the Kittybombers by wireless. An R.A.F. officer was also detailed with a wireless set in an armoured car to be positioned far forward from where he could warn our aircraft if they were shooting up our own troops. Then there was all the detail in connection with landmarks, timings and coloured smoke signals. Later on all these ideas became a matter of routine, but then they were in their experimental stage.

The final air plan catered for a "crump" by forty light bombers on the narrow frontage of attack, to take place just before it commenced. Then, with five Spitfire squadrons as top cover, sixteen Kittybomber squadrons would operate over the battlefield for two and a half hours, at an average density of two squadrons at any one time. These using bomb and cannon would shoot up everything they saw. In addition a specially trained squadron of "tank busters" were to go for the enemy armour when located. In order to cause disorganisation to the enemy's rear areas, it was agreed to carry out night bombing raids during the previous two nights. The pilots were brought up to a great state of enthusiasm, and as will be seen the whole operation was an unqualified success. Montgomery agreed to the final plan that Freyberg and Horrocks hatched out between them. It was simple in the extreme. The attack was on a narrow front, preceded by a heavy creeping barrage, and with artillery concentrations and smoke dealing with the enemy on either side of the valley. Behind this barrage the tanks would move forward, and behind them the infantry. It was hoped that all dangerous minefields had been dealt with, but in case of unexpected trouble sapper parties were available. Then, of course, superimposed on all this were the aircraft, the pilots being able to see exactly how the attack was going by the barrage. They therefore knew what to go for; the barrage gave them the bomb-line. The New Zealanders were to make the hole and the 1st Armoured Division was to be positioned behind ready to thrust through the gap so made towards El Hamma. They were to go by night or day — preferably by night as a good moon would be shining. The attack was to take place at 16.00 hours, as this would give us the sun behind, shining into the defenders' eyes.

The Army Commander sent his blessing to the plan accompanied by two bottles of brandy, but no artificial stimulant was necessary to spur on these two fine commanders!

There was one slight difficulty from the staff point of view, and that was — who was to be head man in this party. I think the Army Commander had more or less laid it down that 10th Corps would take control, but until this was made clear I was a bit worried that Freyberg, who had done all the dirty work so far, might feel a little resentful. I knew once Horrocks and he got together they would work smoothly, but until then I addressed them as a joint authority. I think this letter which I wrote explaining some points for the forthcoming attack may be of interest: —

Main H.Q.,
Eighth Army,
M.E.F.,
March 25th, 1943.

My Dear Generals,

(I feel as if I am writing to the old combination — Hindenburg and Ludendorff!).

This letter gives you the Army Commander's views as to future operations.

1. "Supercharge"[24] is virtually your course No. 1 (N.B., this refers to various plans submitted), with stronger and more intimate air support than we have ever tried before.

2. The Army Commander wants you to go 100 per cent, for "Supercharge" and produce a simple cut and dried plan, and we will give you the maximum air support possible.

3. The Army Commander stresses the need to keep your joint resources concentrated and not dispersed; that is why he

---

[24] Note the same code word for the decisive attack as used at El Alamein.

did not like the Kebili project as it placed a mountain range between the two Divisions.

4. He feels that if we can break into this front facing you, you can take considerable risks, and by pushing on deep, the enemy will be forced to pull back from the hills.

Paras. 5 and 6 contained the latest intelligence reports.

7. We are sending over Darwin[25] Burton[26] and Alex Wallace[27] to help you tie up the air support for "Supercharge." The R.A.F. have ordered an armoured car to report at N.Z. H.Q.; and it is proposed that Darwin should be located in it, and be stationed "cheek by jowl" with Comd. 8 Armd. Bde. or whoever else is in a position to get the latest information as to how the air support is working. It is important that he should be able to see the battle area from a good O.P. and he will then be able to give the pilots the "low-down" as to how they are doing. It is also important that he keeps in the closest touch with one of our Commanders as he must have an up-to-date picture. Sitting back here it would look as if 8 Armd. Bde. is the right location.

8. The following are the main points which have arisen during a Conference held with R.A.F. this morning:

(a) The R.A.F. are prepared to allocate all their Spitfire Sqns. and 16 Kittybomber Sqns. to support your break-in and break-through.

(b) The length of time they can operate over the area continuously depends upon the Spitfire Sqns. These can operate continuously for two hours. Therefore you can

---

[25] R.A.F.-Darwin was a magnificent fighter pilot who was killed in Italy.
[26] Burton lost his life on his way back from England to the Sicily campaign — we missed him a great deal
[27] Our G2 Air, who was killed when flying with a bomber sortie in Tunisia.

expect Kittybomber attacks throughout this two-hours' period at the density of 2 Sqns.

(c) The important thing will be to decide on the correct timing. We feel that it might be best to start this intensive air effort about zero minus 30 mins. This should thoroughly disorganise the defence at the psychological moment and allow the fighter bombers to continue supporting the attack during the most difficult period. Tou may, however, feel you would like a longer preparation beforehand, but it is probable that your artillery will be able to deal with this.

(d) It will be most important to give the Air Force, as soon as possible, the maximum information as to your plan of attack, and the areas and centres of enemy resistance, guns, etc., that you wish to be attacked.

(e) We would also like to know your zero hour as early as possible.

(f) It is hoped that other air resources will be employed on bombing enemy aerodromes during this period and so interfere with enemy air re-action.

(f) The tank busters we feel should be used in the preparatory stage owing to the complication of employing them during the concentrated blitz.

(h) The weather should allow a similar night effort as was put over the enemy facing you last night. From reports received things seem to have gone extremely well, and we feel that two nights like this will not improve the enemy's fighting value. Only the worst type of weather should interfere with the support laid on.

9. The Air Force are going flat out on this low straffing. It may be very expensive owing to flak and enemy opposition, but they have agreed to do it because the Army Commander has told them it is the big thing at this stage of the campaign. They will not be able to stage such an intensive air effort two days running.

Yours ever,

                                                F. W. de Guingand
Lt.-Gen. Sir B. G. Freyberg, V.C.,
Comd. N.Z-Corps.
Lt.-Gen. G. B. Horrocks,
Comd. 10th Corps.

What with the enemy's night straffing and the excitement I felt about the coming attack, I could hardly sleep the night before. I am sure I could never become so hard-boiled that moments such as these would leave me unmoved. The outlook in the morning was most depressing, for a bad sand storm was blowing, and none of our aircraft could leave the ground. We walked about with our fingers crossed. By lunch time there was very little improvement, but by 1.30 p.m. things began to look up, and the R.A.F. said they would be able to carry out their programme. Never have I sent a message with greater joy and relief than when I informed the Commanders concerned. As it turned out, this sand storm worked very much to our advantage, for it gave invaluable cover to our troops during the forming up period. In this way our violent blow fell from the air and ground from out of a sunny and dusty western sky, and undoubtedly caught the enemy by surprise.

The attack went like clockwork. I remained in our operations lorry reading and listening to the reports being flashed back from the "J" Service. One began to think there must be a catch in it. For almost to the minute reports arrived saying that this or that objective had been taken in accordance with our plan. Returning pilots gave vivid descriptions of the battle and of the success they were achieving. They were really enjoying themselves. The battlefield and the rear areas were covered with smoking and burning vehicles. Never before had our Desert Air Force given us such superb, such gallant, and such intimate support.

By dark the New Zealanders and the 8th Armoured Brigade had captured their objectives. The 1st Armoured Division, followed until dark, penetrating to a depth of five miles. They then waited until the moon rose to give them light for their further night advance.

With the rising moon the 1st Armoured Division, acting with great resolution, passed right through the 21st Panzer Division and the other troops holding the defences. By daylight our leading troops were only a few miles short of El Hamma, and here they came up against a strong screen of anti-tank guns. The enemy were now desperately reinforcing the El Hamma area, and units from 15th Panzer Division were in the neighbourhood. There was some grim fighting still going on in the "Plum" bottleneck where the New Zealand Corps was mopping up. Between these two formations were the 21st Panzers, and in the morning they made an attempt to attack the rear of the 1st Armoured Division. For some time our troops were fighting to their front and rear, but they were not caught napping, and the enemy armour trickled off around their flank after suffering severe losses.

By nightfall on the 27th, the enemy had been soundly thrashed, and during that night the bulk of the New Zealand Corps moved forward towards El Hamma, subsequently bypassing the town and making straight for Gabes.

In this battle 164th Division, 15th and 21st Panzer Divisions, and of course the Italians, had been given a tremendous hammering, and the battlefield was littered with destroyed and captured M.T. guns, tanks, as well as with prisoners and dead. We had captured 7,000 prisoners since the battle started.

The effect of the success of the El Hamma battle was decisive. The enemy retired from the Mareth position proper on the night of the 27th/28th, and early the next day 30th

Corps were moving forward confronted by the usual difficulties of mines, demolitions and booby traps.

By mid-day of March 27th the 4th Indian Division had opened up the road to Halluf and Bir Soltane.

On the 29th we captured El Hamma and Gabes, and by this time the enemy had withdrawn his depleted and somewhat disorganised forces to man the Wadi Akarit position. We called this natural fifteen-mile-wide defile between the sea and the Shott El Fejadj the "Gabes Gap." To break through this to the open country of Central Tunisia was therefore our next task.

After the battle I flew over the Mareth defences in a very slow-moving captured German "puddle-jumper" with Broadhurst. We spent a long time studying the layout. There was no doubt about its strength, and we both felt how lucky we had been to win this battle with so little loss. The scene of the 50th Division's fighting was a nasty sight. It was sad that that gallant formation had not reaped more tangible signs of their hard fighting, but in the big scheme of things they had nobly played their part.

V

I feel it only right that I should mention certain repercussions that took place after the magnificent effort put up by the Desert Air Force in the El Hamma battle. The press very rightly made a great business of it. One read vivid descriptions of these "new blitz methods" — the "annihilation of the battlefield by the R.A.F." — "the zero feet attacks by the Desert Air Force." Yet, in spite of its success, I happen to know that there was considerable anxiety shown by those in high R.A.F. places — from the Air Ministry downwards. Great efforts were made to write down the story, and to infer that the support was normal and not out of the ordinary. I suppose the idea behind all this was the fear that the Army would always ask for this kind of support, and that the result might be a heavy drain on our fighter strength, and therefore make the R.A.F.'s primary task of defeating the enemy's air forces more difficult. I felt most bitter about this attitude at the time, for to start with it inferred great ignorance and stupidity on the part of the Army. Only on special occasions would we ask for this intensive type of action. Then it was grossly unfair to Broadhurst and his gallant pilots. They had taken a risk, had fought magnificently, and had got away with it — surely they were entitled to a full measure of praise for the way they had answered the Army's call. It is interesting to note that the losses for the day's operations were eight pilots killed or missing — by no means a heavy bill to pay. To sum up, Broadhurst laid on a type of support that had not been tried before, and made a great success of it. We in the Army were most grateful to him.

VI

After the Mareth battle was over both Tactical and Main Headquarters were moved forward — Tactical to Gabes. It was here that Montgomery met Eisenhower for the first time. He came and stayed a night. We were all greatly impressed by our Supreme Commander: Montgomery, who was rather gauging people's merits by the number of battles they had fought — and won, rated him "a very decent chap"!

Another visitor was Giraud, the Frenchman. We also liked him a lot, and were entertained by his exciting account of how he escaped from prison in Germany. For a man of his age it was a remarkable story. Montgomery was really intrigued by the tale, and made Giraud tell it all over again to some new arrivals at his camp.

To deal with the Wadi Akarit position the Army Commander regrouped on March 31st, placing 30th Corps in command of the New Zealand Division. Once a breach had been made, 10th Corps would take over the New Zealanders, and would strike deep into the open country and make for the Mezzouna group of airfields. 30th Corps would operate along the coastal road axis.

At first Montgomery had considered that two divisions would prove sufficient for the break-in, but later he increased this to three (50th, 51st and 4th Indian Divisions) as the position possessed such natural strength.

The days of preparation were not very pleasant for the troops concerned, as the enemy had excellent observation over the whole area, and his artillery fire became a nuisance. However, by April 5th everything was ready, and the attack went in at 0400 hours the next morning.

As time was important, the Army Commander decided to attack on a dark night — with no moon. We had not attempted this before, and so he hoped to obtain a measure of surprise. And in this he was successful.

The 50th Division had the most difficult task in the centre, and had trouble in crossing the wadi; but the other two divisions on their flank made good progress, and by nightfall were firmly established on the heights. The 4th Indian Division carried out their attack without artillery support — a silent attack especially suited to the Indian soldier. It was brilliantly planned by Tuker, their Commander, and was a great success. I am told that the scene of carnage on top of that hill when daylight came was indescribable. The Highlanders experienced bitter fighting throughout the day, ground being lost and won on many occasions, but in the end they fought the enemy to a standstill.

The 10th Corps with the New Zealand Division leading, were to commence their advance during the afternoon, but they had still not broken out by darkness. We, therefore, arranged for a concentrated air effort to help them next morning. The enemy, however, had been exhausted by the day's fighting, and withdrew during the night. We were now in the open, and the enemy had no suitable position to hold us up, other than far North at Enfidaville. We knew that the ports of Sfax and Sousse would soon be in our hands, and this would greatly improve our maintenance position, for we were still maintaining ourselves from the port of Tripoli.

We were all feeling elated and the two Corps, helped by the Desert Air Force, started chasing the enemy much faster than he wished to go. In this battle we had taken 7,000 prisoners, and this brought the total since the start of the attack on the Mareth Line to 20,000. During the Wadi Akarit fighting we received a report from the troops that the enemy were forming up in considerable strength for a counter-attack. We at once started laying on an air attack. But just as the aircraft were about to take off, we were asked to cancel the bombers. It transpired that this alleged counter-attack was in reality a formation of Italians preparing themselves for surrender! They had been paraded, and they then marched over to us, each carrying a little suitcase, as if packed for a week-end's visit! Surrender *par excellence*! "Sir, I beg to report that my unit is all present and correct for surrender!"

On the other side of the balance sheet this battle cost me, and many others, a very dear friend. Brigadier Kisch, our Chief Engineer, was killed by a mine in the Wadi Akarit when he was examining the enemy's defences after the battle.

VII

It was a thrill to drive northwards through central Tunisia, for spring was upon us, and the countryside was soft and green. Spring flowers were poking their heads out of the grass, and the thousands of olive plantations were a pleasure to the eye, if irritating when encountered during the tactical battle. This was indeed the promised land after our wanderings in the desert.

The line of the enemy's retreat was well marked by deserted and burnt-out vehicles, a shedding of strength that the enemy could ill afford. The end was now in sight. He knew it, and we knew it, and drier weather was on its way in Northern Tunisia which would allow First Army to develop its full strength. Up to this time there had been within Eighth Army a certain amount of criticism at the inability of First Army to perform greater feats. I probably felt that way myself at times. This, however, was very ignorant criticism and made without any knowledge of the true facts. When once one heard the story of those early days after the landing — the "hotch-potch" forces — the distances involved — the supply troubles, it was possible to realise what a colossal task had to be undertaken before any question of a large scale offensive could be contemplated. Then by the time things had been sorted out the weather broke. This weather factor we never properly appreciated. We had been used to operating over a dry desert, where rain storms were mostly freaks, and where dust storms were our only meteorological anxiety. We had our smugness removed in Italy when we met for the first time a European-type winter. It killed our efforts north of the Sangro River. It is, therefore, with no attempt at being patronising that I now say, "Well done, First Army, who under such difficult conditions played so noble a part in the destruction of the Axis forces in North Africa."

Within a few hours of the break-through of the Wadi Akarit position, troops of 10th Corps linked up with our American allies. It was a great moment, and one that called for special celebrations. From the accounts I heard, these took place! Four days later Eighth Army joined up with the 9th British Corps of First Army near Kairouan, as a result of an offensive by our comrades in arms.

During the advance to the north several fierce rearguard actions took place, each of which lopped off more of Rommel's fighting strength.

Sfax was captured on April 10th and Sousse was in our hands two days later. And by the evening of the 13th our leading troops were up against the anti-tank defences of the enemy's Enfidaville position. A re-grouping had now taken place, 30th Corps being held back in reserve in the Sfax area with the 7th Armoured Division and the 51st Division under their command. The final stages of the campaign as far as Eighth Army was concerned was now entrusted to 10th Corps who had been reinforced by the 4th Indian and the 50th Division from the other Corps. Now that the link up with First Army had been achieved, there was hardly room to employ two Corps Headquarters, but there was also another reason behind the Army Commander's decision to place 30th Corps into reserve, and that was the urgent need to start detailed planning for the invasion of Sicily.

About April 10th, Montgomery wrote to Alexander to enquire as to the final plans for this campaign. Which Army was to deliver the knockout blow? In response to this, McCreery, Alexander's Chief of Staff, came to visit the Army Commander at his Headquarters near Sousse. Here he explained the proposed plans, and told us that it was now First Army's turn. This was no doubt the right solution, for not only was the terrain within the First Army's sector more suitable, but we had to begin preparing for Sicily. Our role was to be a holding one, and we were asked to send an armoured division and an armoured car regiment to reinforce the other Army. The 1st Armoured Division was selected for this purpose.

At this same meeting the planning for Sicily was discussed. Montgomery stressed the unsatisfactory state of affairs, in which he as the Commander was unable to devote any time to the business. Further, only one of the Corps selected to undertake the landing had been able to start work. It was not certain when the end would finally come in Northern Tunisia, and until it did the Army Commander felt he could not leave his headquarters. As a result it was decided that I should return at once to Cairo and act as Montgomery's Deputy-cum-Chief of Staff. I would get back the necessary staff from Eighth Army Headquarters as the situation allowed. In this way Admiral Ramsay would have someone to deal with who could make decisions in the Army Commander's name, and Dempsey and 13th Corps Headquarters would be released to carry out their legitimate tasks — the planning on the Corps level. A signal was sent to Alexander putting forward this proposal, and his approval arrived the same day. It was agreed that in view of my new status and responsibility I should be given the rank of Major-General.

VIII

At Sousse the A.D.C.'s laid on a carefully prepared plot, in which a surprise attack was made upon the Army Commander by one of the women of that town. His trained military mind reacted instantly and won the day. It was at a ceremony at which Montgomery was being greeted as the city's deliverer. At one stage a sweet young French woman came up to present the

General with a bouquet of flowers. She duly handed it over to the smiling conqueror. Then came the words, "Vill you kees me?" The Army Commander recoiled slightly, but rebounded to deliver a sharp peck on the lady's blushing cheek. The incident was, of course, a tremendous success and brought the house down. The previous afternoon John Poston and Johnny Henderson had spent some time in rehearsing this episode. How long it took them before they were satisfied, I don't know — but she was a very pretty girl, and knew no English!

After the Sousse conference I returned to Sfax to spend a night with 30th Corps Headquarters. It was here that I was visited by a certain American General who had recently arrived to take up an appointment at Eisenhower's Headquarters. Later he distinguished himself as a very fine divisional and I think, Corps Commander. He arrived in the early afternoon, and I gave him some lunch, during which he asked whether he could have a word with me in private. I, therefore, told the mess waiter to leave. He told me he was rather worried about the fighting powers of some of the American units, the setback at Gafsa was quoted. He knew that there had been a certain amount of criticism by both British and American officers at the time. What did I think about it? Without any hesitation I told him not to worry one little bit, for I was absolutely certain that before very long he would have no more anxieties. I then gave him some of our experiences when troops who had not been "nursed" into battle, and who, having had insufficient training, had produced unhappy results. I explained Montgomery's method of this nursing into battle. Patrol work, raids, small unit attacks, before a big operation was tried out. How certain key commanders and staff officers were superimposed amongst other units in the line in order to get the "form." He seemed somewhat relieved, and later when

I met him in Sicily after Patton's Army had fought so bravely at Gela, I went up to him and said, "Any anxieties now?" He said, "No," and thanked me again for my little chat of three months before.

I had a bit of a celebration that night, drank rather a lot of champagne — a present from the French — and played poker until the birds began to sing. Now that our Army was to carry out a holding role, and Sicily was to be the big thing, I was human enough to be pleased to return to the fleshpots of Cairo and my wife. Later I was just a bit envious when I heard descriptions of the closing scenes of this remarkable campaign. I flew back to Main Headquarters at Gabes to collect my kit and hold a staff conference at which I explained the new plans and my return to Cairo. I selected Richardson, my G.S.O. 1 Operations to answer for me and this meant he became a Brigadier. The next morning I flew to Cairo with my servant, and my faithful Chief Clerk and friend, Harwood, who incidentally remained with me until the war's end. Life seemed good at that moment, the sand of the desert left behind, the good things awaiting me in Cairo, and the thoughts of fresh adventures ahead.

CHAPTER XI: PREPARATIONS FOR AND THE INVASION OF SICILY

I

I ARRIVED back in Cairo on April 15th and spent the next day getting clean and acclimatised to the new conditions. Good food at the Mohammed Ali Club, some new clothes for myself as well as for my wife, Gezira Club, with all its pleasant attractions, and dancing at Shepheard's — a lovely change after our long trek from El Alamein.

On the 17th, I reported at my new Headquarters. The buildings were given the code-name of "George," and were situated in the centre of the residential part of Cairo. Secrecy was, of course, one of our most difficult problems, and looking back, it seems a miracle that we kept our plans from the enemy. The world knew that the Allies were preparing something fresh in the Mediterranean area; that we could not hide. But the place, the date, and the scope of our next venture were denied to the enemy. "George" was completely wired in, and an elaborate system of passes had been instituted. Sentries were posted at every gate, and patrols functioned after dark. An additional protection at night was provided by specially trained police dogs. Every evening some twenty of these animals would arrive in their lorry, each with its master — a military policeman. They were prepared to bite on sight anyone other than their own M.P. I never got tired of watching their arrival from the balcony of my office. It sounded like feeding time at the lion's house in the Zoo. One evening their arrival coincided with the distribution of the men's suppers from the cookhouse. Just below me an orderly had dumped his load of a dixie with a tray of rissoles on top of it, and was talking to a pal of his leading one of these dogs. This dog was of enormous size, being a cross between an Alsatian and a mastiff. It had a particularly evil expression. By some clever manipulation it managed to stretch its chain so that his jaws were within range of the rissoles. Delicately, quietly, and with extreme rapidity, this police dog polished off over half of these dainty morsels. The dog then looked up at me — I'm sure he winked — and I just felt I couldn't let him down and give him away, so I kept quiet and said nothing. The conversation having ended, the M.P. and his dog moved on, and the orderly turned round to pick up the suppers. I shall never know what that soldier really thought. He stared for a moment, scratched his head, looked puzzled, and then picked up his load and walked away. He could not have helped seeing the disappearance of so many rissoles, but he was, I think, the type of soldier who says, "Well, it's happened — I've no idea how or why — but its too hot to understand — so why worry!"

I paid my respects to Admiral Ramsay, and gave him a letter from my Chief which described my appointment. He couldn't have been more delightful and helpful. This also went for his Chief of Staff. I explained what I intended to do. Having heard the Naval story, read the Force 141 plan and discussed things with Dempsey, I decided to write another appreciation for the Army Commander. This took me a day or two, and when it was finished I sent it with an officer to his headquarters in Tunisia. In brief, the examination once more brought out Montgomery's initial reaction that the landings were too dispersed, and that a far more concentrated effort was required if we were to overcome the resistance which we must expect from our experiences in North Africa. The more concentrated the landings, the easier would be the tasks of the Navy and the

Air Forces. The original plan had proposed that the landings should take place in the northwest and south-east corners of the island. There were to be only four assaulting divisions — with a slow build-up — for the south-eastern assault, and these were to be spread between the gulfs of Catania and Gela. So there was to be dispersion in all directions. I was not happy about the intelligence we were receiving, and energetic steps were required to put this matter right. The time factor was most disturbing, as we had only two and a half months in which to prepare the expedition. There was no time to lose before a firm plan was agreed upon, and it was essential that an adequate Army staff should arrive in Cairo at once. There were other matters such as the Air Command proposals which were unsatisfactory.

I then followed up this appreciation with a signal saying that I was convinced that the Army Commander should himself pay a visit to Cairo without delay, in order that he could acquaint himself with the problem in more detail, and discuss matters with Ramsay and others. I was relieved when I heard he had agreed to do so, and would arrive in Cairo in his Fortress on April 23rd.

Whilst the Army Commander is flying over the scenes of his recent successes on his way back to the Nile, I will try and describe some of the major difficulties with which we were confronted in preparing for the invasion of Sicily. They look formidable as is common to all such enterprises when you first tackle them. They were all resolved in time, and this phase in my work provided a good lesson why one should never, save very reluctantly, reject any project because it seems too difficult.

II

To start with, the location of the various Commanders and headquarters is interesting: —

Commanders
Supreme Commander: Algiers.
The Army Commander: Fighting a battle in N. Tunisia.
The Naval C.-in-C.: Cairo.
The Air C.-in-C.: Malta.
13th Corps Commander: Cairo.
30th Corps Commander: Sfax.

Headquarters
Main Army Headquarters: North of Sousse and part in Cairo.
Rear Army Headquarters: End of first week of May, Cairo.
Tripoli Base Administrative link with G.H.Q. Middle East: Tripoli.
Naval Headquarters: Cairo.
Air Headquarters, opening phase: Malta.
Air Headquarters after landing: Tunisia.
13th Corps Headquarters: Cairo.
30th Corps Headquarters: Sfax.
Supreme Commander's H.Q., where co-ordination between Eighth Army and Seventh U.S. Army took place: Algiers.
Middle East H.Q. who were primarily responsible for mounting the operation: Cairo.

From the above it will be seen that the distribution of Commanders and Headquarters didn't make for smooth and rapid business.

As a first step I got 30th Corps, the Desert Air Force, and Air C.-in-C. Malta to send representatives to Cairo, so that all staffs could get on the same "wave length." We also sent an officer to represent us at General Alexander's Headquarters in Algiers.

Then the question of the formations taking part presented another major problem. Some of them were still fighting in Tunisia, and one was in England. Even after the end of the Tunisian campaign the distribution of the troops produced many complications. Here it is: —

    1st Canadian Division: England.
    51st (H.) Division: Tunisia.
    78th Division: Tunisia.
    1st Airborne Division: Kairouan — Tunisia.
    7th Armoured Division: Tripoli.
    5th Division: Egypt — Palestine — Syria.
    50th Division: Egypt — Palestine — Syria.
    231st Infantry Brigade: Egypt — Palestine — Syria (ex-Malta).

Until the end of the Tunisian campaign we were not quite certain which divisions were available for the assault. And of course until a division was nominated and its staff made available, none of the intricate detailed planning could commence.

The numbers and type of ships and assault craft was for ever changing, and only those who have had experience of planning a combined operation will know fully what this meant. Without a firm detailed "lift," plans had to be revised continually.

Another small but worrying thing was the fact that the Canadian Division and other units coming from the United Kingdom were on a different war establishment from ourselves; that is, the various units did not compare exactly with their counterparts in the Middle East as regards number of personnel and vehicles.

None of us was trained or experienced in preparing for a big amphibious expedition of this sort, so a certain amount of planning was by trial and error.

Another matter which took up a lot of time and trouble was the fact that many of the units which had been fighting were low in strength in both men and equipment. Absorbing and training of reinforcements and the issuing of new equipment was a big and complicated affair.

Besides all this, there had to be time for training the formations in amphibious warfare, the waterproofing of vehicles, and the holding of full dress rehearsals.

For the Navy things could hardly have been more complicated. Convoys were to sail from the U.K., Sfax, Sousse, Tripoli, Benghazi, Alexandria, Haifa and Syria. Somehow they had to meet off Sicily at the right time. Many of the troops were to be on board ships for many days, and this raised the question of their fitness for immediate battle.

From the enemy side we were not very happy about the intelligence we were receiving; in particular regarding the coast and the defences. To a large extent this was put right by some magnificent very low altitude oblique photography taken by the R.A.F.

The ultimate size of the German garrison and the strength of the German Air Force in Sicily by the date of the invasion were, of course, unknown, and not very easy to assess. We had therefore to prepare for a considerable reinforcement.

The weather factor, as always in such operations, remained uncertain.

So it will be seen that for novices at this type of warfare we had a pretty full plate. But to counter all this we had one invaluable asset. We were all a team — commanders and staff — who knew each other, liked each other, and knew how to work together. We knew the short cuts, and how to do without red tape and pompous officialdom. There were even times when I became a bit worried that we took things too light-heartedly.

III

On April 23rd the Army Commander arrived in Cairo and stayed at the Embassy for nearly three days. Besides matters connected with the next campaign, I had to arrange visits to the barber, tailor and friends which he had asked for. I had arranged a presentation with the use of maps of all relevant factors. He sat as he usually did on such occasions silently sucking it in, interrupting with an occasional question. After this he had talks with Ramsay and Dempsey. By the evening he had quite made up his mind, and after we all had finished dinner at the Embassy we withdrew to a small room which Miles Lampson, the Ambassador, had placed at Montgomery's disposal. Here a draft signal to Alexander was discussed. In it Montgomery clearly stated his objections to the existing plan, his suggested modifications, and a conclusion that if the revised plan were accepted he was confident of success. He considered it essential that the assaulting formations of the Eastern Task Force should land within supporting distance of each other. It was also important to include in the bridgehead area a port and airfields. Further, as stiff opposition was to be expected, the assault must be carried out within fighter aircraft range of our airfields. In view of the above considerations it appeared that landings in the Gulf of Noto, and on either side of the Pachino peninsula, were the best solution. After a lot of discussion I read out the final draft of the signal, and the Army Commander asked whether the Admiral agreed. "Yes," said Ramsay. "Excellent," replied Montgomery. "Now, Freddie, just add a last paragraph saying that Admiral Ramsay is in complete agreement." The Admiral was not quite sure that he liked this, for no doubt he felt that he should not commit himself to an opinion on more or less an Army matter, without first consulting his own Commander-in-Chief (Admiral Sir Andrew Cunningham).

"But, Bertie, you have just said you did agree, did you not?"

"Er — well, yes," from Ramsay.

"All right, Freddie, send it off."

And off it went. The conference over, we had a drink and a chat, and then made our respective ways to bed.

This signal, however, did not receive a very good reception in Algiers, for neither Cunningham nor Tedder liked the suggested changes; Tedder insisting that the airfields at Comiso and Gela must be included in our bridgehead. Montgomery's counter to this was a request for two more assaulting divisions in order to extend our frontage of attack to include Gela.

On the 26th Montgomery flew back to Tunisia and about the same time we heard that Alexander had called a conference at Algiers in order to finalise the plans.

On the 27th I received a signal from the Army Commander to say that he was sick and that I must fly to Algiers to represent him at the Algiers conference. The R.A.F. allotted me a Hudson aircraft, and I spent the 28th preparing my briefs for what was certain to be a very tough battle. I was due to take off at 10 p.m. at an airfield some few miles out of Cairo. After dinner I drove out with my wife and punctually took off on my journey. We landed at El Adem airfield just south of Tobruk to refuel, and here I was given some supper by the Station Commander. During the halt a mist had spread across the desert, and we were kept waiting for it to clear. As it was of considerable importance that I arrived in time, permission was given to take off in spite of the mist. So off we started. I never heard what really happened, but the next thing I knew was arriving back in Cairo in a Bombay ambulance plane. Apparently we had cleared the ground, but subsequently crashed. The plane was written off, but neither I nor any of the crew were killed. There were some fractures and I was concussed. My wife was told to go out to the same airfield, and was a bit shaken to see me returning so soon on a stretcher!

Montgomery ordered Leese (30th Corps), who was now in Cairo, to go instead, and he took off on the 29th for Algiers.

The result of this accident was that after a few days in bed I was ordered a rest, and my wife and I spent a delightful three weeks' holiday in Syria.

Montgomery being fit again, the Supreme Commander held a conference at Algiers on May 2nd in order to thrash out the final plan. As a result the American assault on north-west Sicily was abandoned, and Patton would now land in the Gulf of Gela. These modifications gave us what we required, and everyone knew where they were.

IV

I feel I had better tidy up the end of the Tunisian campaign, which I rather left in the air in the last chapter.

By the end of April we had yet not been able to break through the enemy's last defences. Eighth Army's attacks in the Enfidaville sector had not produced tangible results, and the country was most unsuitable for offensive action. On the 30th I think, in answer to a request from Montgomery, Alexander flew to his Headquarters to discuss the situation. The former stressed the unlikelihood of achieving rapid success in his Army's area, and suggested that some of his divisions might be more usefully employed elsewhere. As a result of this conference the 7th Armoured Division, the 4th Indian Division and the 201st Guards' Brigade were transferred to First Army. Horrocks went as well, for the Commander of the British 9th Corps had been wounded.

This addition of strength made First Army's offensive irresistible, and Tunis and Bizerta fell on May 7th, and all resistance ceased on the 12th. One of our divisions which had fought all the way from El Alamein — the 7th Armoured — was first into Tunis. Which unit reached the city first will long remain an inter-regimental dispute. Probably the 11th Hussars — possibly the 1st Royal Tanks.

V

During my sick leave in Syria I handed over my work to Graham, and to Belchem (G.S.O. 1 Operations). I arrived back to find that they had done extremely well in my absence, and that preparations were well and truly launched.

In spite of my sore head, this holiday in Syria was a real delight. Springtime in the Levant is hard to beat in any part of the world I have yet visited, and as I derived such joy from the visit, I propose to give a short description of it in the hope that it may refresh the reader who must by now be somewhat weary of tales of war.

We left Cairo by car as the sun was rising, breakfasted at Ismailia, and then across the Canal to the Sinai Desert. The boredom of these leagues of barrenness provides a fitting contrast to the green fields and hills of Palestine. By the time you reach them you are thirsting for shade and looking for relief from the glare of sun and sand. We spent the first night at the King David's Hotel in Jerusalem, and here one appeared to be back in the days of peace — it certainly made it easier to try and forget the war. And so to bed, with the many church bells ringing their awakening some eight hours later.

The drive from Jerusalem to Baalbek — our first perching point — was as lovely as one could hope for. Past the sea of Galilee under the shadows of snow-capped Hermon, through to the Baalbek Plain. The trees, the ripening corn, and above all the myriads of wild flowers, made this long journey a thing of joy. The object of our expedition to this historic town was not to pry into the remains of past eras and of wars, but to use it as a base from which to catch the fine trout that live in the Orontes river between this city and its neighbour Homs. Half the charm of the fishing here is the unexpectedness of it all. When driving along the hot and dusty road to Homs, it is hard to imagine that within a couple of miles there flows an ice-cool river speeding like the Dee or Spey, and within its crystal waters are to be found the most delicious and warlike trout. The river rises from a series of gushing springs, right out of the rocky side of the Lebanon massif. It is ice-cold at first, but as it wends its way towards the sea the sun gets to work, and after a few miles it becomes too warm for the trout to live. But in this cooler stretch which runs through a narrow but fertile valley, the sport is good and well worth a visit. I'm afraid grenades and sticks of dynamite used by both soldiers and the Arab have taken their toll. But I hope the Syrian Government will do something to preserve this unique spot which must surely prove of considerable value to them from the tourist angle.

We spent three days at Baalbek, leaving our hotel each morning before the sun was up, and then moved on to Beyruth and the blue Mediterranean sea. Here we heard of a small inn situated in the Lebanon hills, cool and perched amongst the pine trees. They said the food was good and the hotel clean. We shall never regret our visit. We stayed there nearly a fortnight, leading a really idle life. The food was excellent, and the most lovely walks were to be had. There was even a trout stream within a stone's throw of the hotel, where with luck some sport could be had. Our two hosts were charming. They took life as it came. One had spent some years in the States, but now was prepared to enjoy the lesser *tempo* of his own country. Some days he would remain all day in his pyjamas and dressing-gown — why should he change? — it was warm and there was little work to do. Then on other mornings we would see him all spruced up as if about to stroll down Fifth Avenue en route to a luncheon date. I envied him his contentment and repose. In the evenings we would all sit out on the terrace under the pines, drinking arak and nibbling little Arab delicacies such as olives, sour cheeses and stuffed gherkins.

The days flew by, and I broke the journey back to Egypt by a visit to the Haifa Staff College, where I tried to describe Montgomery's triumphal progress from El Alamein. I'm afraid it was rather long, and perhaps I was a bit too enthusiastic — but we felt very proud of our Commander and the Army's achievements.

During the short period we had been away the temperature of Cairo had risen considerably, and the hot weather had set in. It took therefore a great effort to cast this recent pleasant interlude from my mind, and once again settle down to warlike things — planning in the summer heat.

VI

"D" day was to be July 10th, and so there was still between six and seven weeks to go.

Montgomery's prestige was now very high, which was very noticeable when he paid two short visits to Cairo in this preparatory phase, and he spoke to both officers and men. He would attend a church service at the Cathedral, and then talk to the troops afterwards in a nearby hall. Crowds would attend and listen to these simple and whimsical chats in which the Army Commander told them how he beat Rommel. For the officers, he delivered lectures to many hundreds of them in which he put over the lessons from his own experience. How many officers have I heard change an uninformed opinion of Montgomery after listening to one of these!

During one of these visits he gave out his orders to his Commanders. It was done with the utmost confidence, and if there had been any doubters beforehand, I'm sure they left that room feeling that there was now no chance of failure. The Navy were not so comforting, for we had to listen to a long list of things that might go wrong, but in spite of that we knew that Admiral Ramsay and his ships would see us through. The Army Commander's orders were followed by a sort of "war game." We set problems to the various Commanders and their Naval and Air opposite numbers, in order to test their plans. This lasted a day, and it brought out many useful lessons.

Before the assault took place the Allied Air Forces were to carry out operations to ensure non-interference by the enemy's ships and air forces. This was no light undertaking, for the Axis had concentrated a very formidable air force in the Central Mediterranean area. The seaborne assault had the initial object of capturing the ports of Syracusa. The assault was to be assisted by an airborne operation, and once we had firmly established ourselves, operations were to be developed to capture the whole island. During this phase the seizing of the ports of Augusta and Catania, as well as the airfields in the Catanian Plain, were to be given high priority.

Patton's Seventh Army, after landing in the Gulf of Gela, capturing the port of Licata and the airfields of the Comiso group, was to ensure the security of our left flank during the advance northwards.

Eighth Army was to land with 13th Corps in the Gulf of Noto, south of Syracusa, and with 30th Corps around the point of the Pachino peninsula. The airborne troops were to be dropped an hour or two before the seaborne assault, just west of Syracusa with the main object of capturing a most important bridge over the Anapo river. If this bridge were blown, our seizing of the port might be dangerously delayed. Commando troops were also to be landed to deal with enemy coastal batteries. Dempsey with his 13th Corps had initially the major task, and Leese with 30th Corps was to assist him by establishing contact as rapidly as possible, and then to take over areas captured by 13th Corps, and so allow Dempsey to pursue his main object. 30th Corps had also the responsibility of ensuring the early capture of the airfield area on the Pachino Peninsula as well as to link up with Patton's forces.

The landings were, of course, to be supported by naval guns and aircraft.

Towards the end of June it became clear that the enemy's garrison of Sicily consisted of two German armoured divisions, and five Italian divisions. There were a further six Italian coastal divisions carrying out coast defence duties. The location of these forces showed that he was fully alive to the probability of an assault in the very area which we had chosen, but they also showed that he was worried about the security of the island from landings in the west. All our means of deception were aimed at making him sensitive about this latter area.

VII

During the final phase of the preparations large scale rehearsals were carried out, and the Army Commander toured all formations to give his customary pre-battle pep talk. 13th

Corps carried out practice landings in the Gulf of Akaba, and the Gulf of Suez. They were impressive affairs, and a great many lessons were learnt. Only a fraction of the vehicles were loaded and waterproofed, but it gave us a good check up on such important matters as signal communications, times for unloading, waterproofing and, fire support. I never had a chance of witnessing 30th Corps' rehearsals which took place so far away. The Canadian division's training and rehearsals were completed in the United Kingdom, and it gave some of our staff an excellent and quite justifiable reason for paying a quick visit by air to their homes. Montgomery even found time to pay a visit to England during May.

The Secretary of State for War, Sir James Grigg, flew out to the Middle East on a visit before we set off. He was able to attend at least one of the Army Commander's talks to officers. I drove down with him on this occasion when Montgomery was talking to the officers of the 50th Division near Suez. I knew Grigg well when I was Military Assistant to Hore-Belisha, and he was the Permanent Under-Secretary at the War Office. I had always liked him and admired his outspokenness. We had a very interesting talk on the way down to Suez. He was obviously delighted with the Army's latest successes. He told me it had been his great aim to restore the Army's prestige in the eyes of the nation. Dunkerque, Greece and the setbacks in the desert had made our stock slump pretty low. He now felt that we were back once more in the public favour, and one could sense how thankful he was at this change. His attitude towards Montgomery was most interesting. He did not know him, and although he was most grateful for the way he had led his troops to victory, I think he was prepared to be critical — Grigg is always that. The sudden publicity and the dictatorial tone in some of Montgomery's signals had no doubt worried him a little. I was greatly intrigued, for I knew that he would be converted. We discussed various controversial matters on the way down, and I explained the reasons behind some of my Chief's views.

On arrival at the camp Grigg met Montgomery, and the Secretary of State saw a demonstration — of which we were by now well accustomed — by the soldiers when their Army Commander arrived. They swarmed around his car shouting and cheering. In the big lecture hall Montgomery got up and delivered his address. It was the usual type. He started by explaining some of the things which he considered important in making war. Then he switched to the matter in hand — the invasion. He discussed the plan, the reasons behind it, and his confidence in it. I believe Grigg must have been surprised at the quiet way in which it was all given. No bombastic rhetoric, no pompous boasts, but plain commonsense given out by one who was obviously a master of his craft. No notes were used throughout. At the end there were spontaneous cheers, and then the Secretary of State for War was asked to say a few words. It must have been difficult in front of that audience, and after the last speaker. However, the right things were said, and I'm sure none of us looked upon Grigg as a pompous politician — he got away with it, and went down well. Ever since that day the two men have been firm friends and have held a great respect for one another.

We had decided to move Army Headquarters to Malta for the opening phase and as, by the end of June, nothing more could be done, we sailed from Alexandria at the beginning of July. Montgomery at this time was back at Tripoli, and was to join his Headquarters in Malta early in the month.

A few of us travelled in a cruiser with Admiral Ramsay and his Chief of Staff. The Royal Navy, as is their custom, were most hospitable and gave up their cabins to the soldiers. It was a very pleasant voyage, for we had a rest from work, and it was calm and enemy aircraft kept out of our way. On arrival at Malta we went up to the buildings which had been taken over for our mess, and then I went to have a look at the Headquarters offices, which had been established in the deep underground tunnels that had proved so valuable to the Island during the dark days of the blitz.

I found most of the Army staff already installed and cordial relations had been established with the Naval and Air Headquarters. It was hot in Malta at the time, but down below in the tunnels it was cooler, but rather damp. Excellent operations rooms had been constructed. For instance, in the Naval Operations room you could see the hour by hour progress of the convoys, the position of H.M. ships and any incident caused by the enemy was immediately posted up. The Air Operations room was equally impressive; fighter control, bombing operations, and enemy activity were all to be seen at a glance. In the Army room things were quiet for the moment, just great maps of the bridgehead area, the beaches and objectives marked, and the various flags and tapes ready to show the progress of our assault forces when the moment arrived. Then there was another room which dealt with the "ferry service" which would operate after the assault landings. Here would be controlled the flow of units, vehicles and equipment belonging to the three services.

Once set up in our new offices there was little we could do but wait. One by one the convoys sailed from their various ports, and were dully plotted on the great charts. Enemy submarines accounted for three ships during their passage, but otherwise our losses up to the rendezvous south of Sicily were very slight.

The Army Commander arrived on the 3rd, and by the afternoon of July 9th all the Chief Commanders were there, from Eisenhower downwards. Another visitor was Mountbatten who, as Chief of Combined Operations, had come to see how the new technique was to fare.

One afternoon I went with the Army Commander to be shown by Air Marshal Park the R.A.F. set-up for the initial phase. It was most interesting to see how a very great air force had been housed in Malta. Great ingenuity had been shown in building the airfields. All the Malta personnel were itching to have their revenge against their late oppressors.

For the last week or two very heavy bomber attacks had been made against the enemy's air forces and airfields, and undoubtedly very great damage had been done. But the enemy was obviously endeavouring to conserve his fighters until "D" Day, had withdrawn some units to the mainland, and in any case would not come up and fight. This we felt at the time was a little disturbing, as it might mean that we should be opposed by a strong air force during the landings. In the event, however, our fears were unjustified, and Tedder, the Fortresses and the Allied pilots had seen to that.

We bathed a good deal to keep cool, and afterwards in the evenings I would sit on a rock looking out towards Sicily and wonder what the next few days had in store for us. I lunched with Lord Gort, the Governor, and we chatted about old times — he had been Commandant of the Staff College at Camberley when I was there.

During the last two days the inhabitants of Malta saw many visible signs of the impending operations. Troops were being got ready, and then embarked into various types of landing craft. Vehicles were being waterproofed and shipped aboard the L.S.T.'s and other vessels. We were visited by an American journalist who offered Montgomery £20,000 on account for his diaries. Alexander with an echelon of the 15th Army Group Staff had arrived, and I had various talks with General Richardson, his Chief of Staff. There was little we could do but try to fill in time and so speed on the vital hour. The Army Commander gave his usual pre-battle talk to the staff and radiated his usual confidence. He did, however, predict some difficult fighting ahead.

During July 9th the various convoys which had sailed from so many ports arrived at their rendezvous with clock-like precision. The Navies had done their work well, and I am told that the sight to the east and west of Malta was really impressive. Admiral Ramsay spent the day cruising amongst the armada in his makeshift flag-ship, which in peace time had been employed in the onion trade. Now all hope of deception was at an end — the enemy must know more or less where the blow would fall. Miles Graham and I went shopping in the late afternoon, and thought ourselves rather clever in finding some silk stockings which we sent off to our wives. Our choice could not have been of the best, for later we heard that each had given them away to friends!

About 6 p.m. I strolled along to have a chat with Admiral Power, the Admiral Commanding at Malta. He had shown himself a true friend of the Army, and we liked and admired this breezy and cheerful character. Out came a bottle of gin, and we drank to the success of the landings. A little later disturbing news came in about the weather. A "force 6" wind was blowing and a heavy sea running which made a lot of troops seasick. It also would delay the "marrying up" of the less seaworthy landing craft with their bigger sisters. The Commanders-in-Chief met and decided to let things take their course. There was really nothing else to do — postponement would have been impossible at this late stage, and the resultant disruption would have been worse than any caused by the storm. We saw some of the troops off on their craft and I gave a talk to a number of officers who had arrived out from England as observers. I'm afraid their observing was restricted to the Malta end of things, and they remained there until we were sure that their presence would not embarrass the Commanders ashore.

After dinner I went to bed at the usual time, and was awakened in the early hours when the first reports began to trickle in. By breakfast time it looked as if things were going well and our hopes were high. The wind had abated, and other than some delay in the arrival of landing craft, there had been no serious results. The Allied air forces had gained complete supremacy, and there had been very little reaction on the part of German or Italian aircraft.

VIII

The airborne assault had been the only part of the operation that had not been a great success. Yet in spite of this the troops, showing great bravery, held on to the important bridge south of Syracusa until relieved by 13th Corps. Many of the pilots of the transport aircraft had never flown an operational flight before, and coming up against flak for the first time is most unpleasant. Then the strong wind did not help matters. As a result of all this many of the airborne troops landed in the water and lost their lives by drowning. General Browning, the Commander of Airborne Forces, was always afraid that this lack of training of the pilots might face them with too difficult a test on the day itself. Between Sicily and Normandy great strides were made, and those later landings were a conspicuous success.

The 30th Corps had the easiest task, and by the first evening were in possession of the peninsula and the Pachino airfield. 13th Corps had more difficulties, but secured their beaches, had pressed inland and had captured Syracusa by nightfall. The port, luckily, was found to be undamaged. We had not met any German troops so far, and the Italians — particularly the troops of the coastal divisions — were quite ready to give themselves up. The American Army was not so fortunate, and soon after landing they were counter-attacked by German troops. Some very stiff fighting took place about Gela. The situation was, however, restored by the dogged fighting of the Americans, by the U.S. Navy steaming close inshore and giving very close range support, and by the courageous leadership of George Patton, who had come ashore at the danger point personally to supervise the operations.

Back in Malta we were primarily engaged in the laying on of air support and supervising the Ferry Control Service. I was chairman of the inter-service priority committee and we used to meet once or twice a day to decide in what order the various units, vehicles, etc., should be sent to Sicily. The ports used were Tripoli, Sousse/Sfax and Malta. We had a special wireless link with the former two.

Once the Army Commander realised that the landings had been successful, he decided to move his Tactical Headquarters over to Sicily. He left Malta himself on the 11th, but there was some muddle over the loading of vehicles, and he was without a home on the island for nearly twenty-four hours. I received the sharpest signal I think I ever got from him, and I no doubt deserved it. One thing I know, it never happened again!

I decided to pay a visit to my Chief on the 12th and asked Graham to come with me. Admiral Ramsay gave us a lift in a destroyer. I have found a letter which I wrote at the time describing these twenty-four hours, which I think gives a good impression of what things were like at that time.

Malta,
July 13th, 1943.

"Monty" had gone over to Sicily the day before I left, and Miles Graham and I went in a destroyer with our Admiral with the object of seeing him and discussing the situation.

We left here about 7 a.m. and zigzagged our way to the south-east tip of Sicily. En route we saw a magnificent sight — the two great battleships "Nelson" and "Rodney" and an aircraft carrier escorted by destroyers — sailing majestically by. We had no trouble with enemy aircraft on the way over — in fact, the only excitement was a mine blown up in front of us when approaching the island.

The picture of the beaches was an extraordinary one. Numbers of great ships lying close in with lines of landing craft going to and from the shore, carrying M.T. and stores. Interspersed and outside this great array were warships and destroyers. It seemed incredible that they could all lie there so near to Italy. The enemy bombed them during the night and early morning, but when we arrived Spitfires were already cruising overhead, and the few enemy aircraft that approached were soon seen off.

Sicily from the sea looked delightful and we had a great desire to step ashore on enemy territory.

We first called on one of the H.Q. ships[28] and spoke to the Admiral and Army staff. Whilst there I received a message which suggested that the Army Commander was in the immediate vicinity — the Pachino peninsula — and so I arranged to go ashore to meet him, and be picked up in the evening by Admiral Ramsay. After he left, however, I found that a mistake had been made, and that the V.I.P. was really General "Ike," who was paying a visit to these parts.

---

[28] Headquarters ship of the Canadian Division

I went ashore and had a good look round the Canadian Division's beach. They had not had an easy time as the swell got up each day and only allowed a few hours for working from ship to shore. Some thirty of their seventy L.C.M.'s[29] were aground ashore. There is no doubt that if heavy initial fighting had been required on the part of this division, it would have soon met serious maintenance difficulties.

I then returned aboard the H.Q ship ("Hilary") and sent out signals to try and locate "Master," and whilst awaiting replies had a chat and some excellent cocktails with Admiral Vian who is a most impressive man possessing great charm and drive. No one seemed to know where Monty was; so I asked Vian to lend me a destroyer so that I could catch up with Admiral Ramsay, and then go ashore at Syracusa. This he readily agreed to and sent me off in an M.L. with an order to the first destroyer I met on patrol. We soon hailed a destroyer and I jumped aboard, and immediately we were proceeding at high speed off the east coast of Sicily. The amount of shipping lying off the various beaches was most impressive, and one wondered how the enemy allowed us to land so easily when one saw the formidable Avola plateau which dominated all the beaches in this area.

When off "Acid North" beach we found Admiral Ramsay's destroyer and the H.Q. ship of 13th Corps. After a chat we left for Syracusa with him, and entered the port. It is an excellent harbour and no demolitions had been carried out. It should be able to take up to 4,000 tons per day. The town had been badly knocked about by the R.A.F. The railway is in good working order and there were thirteen locos, in the sidings. These should prove very useful. At about that time we could see some of H.M. ships bombarding targets near Augusta.

I then set out for 13th Corps Tactical H.Q.'s, where I hoped to find the Army Commander. After I left Ramsay's

---

[29] L.C.M.s — a type of landing craft.

destroyer proceeded to Augusta and entered the harbour. Shortly after landing the party and ship were shelled by the enemy, and they had to beat a hasty retreat under a smoke screen.

On the way into Syracusa we saw an Italian submarine which, having surrendered, was being towed into port.

We borrowed a 3-ton lorry and started down the road to Tac H.Q., 13th Corps. There were some gliders lying near the bridge just south of Syracusa which had been the objective of the airborne troops on "D" night. It is a good thing they fought so well and prevented it being demolished, as much bridging would have been required to create a crossing; and the delay involved might have been disastrous.

We found General Dempsey at his H.Q. but no Army Commander, who, we were informed, had gone back to his camp near Tac 30th Corps H.Q., near Pachino. After a chat with Dempsey we borrowed a car and drove down to Pachino. The country through which we passed is delightful. Vineyards, olive trees and plenty of other trees and vegetation. Beautiful wooded hills run down close to the shore. The towns are not impressive — very poor looking. The people's attitude was amazing. They lined the roads and appeared to be most friendly, waving their arms and making "V" signs. We passed many farm carts laden with household effects carrying inhabitants back to their homes — presumably they fled into the country upon our invasion.

We had no excitement on the way down except two 190's dropping bombs well wide of the road which obviously did no damage whatever. We arrived at Tac Army H.Q., which was situated in some trees near the Pachino L.G.[30] next door to 30th Corps H.Q.'s.

I had a long chat with the Army Commander and then dined. After dinner we went over to 30th Corps Mess for a drink, and found them entertaining the Italian General

---

[30] Landing Ground.

commanding the coastal division who had surrendered that day. I had a talk with him. He was obviously very tired of war, and thought that the Italian field divisions had let him down. He is not fond of the Germans.

Later on in the evening Mountbatten came in from the American sector; he reported good progress and told us that 196 Axis aircraft were found on Comiso L.G. A discussion on combined operation questions went on until well past midnight.

From dark that night and practically through until 08.30 hours enemy aircraft came over with the object of attacking the shipping lying off the beaches and the Pachino L.G. It was the noisiest night I have spent for a long time. We were surrounded on three sides by the Beach A.A. defences, outside these the ships' A.A. opened fire, and in and around us were the guns protecting the Pachino L.G. One aircraft was brought down nearly in our camp — quite a spectacular party.

Although the R.A.F. H.Q.'s could not move to Sicily until we captured the Catania airfields we decided that Main Army H.Q.'s must move over at once, and so I asked Admiral Vian to give me a destroyer to take me back to Malta in order to wind up our activities there. He kindly obliged and I left the beach about 8 a.m.

No ships or aircraft were hit in the raids during the night, and a number of enemy aircraft were shot down. The amount of A.A. ammunition shot off gave poor Miles a "pain in the neck," but now with Syracusa open, our maintenance situation should be assured.

I landed back here at about 10 p.m. and immediately held a staff conference to settle the move. I shall leave to-morrow for Sicily again.

On arrival back, I made immediate arrangements to move the Headquarters to Sicily. As the R.A.F. were still using to a large extent the airfields in Malta, their Main Headquarters could not come over with us. In its place an advanced control section was sent, and with this arrangement we managed to run the air support side of our activities for some days. The site chosen was an area on the coast north of Syracusa. It turned out to be rather an unpleasant spot at night, as the enemy raided the shipping and other targets about Syracusa and Augusta each night, and we received a continuous hail of anti-aircraft shrapnel from the guns defending both ports. We also received the enemy's "*overs*" from Syracusa. After some large pieces of shrapnel had hit and near-missed the Army Commander's caravan a couple of nights running, I got the Engineers — unbeknown to him — to reinforce its top with some steel plating. The R.A.F. night fighters and the A.A. guns took a heavy toll of enemy aircraft, but we lost several good ships. One night an ammunition ship was hit, and the firework display was almost too terrible to watch.

IX

First Phase.

I will deal with the operations in three phases. The first phase includes the landings and the rapid advance to the Catanian plain.

Immediately after Montgomery landed in Sicily he decided that he must aim at securing the main road centres. In this way, because of the difficulty of moving off the roads over most of the country, the enemy's movement would be restricted. The 13th Corps was ordered to advance on Catania, and the 30th Corps to move by the axis Caltagirone and Enna to Leonforte — the latter being a major road centre to the west of Mount Etna.

In order to accelerate their advance, 13th Corps staged an airborne attack on the important Prima Sole bridge over the Simeto river, on the night of July 13th-14th. Again only a portion of the airborne force arrived near their target, but they managed to remove the charges, and after some very fierce fighting were joined by the leading troops of 13th Corps on the morning of the 15th. On July 16th we had, after exceptionally bitter fighting, established a bridgehead north of the river, but an attempt to break out and advance towards Catania by 50th Division failed. And here the Corps was held up for some time.

On the left flank 30th Corps fought their way forward, and 51st Division captured Vizzini on July 14th. It was at this stage that the Army Commander decided to order the 1st Canadian Division to continue the advance on Leonforte, and for the 51st Division to change its axis of advance and start an advance towards Paterno on the 16th. The objects were to clear up the area between the two main thrusts, and to assist 13th Corps in their hard struggle towards Catania. This division crossed the Simeto and advanced to within a dozen miles of Paterno where they were held up. By this action they captured the important airfields at Gerbini (July 21st).

The Canadians captured Leonforte on July 21st, and the 231st Infantry Brigade operating between the Canadian Division and the Highlanders had reached on the 19th a point just south of Agira, on the main Aderno-Leonforte road.

Whilst these moves were being carried out by Eighth Army, the Seventh U.S. Army were on the 15th given the task of capturing Caterina. By the 22nd the Americans were in Termini on the coast to the east of Palermo, thereby cutting the island in half.

We had reason to be satisfied with our progress, but from now onwards things were not going to be so easy. In the first place, the enemy had more or less recovered his balance and was able to concentrate his troops in a smaller area. It was now clear that he was determined to delay us as much as possible in our advance towards Messina. Sooner or later he must be forced out of Sicily XVIth the Italians fighting so badly, but the greater delay the better for the Axis. It would give the Germans time to organise the defence of Italy itself, and the denial of the excellent airfields around Catania to our large air forces was another important factor. The enemy was now pivoting on the Catania-Etna positions, the country around there being perfect for defence. The lava and the closeness of the country made movement off the roads almost impossible, and extensive demolitions were met with whenever we advanced. It was now impossible to exploit our great armoured superiority — advances had often to be made on a one tank front. Then of course the observation from Etna and her foothills gave the enemy considerable advantages. Finally, after many days of continuous fighting in extremely hot and unpleasant weather the troops were growing tired. In order to have fresh troops the Army Commander on July 20th ordered over the 78th Division from Sousse.

In order to stem our advance towards Catania the Germans had flown in paratroops from the mainland of Italy, and these men fought with fanatical savagery. One heard several stories at the time which well illustrated the effect that Nazi political injections can have upon basically brave men. During the fighting across the Simeto these incidents occurred. A wounded German was lying on a stretcher at a dressing station having his wounds dressed by one of our orderlies. Directly he recovered sufficient strength he turned over, seized the orderly's hand and plunged his teeth deep into it, shouting some Nazi invective. Another, when being interrogated by one of our officers, drew himself up to attention and spat deliberately into his face. A third, who was wounded, managed to stand up, pulled out his revolver, shouted "Heil Hitler" and shot himself. Then there was a German paratroop officer who had been dropped wide of the mark and landed behind our lines. He managed to get hold of a suit of civilian clothes and was subsequently captured by us. He was brought along to my caravan. He refused to give anything except his rank and name. I then told him that having been captured in our lines wearing civilian clothes, he was liable to be shot — in fact that was to be his fate. His face never showed the least reaction. He said, "That is quite understood. I took the risk and failed — I deserve it — Heil Hitler," and then saluted and was marched away. I did not have him shot, principally because I intended making some capital out of it over the B.B.C. in the hope that the enemy might deal similarly with any of our paratroops who had been dropped wide and were probably trying the same thing. We had far more paratroops at large than had the enemy.

From Syracusa we moved our Headquarters to Lentini. It was very hot and dusty here. I have never met in any part of the world such oppressive heat. No wonder our troops found it so trying — particularly those who were fighting in the plains. Once or twice Graham and I took our camp beds and batmen up into the hills for the night. Here in the cool atmosphere we ate and drank in peace and quiet, arriving back early next morning much refreshed. Corporal Reeves had been with Graham in civil life for many years, and became a soldier to serve as his batman for the duration of the war. He was the perfect batman and never lowered his high standard. At any time, under any conditions, he could answer his master's needs — whether they might be in the shape of a bottle of port, a meal, a cigar, a dry pair of socks! He and my servant, Lawrence, made a good team. The Main Headquarters remained here until the end of the campaign.

After we left the Syracusa area, General Alexander and his 15th Army Group Headquarters came over and established themselves to the south of that town.

Second Phase.

Faced with this difficult situation on his right flank, Montgomery decided on July 21st to switch the weight of his attack to the left flank. 13th Corps and the 51st Division assumed for the time being a defensive role, whilst 30th Corps, reinforced by the fresh 78th Division, continued the attack with the object of advancing round the west side of Etna to threaten the rear of the remaining enemy positions. Aderno and then Randazzo were the key centres on this line of approach. The thrust towards Aderno was made by the Canadians along the axis of the Leonforte road and the 78th Division by way of Catenanuova and Centuripe. Agira fell on July 28th, Catenanuova on the 30th, and Centuripe was in our hands on August 3rd. This latter town was perched on top of a pinnacle of a hill, the road reaching the summit by a difficult and tortuous route. It was the last objective one would choose for an attack, but there was no alternative. I sat and watched this attack from another high hill to the south, and it appeared too much to ask any troops to undertake. Yet with air and artillery support this fine division climbed the height and after the fiercest fighting they captured the town. It was an inspiring sight, and Centuripe will for ever spell valour in the records of the 78th.

On August 4th Montgomery ordered 30th Corps to press on towards Aderno, and after a link up with 13th Corps had been made to the north of Etna, General Leese (30th Corps) was to assume command of all troops necessary for the final drive to Messina. The Army Commander had made this decision in order to allow 13th Corps to start planning the next campaign, i.e. the landing in Italy. He also instructed the Corps to bring into reserve the 5th and Canadian Divisions as soon as possible, with the same object in view.

These tactics began to bear fruit, for on August 3rd the enemy began withdrawing from the Catania sector and this allowed 13th Corps to go over once again to the offensive. In spite of strong enemy rearguards, helped by demolitions and the difficult country, Catania, Paterno and Misterbianco fell on August 5th. The next day Aderno was captured by 78th Division after some very heavy air bombing support. On the same date the Americans were reported in Troina; and so the important centre of Randazzo was now under a double threat.

Demolitions, the lava, and the effects of our own bombing made the advance northwards very slow. Bronte fell on August 8th and Randazzo was captured by the Seventh U.S. Army on the 13th. In order to speed up matters, the Army Commander ordered the 5th Division once again into the line, so that 13th Corps could develop a two divisional thrust on the east side of Etna. This division was, however, relieved almost at once, on August 11th by the 51st. We were due to land in Italy three weeks later.

Whilst all these thrusts were taking place in the shadows of Etna, another American advance was progressing well along the axis of the northern coast road of Sicily. Previous to this Palermo had been captured, and the whole of the western part of the island was in American hands.

On July 28th, Montgomery flew over to visit Patton at his newly established headquarters in Palermo. The A.O.C. — Broadhurst — and I went with him. We took off in the Fortress from an airfield near Syracusa and flew south round the coast until we reached Licata. It was interesting to see the scene of the Seventh Army's great fight at Gela. From here we flew inland and made straight for Palermo. The airfield was not a good one, having a very short runway, and surrounded by hills, which makes the wind rather treacherous. Just as we were landing the wind changed round completely, and for a few moments it looked as if we were certain to overshoot the landing strip. However, by the maximum application of the brakes and by swinging round as we approached the limits, we arrived safely. I remember remarking as we left the airfield that I hoped our brakes hadn't been burnt out.

Patton met us and Montgomery inspected a guard of honour which was formed up in front of the headquarters. There was a band in attendance and everyone was very much on their toes. The headquarters was housed in the Royal Palace which contained many fine pictures and treasures. We immediately sat down to luncheon which was simple but excellently cooked. Patton was a delightful host and was full of good stories about the campaign. One could sense his great love of the American fighting man.

Luncheon finished, we adjourned to another room to discuss future plans. The stage had now been reached when, unless we were careful, we might get in each other's way. With the two armies converging on the restricted area now held by the enemy, questions relating to boundaries, maintenance routes and air support had to be most carefully tied up. We had come with definite proposals, and with slight modifications, these were agreed to by Patton. After the conference, Montgomery gave a short interview to the American war correspondents. We then returned to the airfield and took off for Syracusa.

After we had been in the air about half an hour, the captain of the aircraft came along to Broadhurst and me and told us that the brakes had given out, and therefore a landing at our home airfield was out of the question. This was not a very pleasant bit of information to receive in mid-air. After discussions, it was decided to try and land at the Comiso airfield, as it had a long runway. We altered our course and arrived over our destination. The runway appeared to have been repaired and there were a couple of our own aircraft parked near to it. Off the runway the grass field was studded with bomb craters, some of which had been filled in. Our pilot considered that if we landed on the runway itself, he could never be able to pull up in time and so chose to land on the grass field. There were two snags about this: first we did not know if the mines had all been lifted, and secondly the choosing of a line which was clear of craters was not easy. We flew backwards and forwards at nought feet until the line had been definitely selected, and then the pilot brought the big plane in to land. None of us was feeling too happy, and we were all very relieved when we touched down. But even then it wasn't over, for we bumped our way across the grass apparently losing very little speed. When nearing the end of the field our pilot swung the machine round on one wing, and she came to rest. It was a very fine piece of airmanship, and unless the pilot had kept his head, we might well have had a bad mishap. We sent a wireless message to call up another aircraft, and after an hour's waiting we all flew back in a Mitchell bomber. On arrival back at his headquarters, Montgomery sent a signal to Eisenhower asking for another aircraft. He received a Dakota in the Fortress's place, which was far more suited to the task. This aircraft accompanied him back to England from Italy, and was eventually written off by the Germans during their attack on our airfields in Belgium on January 1st, 1945.

During this period I received the first information suggesting Italy might ask for an armistice. I think the Army Commander and myself were the only ones "in the know," and although we didn't expect the Germans to withdraw from Italy as a result, it certainly gave me some private excitement. To talk about further developments in this matter, as well as other business, I used to meet Richardson (Alexander's Chief of Staff) in the hills at a place called Palazzolo. It was about mid-way between our respective headquarters, and was cool. We used to bring our lunch, and I enjoyed these discussions a great deal. We called them the "Palazzolo conversations."

In addition to all the work in connection with current operations I became deeply involved in planning for the next phase, i.e. the assault into Italy. Our task was made as difficult as possible, as no firm decision as to which plan was to be adopted was made until very late.

The original proposal was for Eighth Army to assault across the Straits of Messina with one Corps, and for the 10th Corps — then in Tripoli — to land in the area of Gioia. These operations went by the code names of "Baytown" and "Buttress" respectively. Even if in early August a firm decision had been given that they would both take place, planning would still have been most difficult. To start with until the Sicilian campaign was over we should not know which formations and units would be available. Then there were no firm figures for landing craft and shipping. Without these detailed planning was almost impossible. But to complicate matters still further, another allied operation for which 10th Corps might be required, was being considered at Algiers. This was "Avalanche" — a landing in the bay of Salerno, south of Naples. I was personally very keen about this project as it would, if successful, speed up matters in Italy, and possibly render unnecessary the obviously long and tedious advance from the toe of Italy. There were, however, some great risks — the main one being that of assaulting so far from our air bases. With the use of long range tanks and aircraft carriers it was, however, considered that adequate air support would be forthcoming.

It was not until August 17th that a decision was made. "Baytown" would be carried out by Eighth Army and "Avalanche" by a new American Army. This meant that 10th Corps passed from our command. I was delighted that we now had something definite to work on, and also that "Avalanche" had been agreed to. But I was not happy about Eighth Army's future role. We received at first no clear directive. We did not know whether we should just land in Italy and open up the Straits, and do our best to contain as many enemy with the object of helping "Avalanche," or were we meant to prepare for a major advance right up through Italy itself? Later we received a directive which more or less gave us both tasks. I think the reason for this dilly-dallying was because some people were pinning too much hope upon the coming Italian surrender and they expected that things would loosen up in Italy, and the need for "Baytown" disappear. This attitude undoubtedly led to insufficient foresight being given to the administrative preparations, and because of this we experienced some very anxious times. Montgomery never had any delusions regarding the effect of the Italian capitulation. He always said that the Germans would fight in Italy, and that they would see to it that there would be no nonsense from the Italians in their zone.

Third Phase.

It was now very plain that the days of the Axis in Sicily were numbered and considerable traffic was taking place across the Straits. The flak had then greatly increased and in spite of the gallant efforts by the Navy and air forces, no very great interference resulted. Every sort of small craft was being used.

It now became a race as to which Army would reach Messina first. Patton was coming along the northern coast road at a great pace. He had his whip out, and brought off a very successful little seaborne landing behind the enemy, which accelerated things.

On August 15th we occupied Taormina, but the going was very bad. The coast road clinging as it did to the steep hills made demolitions an easy matter. Bridges had to be built every few hundred yards, and in spite of the use of landing craft to circumvent the obstacles, progress was very slow. In order to speed up our advance, the Army Commander ordered a seaborne landing to be carried out at Ali on the night of August 15th/16th. It was, however, too late, for the enemy had withdrawn.

The Americans won the race and entered Messina on August 16th, and some of our troops who had landed at Ali joined up with them the next day.

I should not end my account of this phase of the campaign without mentioning the help we received from the Royal Navy in so many ways. There was the protection of shipping, the clearance of harbours, the provision of landing craft, and the bombardment of targets from the sea. Then the few landing operations we carried out were laid on by them. We were fortunate in having first-class men to work with. Admiral McGrigor was in command, and we worked through our Naval

Liaison officer and McGrigor's Chief of Staff. We were very sad to lose our N.L.O. who had marched with us from El Alamein, but were lucky to get Clarke in his place, who remained with Eighth Army until the end of the year.

And so Sicily had been captured after a hard fight and Eighth Army had shown themselves able to achieve success in country other than the desert — much to some people's surprise!

X

August 13th was the anniversary of Montgomery's arrival in Eighth Army, and we had a little dinner party at his Tactical Headquarters, which was then situated on the coast a few miles north of Catania. We all felt very proud of our Army Commander who had led us so successfully and so far; and we were all eager to follow him still further. I reproduce here the message which I sent him from the staff, which I think represents our feelings at the time.

> "Personal to Army Commander from Chief of Staff (.) It is exactly a year ago since you took over command of the Eighth Army (.) The anniversary appropriately coincides with the end of enemy resistance in Sicily (.) Tour staff at Army Headquarters wish to send you their warmest congratulations on so successful a year's campaigning (.) We feel certain that under your leadership still greater victories lie ahead (.) We would also like to say how much we have appreciated your understandings guidance and help during this most eventful period (.)"

Looking back on this campaign there appear to me to be three points about which there was some argument al the time, an argument that will probably continue. Were we too slow, considering the strength of the opposition facing us? Were the Americans given an unfair share of the fighting? In other words did we pass the buck to our Allies? Did the Army use the tactical air forces to the best advantage? I will discuss each of these in turn.

I doubt whether anyone will complain about the initial speed of our advance up to the line of the Catanian Plain; nor do I consider the overall period of five weeks for the capture of the island is anything to be ashamed of. It is, however, the rate of progress after reaching the Catanian Plain which requires some examination. I have already given the reasons which decided Montgomery to switch his main axis of advance from the coastal sector to the west of Etna. They were sound ones, i.e. the difficult nature of the country, and the tiredness of the troops. The total enemy force which fought in Sicily consisted of about four German and three Italian divisions. In view of this strength compared with the Allies, could we have driven the enemy out of Catania much earlier? Did we lose an opportunity? My answer to these questions is a decided No. But I qualify this by saying that had some of our divisions been fresher, we might have just done it. In view of the importance of Catania and the nearby airfields this area was the most strongly defended in all Sicily, and this, added to the natural strength of the country, made an advance on this axis most difficult. I remember, however, being most impressed with the fighting power of the fresh 78th Division. Their capture of Centuripe was a remarkable feat, and made me wonder what might have been the result had fresher divisions been available for the initial battle for the Catanian Plain. The lesson I wish to bring out here concerns the selections of formations for a particular enterprise. A Commander naturally is inclined to rely upon those divisions that have done him well in the past, and be rather shy of those about which he knows little. In this particular case some of our divisions had become rather stale and tired before the invasion of Sicily. Besides having fought almost continually from Alamein to Tunis, some formations and units had been employed in the Desert long before Montgomery's arrival. So the lesson to Commanders is — don't overload the faithful horse; and my conclusion is that had the troops which were used in the initial thrust towards Catania been fresher, we *might* have speeded up the campaign.

Once the enemy had concentrated his resources in the difficult country of the north-east corner of the Island, his lack of numbers did not matter. Even to the west of Etna — the new axis of our main thrust — the country was no better. We could not use our great superiority, and the lava and terraced countryside minimised the use of tanks. The enemy carried out a very thorough demolition plan, and this and the terrain made any exploitation impossible. Critics of our slowness should pay a visit to Sicily, and I'm sure they will be astonished at the natural difficulties which they will find.

I now come to the question of whether the Seventh U.S. Army were given an unfair share of the work, and whether their exploits tended to reflect badly upon our fighting qualities. At the time a number of us were rather worried by the comparison of achievement; and on occasions I had to swallow hard when this was pointed out to me. But after having seen all the country and reviewed the campaign as a whole, I felt that we could hardly be held to blame. The rapid advance northwards through the centre of Sicily and the spectacular occupation of most of the island by the Americans was unquestionably a fine achievement; but the opposition was primarily of a very lukewarm Italian type, and I'm sure that Seventh Army would readily admit that the fighting was not very hard. This was, of course, not the case in the American coastal thrust towards Messina, or in their advance towards

Randazzo. But having seen the country along this northern coast, I would without hesitation say it presented a far easier proposition than our rugged approach from Catania. Then we must remember that the U.S. thrust to Randazzo found the going just as difficult as we did. Given similar country there was little if any difference in the speed of our operations.

So my conclusion to the second question is that the Seventh Army after a more difficult start, fought with great valour and determination, but would not have achieved better results after the hold up on the Catanian Plain, if the Armies' sectors had been reversed.

There is one aspect of the employment of the Seventh U.S. Army which calls for comment. Could Messina have been captured earlier if Patton had virtually ignored the Italians in the centre and west of Sicily, and had concentrated all his resources — troops and maintenance — upon getting to Messina? Personally I feel he could have accepted this risk, and although the available axes of advance to Messina open to the Americans were restricted, a speed-up of the campaign could have been achieved.

We had virtual air supremacy in Sicily and very powerful air forces available to support the Army. Rather in the same way as with the Army, it was found difficult to employ fully this superiority. Once the "sticky" period commenced there was little enemy movement, and what did take place was difficult to spot. Night and the tree-lined roads saw to this. The Army as I have said, found progress slow and experienced difficulty in deploying its supporting arms. The rather natural and human reaction was "get the air to blow the enemy's positions to pieces." Our air forces as usual loyally accepted and carried out the Army's requests. But there was a feeling, not shared by the R.A.F. alone, that the effort employed did not produce commensurate results. It led to very heavy attacks on towns which the enemy were holding, and which were blocking our advance. A typical example was Aderno. On the request of 30th Corps a great many tons of bombs were dropped on the town, and it was completely demolished. In addition to the damage to buildings, a number of civilians were killed. The benefits derived from these attacks are difficult to assess. Certainly a number of Germans were killed, and the place became untenable, but on the other hand the resultant mass of debris took hours, if not days, to clear in order to drive a way through. Therefore, any prospect of rapidly exploiting the situation was out of the question. There appeared to be no alternative solution. How could we destroy the opposition and yet not hinder our own advance. Possibly a more selective use against certain targets might have been the answer. But here we were confronted by the great difficulty of accurately locating the enemy and his weapons in this close country. It therefore comes down to this question of the morale or psychological effect upon our own troops. They were tired and irritated by their inability to surmount the various obstacles confronting them. They asked for heavy air support to help them. To refuse would have had a very bad effect, and in this case we felt the heavy expenditure was justified, and on balance it certainly produced results — but not spectacular ones. As is so often the case in war, one must not calculate expenditure of effort in terms of material destruction of the enemy and his resources, but must be guided by the effect upon the enemy's and our own troops' morale. This, as Montgomery has always held, is the most important single factor in war.

On one occasion I put forward a suggestion to the R.A.F. which they tried out. It was to sprinkle the countryside with oil or fire bombs, and so set the vegetation alight. This would force the enemy to move his vehicles from their place of hiding, and so give the fighter-bombers an opportunity of straffing. The operation was carefully laid on, and the attack carried out just before dawn. We hoped that in this way the movement would be in full swing by the time the fighter-bombers got under way. The results were rather disappointing, for the grass and crops did not burn as well as expected. Given more time, however, I believe we could have developed this form of attack to our advantage.

There was criticism at the rather meagre interference with the enemy traffic across the Straits. Here is a most difficult problem for air forces, and one which deserves special study. On occasions such as this, the enemy strengthens up his flak to a very high density and our losses become too great. Small craft are not easy to hit unless very low attacks are made. The flak makes these most hazardous. We experienced a similar problem when the enemy were retreating across the Seine in 1944. Results were far better, but still not good enough.

This brings me to the end of our campaign in Sicily. We thought it was a great achievement, and also thought we knew all about amphibious warfare. Within four months I was to realise how wrong we were!

CHAPTER XII: ITALY — SEPTEMBER. 1943, TO JANUARY, 1944

I

IT was the day after Messina fell that we at last received a firm decision that operations "Avalanche" and "Baytown" were to take place. As, very rightly, the Salerno landing had priority over "Baytown," it meant that we would have to do things on the cheap. This endeared this strategy less than ever to me. The thought of advancing up Italy from the very point of the toe was not very attractive, for never was a country more suited to delaying action. Roads hugged steep cliffs which jutted into the sea, and there were innumerable rivers over which the bridges were certain to be destroyed. It seemed that, unless we were careful, there would be a great expenditure of effort for very little result. Looking back I question whether our strategy was right in this respect.

If the Germans and some Italians were to continue fighting in Italy, then it was necessary to establish a front right across the country from east to west. The point at issue, however, is this — was there a better plan than the one adopted? — i.e. that of landing at Salerno, and moving Eighth Army from the toe up to the East coast about Bari. There were apparently two possible alternatives to this plan. The first was to reinforce "Avalanche" by Eighth Army after Naples had been captured and put in working order. The second to land Eighth Army in the Taranto-Brindisi-Bari area. The first alternative was too much of a risk, and it would have taken too long to get the ports up to the required capacity for the maintenance of two armies. The second was more attractive. An *opposed* landing was out of the question — our shipping and assault craft resources being insufficient for the purpose. But I am not entirely satisfied that we could not have moved a *sufficient* portion of Eighth Army through these ports with the resources we had available, or *should* have had available at the time. In the event, troops were landed at all these ports without opposition on September 9th, whilst Eighth Army, after reaching the Bari-Altamura line, could not advance in strength before the end of September owing to administrative difficulties. We also had to change our base from Reggio to the Adriatic ports — a very complex and expensive business. The point to decide is whether we achieved a good dividend from this long advance, or would it have been possible to have produced similar results by feeding Eighth Army in via the Adriatic ports?

It was certainly necessary to land on the toe of Italy, and so open the Straits to our ships. Could we have limited our activities to this task, and then concentrated upon establishing ourselves in the "heel" and Bari area? Some would like to think — I did at the time — that we helped, if not saved, the situation at Salerno. But now I doubt whether we influenced matters to any great extent. General Clark had everything under control *before* Eighth Army appeared on the scene. In our advance we inflicted very few casualties on the enemy; demolitions and the difficult country were our principal worries. If this is accepted, then the problem resolves itself into the availability of shipping and landing craft. I knew we were very short to start with. But I also know that after firm representations we were allotted additional resources. The question I would therefore ask is: "If the High Command had decided upon feeding Eighth Army in through the Adriatic ports, would our build-up in the Bari area have been sufficient to produce the results that were in fact achieved?"

In arriving at the answer it must be assumed that we used the very minimum for the "Toe" operation, and that we commenced planning and preparing for the alternative in early August. Also formations were cut down to the bare minimum of transport. I was never in a position to know the overall shipping and landing craft position, but I consider this might prove an excellent exercise to give the Staff College to work out, i.e.: —

"If, in early August, Eighth Army's role had been defined as: —

(a) To ensure safe passage for our shipping through the Straits,
(b) To concentrate in the Taranto-Brindisi-Bari area as early as possible after Italy's capitulation,

given the resources in shipping, transport, etc., that could have been made available; what might have been the result of the Army's activities in comparison with that actually achieved?"

II

To start with the Army Commander had planned to employ two Corps for "Baytown": 13th Corps to assault across the Straits and 30th Corps to take over the initial bridgehead and so allow Dempsey to carry out the advance up Italy. In view of the shortage of landing craft which originally allowed for only a four battalion assault, this proposal had to be abandoned, and both tasks were given to the one Corps (13th).

It looked as if we might be opposed by two weak German divisions in addition to any Italians who had the stomach for a fight, and Montgomery was anxious to assault in sufficient strength to make a certainty of his task. He therefore flew to Algiers to attend a conference on August 23rd to discuss the allocation of craft as well as the provision of adequate naval personnel. There was some slight difference of opinion as to what our needs should be in respect of the latter. As a result of this conference, at which I understand my Chief made himself, as usual, crystal clear, an extra allocation of craft was made, and Admiral Cunningham himself jumped into an aircraft after leaving the conference room, for Sicily. From our point of view we were well satisfied with the results.

13th Corps was to assault on a two divisional front: the 1st Canadian Division on the right and the 5th British Division on the left. The landings were to be made north of Reggio. 231st Brigade and two Commando units were to be held in readiness at Riposto to carry out any subsequent landings that appeared desirable. The first objective given by the Army Commander was to be the Catanzaro neck. The assault was to be supported by the R.A.F., naval craft, and a heavy concentration of artillery from Sicily. The attack was to start on the night of September 2nd/3rd.

In order to obtain information as to the situation on the mainland we sent over several patrols equipped with wireless sets. One which landed at Bova Marina reported that the Italian troops were deserting, and that the civilian population had taken to the hills. The majority, however, did not return. This led the Army Commander to believe that the Germans were well organised and watchful.

As usual we had a race against time. We had only just over a fortnight from the end of the Sicily campaign, and there was a great deal to do. The roads, bridges and railways had to be repaired in order to allow the easy flow of traffic and supplies to the points of embarkation. New airfields had to be constructed, not only for the support of "Bay town," but also for "Avalanche"; the area chosen was on the north coast of

Sicily to the west of Messina. Assembly areas for the transport and concentration areas for the troops had to be prepared, and these were hard to find because the hills in most places ran down to the sea. We used the dry river beds for the marshalling and waterproofing of vehicles. We realised that everything would depend upon adequate bridging resources, and so great quantities of Bailey bridging had to be transported and collected near the ferry points.

Whilst all this was going on, the troops had to be given special training with the landing craft, and the artillery moved up into their supporting positions. Here again the mountainous country around Messina necessitated combing the countryside for every available flat piece of ground that would take a gun. Having put in the guns, they all had to be "tied up" under one centralised command. The Commander Corps Royal Artillery (C.C.R.A.) 30th Corps — Dennis — took on this task and made a great success of it. Shortly before "D" Day any distinguished visitor could go and lunch at his Headquarters and witness an impressive display. He would be allowed to sit on the sunny veranda of a charming villa overlooking the mainland of Italy. It looked a mere stone's throw away. With the luncheon cocktail would be brought a target map. The guest would then be asked to choose the place which he would like to see shot up. In would go the pin, and within a matter of a minute or so a roar would be heard, and then columns of dust would indicate where the shells from several hundred guns had burst. It was most spectacular.

During this preparatory period Montgomery kept his Tactical Headquarters at Taormina, whilst for most of the time Main Headquarters remained at Lentini. The villa in which we lived was a charming one belonging to an Italian fascist. All beautiful villas were conveniently owned by Fascists. It was most comfortable and was perched on the cliff overlooking the Straits and the area of our next assault. I spent a number of nights here, and it was pleasant to feed off a polished table and eat from perfect china once again. I enjoyed these visits and sometimes came by sea in Broadhurst's captured Italian speed boat. They were happy days, for we made a picnic of it, and would bathe *en route* in the deep blue sea. Montgomery had several visitors to stay, and he was in his very best form, supremely confident and provocative. One night after dinner, when the Army Commander had retired, several of us were playing a quiet game of *chemin-de-fer*. A very charming and high-powered Civil Servant[31] on a visit from the War Office was watching us. He said he didn't play, but appeared quite interested. Shortly before we closed for the night I had a very good bank. Our guest, who had had a long experience at the Treasury, must have suddenly decided that there was money in this game, for he quietly said he would like to join in. The result was, however, rather painful. We first took his Italian lira, then his French francs (he was visiting Algiers), and finally his few remaining English notes found their way into our pockets! Besides this sharp tactical success, however, we profited further by the visit. He would patiently listen to our grouses, and although he never promised anything, we found that in the course of time various changes were made in the Army regulations which we knew were a result of his activities. We all enjoyed his visit and were sorry to see him go.

For the operation itself we moved our Main Headquarters to a place near the north coast, some thirty miles west of Messina. The R.A.F. Headquarters were close to their airfields, and this fact determined the locality. It was, however, most inconvenient for other reasons, and meant long journeys by air,

---

[31] Sir Eric Speed now P.U.S. at the War Office.

sea and car. I will explain later how I worked during the first phase of the operation.

By September 2nd everything was in readiness. Montgomery had forsaken the comfortable villa for his caravan and tented Tactical Headquarters, which was now in position on the coast further north. I decided to stay with the Army Commander during the opening stages of the landing, and by mid-day I found that I was at a loose end, and so took a sandwich lunch and drove up to the top of a prominent hill overlooking several of the assembly and embarkation points. It was a lovely day, and I felt that there must be something "phoney" about this operation. Below me on the beaches and dry river beds there was intense activity. Transport moving to their allotted positions, landing craft being loaded, and all this within what appeared to be a stone's throw of Italy. In the hills around me I knew there to be several hundred guns, which now and then sent a covey of shells to some target on the opposite shore. On the enemy's side of the Straits all seemed to be quiet. Sailing in those peaceful waters were some of His Majesty's ships — a monitor and others — which at intervals would bombard the hostile shore. In the air our aircraft were flying to and fro, busy with their various missions. We had assembled and prepared a formidable force. Were we using a sledgehammer to crack a nut?

I rose in the early hours of the next morning in order to have a view of the assault. Before 4 a.m. the convoys of landing craft were streaming across the Straits moving to the accompaniment of bomb and shell. At 4.30 a.m. our troops were landing on the beaches north of Reggio. It turned out to be virtually an unopposed landing. The Italian troops, as in Sicily, showed great joy at having the opportunity of surrendering. The only German opposition was from long-range artillery fire, and the occasional fighter-bomber attack. It is not surprising, therefore, that good progress was made. Both Reggio and San Giovanni were captured during the morning. By the evening the 1st Canadian Division was in San Stefano and the 5th Division had occupied Scilla. The beaches were not mined and the port of Reggio was not badly damaged. Therefore the ferry service for reinforcement and supply got going to a flying start.

During the morning the Army Commander crossed to Italy and ordered a Commando landing to take place at Bagnara during the next night. This was successful and got behind the small German rearguard party. After rather slower progress the Canadian Division were nearing Cittanova and the 5th Division had secured Gioia Taur by September 6th. It was now that Montgomery switched the Canadians to the east coast road axis and directed them on Catanzaro. The 5th Division was at the same time given Nicastro as their objective. To assist the advance 231st Infantry Brigade were landed at Pizzo and successfully engaged a German detachment, destroying some of its transport. By September 10th the Catanzaro-Nicastro objective was reached, some hundred miles from where we landed. Our maintenance situation had now become stretched and necessitated a pause in our forward movement.

This advance up Italy was a veritable Calvary. Our speed was determined by the capacity of the sappers to repair bridges and other demolitions. As I have already said, the country was ideal for delay, and the Germans had evidently worked out a most efficient plan. We were using a great deal of Bailey bridging, and the transporting forward of this war winner and the building of bridges and repair of demolitions, can be said to have been the factors limiting the speed of our advance.

Rightly or wrongly I know I felt most dissatisfied about this expenditure of effort and of valuable resources. Where was it getting us? Was it necessary? These were questions I could not help asking myself.

III

It was fortunate that the fighting was not very heavy during this period, as control was far from easy. Distances were now very great. The Army Commander was moving close up to the forward troops with his Tactical Headquarters. Main Headquarters and the Headquarters of the Desert Air Force were thirty miles west of Messina. We had an administrative organisation at Messina, whilst General Robertson's "Fort Base" administrative set-up was at Catania. Ferry Control was, I think, at Messina. It would have been far better if our Main Headquarters could have been at Messina itself, but there was neither a free area to house it, nor could the numberless telephone cables be laid to the airfields from there in time. The Army, therefore, at great inconvenience to themselves, had to bow to the R.A.F. needs. The decision was, of course, a correct one. We were at first out of telephone communication with all headquarters over the Straits, and so many of us spent most of our time on journeys. I had a light aircraft, and a L.C.I.[32] as a "yacht." During the first few days I paid about four visits to Italy. The first on the second morning when I saw both the Army Commander and Dempsey; the next for a conference between Montgomery and Alexander on the Reggio airfield. Here the prospects of the forthcoming Salerno landings were discussed, and Montgomery warned against expecting too much from the Italian armistice which was shortly to take place. We had a nasty flight back, what with a bad

---

[32] Type of landing craft.

thunderstorm, an over-anxious anti-aircraft gunner on a landing craft, and a violent cross wind on our airstrip. After the Pizzo landing I sailed there in my "yacht." I took a party of staff officers up with me so that we could together transact as much business as possible on the spot. It was a lovely trip in a calm blue sea. Lying on the deck we might have been sailing off Cannes. Both Montgomery's and Dempsey's Headquarters were quite near the little port, and so after spending the night we sailed back again the next morning. By about the 9th an ex-enemy airfield had been put into commission a few miles from Pizzo, and so the next trip was possible by air, which I made on the 9th.

The evening of September 8th was exciting. I knew the Italian armistice was due to be announced at 6 p.m., but this was a closely guarded secret. At 5 p.m. George and Beryl Formby started to give an excellent concert to all the troops at the headquarters. Unfortunately just after it had finished I received a message to say that the Italian wireless was broadcasting the armistice. It would have been a wonderful last turn to have been able to announce this news to the large assembly. However, the news soon spread round, and great rejoicing took place. We asked the artistes to dinner, and they entertained us until the early hours. The next morning we began to receive the first reports of operation "Avalanche."

During the night of the 9th/10th, when I was staying at Tactical Headquarters, a signal was received from Alexander. In it he stressed the importance of Eighth Army bringing all pressure to bear on the enemy, and so assisting the progress of the new landings. The situation at Salerno was difficult and very fierce fighting was in progress. In the same signal we received the news that troops were to be landed at Taranto and that by the 15th it was hoped to have available in that area several thousand men.

As always in such cases Montgomery responded wholeheartedly and with speed. He called a conference after breakfast to examine what could be done. We hoped that additional resources in shipping, landing craft and units would be allotted us, and so I suggested I should fly back to Messina and hold a conference with everyone concerned to speed up supplies and transport, and so allow our advance to be accelerated. Whilst these matters were being examined the Army Commander ordered light forces to advance north of the Catanzaro-Nicastro line. In order to use our air forces against the enemy with more effect, and also to support our advancing troops, it was essential that the Crotone airfields should be occupied and put into use by the Desert Air Force. Crotone was also of considerable importance because of its port. With this in our hands, the maintenance problems would be eased. In order to allow these objects to be attained we had to alter the priorities in the Ferry Service. For instance, R.A.F. transport and equipment became all important. Such matters as these were dealt with at the Messina conference. We also decided to use the small port of Pizzo to its full capacity.

On arrival at Messina I was sorry to hear that Admiral McGrigor had been wounded during an enemy bombing attack. He was, however, very cheerful about it all. The Navy rose to the occasion magnificently, and as a result of the conference a good speed-up in traffic was arranged. This reacted right up the line. By September 11th Crotone was captured with its port undamaged, and our advanced forces had reached the general line Castrovillari-Belvedere.

On September 13th Montgomery was ordered to take command of the troops now arriving in the Taranto area as soon as this became feasible. At the moment they were under General Allfrey, the Commander of the 5th Corps.

It was not until September 16th that General Clark said he considered the situation at Salerno was well in hand. The preceding days had been full of anxieties.

Now let us see what Eighth Army had been doing during this critical period. After reaching the Castrovillari-Belvedere line on the 11th, Montgomery ordered on September 14th, 13th Corps to move a brigade forward to Sapri, and having reached this area to operate light forces as far north as maintenance conditions would permit. On the 16th our patrols linked up with the Fifth U.S. Army, and by this time the enemy had swung back his southern flank. Undoubtedly this threat from the south must at least have had a psychological reaction on the German Command, and possibly may have decided them finally to abandon their efforts to destroy General Clark's bridgehead — it at any rate gave them a very good excuse. But on the other hand, our pressure was never very weighty, and the enemy were moving back as quickly as they could. It must be remembered that the situation at Salerno was well in hand *before* we established any pressure in that neighbourhood.

In considering this problem the influence of the landings at Taranto should not be forgotten. We were bringing in resources at a good pace, and the organised enemy resistance was negligible. I feel myself that the situation here must have been just as, if not more, disconcerting for the Germans than our move northwards. As I have already said we were all patting ourselves on the back at the time saying, "We've done it again." I now realise how very irritating this attitude must have been to the Americans and to General Clark!

On the 16th, patrols from the Taranto area made contact with the Canadian division. These patrols could work unmolested at least 40 miles from the port — which shows what the situation was like on this side of Italy. I therefore still ask myself "Would we not have done better to have concentrated on entering Italy via the Adriatic ports after we had established ourselves on the" Toe "of Italy in sufficient strength to command the Straits." To carry out such a plan it would have been necessary: —

(a) to have made the decision by mid-August, and
(b) to have given us the shipping and landing craft, which were ultimately made available, at an earlier date.

After a great effort by Signals to lay the necessary communications, we achieved on September 15th the desirable objective of having Tactical, Main and Rear Headquarters located in the same area. This was a few miles east of Pizzo.

It was not until September 19th that the advanced troops of the 5th and 1st Canadian Divisions reached Auletta and Potenza respectively. To indicate the strength of the enemy resistance which we were up against at the time, in the whole area bounded by Taranto-Bari-Foggia and Potenza, there were only about 8,000 German troops of the 1st Parachute Division. Having reached the Auletta and Potenza line, Eighth Army had to more or less turn itself inside out. We had advanced 300 miles and were being maintained mainly by road from across the Straits of Messina. This was a most uneconomical and wasteful effort. It now became necessary to switch our base to the Adriatic ports, and obviously this would prove a big undertaking and would take time. We had also to re-group our forces to carry out the future role allotted to us by 15th Army Group, i.e. to operate up the eastern side of Italy. On the 24th there was no further need for us to keep forces in the Auletta area, and so the Army Commander gave out his orders for the next phase.

Before passing on, however, I will describe a visit I paid with the Army Commander to Taranto on September 22nd. We left the Pizzo airfield after breakfast, and were met at the Taranto airport by General Allfrey (5th Corps) General Mason-Macfarlane who was Head of our Mission to the Italian Government, and the Italian Army Commander of that area. Before Montgomery spoke to the Italian he had a talk with Mason-Macfarlane. Apparently our co-belligerent had been enquiring as to Montgomery's seniority, no doubt with the object of working out who was to command the other! Any doubts as to this matter were however soon removed, for the Army Commander shook hands, said he welcomed his co-operation, and then very concisely gave out his orders. All Italian Commanders must obey his orders. The troops must stay where they were. He was arranging for a British Commander and staff to form a Mission for dealing with the problems of the five Italian divisions located in the region of Italy which we now occupied. All requests for assistance and material must be instantly obeyed. The Italian Army Commander said he understood, but that his great desire was to fight the Germans — when would he be allowed to march against the enemy? Montgomery passed this one aside by saying that at the moment the Allied cause could best be helped by doing as he said. Later perhaps, a more active role would be allotted. We then drove to the headquarters of 5th Corps where the Army Commander spoke to a gathering of officers. They were mostly new to his command, and so they received an injection of the Montgomery virus — and seemed to like it.

Besides the troops of the 1st Airborne Division, the 78th Division had been ordered over from Sicily, and some advanced elements landed at Bari on September 22nd and 23rd, the whole division being due to concentrate in this area. Behind this formation the 8th Indian Division was expected from Egypt. The Army Commander went on to explain how he was having to switch his base, and also the axis of his main thrust. Time would be required to organise our maintenance before a full-blooded attack north of Bari could be undertaken. In the meantime 5th Corps was to carry out very active patrolling, and so find out the enemy's dispositions and strength.

After lunch we flew back to our headquarters. It gave me quite a thrill flying over these great Italian cities whose capture had been made possible by allied arms. Here there was more to show for our efforts than the leagues of desert sands.

IV

From now onwards we were to have two armies operating side by side in Italy: the Eighth Army on the right and the 5th U.S. Army, containing some British formations, on the left. There was a feeling of competition in the air, and we were both, I'm sure, very interested in, and perhaps professionally critical of each other's doings.

The next objectives given the two Armies were the Foggia group of airfields and the port of Naples. With our long-range fighters based around Foggia it would then be possible to escort the day bombers over the parts of Axis territory that had hitherto been difficult to reach. Later the heavy bombers would be able to use the airfields themselves. This objective was, therefore, of considerable importance in Allied strategy. In order to operate with security it would, of course, be necessary to drive back the enemy to a considerable distance beyond.

Whilst all this re-organisation was taking place within Eighth Army, and whilst we were accumulating maintenance resources in our new area, Montgomery had laid down that no main bodies would advance forward of the Bari-Altamura line before October 1st. Dempsey's 13th Corps was to lead the advance and 5th Corps was to move in rear, watching the left flank. Later this Corps would be brought up and allotted a sector of the main front.

Allfrey very rightly gave a very liberal interpretation to his orders regarding "aggressive patrolling." His airborne troops showed great dash and resource, and pushed far and wide. The advanced elements of 78th Division and the 4th Armoured Brigade which landed at Bari "patrolled" so effectively that by October 1st the Ofanto river had been crossed, Foggia and its airfields occupied, and the Gargarno peninsula was in our hands. By now, however, the enemy had sufficiently re-organised his resources to have collected forces to oppose our advance into the hilly country to the north and west of the Foggia Plain.

During this period of re-organisation we moved our various headquarters to an excellent area about 15 miles west of Bari. So by the 26th we were once again all together. In addition 15th Army Group Headquarters was arriving at Bari, and so future planning became a simpler process.

Whilst the move took place, I cut myself off from the war for a couple of days, and drove an independent course to Bari. I had a wireless set in case something unforeseen turned up, but otherwise I was not to be disturbed. My companions were my servant and my faithful Serjeant-Major Harwood. On the second day we found a lovely spot a few miles from Bari, and after we arrived I suddenly developed a fierce craving for beer. I drove into the city but was bitterly disappointed to find that none was obtainable. Bari was a pleasant city, and we were all astonished at the goods they had to sell in the shops. Silks and satins, stockings, and all the perfumes and cosmetics you required. Many must be the wives, relations and sweethearts who profited from the capture of this Adriatic port! Conditions appeared to be quite normal and were not in accordance with what we had been led to expect from listening to our propaganda telling us of the horrors of living under the Axis yoke!

The first serious action fought by 13th Corps was across the Biferno river, and around the port of Termoli. In order to assist the crossing, Commandos were landed on the night of October 2nd/3rd, at Termoli. A bridgehead was established across the river, and on the following night a brigade of 78th Division — the formation which was leading the advance along the coast — was landed to reinforce the Commandos. The enemy was very worried by this success for he moved over from the Fifth U.S. Army front a Panzer Division (16th) and during the 4th and 5th some very bitter fighting took place, one of his counter-attacks penetrating as far as Termoli. We were handicapped during this period by the flooded river, which had interfered with our bridging, and therefore with the passage of tanks and supporting weapons. The Desert Air Force fought valiantly in our support, and Dempsey's cool handling of the situation backed by the dogged fighting of his troops finally forced the enemy to withdraw. On the 7th he withdrew to the next river line — the Trigno. As maintenance considerations prevented an immediate follow up in strength, I will explain briefly the progress made by the other flank of the 13th Corps' advance.

The 1st Canadian division had been directed across the mountainous country on Vinchiaturo. But they experienced considerable difficulty in capturing this small town, which did not fall until about October 10th. Again supply prevented any further immediate major advance on this axis, lack of petrol being one of the principal limiting factors.

The front was now becoming too wide for control by one Corps, and therefore on October 9th, Montgomery brought up 5th Corps to the coastal sector, taking over 78th Division in the process. The 8th Indian Division was also under Allfrey's command, and was located in the area between Bari and Barletta. 13th Corps was now to have the 1st Canadian and 5th Divisions — the latter having followed up our advance and now positioned around Foggia. Montgomery was always most careful of what he termed preserving "correct balance," and had been most insistent that the 5th Division should form a firm base in the Foggia region.

About this time our old desert friend Freyberg, and his New Zealanders were arriving in the country, and were to be ready for operations about the middle of November.

The next task given us by 15th Army Group was to advance to our sector of the "Rome Line." This was the road running across Italy between Pescara and Rome. But as I have already said, maintenance was holding us up. At the time we were rather fractious about this brake upon our activities, and were inclined to blame those behind us. We were undoubtedly suffering from the results of the somewhat nebulous appreciation of the development of operations when we first landed in Italy. I don't say the High Command had an easy task, but I believe that greater administrative foresight might have avoided some of the delay — but perhaps not a great deal. Ports, shipping and lack of certain administrative units were the principal difficulties. We, of course, watched rather jealously the administrative appetite of our sister Army to the west. It was only human nature that we felt they were getting too great a slice of the administrative pie. Whether they got too much I can't say, but they should certainly have had first priority. Theirs was the more important axis of advance. Then there was a very big air force demand at this time. All the material for constructing the all-weather airfields at Foggia had to arrive through our ports, together with petrol and bombs. Winter was around the corner, and so there was not much time to lose. When at times our petrol was almost exhausted, and our ammunition fairly low, we became a bit worried, but there was never any chance that the enemy could have staged a major counteroffensive against us at that stage of the campaign. It is, however, natural that we should have been rather sensitive about these administrative shortcomings, and it was our duty to see that our troops were adequately supplied.

Montgomery planned for the crossing of the Trigno operation to be preceded by a drive by 13th Corps on Isernia. This was to take place on October 23rd, two days before the main attack was due to start. Bad weather and successful action of patrols, however, interfered with these plans. On the 22nd, the 78th Division obtained a footing over the Trigno, but extremely heavy rain on the 27th and 28th prevented a further effort at enlarging this bridgehead from achieving success. In the meantime rain postponed the 13th Corps' attack by a day, and the 5th Division eventually started in the rain on the night of October 29th/30th.

On the night of November 2nd/3rd, the 78th Division attacked with heavy artillery support, and after two days' fighting the enemy started to withdraw to the Sangro river. By November 8th, 78th Division had established themselves on the high ground overlooking the river; the 13th Corps had captured Isernia, and the 8th Indian Division was being moved up on the left of 78th Division. Once again a pause was necessary for maintenance purposes, before we could stage a major attack across this formidable river obstacle. The New Zealand Division had been ordered up to the Foggia area. Montgomery was once again ensuring that he kept his Army balanced.

V

We were now beginning to experience the trouble of a European climate. The days of the dry desert were over, and rain and mud presented us with new problems. The 5th U.S. Army had captured Naples and so all eyes were now focused upon Rome, and the plans of both armies were directed to the capture of the Italian capital. We spent a lot of time in early November studying all the climatic information we could get hold of. On the average it appeared that November and December should not prove very wet, and that the lateral roads, over the back-bone hills of Italy might not be made unusable by snow. We, therefore, were fairly optimistic as to the prospects. In the event, although we had considerable fine periods between rain, the cumulative effect played havoc with the roads and made movement off them increasingly difficult.

On November 8th, Alexander called a conference at his headquarters at Bari which I attended with the Army Commander. Montgomery had ready his plan for Eighth Army if Rome was still to be the winter objective. This was to drive across the Sangro river, and, having secured the Pescara-Popoli road, to send forces towards Avezzano, and so help to loosen up the resistance in front of the 5th Army. Montgomery, in his usual confident style, gave out his proposals, and these were accepted by the Army Group Commander. General Clark, unfortunately, could not attend because of poor flying conditions, and so we did not have a first hand impression of what he felt about the future. Sitting in that conference room in the dry, warm atmosphere, and looking at the maps with their confident coloured arrows indicating the future proposals, the capture of Rome before the spring still looked a possibility. Mud, that arch enemy of the offensive soldier, however soon showed us how wrong we were.

Having received our orders we returned to complete the preparations for the first phase of the plan — the crossing of the Sangro river.

Montgomery after considerable thought had chosen the coastal sector for the main punch. This was to be carried out by the 78th and 8th Indian Divisions and by the 4th Armoured Brigade on a very narrow front. The New Zealand Division was to be moved up into the sector previously occupied by the Indian Division. It was hoped to launch the attack on November 20th, but heavy periods of rain caused continual postponements, and modifications to the original plan.

The 78th Division once again beat the gun, for in spite of the bad weather, they managed to establish themselves across the Sangro by the middle of the month. We now required a good spell of weather to allow us to put in our big attack, and to employ the large forces which we had available. Further, the rains caused flooding of this wide river and therefore made bridging operations most difficult.

By November 24th the bridgehead had been expanded to a width of 10,000 yards stretching to a depth of 2,000 yards. By this time we had advanced elements of three divisions across. The 78th on the right, the 8th Indian Division in the centre, and the New Zealand Division on the left.

The weather now made a large scale attack with deep objectives out of the question, and so Montgomery changed his plan to take the form of limited objectives supported by a heavy weight of artillery. The first essential was the capture of the Sangro Ridge, from which the enemy could overlook the crossings. By this time 13th Corps had cleared up the area to the west of 5th Corps, but the country was in a very bad state.

We had now moved our Main Headquarters with the R.A.F. to Vasto, whilst Montgomery's Tactical Headquarters was farther forward. Never have I admired the soldiers of the British Empire more than during this period, for the condition of the country was appalling. It was cold, wet and muddy, and they had the greatest difficulty in keeping themselves in fighting trim. The road along which the supplies of all kinds had to go was a nightmare, covered in mud and saturated with traffic. I used to marvel at the good humour of the drivers, who remained so cheerful under these conditions. It was very difficult to find areas sufficiently dry to establish dumps — the surrounding country was so soon cut up by the lorry traffic. Our main forward administrative area was laid out on the shore at Vasto, and at one period was partially inundated by the sea. It was amazing how the guns were got into positions and the ammunition brought to them. The more I drove around, the more I realised that Rome was a very far cry; and incidentally I paid silent tribute to First Army's efforts the winter before.

The attack commenced at 9.30 p.m. on November 28th, after a day or two of fine weather. The 8th Indian Division with the help of the 4th Armoured Brigade, captured Mozzagrogna. It was possible to get a grandstand view of this battle from the hills on our side of the Sangro, and when one watched the heavy scale of bomber and artillery support, it was difficult to see how the enemy could stand much more. I saw some of the prisoners being brought in and they were quite dazed and all spoke about the terrific bombing and shelling which they had experienced. By the evening of the 30th the whole of the Sangro Ridge had been captured, and the New Zealand Division fought their way across the river and linked up with the 5th Corps. The German 65th Infantry Division had had a bad time, and elements of a Panzer Division were brought to their assistance. Nevertheless they failed to hold the ridge.

Until a high-level bridge had been built across the Sangro, our forces to the north were dependent upon reasonable weather for their senility and supply. Sudden storms caused great damage to the other types of bridges. Working with great courage and fortitude the Sappers built this bridge by December 6th. It was the longest yet built by Eighth Army, and I think was called the "Montgomery Bridge." We blessed the Bailey equipment. After hard fighting the general line Saint Vito-Lanciano — just short of Orsogna — had been reached by the 4th. The weather, the River Moro, and enemy reinforcements combined to hold up our advance. The Army Commander re-grouped with a view to a continuance of the offensive. The 5th Corps now with the 1st Canadian and 8th Indian Divisions under command, still operated on the right flank, whilst the 13th Corps was given a sector farther west with the New Zealand and 5th Divisions. The 78th Division which had fought so well over a long period, was now pulled out and given something of a rest by holding the mountainous country on the left flank directly under command of the Army. These moves, carried out over appalling roads, gave the staff a difficult time, but in the end the re-shuffle was tidily accomplished.

It was not until December 10th that a bridgehead had been established over the Moro river by the Canadians. The advance from here towards Ortona was fiercely contested and the German paratroops in the town were fanatical in their resistance. By Christmas Day our line ran from just short of Ortona on the right (1st Canadian Division), Villa Grande (8th Indian Division), Arielli (5th Division), and on the left the New Zealand Division had all but captured Orsogna.

The fighting during this period had been fairly costly, and one rather wondered what we achieved. Enemy formations were certainly pulled over from opposite the Fifth U.S. Army, and heavy casualties had been inflicted on the Germans. With snow in the mountains, and mud everywhere else we began to think about Passchendaele. Had we gone on too long? Were the troops being driven too hard? I feel very definitely that a mistake was made in pressing the Sangro offensive as far as it was. When once the weather had broken it was extremely unlikely that we could have advanced across the mountains, even if we had reached the Pescara-Rome road. Perhaps we were still not prepared to give the weather best, resenting her behaviour after the dryness of the desert. Who should have stopped the operations — the Army or the Army Group? The Army Group, I suppose, for its job was to assess whether our contribution was proving worth while within the bigger picture.

VI

During this period of the Sangro fighting we had several distinguished visitors. The Russians sent a mission to view our front. We noticed one old friend amongst them who, during the Desert days, was attached to us as a war correspondent. Now he was wearing the regalia of a General! We pulled his leg about it. They dined with me their first night at Main Head quarters in Vasto, and we spent a really interesting and enjoyable evening. The Russian officers were extremely well informed and wanted to know everything. They expected a "standard solution" for all problems. "How many guns do you use to support a certain type of attack?" Answers such as "Depends on the targets or the air support" or "as many as we can scrape together" would not do. "What proportion of fighters to bombers do you have?" Here again a standard yardstick was required. We talked long and late. I think I was most interested in hearing about how they, the Russians, had kept their great armies maintained during the long advance back from Stalingrad. We heard a saga of guts, improvisation, and the will to succeed.

The next day we took them up to see some of the fighting and they were shown round by Freyberg and others. They had come to see whether we really fought, and so they were "taken places." They witnessed some pretty sticky fighting, and one of them is alleged to have said after the second day: "We have seen enough bravery for one day, we now would like a little sleep!" We enjoyed their visit greatly, and I only hope they felt the same. At any rate I received a very charming letter from the head of the Mission a few days later.

The Chief of the Air Staff — now Lord Portal — came out. I was asked to lunch with the R.A.F. at Vasto. It was very interesting for me, as I heard for the first time something concrete about the possibility of the Germans using their "V" weapons. I remember it gave me an uncomfortable feeling. Surely weapons of this nature could not rob us of the victory which now looked so certain?

When everyone was speculating who would be the Commanders for the "Second Front" we were visited by the

Prime Minister, the C.I.G.S. and Eisenhower. They were flown up to Montgomery's Head quarters near the Sangro river and had lunch. We all thought we would hear the answer — but we didn't. All sorts of rumours were circulating. We were naturally very interested in our Army Commander's future. First it was to be General Marshall, the U.S. Chief of Staff, as the Supreme Commander, with Alexander commanding the armies under him. It might be Alexander as Supreme Commander and therefore Montgomery would take his place at 15th Army Group. Every possible combination was worked out, but still nothing official was heard. The C.I.G.S. had tea with us in my mess on his way back to Bari, and no fly that we dropped produced any reaction. But then he is a keen fisherman and knew the game.

Time was creeping on and still no news, and it looked as if once again the "great ones" had made the fatal error of appointing the Commanders of a great enterprise too late. If they had only known how such an omission complicates and increases the work of the staff, I'm sure they would have acted otherwise. I realise that there were certain political and strategic considerations that made them delay. In the first place, they still hoped to capture Rome by the end of the year, and the effect upon Russian opinion, if we withdrew all our high commanders from the Central Mediterranean front, had to be taken into a count. In spite of such factors, let us hope in the event of another war commanders and their staffs will be appointed in good time.

In the middle of all this uncertainty as to the future, and when our operations across the Sangro were slowly but surely being paralysed by mud and rain, I received a tip that the convoy in which my wife was sailing to England was putting into Augusta in Sicily and might be there for a day or two.

Montgomery gave me leave, and I flew down to Catania, arriving at Augusta just after the great collection of ships had anchored in the bay. She was, of course, very surprised to see me, and we spent three very happy days on the island. I took her along the route of our advance, and to lovely Taormina. Here we stayed with General Crerar, the future commander of the Canadian Army, who was then in command of a corps. We were both deeply touched by the kindness we received from Crerar and the officers at his Headquarters. I was to meet many of them again in northwest Europe. I was most impressed by the way the Sicilians had worked to repair the ravages of war — Catania was once again a flourishing town, throned with happy smiling people. On the last night that I spent on board the transport I was asked to give a talk over the ship's loud speaker system. I shudder to think what I said, for I was so steeped with pride at Eighth Army's achievements I probably suggested that we alone had won the war!

Whilst in Sicily I heard that Eisenhower had been appointed Supreme Commander for the "Second Front." But still no news of Alexander's and Montgomery's future. And it was not until I returned to our headquarters on December 24th that we heard over the B.B.C. that our Army Commander had been made Commander of the 21st Army Group in England vice General Paget.

I said good-bye to my wife at Augusta, little thinking that I should reach England before her.

Christmas Day was great fun. Montgomery stayed at his Tactical Headquarters, and so I had to visit the sergeants' mess and go round the men's dinners. The "Q" side had done their work well and there was turkey, pork, pudding and all sorts of other good things. It was on occasions like this that one felt the spirit and the comradeship of this fine Army that had come so far. In the afternoon I drove up to Tactical Headquarters to dine with my Chief and to stay the night. After tea he called me into his caravan and told me that he had signalled home to say that he wanted to take me back as his Chief of Staff of the Army Group. I was naturally overjoyed at the news for, besides wanting to follow Montgomery, I was becoming a little stale, and required some fillip such as this to give me a new lease of life. I enjoyed that Christmas dinner, for there was a feeling of new adventure in the air, but we also talked of the past. Montgomery, I believe, was always happiest when he was surrounded at his dinner table by a few of his staff, and could relax and talk without restraint.

The date fixed for Montgomery to leave Eighth Army was December 31st, and about two days before he arranged to say farewell to his officers. The local Opera House at Vasto was in a sufficient state of repair to be used for his address. There was a great gathering including a proportion of officers down to and including those of the rank of lieutenant-colonel. I drove with him to the hall, feeling as I always do on such occasions, sad and sentimental. My Chief was very quiet and I could see that this was going to be the most difficult operation he had yet attempted. We arrived inside and he said, "Freddie, show me where to go." I led him to the stairs leading up to the stage. He mounted at once, and to a hushed audience commenced his last address to the officers of the Army which he loved so well.

He started very quietly, apologising in case his voice might let him down for, as he said, "this is not going to be easy, but I shall do my best. If I happen to find difficulty in speaking on occasions, I hope you will understand." I felt a lump coming in my throat, and one could feel every one of his audience was perfectly tuned into his mood. He then very simply and rather slowly explained about his coming departure, and what responsibilities lay ahead. He touched on the past — upon the successes we had gained together, and of the things which he considered important, and which guided him during his command. He summed up the situation, and expressed his thanks to everyone for the support he had received, and for the way they had fought. He then asked them to follow the new Army Commander, Leese, as they had followed him. There were no great feats of oratory and no false note. It was exactly right, and I found it intensely moving. He finished quietly by reading his last of many personal messages to the Army — his message of farewell. (See Appendix A).

We cheered him and then he walked slowly out to his car. I followed feeling very uncomfortable, for I had tears on my cheeks and we were riding in an open car. We drove back to Main Headquarters, which was only a few hundred yards away, where some of the senior commanders had been asked to come and have a chat. It was a wonderful gathering of old friends. As my Chief talked to this trusted few I could not help thinking of Napoleon and his Marshals, for here surely there was to be found the same relationship, born and tempered by mutual esteem and success in battle. Later Freyberg, Dempsey, Allfrey and the others departed, and I had a feeling that something rather terrible was happening — I was leaving this great family. But then again I remembered that I was leaving in company with the one who had given us that inspiration, and that guidance, and so although sad I felt content with fate.

Our hand-over and departure was a speedy affair. But this did not matter much as the new Army Commander and his Chief of Staff were old friends and knew the form. They did not arrive at Main Headquarters at Vasto until 7 or 8 p.m. on the 30th. Leese drove straight on to see Montgomery, whilst

George Walsh remained with me to take over. This we did over whiskies and soda's in the mess. We had worked together for over a year before in the Army, when he was B.G.S. of 30th Corps, and so there was not much to say. About 9.30 he said he was satisfied, and so I took him over to my old caravan in which I had lived from El Alamein. I patted it affectionately and turned it over to its new master. We then said good-bye and I drove forward to Tactical Headquarters for the night.

The next morning we all took off in the half-light in Montgomery's Dakota from the small airstrip at the mouth of the Sangro river. It was a heavy load for, besides my Chief and myself, there were two or three other members of the team — Miles Graham, Williams who had been the head of our Intelligence, and Richards our tank expert. There were others to follow, but with a servant or two, and kit and a full load of petrol, we only just got off in time. On our way down the coast the Desert Air Force paid the Army Commander a last salute, and we were escorted well on our way by a squadron of Spitfires, flashing in the morning sunlight.

Our course allowed us a glimpse of Etna and then nothing until the North African shore. We landed to re-fuel at Algiers, taking off immediately for Marrakesch, where we arrived about six in the evening. Here we changed aircraft. Montgomery went off to spend the night with Winston Churchill, who was convalescing there, whilst the rest of us, after a good dinner at the local hotel, took off for Prestwick at 10.30 p.m. As I sat back in my comfortable seat of that steady C.54, I suddenly realised that at that very moment the year was changing — 1944 was upon us. Would it be the year of victory?

VII
TAIL-PIECE (A TRUE STORY).
"Have plans ready to exploit every situation."

— Eighth Army principle.

During our trek from Bari to Vasto, hospitality was occasionally accepted by officers at Italian houses. There was one house in which lived a very charming and pretty woman, but her husband was both fierce and ugly. He had no human understanding, was an ogre, a veritable Gestapo! Our Headquarters passed on, and this charmer and her gaoler were left far behind.

It was a stormy evening at Vasto. The wind was blowing and snow was falling. At No. 37 Pigeon Loft, where the Signals carrier pigeons lived, the sergeant was blowing his cold hands to keep them warm, and thinking of packing up for the night, when suddenly out of the blizzard a miserable little bird appeared and perched exhausted on the ground. With expert fingers the sergeant detached a message from its leg and despatched it up to those who dealt with such things. "It must have been mighty important," mused the sergeant, "to have released him on a night like this." Perhaps from some agent across the Adriatic, or from an airman who had crashed.

It was not long after the message had been delivered to the officer to whom it was addressed that this same officer could have been seen leaving the camp area in a jeep. He had a look of grim determination on his face, and his car was pointing south.

The next morning an orderly was clearing up the office when an unusual little piece of paper attracted his eye. He unfolded it and read "Antonio has gone to Naples."

CHAPTER XIII: BUSY DAYS

I

WE landed at Prestwick and flew on to Hendon. It was good to see London again after four years' absence. Cairo had been the only large city I had visited during that period, and there every form of luxury was available, as well as servants and transport. The things that struck me most about war-time England were the fortitude of the people, the monotony of the food, and the way in which the bomb damage had been tidied up. I also found a very deep affection for the Eighth Army, and some of the simple remarks that were made to me because I wore the Africa Star with the "8" on it brought a lump to my throat.

The way in which the British people worked together to launch this colossal expedition — the Second Front — was truly wonderful. They realised that the end was in sight and in whatever sphere one moved there was to be found that unity of purpose, that self-sacrificing devotion to duty, and that characteristic cheerfulness. The workers in the factories who were asked to accelerate production to give us the tools; the railwaymen who bore such a heavy burden; and in fact all sections of the community who were harnessed to bring us victory responded as never before in our long history.

The next morning, January 2nd, I reported at "Cossac," which was the headquarters that had been working out the plans and preparations for "The Second Front."

Eisenhower, who had to pay a visit to America, had named Montgomery his Land Force Commander, who during the former's absence was permitted to give decisions in his name.

It had been arranged that Bedell Smith, Eisenhower's Chief of Staff, and I should discuss the existing plan together, and give Montgomery our views on his arrival from his visit to Churchill at Marrakesch. The existing plan which we found was briefly as follows. An assault by three divisions and tanks between Grandcamp and Caen. Behind these were two follow-up divisions, and behind them two more divisions which would be afloat in ships on "D" day. Given *exceptionally* good weather conditions it was calculated that we should have nine divisions ashore by the end of the sixth day. As the landings were to take place to the east of the River Vire, it was not anticipated that we could capture the port of Cherbourg for at least a fortnight. The use of the artificial harbour "Mulberry" was therefore of great importance. Besides the sea-borne assault it had been calculated that about two-thirds of a division would be dropped by air. This estimate was based primarily upon the air-lift available. It was proposed that the assault would be in charge of an American Task Force Commander with both British and American formations under his command.

Bedell Smith's and my reactions were, I suppose, similar to those of any other trained soldier. We wanted a greater weight of assault, a quicker build-up, a larger airlift, and we thought the area of the assault too restricted. I put it this way in defence of the "Cossac" planners, who would also have liked these modifications, but they were having to plan on certain given assets, and such changes would mean an additional allotment of landing craft, ships and aircraft. It required the appointment of a Commander who could bang the table and say what he wanted. It was only as regards the questions of the command set-up and the extent of the frontage of attack that there was any real difference of opinion.

I had of course not had time to undertake a detailed study of the whole problem, but an assault *on either side* of the Cotentin peninsula looked an attractive proposition, and if that was found to be impracticable, then an extension of the selected area would be an alternative solution. The only other comment I had to make was that in my opinion the estimates of port capacities were too low. With modern unloading facilities, and despite extensive demolitions, it was extraordinary what tonnages we could hope for in practice.

As always Bedell Smith gave me a very warm welcome, and he arranged for a presentation of the existing plans by the "Cossac" staff for Montgomery when he arrived. The full appreciation would be gone through with the aid of maps and diagrams. The Naval C.-in-C. (Admiral Ramsay) and the Air C.-in-C. (Leigh-Mallory) would also be present.

Montgomery duly arrived, and the presentation took place. It was admirably staged, and to those of us new to the problem we realised what an amount of work had been done, and also how easy it is to think you can produce strategical solutions without having first examined *all* the relevant data. Here are some of the factors that had to be taken into consideration in arriving at the "Cossac" plan. General "Freddie" Morgan and his staff had certainly thought of most things.

There were the *ports* which were essential for the ultimate maintenance of our forces on the continent. Their existing capacities were misleading, for it was certain that extensive demolitions would be carried out before we captured them. Here practical experience was a pearl of great price. The "*Mulberry*" was explained and the forecast of its value produced. It was essential that *fighter cover* be given to the expedition from air bases in the United Kingdom, and so this limited the area which was "open" to invasion. The *beaches* had to be of the right type and gradient. There must be sand and not mud or clay, otherwise the vehicles could not be got ashore. The *tidal factor* had to be taken into account, as the rise and fall differed considerably in accordance with each particular sector of the Invasion Coast. The prevailing *wind* was from the south-west and therefore the Atlantic swell should if possible be avoided. The *hinterland* had to be closely studied. Were the *exits from the beaches* practicable? What *inundations* had been carried out, and did the country lend itself to further treatment of this sort? Could our armoured strength be exploited? And did a tactical analysis of the whole region favour the establishment of a lodgement area? These were some of the matters that had to be examined. Then there were the naval problems. The availability of the home ports for launching the invasion, as well as the enemy minefields and depth of water.

Besides the question of fighter cover, it was important that the Allied Air Forces should have suitable ground for *airfield construction* on the continent soon after we landed.

Finally, there was the question of the *enemy*: the strength of his fortifications, the location of his garrison and of his reserves. This was not easy, for a lot could happen by the time the expedition sailed, and so an assessment of the force we should eventually be opposed by was to some extent guess work.

The presentation was conducted with great lucidity, and at the end Montgomery got up and gave his first reactions. He stressed that he was new to the problem, but that before being satisfied that the best sector had been selected, he would like an examination undertaken of the possibilities of a landing in Brittany, and on either side of the Cotentin peninsula. Although these areas had of course been considered already, it was only right that the Commander-in-Chief of the assault should hear the arguments himself, and be sure that he was satisfied with the conclusions reached. A second presentation therefore took place, and at the end of it Montgomery agreed that the "Neptune" area (the code name given to the selected sector) was the right one. Brittany was too far away from the United Kingdom and insufficient beaches and ports existed. And, above all, it would have been impossible to provide the air cover on the necessary scale. A landing on the west side of the Cotentin peninsula had several major snags. To start with, to reach the beaches the convoys would have had to run the gauntlet past the strong defences of the Channel Isles. Also there was a tremendous rise and fall of tide; and finally the Atlantic swell was a risk that could hardly be accepted.

Montgomery now set about modifying the existing plan in accordance with his views. The changes which he aimed at were broadly: —

(a) To extend the frontage of attack.
(b) To increase the strength of the assault, and subsequent build-up.
(c) To alter the command set-up for the opening phase.

At first sight an extension of the frontage of assault either to the right or to the left did not appear very attractive. On the right it meant assaulting to the North of the estuary of the Vire, and this would not only tend to isolate the forces so employed, but already a large area of inundations had appeared immediately behind the beaches. On the other hand, the beaches were of the right type, and a successful landing here would make it possible to threaten Cherbourg at an earlier date. Moreover, because of the apparent unsuitability of the terrain through flooding, surprise was likely to be achieved.

Montgomery, after discussion with General Bradley, therefore suggested the use of airborne forces to assist this new landing, and asked the staffs of the three services to examine the problem and suggest answers.

On the left, the beaches to the east of the Orne river were within range of the formidable Havre defences, but even so, it was still possible to extend the proposed eastern boundary further towards the Orne. The area immediately to the east of the Orne was, however, very suitable for airborne operations, and so the staffs were ordered to include this project in their studies.

Without considerable additions of landing craft and shipping the strengthening of the weight of assault would not be possible. Montgomery therefore appealed to Admiral Ramsay for his help in this direction, and also asked Eisenhower for additional resources. The staffs were set the problem of examining the ways and means of complying with the Commander-in-Chief's views.

There were certain Naval and Air difficulties which would have to be overcome. The broader the front the less would be the density of air support, and the more difficult the protection of our shipping from air attack. The Air Commander-in-Chief, however, after examination agreed to accept these drawbacks. On the naval site it would mean extra swept lanes, and more escorting craft. Mine sweepers and destroyers were, however, in short supply. And further it was difficult to find additional accommodation in the U.K. ports. Ramsay eventually undertook to accept these added commitments.

Obtaining our landing craft and shipping requirements was an exhausting business, and it was a long time before we reached finality. There were so many factors which influenced the problem. The Anzio operation, which was about to take place, needed landing craft. Then the assault in the South of France (operation "Anvil") had to be catered for, as also the needs of the Pacific War. There was also a back log on the repair and overhaul of landing craft that were now leaching England from other theatres.

Representatives from the U.S. Naval staff in Washington arrived over in England to discuss our landing craft needs with particular reference to "Anvil." We had several hard-fought battles with them. They produced certain suggestions which made for economies in requirements, but they left with a clear understanding of our needs. They agreed to certain exchanges in the types of ships and craft, as well as to a further allocation.

It soon became apparent that if we adhered to the original planning date, none of the suggested palliatives would produce our requirements. And so the question of a postponement of "D" day was opened up. The date which we were working to was May 1st, and even provided adequate landing craft had been available, I doubt very much whether we could have prepared the expedition in time. Our respective Governments were not keen on a revised date, particularly as Stalin had already been told when to expect the "Second Front." Further, a delay would give the enemy that much extra time in which to improve his defences, extend his inundations, and generally strengthen his western wall defences. There were, however, considerable advantages in a postponement. For besides having more time to train, equip and prepare the invasion forces, it would also give the Allied air forces more time to paralyse German industry and her railways. Also the weather in June should be more favourable. As far as the landing craft were concerned it would give more time to complete repairs and make available those from new production due in the extra period.

Eventually on February 1st it was agreed by the Combined Chiefs of Staffs and the British and American Governments, that "D" day should be put back until June 1st or thereabouts. Stalin, I understand, took the news extremely well.

So with the extra production, the repaired craft to be made available through the revised date, the postponement of "Anvil" until August, and by ingenious juggling on the part of the Naval and Army Staffs, we found that it was possible to comply with Montgomery's wishes. The invasion should be carried out by five divisions in the assault and two in the immediate follow-up, excluding the employment of airborne divisions.

A similar struggle went on to increase the allocation of aircraft and gliders for the airborne operation. Here again "Anvil's" demands ran counter to our own. In the end, however, additional resources were made available, which allowed for an initial lift of between two and three divisions.

On January 21st the Supreme Commander had given his blessing to the new plan in general. There was, of course, a lot of detail work still to be done, but from that moment all the staffs knew what was wanted and could get to work in earnest. By February 1st we had produced with the Naval and Air Headquarters an "Initial Joint Plan" for Eisenhower's approval, and having received this, the inter-service detailed planning could then go ahead. I will touch on the actual plan of assault later on when I describe the presentation of the plans in April 1944.

The third major point about which Montgomery was not satisfied was the command set-up for the assault. Previous experience had taught him that it was necessary to assault by formations in depth — i.e. Corps and Armies. He, therefore, decided that the 1st U.S. Army and the 2nd British Army should land side by side, each on a two Corps front, the Canadian Army and Patton's Third U.S. Army coming in later when there was sufficient room. He would command personally these two Armies from the start, and so the single Task Force Commander principle was given up.

II

It wasn't until January 9th or 10th that I formally took over Chief of Staff 21st Army Group. It was very bad luck on Morgan (not the "Cossac" planner) who had held the appointment for some time, for because of the change, he missed being in the invasion. He later became Chief of Staff to Alexander in Italy, and subsequently Supreme Commander in the Mediterranean (the Morgan Line bears his name). So he got well-deserved recognition for what he had done. There was no one more pleased than myself to see his advancement, for leaving 21st Army Group through no fault of his own must have been a bitter blow. He couldn't have been kinder and more helpful either before or after I took over.

It was rather an ordeal arriving at this enormous Headquarters composed of entirely new faces, the majority of whom had not had much practical experience of war. In order to get things done in the time it was therefore necessary to bring back from Eighth Army several officers to take on certain key positions. We re-assembled to some extent the "old firm," the team which had worked so well together. This was, indeed, a wise move on Montgomery's part, for I am entirely convinced that it would otherwise have been quite impossible to have completed successfully all the planning and arrangements in the time. It was hard luck on those officers who had to make way, but then one has to be ruthless in war to be successful.

I have always felt most grateful for the way the officers of this Headquarters helped me during this period, for it was only natural that they should have resented my intrusion. I received nothing but kindness and whole-hearted support.

Besides the absorption of the new arrivals from Eighth Army, another and greater re-organisation had to be undertaken. By virtue of Montgomery's position as overall Land Forces Commander we became an Allied Headquarters. The Supreme Commander left it to us to decide what the set-up should be. I talked it over with Bedell Smith and he gave me a pretty free hand. One of the problems was that at some future date Eisenhower would take personal command of the Land Forces, and so we would then cease to command American Armies. Therefore, it was not possible to have an entirely integrated Anglo-American staff, for when the change round came about, there would be many gaps without experienced officers to fill them. Then again, most of the American officers whom I was going to get were required for the 12th U.S. Army Group Headquarters when it started to function as such.

In the end I produced a compromise. Some of the branches of the staff were integrated, and in some we produced parallel British and American elements. This compromise would avoid any hiatus when the Americans left our command, and would compensate for differences in the two staff systems. I was lucky to obtain a first-class lot of officers who whole-heartedly accepted the situation. It must have been disappointing to many of them, for according to the original proposals an American and not an Englishman would be commanding the assault.

21st Army Group Headquarters was initially located in St. Paul's School, whilst SHAEF with the Naval and Air

Headquarters were in Norfolk House. Later the Supreme Commander's Headquarters moved to Bushey Park.

The 12th U.S. Army Group Headquarters was in London, the First U.S. Army at Bristol, the Second British Army in Oxfordshire. For part of the detailed planning stage the armies sent skeleton staffs up to work close to us in London. We had to plan with two Air Headquarters, Leigh-Mallory's as well as the British and Tactical Air Force Headquarters under Coningham — the reason being that after 12th U.S. Army Group took over, we would not be controlling the whole land battle. Other Headquarters which functioned directly under our command were Airborne Troops, L. of C., G.H.Q. Troops, and the 79th Armoured Division (of which more will be said later).

Nearer the day of the invasion the various Headquarters took up their battle locations. We lived in various flats and messes in the neighbourhood of St. Paul's School. Montgomery had a flat in Latymer Court, with a mess attached. Graham (Major-General Administration) and I shared another in the same building. It was, therefore, very convenient.

Once Eisenhower had approved the outline plan, Montgomery gathered together his four Army Commanders[33] to explain his plans. The meeting went off very well indeed, and everyone appeared quite clear as to what his role was to be. Bradley was most co-operative and charming as always. Patton was full of fight and a bit disappointed that he was not going to be let loose in the opening stages. However, when he heard what his task was to be — to over-run the Brittany peninsula and exploit the break-out by the First U.S. Army, he

---

[33] Dempsey — Second British Army; Crerar — First Canadian Army; Bradley — First U.S. Army; Patton — Third U.S. Army.

cheered up, and told us what he would do to those "Goddamn sons of bitches." It was a friendly and happy meeting.

III

I will try and give some idea of how I spent my time during these busy days.

Each morning I would start by holding a full scale staff conference at which I would give out any instructions regarding the day's work — conferences — meetings — visits, etc. The various branches could then raise points for decision and co-ordination. I was a great believer in these conferences, for they saved an immense amount of paper work, and quickened things up generally. I liked some of the lower levels of the staff to attend as well as the heads of branches and sections. I found this paid and their time was not wasted.

More often than not there would be a full scale interservice staff meeting presided over by each of the three Chiefs of Staff[34] in turn. These were exhausting affairs at which we would thrash out all the current planning problems that had reached our level. Modifications to existing plans; requests for more shipping; selection of bombing targets are examples. The atmosphere became very heated at times, but we never failed to find an agreed solution. There had to be a lot of give and take, and we rarely worried our respective "Masters." I was very lucky in having such delightful colleagues. Leigh-Mallory's Chief of Staff was Wigglesworth. We knew each other well, both from planning days in Cairo as well as during Eighth Army's campaigns when he was with Tedder. I was so glad to see him given the important post of Air Commander-in-Chief in Germany. Then my Naval opposite number was Admiral Creasy. He never minced his words and you knew just where

---

[34] Montgomery's, Ramsay's and Leigh-Mallory's.

you were with him. The Army can be truly grateful for the way he helped us, and I take this opportunity of saying how sorry I am that the Army had so often to ask the Navies to change their plans!

Then each week the Supreme Commander held a conference attended by the various Commanders-in-Chief and their Chiefs of Staff. These were used to check up upon progress, and any troubles could then be aired.

The conference finished, we would usually adjourn to the V.I.P.'s mess where you found yourself inside a little plot of America, and could eat juicy steaks, fried chicken, and other delicacies not often seen in rationed England. I enjoyed those lunches a lot, for not only was the food good, but we did a great deal of business over the luncheon table. Bedell Smith was usually my host, and we built up a firm friendship on these and other such occasions. He has a ready wit. One morning at Norfolk House, after there had been a heavy raid on London, and my daughter had been born during the night, he sent the following signal to my wife. "Many congratulations (.) But why all the gun-fire; it was only a girl (.)"

Besides these regular meetings there were, of course many others. Discussions with various members of the staff. Conferences on specialised matters such as medical evacuation, the "Mulberry," waterproofing, equipment production, etc.

When once the Joint Plan had been agreed to, I did not see my Chief very often. He would pop in now and again in between his travels, and when in London would dine in our mess. He possessed that priceless asset — of letting one get on with the job, and if you were stuck for a decision, you knew you could get it immediately.

I found it very difficult indeed to get out of London, but managed to see one or two rehearsals and trials, and also paid visits to 79th Armoured Division. I must now say a word about this remarkable formation.

IV

In April, 1943, General Hobart was charged with the task of developing a new technique for the assault in Western Europe. His old division, the 79th, was to be used for the purpose. All kinds of tank and engineer units were collected together under his wing, and all the resources of the country, brains and industry, were put at his disposal. But the full credit must go to "Hobo" (General Hobart), for his drive, personality and resource were primarily responsible for the great success of these developments. Without his "babies" or "funnies" as they were often called, the assault against the West Wall would have been more difficult, and much more expensive in lives. Even after the successful assault, his units were in continual demand.

The following are some of the machines which were developed: —

> The D.D. — amphibious tank.
> The C.D.L. — a tank carrying an armoured protected searchlight which could flicker and temporarily blind the defence.
> The CRAB — a tank carrying a "Flail" for exploding mines.
> A.V.R.E. — assault engineer units which handled a number of vehicles and machines designed to deal with various types of defences. These included flame throwing tanks.
> The Armoured Bulldozer — a most important item.

Later on the 79th Armoured Division was also equipped with other amphibious vehicles such as the Buffalo (tracked amphibian) which proved so useful in the fighting in the waterlogged country of Holland and Belgium, and also for crossing the Rhine.

Some of the staff under me would become terrified when they knew General Hobo was about, He was such a go-getter that they never really knew until he had left what new commitment they had been persuaded to accept. I found his visits acted as a tonic, for his enthusiastic and confident nature would never consider failure. An answer *would* be found — and it usually was. I paid two or three visits to the Division and was always heartened by what I saw.

The first rehearsal which I attended was carried out at Studland Bay in Dorset. Admiral Ramsay and his Chief of Staff travelled down with us in Montgomery's train. The train was named "Rapier" and was a most comfortable affair. There were sleepers, restaurant coach, saloons and compartments for the train staff. Several cars could be carried in a specially designed "gutted" coach. Without this train I am sure the Commander-in-Chief could never have carried out the immense programme which he had set himself. He usually travelled by night, and it meant he could accomplish his visits with the minimum fatigue.

This exercise was of an experimental type, and the assault was in skeleton only. The D.D. (Amphibious) tanks were used with the leading waves, and Naval rocket fire, and fire from L.C.T.'s supported the landing. The operation started at first light and was watched by a distinguished gathering headed by H.M. the King himself. Eisenhower was there, and all the leading commanders. Many lessons were learnt, particularly as regards timing, and the usefulness of the various machines and craft employed. On our way back to London in the train Montgomery held a conference at which the problem of the composition of the assaulting waves was discussed. Everyone had been trying to find the "school solution." There were so many things to be considered. D.D. tanks — forward observing officers for the artillery — assault engineers and their several machines of war — landing craft carrying various types of guns — rocket ships and landing craft containing self-propelled artillery; all of which could be used to support the actual landing. It was agreed at this conference that the D.D. tanks would be the first to land, and that the self-propelled artillery would be positioned in rear, firing over the leading waves. Naval ships would support the assault from the flanks. No fixed rule was made as regards the various assault engineer machines, or for the different gun devices. A "menu" would be selected to suit the problem presented by the particular beach in question. This arrangement worked very well.

Much nearer "D" day I witnessed a rehearsal by the First U.S. Army near Dartmouth. It was upon a far bigger scale and the great fleet of ships and landing craft were supported by air attack. The operation went on for over 24 hours, and the beach maintenance arrangements were tried out. To be able to undertake such large scale rehearsals without interference from the enemy's air forces said a lot for the degree of air supremacy we had already attained.

Another exercise worth mentioning was one to test the air support plans. This took place at Studland Bay and was most impressive. Wave upon wave of heavy and medium bombers flew over the beaches releasing their loads. The weather, unfortunately, was poor and the heavies were forced to fly too low to allow really accurate bombing. In spite of this, however, we all came away most optimistic, for it was difficult to see how the enemy could be anything but dazed after such a frightful plastering. The final phase of the air support was conducted by fighters using rockets, bombs and cannons. After all such exercises a very careful analysis and examination was carried out by the services concerned, in order to arrive at the optimum technique.

There was one incident which upset the usual routine at St. Paul's, and that was the christening of my daughter. Montgomery had agreed to become a godfather and he suggested that the tea-party should be held at our headquarters, and he gave over his own offices for the occasion. The A.D.C.'s were ordered to assist, and our A.T.S. produced a magnificent tea. When inspecting the scene before the arrival of the guests, Montgomery pointed to the "Pending Tray" which still remained on his desk. He said:

"I've left it there so that you can park the baby when it gets tired!"

V

Very shortly after taking over the new Commander-in-Chief held a big conference at St. Paul's to which all General officers and senior staff officers were invited. Here he introduced himself and then proceeded to explain his views on "How to make war." He laid down a very clear tactical doctrine, and certain principles which were to apply to command and organisation. He took the opportunity to give out his rulings upon some of the controversial subjects that existed at the time. Finally he described how he worked himself, and also something about his habits. This was all of great value and it ensured that everyone was tuned into the same waveband.

Having got the Joint Plan off his chest, Montgomery now concentrated upon his soldiers. He was new to many of them, and he lost no time in ensuring that they both saw and heard him. He travelled round and visited all the formations. He would often use a jeep, and tell the soldiers to gather round and, standing up, would give them a few minutes of the

"Monty tonic." As in the past, he produced in this way great enthusiasm and confidence. He did not only attend to the soldiers, but also visited some of the war factories, and ceremonies in connection with the "Salute the Soldier" campaign. Here again his object was to assist this great crusade which was gathering momentum day by day.

It made me very angry when I heard disgruntled officers in the clubs and others criticising these activities as being done merely for personal publicity. It was all part of a carefully thought out plan, and one based upon practical experience.

Concurrently with these visits he set about examining the various commanders and staffs. Many were quite new to war, and so a lot of shuffling around took place in order that at least the commander or his senior staff officer should be one who had proved himself in the war which was then being waged.

VI

On April 7th Montgomery held a Presentation of Plans in the big lecture hall at St. Paul's School. The Prime Minister and the British Chiefs of Staff were invited. All General Officers of the four Armies attended, as well as their Naval and Air counterparts. Certain senior staff officers were also present. The proceedings started with each Commander-in-Chief in turn explaining his broad plan, and this was followed by talks by the various commanders concerned. In this way everyone became acquainted at first hand with the complete plan, as well as with the various ingredients. It was a great success, and at the end I am sure there were no doubters as to what the outcome would be. Montgomery made a big impression that day, especially amongst some who were still not quite convinced of his true ability.

Admiral Ramsay, in giving out the naval picture, was inclined to put too much stress upon the difficulties that might arise. He felt it was only right that the Army should realise how easy it was for the Naval side of the operation to be put out of gear. He finished, however, on a confident note, saying he was perfectly certain the Navies would land the armies in the right sectors, and would ensure their subsequent supply.

The Air side was admirably put across by Leigh-Mallory. He was quite confident the German Air Force would be well under control, and he lucidly explained the various plans. It was either Leigh-Mallory or Coningham (Tactical Air Forces) who stressed the importance of the early seizure of the good "airfield area" to the south-east of Caen.

The American Commanders were particularly impressive. Collins[35] I think, would have won a Gallup poll, and there was no doubt that he lived up to the feeling he then gave us all, as being a forceful and able commander.

There was a very large layered map on the floor upon which the various speakers could walk. The boundaries and objectives were marked upon it. Arrows and models were used to denote the ships and formations during each explanation. On the walls behind, several large maps were available. I think the Army's contribution consisted of a "Phase line" map (of which more anon), a map showing future developments of the operations, the administrative plan, and one showing the arrangements for concentrating and mounting the expedition.

Montgomery started his talk by explaining the purpose of the Presentation, and the importance of preserving secrecy. He touched upon the object of "Overlord" (the name given to the whole operation) and stressed the significance of this great Allied team. He then went on to describe the enemy picture,

---

[35] Commanded the U.S. VIII Corps.

which two months before the landings were to take place was not an easy matter.

In view of the controversy which has been going on as regards Montgomery's plan in Normandy, I will give the Army tasks as given out by him that day: —

The First U.S. Army, having assaulted astride the estuary of the Vire river, was to capture Cherbourg as rapidly as possible, and then, east of Carentan to develop operations southwards towards St. Lô — conforming to the advance of the Second British Army.

After the capture of the area Cherbourg-Caumont-Vire-Avranches, the Army was to drive southwards with the object of capturing Rennes and establishing our flank on the Loire river.

The Second British Army, after assaulting to the west of the Orne river, was to develop operations to the south and southeast in order to secure airfield sites, and to protect the eastern flank of the First U.S. Army while it was capturing Cherbourg.

In its subsequent operations the Army was *to pivot on its left flank and offer a strong front against enemy movement towards the lodgement area from the east.* (The italics are mine.)

The First Canadian Army was to come in later and take over the left sector of the lodgement area.

The Third U.S. Army was given the task of clearing the Brittany peninsula, and subsequently of covering the flank of the lodgement area whilst the First U.S. Army moved northeastwards towards Paris.

After this came some details of the composition of the assaulting force, and the Fire plan to assist it ashore.

The two U.S. Airborne Divisions (82 and 101) were to be dropped behind the beaches north of the Vire estuary, and also in an area on the west side of the Cotentin peninsula in order to prevent the movement of enemy reserves northwards. Subsequently, however, as I will explain, this plan was modified, and both divisions were dropped behind the "Utah" beaches in order to secure the beach exits and assist the troops across the difficult inundated country.

On the British front a portion of the 6th Airborne Division was to be landed to the east of Caen and its main task was to seize the bridges over the Orne at Benouville and Ranville.

Next came a description of how the Commander-in-Chief hoped to develop the operations, and to assist him a "Phase line" map was exhibited. Let me explain what is meant by a phase line. A Commander must have a definite idea how he intends to swing the battle. He must aim at a definite pattern. Having given this, the staff work out the *optimum* progress of development in accordance with that pattern. Upon this all planning is based. The amount of transport, the number of airfields to be constructed, the amount of bridging material; all such items as this have to be equated to the time factor. These decisions reflect back upon the loading of ships, and the planning of the build-up. I stress the "optimum" classification. A phase line does in no way imply a guarantee that we shall reach such and such a position by a certain date. It should mean that the armies will not be caught napping if things go really well, by being held up through some shortage or another. I am afraid a lot of the controversy in respect of developments in Normandy originate from this misconception of the true significance of a phase line.

Montgomery always meant to swing upon the "Caen hinge," and that even in the best of circumstances he only intended to move this flank eastwards some ten miles in the first month.

The rate of build-up was then dealt with. The plan was to be as flexible as possible so that the Armies' requirements relating to types of divisions and maintenance needs could be adjusted. An Anglo-American organisation named "Buco" (Build-up Control) was established at Portsmouth, and this body, although confronted with the most intricate problems, fulfilled their tasks with complete success.

Montgomery then gave the planned build-up for the first ninety days. This was as follows: —

D Day (including airborne): US Divisions: 3⅔, British Divisions: 4, Total Divisions: 7⅔

D+1 (including airborne): US Divisions: 5⅔, British Divisions: 4⅔, Total Divisions: 10⅓

D+4 (including airborne): US Divisions: 8⅓, British Divisions: 6⅓, Total Divisions: 14⅔

D+12 (excluding airborne): US Divisions: 9, British Divisions: 9, Total Divisions: 18

D+20 (excluding airborne): US Divisions: 9, British Divisions: 15, Total Divisions: 24

D+35 (excluding airborne): US Divisions: 15, British Divisions: 15, Total Divisions: 30

D+90 (excluding airborne): US Divisions: 20, British Divisions: 15, Total Divisions: 35

He then spoke of the assistance we could expect from the Resistance Groups on the Continent, and of some of the Engineer problems which confronted us. The latter were divided into the following categories: on the beaches — dealing with obstacles to our advance — bridging and airfield construction.

Montgomery drew attention to the mounting arrangements. These were very complicated. Troops and vehicles were to be moved first to concentration areas, and from here to marshalling areas, and finally to the embarkation areas. In each embarkation area there were to be a number of embarkation points.

I said the mounting arrangements were complicated and so they were. To start with several agencies were involved, and their work had to be co-ordinated, e.g. the War Office, the Air Ministry and "Etousa" (in respect of the American forces). Then there was the problem of finding sufficient accommodation, particularly as the concentration and marshalling areas had to be within one day's march of each other. Another restriction was the fact that once waterproofed, vehicles could only travel a certain distance.

The security arrangements had to be very carefully watched. At the marshalling areas the troops would be briefed, i.e. have their tasks explained to them. Models were provided at all the briefing points, and once troops had been let in on the plan, it was important that they should cease to have contact with the world outside. The war correspondents had to be included in the briefing arrangements, and steps had to be taken to prevent widespread comment on this sudden disappearance of so many well-known journalists. The stoppage of leave so as to avoid an indication as to the real date of assault, and the temporary suspension of the use of diplomatic mail bags by the representatives of certain countries, were other matters requiring special handling.

The arrangements for map distribution — a big task — and the handling of "Residues" (the portion of formations that were left out of the initial assault) were also explained.

The repercussions if a postponement became necessary were of course tremendous. Montgomery explained briefly the two types — of one or two days, or for the alternative, a month.

Various measures which were being taken to mislead the enemy as to our real intentions were then described. These were aimed at making him think we were going to invade the Pas de Calais.

Montgomery's address finished with the main administrative points. As can be well imagined, the problems encountered were vast. To start with, the American and British systems were different and had to be blended to meet the needs of this great operation. The uncertainty of the value of the "Mulberry" artificial harbour, and the dangers from bad weather necessitated the preparation of emergency maintenance plans. I will leave it to others more qualified than myself to tell the full administrative story. We were indeed lucky in our head administrative staff officer and in the heads of the Services. Graham was able to bring his resourceful business brain to bear on the many problems, and he was ably backed up by Brigadier Fielden, who possessed just exactly the right temperament for his exacting appointment.

Towards the end of the afternoon Churchill got up and made a speech. He appeared rather tired and grave at first, but finished with great strength. We were left in no doubt as to the vital importance of this great enterprise to the Allied cause. In our Commander-in-Chief's final remark he had stressed the need for the various Commanders to show great resource and initiative, and to move inland even if things were sticky on their flanks. He instructed them to "peg out claims" as deep as possible. This conception pleased the Prime Minister a great deal, and he stressed the need to take great risks.

It had been a most satisfactory day, and at the end of it there was a confident feeling that we would not fail.

We held a "war game" on April 8th to test out the plans and to find out any weak links in our preparations. We chose a number of situations before, during, and after the assault, and the various Commanders concerned were confronted with them.

The Allied air forces, unlike the Armies, had already started their air offensive in support of operation "Overlord." Their activities included:

(a) Destruction of the enemy's air forces.
(b) Attacks to reduce the enemy's war industry, and his morale.
(c) Destruction of the German oil production.
(d) The rail interdiction programme.
(e) Bombing attacks against the "V" weapon sites.
(f) Operations against the West Wall defences.
(g) Attacks carried out to support the cover plan.
(h) Photographic reconnaissance.

Besides the above, specialised training had to be done with the Armies, and with the airborne troops.

It was a very big programme, and it was most efficiently completed. Several controversial matters arose. For instance, numerous meetings were held as to the value of an intensive effort to dislocate the enemy's railway systems. Some argued that it would be impossible to reduce the rail capacity below the strictly military needs. There was also divergence of views as to the type of targets to go for — the locomotives, the repair shops, the marshalling yards, or the bridges. Leigh-Mallory never wavered in his opinion that the "Railway Interdiction" plan, as it was called, would produce a good dividend, and events, I am sure, justified his attitude. By the time we landed the enemy's railways serving the invasion coast were virtually at a standstill. It must be remembered, however, that the comparatively late development of a successful technique for bombing bridges was largely responsible for this.

There were few railway bridges remaining over the big rivers such as the Seine and Loire by "D" day.

The attacks upon the enemy's oil production did not commence in real earnest until about May. Spaatz[36] pressed for an earlier start, and in view of the great success that was eventually achieved, and remembering the vital effect it had on the German collapse, it would have paid us well.

The attacks against the enemy's coast defences were a big commitment. In order not to give away the sector of coast chosen for the landing, these operations had to be spread equally all along the invasion coast. It involved a maddening waste of effort, but this was inevitable. The Navy and ourselves were continually pressing for these attacks to be undertaken in good time. In some cases, however, the concrete defence works were so strong as to be hardly susceptible to destruction.

We were very grateful for the brilliantly executed low oblique photography of the actual beaches and the waterfront. It gave us detailed information as to the type of beach obstacles to be met, and the attacking troops had pictures showing exactly what their particular beach would like look as they landed.

In view of the diversity of the demands made upon the Allied Air Forces, it will be interesting to know how we could have produced better results by alterations in the distribution of this preliminary air effort. I understand that investigations are being carried out with this end in view.

VIII

To get finality for the airborne plan was not easy. It was decided after the "Presentation of Plans" that the two American divisions should, if possible, be dropped in

---

[36] Commanded the U.S. Strategic Air Force.

supporting distance of each other. But the trouble was to find suitable D.Z.'s (Dropping Zones). The Bocage country, with its small fields, hedgerows and trees, was hardly suitable for the landing of gliders. Numerous experiments were carried out in order to see whether it was possible for the chosen areas to be used. Eventually a plan was agreed to, and General Bradley, whose right corps depended to so large an extent on a successful airborne operation, breathed again!

A crisis occurred either in May or early June, when the Air Commander-in-Chief became very worried about the hazards of the airborne plan. Owing to the danger from our own ships' A.A. the fly in, which was to take place at night, could not be made from the east, and in addition the aircraft had to avoid the heavy A.A. defences of Cherbourg and Le Havre. This meant that the American divisions would have to approach from the west side of the Cotentin peninsula. The defences of the Channel Islands were one problem, but our information now pointed to a strengthening of enemy troops in the very area over which the air convoys would have to fly.

This airborne operation was vital to our plans, and Montgomery had instructed me to remain quite firm on the issue. I spent a long day at SHAEF Headquarters in Bushey Park arguing our case. Leigh-Mallory was very understanding, but he felt it his duty to represent his assessment of the probable casualties. We in the Army were not so alarmed, for we knew that unless a formation was prepared for such a target, it would take some time — especially at night — to appreciate first what was afoot, and then to concentrate the A.A. artillery in the right place. An impasse was reached in the afternoon, and I referred the matter to Bedell Smith. I found him entirely in agreement with the Army's point of view, but it was a matter which required the decision of the Supreme

Commander. Eisenhower never hesitated; he said that he appreciated his Air Commander-in-Chief's attitude, but that in view of the importance of this operation it must take place, and he would accept the risks involved. The air was now cleared and planning could go ahead unhindered. Leigh-Mallory of course accepted the Supreme Commander's decision without question, and concentrated upon doing everything possible to ensure the minimum of losses. When after the airborne assault was over, and it was found that the casualties had been astonishingly low, he was the first to ring up Eisenhower and tell him how glad he was that the latter had accepted the risks, and admitted that he had been wrong. This was typical of the man — always frank and generous-hearted.

IX

It is always very easy to stress the difficulties that are encountered, and then to explain how brilliantly these were overcome. But, on the other hand, I think it may be of interest if I select a few of the snags which cropped up, particularly during the latter part of the planning period.

Ensuring the timely arrival of the various machines and equipments was a complicated business. A slight adjustment in a plan might have repercussions upon the numbers of tanks, machines for the 79th Armoured Division, or some specialised type of transport. I kept an enormous list of all the various items of equipment, and it fell to me to revise the priority categories each week. I was lucky in having Brigadier Herbert on my staff who dealt with these matters, and it was due to his efforts, coupled with the unstinting support we received from the War Office and Ministry of Supply, that this complicated process was successfully solved. We had some nasty shocks, but a little pressure here, and a pat on the back there in the end produced the right answer. Waterproofing material was, for instance, one of our particular headaches. The many thousands of articles necessary to permit vehicles to "wade" ashore were being made in factories in many parts of the country. These had all to be "married up" and delivered at the right place and the right time.

Another major worry was the late appearance of beach obstacles in the "Neptune" area. There were various types of steel devices and posts, some of which had mines attached. The Navy carried out trials to see what effect they had upon the different landing craft, and we handed over the other investigations to General Hobart and his 79th Armoured Division. In his thorough way he developed several methods for defeating these obstructions. He evolved rapid methods for blowing them up with prepared charges. Grapnels were available for pulling them aside to form a fairway. He also found out the best point of aim for the D.D. tanks' guns. I paid a visit to see these activities, and I returned feeling that yet another "horror" had been laid low. Inglis, our Chief Engineer, was of course intimately connected with all these problems.

Clay and peat on the beaches was another matter which worried us. Our information was not complete as to the whereabouts and extent of such patches. Unless there was sufficient covering of sand over the top, tanks and vehicles might get stuck and never arrive ashore. We consulted every expert on the subject, examined many books, interrogated those who knew that coast, and took air photographs. Some very gallant men were used to obtain samples of the beaches. They would swim ashore on a dark night from a submarine, bringing back samples of the beaches by screwing in a type of hollow cylinder. We also carried out experiments on similar types of beach around the Wash, to determine the amount of sand cover that was necessary, and also to develop types of track-way that could be laid over such patches. In the event we had little difficulty on this account, but we could not afford to neglect any difficulty. This clay problem also affected the bombing policy, for we had to experiment with fuses in order to ensure that the bombing support would not defeat its object by churning up the ground and spreading layers of clay all over the place.

Many of the ships carrying vehicles and equipment, although not required at once, had to be loaded before "D" day. Relative priorities so much depended upon the course of the campaign, and therefore decisions at this early date were not easy. For instance, by what date would another load of bridging be required? This depended, of course, upon our rate of progress. When would the 12th U.S. Army Group take over? If we shipped over all their vehicles too soon, valuable space might be wasted. Such problems came up each day.

The provision of suitable areas to carry out rehearsals was another difficulty we met. The Government were naturally very loath to cause the hard tried British people any unnecessary inconvenience. These exercises often meant clearing a large area of all its inhabitants and often damage would be done. There were some difficulties but the War Office fought successfully on our behalf.

As can be well imagined the signal complications were considerable. The provision of the communications for the mounting, and for the headquarters which we used in England was undertaken by the War Office, and was remarkably successful. The question of frequencies was a matter which gave the Joint Signal Board a lot to think about, for there was a danger that on "D" day the air might become saturated with wireless traffic. There were so many applicants — the Navies,

Armies, Air forces, resistance groups, the B.B.C. and many others. Some demands had to be reduced considerably.

One of the most complicated matters with which we were faced was the question of "D" day and "H" hour. "H" hour being the time at which the leading wave of the assault touched down on the beaches.

It was decided from the Naval point of view that moonlight would be required for the final approach, and because of our great superiority in Naval guns and aircraft, a daylight assault was agreed to. The Army, however, very naturally wanted the period between moonlight and the assault reduced to the very minimum so as to give the enemy as little daylight as possible during the initial approach. There had to be sufficient time, however, to allow the navies and the air forces to engage the enemy's coast defences. Agreement was eventually reached that a minimum of forty minutes was required between nautical twilight[37] and "H" hour.

The tidal factor was an even more complicated affair. In order to clear the beach obstacles, the lower the tide the better. But at low water the troops would be faced with a very long approach to the shore, and the uneven ground so uncovered would here and there necessitate a swim. Therefore a landing at low water was not acceptable to the Army. The need to ground the landing craft on a rising tide and so allow them to get away quickly and prevent congestion on the beaches was another factor to be considered.

Because of these and other influences it was decided that "H" hour was to be at 40 minutes after nautical twilight, and this to be when the tide had flowed for three hours. But because of the differences in tide timings between the various

---

[37] Best defined as when it is just possible to notice a change from night to day.

beaches, and because of rocks in one particular area, different "H" hours for each beach had to be accepted.

These conditions would only allow an assault within a three-day period once a fortnight. And June 5th was the start of the nearest such period to the provisional date of June 1st already fixed. We therefore agreed to the former date. But then everything would depend upon the weather.

Perhaps the most irritating of all our problems was the uncertainty as to the enemy's final dispositions. Other than the possible use of air attack against a new arrival, little could be done, for our plans were completed. We just had to hope and pray that any reinforcement would not be on a major scale. Nearer the day, however, we could breathe more freely for the railway interdiction plan had been so successful that the movement of reserves by the enemy had become a matter of extreme difficulty.

X

About the close of April, Main Headquarters 21st Army Group moved down to the Portsmouth area, Rear (administrative) Headquarters remaining behind in London. Except for one or two rooms in the large house which was requisitioned for the Naval Headquarters, we now functioned on a tent, hut and caravan basis. These were scattered about the surrounding park, and except for the Commander-in-Chief's mess which was in a small house, the remaining messes were under canvas. It was a pleasant change to be working once again more or less under field conditions.

The vehicles comprising Montgomery's Tactical Headquarters were either being waterproofed at some assembly area or were concentrated around the house where he had his mess. It was a charming house and we lived in comfort.

The C.-in-C. had his office there, and his personal staff, myself and Graham had bedrooms as well. The remaining Generals who messed with Montgomery either slept in tents or in their caravans.

During the few weeks before the assault many distinguished visitors came down for lunch or dinner as Montgomery's guests. There was a visit by H.M. the King, as well as by the various Dominion Premiers. Then Churchill dined with us one night, and we experienced one of those unforgettable occasions. He was in great form, and prepared to talk — we let him. The Commander-in-Chief's betting book was brought out, and several wagers were laid on diverse subjects. The date by which the war in the West or in the East would end. The type of Government we would elect after the war. These were examples. Montgomery never *laid* a bet himself, but he was always prepared to *accept* one. The procedure was something like this. Someone might say:

"We'll have those Germans licked by Christmas, 1944."
Very quietly Montgomery would say:
"What was that you said?"
The statement would then be repeated — possibly with not quite its previous conviction:
"All right, are you prepared to bet on it?" Answer, "Yes."
"How much?" from the Commander-in-Chief.

A sum would then be arranged, and down it would go in the betting book, and the two concerned would sign. It is a vastly interesting book, and many famous names appear — but it's probably not for publication!

Whilst down at Portsmouth I made a change in M.A.'s. (Military Assistant). Harry Llewelyn who had acted in that capacity since my return to England had run the liaison staff in

Eighth Army, and I had promised him that nearer the day I would return him to his old calling. I was sorry to see him go, but I was lucky enough to get a delightful officer in his place — Bill Bovill of the Inniskilling Dragoon Guards. He was the ideal friend and companion during such an enterprise as this. I am sure it was largely due to his efforts that I remained more or less sane. Quiet, popular and possessing great personal charm, I can never be too grateful for all he did.

In addition to the M.A., I became the possessor of an A.D.C. — not a Britisher, but an American. Early in the year, with the new command set-up, Montgomery had asked Eisenhower for an American Aide. Two men were sent along to choose from. They were both so good, however, that my Chief felt the problem was altogether too difficult. So he asked if one of the officers could be allotted to me. This was agreed to, and, of course, I was delighted. Again I was extremely lucky and I'm sure "Bill Culver" will be long remembered by many in 21st Army Group. He served me well and kept me cheerful. He was full of the enthusiasm of a typical young American, and he was a great master at getting what I, and incidentally what sometimes he, wanted! We had some happy times together.

During the last two or three weeks Montgomery travelled around a great deal, speaking to various groups of officers of Lieutenant-Colonel's rank and above. He was in the process of producing that enthusiasm and confidence that was a keystone in his method of command. He then decided to take two or three days' rest in Scotland, It was arranged that "Rapier" (Montgomery's train) would be parked in a siding in the Highlands, and that he would pass the time walking and fishing. I found some important papers needed signature, and so followed him up, and spent two glorious days fishing on the

Spey! We then all travelled down together — a very pleasant interlude.

We spent a good deal of our time in planning for the future — trying to think out the various ways the operations would swing, and so have plans ready to meet such situations. We gave the Canadian Army the particular task of studying the operation for crossing the Seine. They produced some excellent material which proved of immense value when the time came. Then in accordance with Montgomery's proposed development of the campaign we prepared plans to help the "right hook" towards Paris. The use of airborne troops for this purpose was gone into, as well as various methods of solving the maintenance problems.

I'm afraid we gave the headquarters of the Airborne Troops a very bad time of it. For they were ordered to plan for one possibility after the other. They played up magnificently, but in retrospect I am convinced we were too anxious to have an answer for everything. In the event things moved so quickly that an airborne operation was not necessary, and so all their labours were wasted.

We produced plans for landing on the coast of Brittany to assist Patton in his advance. And then also there was a project for seizing Quiberon Bay, and establishing there a supply base.

Two or three exercises were held to test out the machinery for the invasion. One of these concerned the Tactical air support of the armies for the opening phase. This was very complicated, for until the Army and Air Headquarters with their appropriate air control staffs had been landed and were functioning overseas, the control of these operations was to be exercised from England. A further difficulty arose over the location of the different headquarters, for as I have already mentioned the headquarters of the Allied Tactical Air Forces was at Uxbridge, and the Naval and Army Group Headquarters were at Portsmouth. To meet this situation we set up a small Army staff at Uxbridge, composed of elements of the air support control and intelligence set-ups. This was, of course, Anglo-American. General directives were issued from our Main Headquarters at Portsmouth which contained an up-to-date appreciation of the Army situation and a forecast as to the future. We laid down the broad priorities. Contact between Portsmouth and Uxbridge was also maintained by frequent visits, and, of course, there were direct secret telephones available. On the far shore "tentacles" were allotted to all the assaulting brigades so that they could request immediate air support in their particular battle. These consisted of a small group with a wireless set that would deal direct with Uxbridge. The Army Headquarters could listen in to these requests for support, and if necessary could comment on them. In addition we planned to have a number of squadrons in the air ready to take on targets, and working on orders from the Divisional Headquarters ships. So it can be seen that it was very necessary to try out this rather untidy system before "D" day. The exercise was certainly successful in bringing forward weaknesses.

Another exercise was carried out to test the movement and embarkation machinery. This was called "Fabius," and again it proved most valuable.

Then we tested out the working of our own headquarters from the purely planning to the full operational basis. The handling of information, the co-ordination of staff work, liaison duties, and all the machinery connected with a full scale campaign were tried out.

Montgomery invited the four Army Commanders to dinner at his mess near Portsmouth two or three days before the assault started. Things couldn't have gone better. Everyone was in their best form, and all appeared supremely confident. During dinner many bets were made as to the duration of the war — when the next war would start, and kindred subjects. After dinner we gambled at some "racing" card game and we went to bed thinking we had taken money off George Patton. However, in the morning he came down to breakfast as pleased as Punch saying he had taken *our* money. So I don't know who won that night!

The Commander-in-Chief's Tactical Headquarters was now all loaded up ready to sail to Normandy. Everything was ready for the assault, and we now had little to do except wait for "D" day — and pray for good weather. The various Commanders-in-Chief issued their Personal messages (see Appendix B) and calm descended upon our headquarters.

The only other matter of interest which I will deal with in this chapter is the Supreme Commander's weather conferences. These showed Eisenhower at his best, and I was present at each one of them. As I recounted the events to Alan Moorehead and he has so vividly described them in his book "Eclipse," I am reproducing, with his permission, the story.

> On June 3rd, unknown to nearly everyone in the world, General Eisenhower called his senior commanders to the country house he was using as a headquarters in southern England. There were present Air Chief Marshal Tedder, the deputy Commander-in-Chief; Admiral Ramsay of the Allied navies; Air Marshal Trafford Leigh-Mallory of the air; Montgomery, with his chief of staff, de Guingand; Eisenhower's chief of staff, Bedell Smith; and one or two others. Of that company, two, Ramsay and Leigh-Mallory, were soon to die, but for the moment they were met to decide on the fate of a million other men. Although it was already past nine o'clock the gentle light of the long English summer

day was still coming through the windows. Coffee was poured out, and there was desultory conversation round the room until Eisenhower called them down to business. Three men, the best weather experts England and America could provide, came in, and one of them, a Scot, acted as spokesman. He was gloomy. A series of depressions was approaching the Channel. Wind, waves and cloud, that was the prospect. And the invasion fleet was due to sail on the following afternoon. One by one Eisenhower questioned his three chief commanders. Could the Navy manage it? Ramsay thought not. The assault might go ashore all right, but if the weather worsened there could be no adequate build-up. Same thing with Leigh-Mallory. Plan "B" would have to go into operation, the lesser plan. His crews would have to bomb on instruments through the cloud without seeing what they were hitting. No. The weather was not good enough for the air. Montgomery? Montgomery alone was favourable. "I'm ready," he said. But just for the moment this was more of a decision for the navy and the air force.

It was an immense undertaking to postpone "D" day. The troops and tanks and guns were embarked and waiting at scores of secret ports around the coast of England. The bombers were waiting on the airfields. The whole elaborate machine was poised to move on this day, and to upset it now, to let some ships put to sea and then bring them back, to retard the immense and exact programme of the build-up, to alter the schedule of the trains and the convoys and the loading, to keep the waiting million of men strung at high tension — all this was a fearfully dangerous prospect. Worse still, the meteorologists warned the meeting that if these next few days were lost in inaction then a week or a fortnight might go by before the channel tides would again be suitable for the landing.

"We will meet again to-morrow morning at 4.30," Eisenhower said. As the commanders went off to their rooms in the building, already the machine was beginning to turn over. Already some of the assault gunboats were putting out to sea, the glider troops and the parachutists were waiting with their harness. The early hours of the following morning were the latest possible moment when a decision could be taken. After that the thing would roll on inevitably and nothing could stop it short of a victory or a disaster on a scale that would eclipse anything that had passed in the war. The history of Europe depended entirely on the rising and falling of the wind.

At 4.30 a.m., June 4th, the same scene again. The same room. The coffee. The men feeling grey and a little unsteady., The meteorologists came in and it was seen at once that they had no better news. Again Eisenhower questioned his commanders. The Navy? No. The Air? No. The Army? Yes. "We will postpone it twenty-four hours," Eisenhower said. Officers ran to send the signals to the ports and the airfields. All over England the machine sighed down into a standstill. There was nothing now to do except wait.

On the evening of June 4th, the third meeting was called. From the meteorologists this time there was a definite flicker of hope. Most unexpectedly the weather had not worsened. It was dark, it was far from favourable, but it was no worse. And there was a hope that it would continue evenly like this for a few days.

Admiral Ramsay was not enthusiastic. He was still worried about the build-up. And yet — the chance was there. It could be done. Things could easily go wrong on the beaches, but still the landing was possible. Leigh-Mallory, too, thought that he could manage to put up his bombers and fighters. But they would have to go in on a modified plan. Montgomery again was all for sailing. The men sat round the table going through the possibilities over again, trying desperately to bring the facts to the point where they would produce a hard inevitable decision. But that was not possible. The element of luck remained.

> Suddenly Eisenhower came forward. "This is a decision which I must take alone," he said. "After all, that is what I am here for." The meeting waited. Then the Commander-in-Chief said "We will sail to-morrow."

And so the decision was made, and the convoys sailed from their many ports. On the afternoon before the landing I drove down to Southsea and watched the ships go by. The weather was not good, but because of it the German Air Force was not inquisitive. As I gazed at this great array of ships heading south, I asked myself whether it was really possible that at long last our months of planning in stuffy offices had reached fruition.

CHAPTER XIV: THE PRESS IN WAR

I

DURING the war in my various appointments, I found myself heavily involved with press matters. When Director of Military Intelligence in Cairo, press censorship and guidance came within my orbit, and as Chief of Staff, press problems were part of my daily bread. There are so many pitfalls, and good relations between the soldier and the press are so important, that I often felt I would like to commit my views to paper. This book has given me the opportunity.

One of the freedoms for which we were fighting was freedom of the press, and yet to achieve this end it was inevitable that on security grounds alone, the press was subject to considerable restriction in the process. In fact, they agreed to a sort of voluntary censorship. In the field, the Commander could impose certain restrictions in the interests of security, and it was inevitable that differences of opinion occurred as to what should or should not be withheld from publication. There was sometimes lack of understanding on both sides. It was quite natural that the press would often want more information as to our plans than we felt we were justified in giving. This was a healthy sign, and I admit sometimes feeling that the military were too "sticky" in this matter. On the whole, however, I was very much struck by the way our press was handled during the war. Hardly ever did their attitude embarrass our Commanders, which is more than can be said about the press of America.

As for the War Correspondents, I can say nothing but good. I have the greatest admiration for them and for the way they worked. I cannot recall any occasion where they let me down, betrayed a confidence, or did not within their unbiased judgment answer an appeal for assistance. I made many friendships amongst this cheerful and brave fraternity, which I hope will persist during the years to come.

In this chapter I will endeavour to analyse the relationship between the soldier and the press; bring out some of the weaknesses I found, and suggest certain improvements.

When I first came in contact with the "gentlemen of the press" in Cairo in 1942, I thought the relationship between us was bad. It looked to me as if the war correspondents were considered dangerous people who had to be very closely watched, in order to prevent them sabotaging our efforts. On the other hand, the war correspondents, I'm sure, felt the soldiers were not treating them with sufficient trust, and were not making it easy for them to carry out their exacting tasks, and their duty to the public. I found the average soldier's reaction towards press control rather narrow. He would have liked to have seen a censorship and control similar to that exercised by the Axis powers, where the truth was not strictly adhered to, and reports on operations were not released until the situation had clarified. I don't think the need to keep a free people fed with up-to-date and accurate news was sufficiently appreciated. A shift of attitude was required. Here is a great organisation with tremendous power; how can we best work together? That should have been the method of approach.

I admit that I was terrified on becoming D.M.I. when I found that included in my duties was censorship and a degree of press guidance. Shortly after I took over I was invited to a special party given by the war correspondents, when I met them "close-up" for the first time. They were friendly and amusing, but from the number of times that I was taken aside and given a bit of advice I realised that they were not very happy. From that moment I vowed I would do what I could to help. I was determined not to be pompous, always be accessible, and do my level best never to mislead them.

In the censorship sphere I was continually receiving appeals from correspondents to have some decision revised, or sometimes they would send me a despatch to read myself before it was submitted to the censors. On many occasions I found it very hard not to take the war correspondents' side when disputes arose, but one had so many "masters" to please. Commanders in the field were extremely sensitive, and would often attribute unwelcome enemy action or some other trouble to what had been allowed to be published in the press. In most cases there was no evidence to support this attitude. The censor's job is a thankless one, and he is continually receiving kicks from the various individuals who think they are likely to suffer from what is said. It is, of course, most important that the Commanders and troops should not get the impression that the press, and war correspondents, are letting them down, and therefore one often had to err on the side of severity. But I do feel that the services and the higher command should be educated more in this matter of the press and censorship. So much which the war correspondents put in their despatches was merely an expression of opinion based upon intelligent anticipation. Because this would sometimes touch on coming events, it was cut out. It was most irritating for the correspondents to see similar views expressed in the American, and even in enemy and neutral papers. For instance in 1942, when it was obvious to the whole world that we were not going to remain on the defensive for ever in the Western Desert, any suggestion that we were preparing for an offensive was for a time forbidden. Then there was a case where two correspondents with Eighth Army had been shown a map with arrows giving the intended direction of a thrust which was being made during the confused fighting shortly after we arrived back at the Alamein position. In a despatch they indicated what was hoped to be achieved. A terrible flap started. Army Commander, Commander-in-Chief and Prime Minister were all brought into it. Although technically wrong, I was sure it made not the slightest difference to the failure of this particular operation. The plan was a bad one in any case. I was equally sure the two men concerned were not deliberately trying to jeopardise our plans, and so I interceded on their behalf. They had been ordered home, and fortunately we got this order rescinded.

Montgomery was very good in dealing with this sort of thing. He disliked "bellyachers," and if during my days as his Chief of Staff I found that there was unnecessary grousing about what the press was saying I had only to go to him, and he would say a word here and there that would put a stop to it.

One must be human in these things, and one so often heard bitter remarks aimed at war correspondents because they were alleged to be trying to get a scoop. I won't deny that such things did happen, but it should be remembered that reporting was their profession, and for those who had not yet made their name this was their great opportunity for laying the foundation of a successful career. So it was certain one would sometimes meet a little over-keenness in this community of intensive-competition. I hold no brief, however, for the man who deliberately tries to evade censorship by getting his copy back through irregular channels, or who tried to trick the hard-worked censor. This individual should be blackballed by his colleagues.

In Cairo I used to hold weekly press talks on the local and general war situation. Why this duty fell upon the D.M.I. I never really understood. It should by rights have been undertaken by the operational staff of the Headquarters. As can be realised, I was often in receipt of very secret information, and I had therefore to watch my step when under the fire of highly intelligent interrogation. A slip might well compromise some source or other.

The war correspondents often used to ask me: "Why can't the press help more?" "Can't we prepare the people for good or for bad news?" etc., etc. In many cases this was not possible as something would be given away in the process but, as I have already said, we often went too far in our restriction. Once I asked them whether they would like to be used like the Axis press. That is, to put over news that would delude the enemy. Here, I said, was an excellent way of assisting the soldiers! But they would not hear of this. "We could never deliberately mislead the public" was what they said, and of course with a free people and a free press, such action would be intolerable.

II

Within the broad term "press" one was concerned with four separate echelons which produced considerable problems, and which sometimes became quite angry with one another. These were: —

(a) The war correspondents at the front.
(b) The war correspondents at the base.
(c) The Empire and Allied press.
(d) The B.B.C.

In the first place, one was continually being faced with the question of priority of releases. It was only natural that those correspondents who were covering the front which was producing the news did not want their "thunder" taken by those situated further afield. We did our best for them, but in practice it was very difficult to prevent mishaps. The B.B.C. was always in a position to get the news out first, and then the higher headquarters behind had war correspondents, and they had press conferences, and therefore they had to be told the news.

When we were dealing with the Empire and Allied press it was extremely difficult to reach agreement on the opportune *time* of release. One or other country would obviously be in a position to publish the news in their press before some other. At these times one cursed the earth for gyrating round the sun!

The soldier who was fighting the battle very naturally wanted to have his exploits made known to his people at home, but he also wanted accuracy. You sometimes got the case of a particular action or battle being reported from the front, and then "written up" by the B.B.C. or press at home. On occasions, no doubt with the best intentions, the soldiers' exploits and his difficulties were expanded. For instance, I have received fierce protests from the fighting soldier because a certain action was described in such a way as to suggest the enemy put up a desperate resistance, when in fact it had been extremely weak. I took up this issue with Haley of the B.B.C. when he visited Eighth Army in Italy. He was most helpful and sympathetic, and after half an hour's talk in my caravan I began to appreciate better some of his difficulties. I drew his attention to the fact that their representatives in North Africa would sometimes describe actions inaccurately. As far as the general public was concerned little harm was done, but the soldier was very sensitive and would ask why a man in North Africa who was out of personal touch with the situation should be allowed to broadcast in this way. I had every sympathy for the B.B.C. reporter concerned, and I am glad to say that a much better system was evolved as a result of Haley's visit.

We were very far behind the Americans with regard to the facilities provided for the transmission of the correspondents' despatches and messages. Our Allies generously helped us out with some of their high-speed equipment for the Normandy invasion, otherwise I believe we should have had a crisis in our press relationships. I don't think our war correspondents were ever really satisfied with the communications which we provided. We did our very best for them, but as the equipment was very scarce and was made in the States, it was obvious that our requests came second. This discrepancy between the communication resources of the two nations meant, of course, that the American press was often ahead of our own with the stories.

Our decision not to allow "beach broadcasts" from the moment we landed in Normandy was not popular. Such talks would have had a wonderful news value, but on the other hand they might have proved very dangerous. It would have been most unlikely that a correspondent, in the excitement and enthusiasm of the moment, might not say something that would have assisted the enemy. It is difficult to see how he could have avoided doing so.

I have known some of our accredited correspondents becoming very angry indeed with the way certain controversial matters were being handled by their papers at home. They would on occasions come to me and try to excuse their papers' attitude, saying that no notice was being taken of their views. And this leads me to the desirability of visits by the editors of our press to the front. I don't recall more than one such organised visit, and that was carried out at my own suggestion with the primary object of obtaining information of Nazi atrocities in Belgium. We all enjoyed having them amongst us, and I regretted that one had so little time available to talk to them. Nevertheless, I am sure good came of the contacts they made. I think it should be an accepted practice that the editors should pay periodic visits to the various theatres, and so gain first-hand impressions of the problems and opinions in those areas. They should help in framing a fair and informed policy for their papers.

III

I held many press conferences during my time as Chief of Staff. I tried to give the war correspondents some background, hints as to the future, and any bits of gossip that might be of use to them. They naturally wanted to quote me, but all that was allowed under the existing regulations was some reference such as "information gathered from a staff officer at Field-Marshal Montgomery's Headquarters." After each talk, I would have to give out the various "stops." These usually only referred to anything I had said about future intentions. On occasions some correspondents got a little tough, but on the whole they were very understanding.

Here are some examples of press conferences to show how difficult they can be.

My predecessor as D.M.I. in Cairo suffered from certain press conferences which he gave under the name of "Military spokesman." He was blamed for giving too optimistic a picture during the early days of Auchinleck's "Crusader" offensive in November, 1941. I believe he was absolutely right as regards the figures which he gave concerning the enemy's tank losses in the initial phase, and, reading this alone, one was tempted to think that the battle was all but won. Our own losses, however, had also been extremely heavy, and in addition the enemy's recovery system performed wonders. This reinforces my previous argument that it should be the task of the operational staff to hold press conferences on current operations — not the intelligence staff.

When Rommel attacked on May 27th, 1942, it fell to me as D.M.I. to hold the press conferences. For the first two or three days it looked as if we were going to give the enemy a sound beating. I very much doubt whether I managed to hide my optimism, but I also know that I remembered past lessons, and was careful to preach a note of warning.

During the period that we were preparing to break out of the Normandy bridgehead, the Allied press became very critical of the situation and suggested that a stalemate had been reached, and hinted that the High Command was not all that it should be. It was during this phase that Montgomery gave a press conference. I watched from the wings. It was not a success, for I believe the war correspondents went away feeling that all was not well, and that possibly something was being held from them. My Chief was not at his best. I believe the press agitation was worrying him, and he was, whether he knew it or not, rather on the defensive and, in addition, talked down to his audience. He said that everything was going according to plan, and that he was perfectly satisfied with the situation, but in spite of it all this did not get across. I was not at all happy, for I realised the danger of a lack of confidence springing up between the press and the Commander-in-Chief. However, not long afterwards the victorious break-out occurred, and this put matters right. It is well that the press should realise how even the most dogged and determined characters are influenced by what they say.

After Montgomery gave the order to withdraw the Arnhem bridgehead, he rang me up at Main Headquarters and asked me to explain the situation to the press, making the particular point that it was his personal decision.

I talked to the war correspondents on the evening of September 27th, and found a rather critical audience awaiting me. There were complaints because the release of the news had been delayed until that evening, and I was pressed to admit that the whole operation had been a failure. I was also asked to say what percentage of success had been achieved.

I started by explaining that the reason for the delay in the release of news about the withdrawal had been imposed entirely to help the soldiers. For it had been hoped that more troops could be got across the river on the night of the 26th/27th. An official announcement, before this operation had been completed, might possibly have encouraged the enemy in his efforts to eliminate the pocket. I then tried to put things in their right perspective, but I found that I had to be very careful not to refer to the Arnhem operation as a "gallant failure," or to suggest that it was anything but a defeat. I quite saw the point — the British people were rather tired of hearing defeats described in this way. Dunkerque and Greece were examples. I analysed the reasons for failure, and pointed out the contribution this action had made towards the capture of the important Nijmegen bridge. I then produced the latest figures — as far as we knew them — of the numbers dropped, those who had got back, and the numbers left in enemy hands. Finally I gave it as my opinion that the whole operation from the neighbourhood of the Dutch frontier had been about 70 per cent, successful.

There were one or two particularly critical correspondents who made frequent interruptions. I was glad to see that their action was not approved by the majority, and they were more or less told to keep quiet.

Most of the war correspondents I believe appreciated the picture correctly, and produced excellent despatches. There was a danger that a hunt for scalps might have had an adverse effect upon the morale of the fighting soldier. I am not trying to suggest that unsuccessful commanders should shelter behind this formula; but I was convinced this setback provided hardly sufficient reason for stirring up trouble.

The result was that the 1st British Airborne Division became heroes as they deserved, but perhaps no more so than formations that had been fighting continuously for years.

One of the greatest dangers for which I had to watch was the advent of an inter-Allied press battle. The controversy on Montgomery's leadership in Normandy, and the recriminations after the Ardennes offensive were cases in point. But I will refer to these in later chapters. Suffice to say at this stage that there was a great danger of being too nationally biased in one's outlook at these conferences, for, by doing so, one might well be heaping the coals on the fire of inter-Allied disharmony.

IV

I think Eighth Army's publications deserve a special mention. The *Eighth Army News* and *The Crusader* came out daily and weekly respectively. They were virtually a one-man effort, and that man was named Warwick Charlton. He was an odd type, and on occasions had to be handled pretty firmly. But he certainly delivered the goods. The arrival of these journals under all kinds of conditions was entirely due to his energy, enthusiasm and resource. He was editor, publisher, leader writer, gossip column contributor, and everything else rolled into one. The papers were very popular with the troops, and besides acting as an excellent means of getting the latest battle news to them, it also offered opportunities for putting over official propaganda dealing with such matters as discipline and anti-waste. There were few towns which we captured that did not provide Charlton with some additional resources for his work. A printing press here, and a stock of paper there. He started papers for the occupied towns, such as the *Tripoli Times*, which incidentally proved of great use to our Military Government authorities for issuing instructions to the Italian population.

In Italy *Eighth Army News* attracted the notice of the very great. Questions were asked in the House, and the Secretary of State for War objected to its policy. There had been some rather outspoken articles about Gracie Fields' non-fulfilment of her promised visit, and other controversial subjects had appeared. I fully realise that our press is free, but with a paper having official backing such as *Eighth Army News* care must be exercised as to what appears.

When we planned to start a paper in 21st Army Group, we applied for Charlton to come and run it. We felt we could accept the risks incurred from his flair for sensation in view of his other undoubted assets. The reply we received said that he was not available!

In *The Crusader* appeared Robb's cartoons, which to my mind are the most clever and witty war sketches I have met. No "Desert Rat" should be without a copy of "My Middle East Campaigns."

One of Robb's cartoons got me into a bit of trouble on one occasion. It was from a series called "Little-known Unite of the Western Desert," and was named "Officers of the Heavy Gaberdiniers." It depicted two staff officers of G.H.Q., Cairo, walking into the Headquarters' building. They were wearing gaberdine uniforms, and a good old Army joke at the time was that staff officers in Cairo were called "Gaberdine Swine." It was a rather clever pun, and I don't think it was used unkindly. I know when I was on the staff in Cairo I thought it very funny. McCreery, Alexander's Chief of Staff, one morning arrived in my caravan near Tripoli and thrust the current copy of *Crusader* on my table, pointing to this cartoon. It is sometimes rather difficult to know when he is laughing and when he is angry, for he has a slight stutter. On this occasion, when he put a trembling finger on the picture and said, "Look at this," I thought he was amused and replied, "Yes, isn't it a wonderful one — about his best yet!" In a very short space of time, however, I realised my mistake, and was told to ensure that no more cracks at those behind us were to be produced.

Richard Dimbleby also got into hot water over this same joke. He produced a despatch — a clever one — in which he made certain references to the "Desert Rat" and the "Gaberdine Swine." This caused a violent reaction in Base circles, who objected to the latter expression. I was ordered to interview Dimbleby and deal with the matter. Poor Dimbleby, he had no intention of offending anyone, but he accepted the situation understandingly.

V

The accredited war correspondents formed their own committee, and I used to deal with this body when any difficulties arose. We would discuss frankly the snags as they arose, and I never had occasion to be dissatisfied with the result. Alan Moorehead, and Paul Holt of the *Express*. Christopher Buckley of the *Telegraph* and Alexander Clifford representing the *Daily Mail* were amongst those I knew best. At intervals they would ask me out to dinner, when we all said exactly what we thought. Because of their unique position they could convey a very useful impression as to what the troops were thinking. I often got a valuable tip from talks I had with these men. The food and drink we consumed on these occasions was of the very best, for their ability to nose out such good things appears not to conflict with their legitimate duties. The work of these war correspondents was outstanding; they were all intensely interested in every stage of the campaign, and it would appear to be an unfortunate oversight that so few high honours came their way.

I had very few dealings with women war correspondents, for in North Africa they were forbidden to appear by the Army Commander. I remember a hectic chase for Clare Hollingsworth in Tripoli. I believe she had arrived by air at the invitation of the R.A.F., but in spite of this, I had orders to see that she was on her way back to Cairo before the sun set. She was — and I hope she will forgive an apparent lack of hospitality!

At times it was suggested that war correspondents should be given the executive powers of an officer. This request usually came to the surface when difficulty was being experienced in producing adequate accommodation, transport and supplies. But such a step could only prove a source of embarrassment in the end, for they could never enjoy the freedom which must be theirs, if they were also subject to normal military discipline. The proper answer is to see that they are adequately provided for, and this is why the Public Relations officers should be most carefully selected.

Observer officers deserve a special mention. They spent their time in the thick of the fighting, and were responsible for writing up first-hand accounts of various actions.

To ensure smooth working and the minimum friction with the war correspondents, I suggest the following are the four main essentials: —

(1) Ensure that there is an efficient censorship and furthermore, that the Commanders and the correspondents appreciate the need and reasons for the "stops."
(2) Communications for the press must be of the highest order, and should not be below the standard of efficiency of another ally.
(3) Make certain that the war correspondents are given adequate guidance and background talks.
(4) See that the machinery for "bear-leading" the correspondents, and for providing their transport and accommodation is well organised.

And finally, here are three requests to the war correspondents themselves: —

(1) Check up to see whether a personal "scoop" may not embarrass the soldier unfairly.
(2) Before starting off with some controversial line, please first be sure of your facts, and make certain you appreciate fully the repercussions.
(3) Remember the majority of commanders — the simple soldiers — are easy meat in your practised hands!

CHAPTER XV: NORTH-WEST EUROPE — I

I

FROM now on my narrative will differ from that of my days with Eighth Army in that I shall not give a complete description of the tactical battles. This I will leave to the military historian and others. In any event, being on an Army Group level instead of an Army level, I was not in such intimate daily touch with the battles; but I was in a better position than ever to watch the higher direction of war. The events to which I shall confine myself inevitably include those high-lights which have become matters of controversy amongst Allied commentators. So much the better, for I at least can give an authentic account of what actually took place, instead of relying, as has sometimes happened, upon hearsay evidence and guess work. It will be seen that these great men who gave us victory pulled together with this object always foremost in their minds and, being human beings and having, as was right, minds of their own, did not always entirely agree as to how best this result could be achieved. Nevertheless, when once the Supreme Commander had given his orders, they were invariably loyally carried out.

II

Sitting back at headquarters at Portsmouth on that morning of June 6th, I felt considerably excited. Reports were now coming in. The airborne operations had been outstandingly successful. The landings were going well. The resistance organisation, which had been given the word "Go" some hours beforehand, was enthusiastically implementing its carefully prepared plans. Our massive air forces were getting into their stride in support of the land battle. The navies, the armies and the air forces were happy. The loud-speakers around our headquarters were broadcasting Eisenhower's proclamation to the Europe that had been so anxiously awaiting this day.

Montgomery kept to his office most of that day waiting to see when he should move to Normandy. His Tactical Headquarters was now on its way across, and he was champing at the bit to get going himself. As the day progressed it became clear that Bradley and his First U.S. Army were having a very sticky time of it at Omaha beach (the left-hand sector of First U.S. Army's front), otherwise things were going more or less to plan.

Besides working on the future and seeing that existing plans were being smoothly implemented, our principal occupations at this phase were to ensure, in conjunction with the Air Headquarters, that the Armies were getting the best air support, and watching to see that the build-up organisation ("Buco") was functioning correctly.

It took some little time to organise the arrival of really accurate and up-to-date information back at Portsmouth. In the early stages it was obvious that some reports were highly coloured and distorted. But within a couple of days things were running well. There were the normal situation reports from armies and formations; air reports; messages from the specially equipped "J" parties; and verbal reports from returning liaison officers. These with the information we received about the enemy gave us a very excellent picture. For the first few days, Broadhurst, who was commanding the Tactical Group (83) which was supporting General Dempsey's Army, flew over the bridgehead area each evening in a Spitfire and gave me an account of what he saw.

Montgomery left for Normandy on June 8th and for several weeks Tactical and Main Headquarters were separated by the English Channel. This was, however, no great inconvenience, for we soon had a good telephone service working, and I could fly over to see him within the hour.

Although the R.A.F. would always provide me with an aircraft, it was not the same thing as having one's own, and so one morning when Eisenhower was visiting me in my office near Portsmouth and had asked whether there was anything I needed, I replied: "Yes, an aeroplane!" He took it very calmly, and said that it would be arranged. Half an hour later I was rung up by General Spaatz who asked me where would I like the aircraft delivered? He told me that I was to use this Dakota until another one had been properly fitted out for me. The first model arrived that very afternoon, and was followed by a most comfortable successor some three or four weeks later. I shall be eternally grateful for this kindly deed, for it was a tremendous help to me in my work. There was hardly a day it was not in use. I could take a number of officers with me for conferences, and could have people delivered or fetched at will. I was lucky to have a really first-class pilot — Jack Race — who stayed with me until the end of the war. Our aircraft got destroyed by the Germans during their New Year's Day attack against the Belgian airfields in 1945, but a replacement was provided a short time after.

There is no doubt that the Americans had less rigid and narrow-minded ideas about air transport. They looked upon it as a normal and necessary part of a senior commander's and staff officer's equipment. And so it should be. I'm afraid the R.A.F.'s reputation in this matter has not been good. It was not until nearly the end of the war that the Army was provided with its needs. During the early years of the war, one had to go through a difficult procedure, or rely upon the kindness of some friend, and even then no satisfactory type of aircraft existed. I fully realise that the shortage of aircraft was probably the basic cause of this attitude, but one often found a sort of resentment on the part of senior officers in the R.A.F. towards the Army's demands for air transport. Again often the aircraft provided was not such as to give one great confidence. It is up to the Army to ensure that in future our needs are fully catered for in this direction.

III

American writers have accused Montgomery of having failed to carry out his original plan in Normandy, of slowness, and even of bad generalship. There have also been suggestions that both Eisenhower and Tedder were displeased with his conduct of the campaign. I will now describe my views and experiences of these matters, and I hope they may result in showing that things were not so bad after all.

First, let us go back and see what tasks Montgomery gave out to his Armies at the Presentation of Plans in early April, 1944. In brief these were: —

First U.S. Army.
  (a) To assault.
  (b) To capture Cherbourg.
  (c) To develop operations towards St. Lô.
  (d) After capture of the area Cherbourg-Caumont-Avranches, to advance southwards, capture Rennes and reach out to the Loire.

Second British Army.
  (a) To assault.

(b) To protect First U.S. Army whilst it captured Cherbourg.

(c) To secure the airfield sites south-east of Caen.

(d) In subsequent operations to pivot on its left and offer a strong front against enemy movement towards the lodgement area from the east.

I have already described the "Phase Line" map that was prepared for the occasion. This showed Caen and the airfield sites in our possession early on in the campaign, but after this, Second Army was virtually to pivot on their left flank for approximately five weeks. I also explained that these phase lines were not guaranteed promises, but presented a general indication as to how things might go. They had to cater for the best so that we would not lose an opportunity.

It will be seen, therefore, that the general pattern of the plan was fulfilled, although the initial phase was slower than we had *hoped* it might be, and Caen and the airfield sites were well behind the *phase line* forecast. But it will also be seen that by the time we reached the Seine we were in advance of our forecast.

Now I am quite certain no promises were made about Caen and these airfield sites. Many times during meetings I was pressed to say we would get them by a certain day, but I would never make such promises. I think if the minutes of those meetings[38] still exist, it will be found that I warned the R.A.F. against relying upon acquiring airfields in that particular area, not only because we realised the enemy would be fully wise to the importance of Caen and the surrounding country, but because even if we achieved the phase line forecast, airfields stuck out on the extreme flank could not be considered very

---

[38] I now understand that the minutes do in fact show that on several occasions I held that Montgomery could not make promises regarding the airfield area.

secure. Looking through some notes for a press talk I gave on "D" day, I find that I warned the correspondents in answer to their questions that it would be very dangerous to assume that the capture of Caen would be easy. This shows our state of mind on this issue, even on a day when everything appeared rosy.

The R.A.F.'s anxiety concerning these airfields was understandable, and during those early weeks they were not very pleased at our inability to capture them. A Commander must, however, be allowed to conduct his campaign in his own way, and not be held rigidly to any particular ingredient of the original plan. Remember this — the original conception was followed and worked. And the R.A.F. despite the non-availability of the airfield site? south-east of Caen did manage to provide the support the Army required. The enemy concentrated the bulk of his armour against the Caen hinge, and we held him there whilst Cherbourg was captured, and the lodgement area was seized.

Montgomery had some very good reasons for not continually pressing the attack on Caen and beyond in the early stages. To start with, the enemy was there in considerable strength. Then a failure here might jeopardise the whole plan, for it should be remembered that an enemy success against our hinge would have meant the over-running of our beaches and of our supplies. The country was suitable for defence in the area which we held — Bocage country, and the Orne and Odon rivers supplied natural obstacles. Further to the East it was more open, and not so suitable. So once our initial efforts to rush Caen had proved unsuccessful and the enemy had reinforced that area, the whole aspect had changed. Another reason for the delay in capturing Caen was the bad weather. This delayed the planned build-up in both formations and supplies, and it was not until June 25th that a determined attempt was laid on to take the town. Success was not achieved however, principally due to the arrival of portions of several S.S. divisions. There had been a very heavy gale between June 19th and 22nd, and without the delay caused by this and other bad weather, it is possible Caen would have been ours before these reinforcements arrived.

I do not quite understand some of Ingersoll's comments about the battle for Caen. He says, for instance, that the effect of the Bocage country had never been appreciated by Montgomery and his staff. And that during the conferences that planned the battle of Caen a minority opinion pointing out these dangers was led by an American staff officer named Bonesteel. Now in the first place an Army Group Headquarters does not plan the detailed tactical battle fought by an Army, this task falls upon the Army Headquarters staff. "Tic" Bonesteel was a brilliant staff officer whom I was very sorry to lose when Twelfth U.S. Army Group commenced to function. He was on the planning side of our headquarters, and one of his tasks had been to study the topography of the country over which we were to fight. I remember well listening to the conclusions which he reached. Ingersoll is quite right that he pointed out the dangers of the Bocage country, and how difficult the employment of our armoured strength would be. I can, however, assure Ingersoll that these dangers were fully appreciated; I discussed them with Montgomery on many occasions. I don't see what Ingersoll expected us to do. We were committed to this sector and we would just have to fight our way out. This was only one of many such horrors that were continually cropping up. If we had sat back and said, "the Bocage is too difficult to fight in," what was the alternative? No, we had to accept the dangers though appreciating the difficulties. We had, as I have already said, *hoped* to take Caen and get out into the open country beyond in the first few days, and in that event we should have been able to make the fullest use of our tanks. Tanks were certainly used in support of the infantry in this thick country. I agree it was not ideal tank country, but nevertheless the infantry expected this support. The Americans used tanks as we did in the Bocage country, and incidentally some of Bradley's engineers designed a most ingenious contraption for fixing to the front of a tank for cutting their way through the hedges and banks of the Bocage. I always quote this as an example of the go-getter methods of our Allies. I was staying with Bradley when the experimental model had proved its worth. In order to equip the necessary number of tanks for the coming battle no time could be lost. The steel required was being salvaged mostly from enemy beach obstacles, but a large number of oxyacetylene cylinders were needed for welding. I was in Bradley's Chief-of-Staff's caravan when the officer in charge of the work reported his requirements. It was about 6 p.m. Phone calls were immediately put through to the United Kingdom and to the local Air Headquarters. Two or three Dakota transport aircraft would be ready to take off at 8 p.m. By 4 a.m. the next morning it was hoped to have collected the number of cylinders required at an airfield in the West of England. This was no easy matter as they were in short supply. By breakfast the next morning the cylinders had arrived in Normandy, and the tanks attacked fitted with their anti-bocage attachments. At the time I compared the trouble we would have gone through to produce similar results. To get the aircraft alone might have taken us a day or so. This is not a crack at the R.A.F., it is a reflection upon the cumbersome machinery which existed for getting aircraft, but then of course, they were very scarce.

Ingersoll then suggests that we had been surprised because the Germans had used their numerous 88-millimetre A.A. guns in the anti-tank role. To suggest this about Commanders and staffs who had fought in Africa, Sicily and Italy is rather overdoing it. We had met this sort of thing for the last two years, and if anything, I think we might be accused of having been too apprehensive of their employment in this way.

He also stresses that our troops were not trained to fight in this close country, having learnt their trade in the desert. Looking at the order of battle of the operations around Caen towards the end of June, I find that the majority of divisions employed had never fought in the desert. Here are some examples — 11th Armoured Division, 3rd Division, 15th Division, 43rd Division and 49th Division.

Montgomery's tacticians are accused of expecting the strategic bombing, which preceded our attack on Caen, to have caused "even more disruption" than it did. The first time we used the strategic air forces in this tactical role was on July 7th in front of Caen. The trouble then was that *too much disruption* was caused, and our advance was impeded by the effects of the bombing.

From the problem of Caen I now come to the more general criticism of Montgomery's slowness in breaking out of the bridgehead. We can all form our opinions as to whether another General might have broken out before, if he had been in Montgomery's place. I am not so bigoted as to say this was quite impossible, but I am prepared to say that we might well have lost a lot by doing so.

Throughout this period the enemy was fighting at a great disadvantage. His reserve divisions, which to his mind were limited in number by the need to defend the Pas de Calais, had to move great distances under day and night attack by our overwhelming Air Forces before they could reach the bridgehead. On arrival, the situation was always so threatening that they were thrown hurriedly into battle. Thus, after a severe hammering en route, they were further blunted by ill-prepared stop-gap attacks. On our side, our position was secure and becoming stronger every day as further troops and supplies were brought ashore. Moreover, it was important that we should build up sufficiently to ensure that we could exploit success to the full when the break-out occurred. In the event, we were in a position to reap a rich reward.

The degree of pressure to be applied at any time on the left flank of the Allied bridgehead, where the enemy's greatest strength was concentrated, therefore called for a careful balancing of advantages: an "all-out" attack before the enemy had been weakened was to risk blunting our own offensive powers which were limited: to wait too long was to risk a stalemate. Such a balance can only be drawn by the tactical commander in touch with the whole front, and the proof of the pudding is in the eating.

My Chief undoubtedly suffered a lot from the criticism that appeared in the press and elsewhere about the slowness of progress in the bridgehead. "Had we reached a stalemate?" "Had Montgomery failed?" These were typical expressions used. I agree that a Commander in that position should be unaffected by such things, but on the other hand, there were considerable dangers that these outspoken comments might have had an effect upon the fighting qualities of the troops. Unlike in the Middle East, the troops now read the press from England, often delivered the same day. If they continually read articles criticising Montgomery, or at any rate suggesting that all was not well, they might lose faith in their Commander-in-Chief. Here then was the danger.

I had every sympathy for Montgomery and Dempsey during this difficult period. They were working to a fixed plan, in which the British role was not a spectacular one. They had to grin and bear it, and await the day that they were quite confident would soon arrive. Throughout the bridgehead fighting the British had a far greater weight of armour against them in comparison with that employed against the Americans. The following information shows the position: —

    Caumont-Caen Sector
        Mid-June: 4 Panzer Divisions
        Early July: 7+ Panzer Divisions
        Mid-July: 6 Panzer Divisions
        July 20th: 5 Panzer Divisions
    Remainder of Front
        Mid-June: Nil Panzer Divisions
        Early July: ½ Panzer Divisions
        Mid-July: 2 Panzer Divisions
        July 20th: 3 Panzer Divisions

I now come to the alleged criticism of Montgomery by Eisenhower and Tedder during this period. As I was in close personal contact with all three of them, I feel I am in a position to give a fair version of the facts. Let me start by saying how easy it would be for me to write down criticisms and remarks I have heard about the slowness in Normandy. Throughout the war I constantly heard people complain when things went slowly. It is just human nature that produces such remarks. When things go well the same people are very generous in their praise. I have myself on many occasions thought and complained about the slowness of some commander or formation. I should hate to see some isolated remarks of mine put down on paper. It is unfair to quote such remarks alone;

the individual's general attitude, and samples of his favourable remarks, must be taken into account as well.

In my dealings with Eisenhower and Tedder during this difficult period, I can honestly say that although at times they were like many other people hoping for a speedier breakout, they certainly never showed me any attitude except one of understanding of Montgomery's difficulties, and a great willingness to help him by every means, and so, if possible, accelerate the *tempo*. Both these Commanders used to pay me frequent visits at Portsmouth; we discussed the situation in all its aspects. When the Headquarters moved to France, Eisenhower had his advanced Command Post within a few minutes of our location, and so I saw a great deal of the Supreme Commander. Never to my knowledge did he criticise Montgomery's tactics during this phase. He was being subjected to a pretty violent press campaign in America about the slowness in Normandy, and the results achieved by U.S. troops compared with those by our men. "Why don't the British do some fighting?" This was rather the attitude. Eisenhower, of course, knew Montgomery's plan, but he couldn't announce to the world what was going to happen. It is obviously the task of a Supreme Commander to ensure that the best was in fact being done. On one occasion he was in my office at Portsmouth, and I had just been talking to my Chief about a coming attack by the Second Army — this was in July. On hearing the date, Eisenhower said he thought it was important that it should start off earlier. His words were, "I know Monty's difficulties, but from the bigger point of view it is important that the attack should go in before then. Do you think it can be speeded up?" I suggested he wrote a signal. This he did in a very straightforward yet friendly way. Later I phoned through and explained my talk with Eisenhower, and

Montgomery responded immediately. He would do his very best to speed up the attack, and this he subsequently managed to do.

A remark Eisenhower once made to me after the battle of the Falaise Gap shows that there had been no major disagreement with Montgomery. He was discussing an alteration of boundaries between the Second Army and the First U.S. Army. He said, "This is the first time when I have ever had occasion to question a tactical decision made by Monty." I will discuss the circumstances of this particular decision a little later on.

Tedder was being pressed by the Air Commanders to see that the airfield sites south-east of Caen were captured. This no doubt made him somewhat apprehensive at times. But in the talks which he had with me, there was never any suggestion that he considered Montgomery was making a mess of things.

Ingersoll is quite right when he suggests that Montgomery knew after the fighting in Normandy that the British Empire forces would require some American assistance for future major offensives. This was fully realised before the assault took place, and was not a result of the battle of Caen. Eisenhower had made it quite clear that he would, when necessary, place American formations under Montgomery's command, even after the 12th U.S. Army Group took over. If Montgomery wanted American troops, it was not in order to provide him with fresh honours, but as a means to help finish the war. No one can blame my Chief for wanting more troops, or for being proud to command Americans.

Undoubtedly towards the end of the campaign Montgomery had to be extremely careful how he employed certain formations. It is inevitable that after a long period of fighting the efficiency of formations drops. Dilution, staleness and war weariness are some of the reasons. Some of them had been fighting for five years, and it was understandable that they were not what they were. The Americans on the other hand were continually receiving fresh divisions, and in any case their period of war service had been shorter. It therefore angers me when I read criticism of Montgomery's handling of his troops. How can he be blamed for ensuring that these hard-tried men were given the best of support, and the best conditions for a particular operation? It is a commander's *duty* to his troops.

To sum up, I would say that Montgomery was entirely justified in putting off the capture of Caen and the airfield sites to the south-east. The Second British Army and later the 1st Canadian Army fulfilled the roles originally allotted them, by containing strong enemy forces on the eastern flank and holding the hinge of the lodgement area. No one can say whether some commander other than Montgomery might not have accelerated events in Normandy, but I very much doubt whether an earlier timing would have been to our ultimate advantage. Finally, I was quite unaware of there having been a "crisis" in Montgomery's relations with either Eisenhower or Tedder.

III

The story of the employment of heavy bombers in close support of the land battle is worth recording.

Back in the planning days at St. Paul's School the Army was giving a great deal of thought to this subject. We fully appreciated the primary role of the strategic air forces, but nevertheless we considered that we should on occasions harness their great power to the immediate support of the land battle. For by now few thought the war would be won by strategic bombing alone. The enemy's army had to be defeated.

General Rowell,[39] who is now Vice Chief of Staff in Australia, and General Crawford (Director of Air, War Office), together with Air Ministry representatives, had studied the technical problems involved. We had several talks together. There were of course many difficulties. To start with, as was only natural, certain personalities in the R.A.F. were not enthusiastic. The usual old arguments were produced about the wrong use of that type of aircraft, a great waste of bombs, and dangers to the troops. I must say this attitude was not shared by the commanders of the strategic air forces, Harris and Spaatz. Their attitude was always helpful.

There were really three main problems which had to be solved before the use of the heavy bombers would be worth while. The bombs had to be accurately placed. The damage caused must neutralise the opposition but not interfere with our own activities. Safety measures must be more or less foolproof.

We did a lot of investigating on the staff level with the R.A.F. in order to find answers to these problems. Modern radar instruments developed by Bomber Command went a long way in solving the accuracy problem. We formed ideas as to the type of target that should be selected for treatment. Obviously, unless the enemy's positions were very strong, accurately known, and the battle of particular importance, it would be wrong to divert the strategic bombers from their normal role. The questions of cratering and bomb fuses were also examined. Besides the technical safety precautions that the air forces devised themselves, we developed all types of landmarks for both day and night use.

In the early days of Normandy an occasion arose when we thought the use of heavy bombers might prove very effective.

---

[39] Was then Director of Tactical Investigation at the War Office.

The Air Commander-in-Chief, Leigh-Mallory, was of the same opinion, and we flew over together to see Montgomery and discuss the matter. So far, so good, and a conference was arranged with the Corps concerned for the next day. The result of the conference was that the heavy bombers were not employed. I blame ourselves for this. In the first place, the Corps had not prepared their case sufficiently, and we had to admit that the tasks appeared to be within the scope of the Tactical Air Forces. I was very disappointed, however, for we were most anxious to try out the machinery. Leigh-Mallory, I know, shared this disappointment.

Before long, however, another occasion arose, and this was the attack on Caen on July 8th. Montgomery requested the aid of Bomber Command from the Supreme Commander, and Harris agreed at once. We gave as the target an area on the northern outskirts of Caen containing the enemy's defended localities and artillery positions. Besides the destruction of these defences it was hoped to cut off any survivors from their supplies in rear. The area was about 4,000 yards wide by 1,500 yards deep. As this was the first attempt, we placed the "bomb-line" (i.e. the nearest point at which the bombs were to be dropped to our own troops) 6,000 yards in front of our forward troops. The enemy's defences in between our troops and the bomb-line were to be dealt with by artillery fire.

At ten minutes to ten on the evening of July 7th 460 aircraft commenced to bomb. The attack lasted for fifty minutes. Early next morning our infantry and tanks went forward, and by the same evening we were in the outskirts of Caen. The town was in our hands on the 10th.

A great deal of damage had been done by the bombing. The defenders had been completely stunned, and cut off from their supplies and reinforcements. They had also suffered considerable casualties in both men and material. The damage caused by the bombing did, however, obstruct our own advance, and as a result of the lessons learnt here, we decided to alter the types of bombs and fuses in the next attack.

Even after this success — and we frankly admitted that Bomber Command contributed very largely to the result — there were some who wanted to assess the merits mainly upon the actual destruction compared with the weight of bombs dropped. They never sufficiently considered the question of morale, the effect upon the enemy's as well as upon our own. If we adjudged the effectiveness of artillery fire purely upon the actual destruction achieved, the answer would be most disappointing.

I believe Harris and others criticised the Army for having given the R.A.F. an untrue picture of the enemy's defences which were to be bombed, the main point being that the expected concrete works did not materialise. The expectation of these no doubt led to the use of the heavy type of bomb with delayed fuses. Unfortunately I have not available any documents showing what enemy picture was given by Second Army, but it is more than probably that concrete was mentioned. When hearing such criticisms it should be borne in mind, however, that we were to some extent experimenting at this stage, and that the final say in bombs and fuses rested, of course, with the Air Force Commanders.

There is more substance in the R.A.F. criticism that the Army often asked for the unnecessary bombing of towns. This is a very difficult question and one that I have already discussed in the chapter dealing with the Sicilian campaign. Undoubtedly the results often impeded our own progress, and destroyed little of a strictly military character. On the other hand the destruction certainly interfered with enemy movement and supply; played havoc with his communications; and as always, gave the attacking troops a most desirable fillip to their morale.

On July 18th the strategic air forces were again employed in support of Second Army. This time in their attack to the east and south of Caen. This time a far greater number of aircraft were used, including Fortresses of the Eighth U.S. Air Force. The details were: —

Bomber Command: 1,100
Eighth U.S. Air Force: 600
Ninth U.S. Air Force (medium bombers): 400

A considerable time had been spent in arriving at the final plan and the lessons learnt on July 7th were taken into account. The heavy bombers were to be used on the flanks of the attack as well as against certain good targets in rear. They would use a number of delayed fuse bombs and so keep the enemy occupied during the attack itself. The medium bombers would deal with the actual corridor of the advance, and only fragmentation bombs with instantaneous fuses were to be employed. We did not want our movement obstructed by craters. The air attacks lasted for two hours from 5.45 a.m., and an advance of several miles was made in a very short time.

I drove out with Air Marshal Coningham to see the bombers attack. It was a perfect opal summer morning. It seemed a sacrilege that this great fleet of aircraft carrying destruction was already in the air. We climbed up into a haystack from which we could see the factory area of Caen and waited for things to happen. Before long we could hear a drone, and almost immediately the northern and eastern skies were full of aircraft. It looked just like a swarm of bees homing upon their hive. I thought how terrible it must be to suffer under the Harris technique in a German town. Just as the leading machines were overhead a loud explosion occurred about one hundred yards away. Just for a moment I wondered whether a marker bomb had been dropped near us by mistake and that it would be followed by many others. Fortunately nothing further happened, and so it was probably an enemy long-range shell. One appreciated the great bravery of those pilots and crews as they flew straight into the most ghastly looking flak. Every now and then an aircraft would burst into flames, and usually shortly afterwards a few parachutes could be seen making their way to earth.

A tremendous amount of dust and smoke was produced by these attacks, and if the wind was unfavourable it presented a problem. It made it difficult for subsequent waves to identify their targets, and sometimes worried our infantry and tanks during their advance.

We were learning bit by bit, and it had now been accepted that this was a legitimate task to give the heavy bomber. A great step forward had therefore been made.

The next occasion on which the strategic air force was used to support the land battle was during the break-out of the First U.S. Army at St. Lô. After a delayed start, owing to bad weather, the real attack took place on July 25th. In order to ensure that the heavy bombers dropped their loads on the enemy's foremost defended localities, a new method was employed. The forward troops were withdrawn back a distance of over a thousand yards, so as to increase the margin of safety. An area of 6,000 yards wide by 2,500 yards deep was taken on by 1,500 heavy bombers of the Eighth U.S. Army Air Force. In addition about 400 medium bombers were used on other targets.

The result of this bombardment was terrific. The enemy in the area was either destroyed or stunned, while few items of his equipment escaped damage. It certainly paved the way for the ultimate success of the battle. I both flew and walked over the area afterwards, and the scene of desolation was complete.

In August the "heavies" supported an attack by the Canadians, but the results were disappointing.

Every now and then some bombs would fall on our own troops. This was naturally very worrying, but I am glad to say the impression created was soon forgotten. What it came to was that the Army was prepared to accept such slips provided they obtained this otherwise magnificent support. After any such incident an exhaustive inquiry would be held in order to ascertain the reason for the error. Steps were then taken to devise means of preventing a repetition.

The technique was gradually improved, and I think it only fair to say that the Americans were more resourceful than we were in their efforts to achieve perfection. In the autumn, for instance, they felt so sure of themselves that they were prepared to (and actually did) employ their bombers in the close support role through thick cloud conditions.

I don't want to be critical of the air support the Army received from the R.A.F. I am the first to say how magnificent it was. To get new ideas accepted, however, did sometimes require a great deal of lobbying, and on occasions smooth relationships were endangered. Many of us were very struck by the different attitude to some of the problems adopted by the U.S. Air Force. But then this is understandable, for their Air Force was part of the Army and the Army Commander would just give orders. I hope that in this period of peace the two services will not drift apart as happened during the years between the last two wars.

IV

The battle of the Falaise Gap resulted in a very great victory. It was the consummation of Montgomery's original plan for using Caen as the hinge upon which the armies would swing. Hitler, by his opposition to any withdrawal and his insistence upon the Mortain counter-attack early in August, certainly played into our hands. The tactical handling of this battle was by no means easy, as both the Americans and ourselves were converging towards the German pocket west of the line Falaise-Argentan. This particularly applied to the question of boundaries and control of the air forces.

At the beginning of August, Bradley's Army Group had forced its way through the Avranches-Mortain bottleneck, and Patton was preparing to advance into Brittany. The First U.S. Army had started to swing round in the direction of Paris, and at the same time were compressing the pocket from the west and south. The 21st Army Group were attacking against the north-west edge of the pocket with the Second British Army, and the Canadian Army preparing for their attack, which it was hoped would reach Falaise. The Canadian attack went in on August 7th and came up against stronger opposition than anticipated, and it became obvious that it would still take some time to reach Falaise.

The German counter-attack from Mortain towards Avranches started on the 7th, but was successfully held by the Americans.

Montgomery's original intention was to carry out a wide envelopment towards Paris by the 12th U.S. Army Group, for he had expected that the enemy, once he realised his hopeless position, would withdraw towards the Seine. The northern boundary for the Americans had been laid down on the general line Domfort-Alencon. But this counter-attack from Mortain showed that he was still hoping to fight it out in his present positions. Montgomery therefore decided to try a short envelopment about Argentan and Falaise as well as the larger one towards the Seine and Paris.

The XVth U.S. Corps had done magnificently and had reached Le Mans on August 8th.

Bradley and Patton both saw the prize ahead, and on the 9th a re-grouping took place to strengthen up XVth Corps. Montgomery now ordered Bradley to move northwards on Alencon and the latter naturally used the XVth Corps for the purpose.

It was not until the 19th that the Falaise pocket was finally closed. The link up between the First Canadian Army and the Americans occurred at Chambois. During this ten-day period Montgomery still went on with the bigger plan of envelopment while he endeavoured to surround completely the Germans in the pocket. My impressions at the time were that he had been a little too optimistic about the probable progress of 21st Army Group. Bradley was given several changes of his northern boundary. First the line Dromfort-Alencon, then Argentan, and finally Chambois. It is just possible that the gap might have been closed a little earlier if no restrictions had been imposed upon the 12th Army Group Commander as to the limit of his northward movement. In any case the Americans felt this. It should not be forgotten, however, that Montgomery had to be very careful to ensure that the two Army Groups did not become entangled.

21st Army Group's progress looked rather meagre in comparison with the Americans. I am the first to agree that our Allies' leadership at this time was bold and resourceful. The way their administrative organisation served their far-flung armies was a veritable triumph. But it must be remembered that by this time they had made a clean break-through, whilst we were still fighting an organised enemy on his chosen ground, and ground that he knew was absolutely vital, and upon which much time and effort had been spent in preparing for defence. Both our armies had some extremely sticky and difficult fighting at this stage.

We were kept pretty busy with the various problems connected with the battle of the "pocket." The co-ordination of air support was the most difficult of them all. When once the area had become reduced there was a great danger of the Tactical Air Forces supporting each Army Group becoming mixed up. It was very difficult to select bomb-lines that would suit everyone. Eventually the task of co-ordination was given to Coningham.

During this time pilots reported a large proportion of the enemy's vehicles were carrying red cross flags and emblems. It was obvious that this was merely a ruse to avoid having their transport attacked. I believe these flags were even seen on tanks. What were the pilots to do? The decision was to avoid attacking them, for it was thought that the Germans in their present mood might well take reprisals against our prisoners and wounded. A difficult decision, but probably the right one.

We had to lay down various recognition signals between the Americans and ourselves so that we would not shoot each other up. We also exchanged artillery observation parties so that we could direct each other's guns. These arrangements proved most successful.

Returning to this inter-Army Group boundary question. After the link-up at Chambois had taken place, Montgomery decided to shift it back again. The new boundary gave the road Argentan-Evreux to the Second British Army.

The decision was not very popular with the Americans, and their attitude was understandable. They argued that having been asked to come and help north of the old original boundary, why couldn't they be allowed to "crack" straight on to the Seine. The change necessitated some complicated manoeuvring, and it was very nearly forty-eight hours before the armies were sorted out again in their correct sectors. It was a great pity that this had to happen, but Montgomery felt that it was necessary in order to get the armies which he controlled tidied up, and each with sufficient major road axes. If this had not taken place the extremely rapid advance northwards into Holland might not have been possible.

Despite these little troubles, however, the victory of the Falaise pocket was a great one, and there was ample honour for all. The destruction caused to the enemy was terrific. I have never seen it equalled before or since. The tens of thousands of prisoners, the wounded and the dead. Thousands of tanks and vehicles lying all over the countryside, some burnt out, some abandoned. The roads that were still open to them were packed with transport, nose to tail. Our aircraft had got to work and record bags had been obtained by our pilots. There were hundreds of dead horses rotting in the hot sun. Never have I seen such a scene of desolation. I flew over the area once or twice in a puddle jumper. It was an unforgettable sight, and the smell of decay was strong in the air above. It seemed difficult to imagine how any army could survive a defeat of this sort. I put our scientific section on to producing a detailed analysis of the destruction. Their report prepared under the direction of that very able South African, Brigadier Schonland, was of very great interest. They made a count of the enemy vehicles and plotted them by types and areas. A percentage were examined to find out the cause of failure — abandoned, hit by aircraft rockets, or destroyed by artillery, etc. One of the lessons which we learnt from this report was that the rockets had not caused as much destruction as most of us believed to have been the case. Probably these terrifying weapons had, however, been responsible for many of the abandoned vehicles and tanks.

This disintegration of the enemy's forces in Normandy made us all wonder whether the end was not far off.

V

I will end this chapter by dealing with the problem of the Allied strategy after the defeat of the enemy in Normandy. A great deal has already been written on this subject. Montgomery has let it be known that he advocated a plan which Eisenhower found himself unable to accept. Press articles have asked the question — "Would Montgomery's plan have finished off the war in 1944?" I will describe therefore the situation as I saw it, and bring out the reasons which I believe led the Supreme Commander to his decision.

During the fighting in Normandy, Montgomery had been considering how best the Allied armies should be handled after the breakout had taken place. He was, of course, at the time Eisenhower's Land Force Commander, but before long he was to revert to the command of an Army Group, and so it was natural that he wanted his future role defined as early as possible. In brief, Montgomery advocated that there should be only one major offensive effort — and this to be across the Rhine, north of the Ruhr into the heart of Germany. In the process he hoped to see this great industrial region denied to the enemy, and because of this, a German collapse within a matter of a few months. It was his opinion that such a decisive result might be achieved provided that the remaining sectors of the Allied front reverted to a purely static role, and all the administrative resources and transport so saved, be allotted to support this one offensive effort.

It is only fair to say that throughout the war, this was the only major issue over which I did not agree with my Chief. I have always held the contrary view, and in the event, I am more than ever convinced that I was right. It fell to me to discuss these matters with the Supreme Commander on a number of occasions. His advanced command post was near our Main Headquarters in Normandy, and as Chief of Staff I had to put over my Commander's views. In general, Eisenhower was agreed that the major effort should be North of the Ruhr, but he did not believe that the strength of forces which we could maintain without the use of Antwerp would be sufficient to finish the war — especially in view of the nearness of winter. He also could not agree to relegating a large portion of the American armies to a purely static role — virtually without the means to manoeuvre. He, therefore, agreed to Patton's Army advancing towards Verdun. Montgomery felt that it should be halted protecting Paris from the east. There were, I think, certain factors that the Supreme Commander had to take into account which Montgomery did not perhaps fully appreciate.

Let me explain how I came to my conclusion.

Undoubtedly the victory in Normandy and the general position of the German Army in the West did produce a great wave of optimism. The enemy did not have immediately available the resources to man a new defence line in strength. He was hastily forming new divisions of a smaller type in order to be in a position to hold once again an adequate Western barrier. It certainly did look as if a thrust of some dozen divisions, provided they could keep up their momentum, would be able to deal with the initial opposition which they would meet north of the Ruhr.

Without the railways and the port of Antwerp, and even given the transport and administrative resources from the Third U.S. Army, I very much doubt whether we could have kept that sized force maintained at full operational scale east of the Rhine. The carry from the Normandy beaches would have been enormous, requiring, I believe, more transport than could have been spared. Then the road and bridge capacities en route, particularly at the far end, would have proved insufficient. We would have been very lucky to find the Rhine bridges intact, and to bring forward the necessary bridging material would have been a lengthy affair. And in any case we had not yet "phased in" the bridging material that would be required for the Rhine. Even assuming that such a force or spearhead did cross the river, I cannot see how it would have produced a German capitulation. If there was a good chance of Hitler throwing up the sponge, then it would have been worth the gamble, but we now know there was never any chance of that. The Generals knew that the war had been lost soon after we landed, and told Hitler so, but the German nation were prepared to accept untold horrors and misery for long after this. It took a Russian offensive using about 160 divisions, massive offensives on our part, as well as eight more months of devastating air attack, to force the Germans to capitulate. And even then Hitler and his gang never gave up.

I feel myself that even if we had been able to get a sizeable force across the Rhine into Germany in the autumn, the Germans, after a period of crisis, would have produced sufficient troops to strangle its effectiveness. The flanks of our salient would have been particularly vulnerable.

The weather was another factor that had to be taken into account. There were only another few weeks available for good mobile campaigning before the winter set in. Not long enough to get this decisive result.

Then there was "Anvil" — the landings in the south of France. The Supreme Commander considered that he must join up with these forces as soon as possible. There were a large number of Germans moving about in the area between the two invasion forces, and he felt it necessary to tidy up the whole front. Who can blame him for that? Being wise afterwards, however, it looks as if some of the effort used in this connection might have been employed further north, without any particular danger arising.

It should also be remembered that Patton's activities in the Verdun-Metz direction drew German formations against him that might well have been sent elsewhere. If my memory serves me right, two or three comparatively good divisions from the south were hurriedly moved to this sector.

Finally, one should consider the repercussions if this gamble had not come off. The Supreme Commander would have been in for a very difficult time. What would his commanders and troops who had been "grounded" say about it? What would their morale have been like? Surely they would have felt rather sore? Their resources had been given to the British just when they had the ball at their feet, and even with that help nothing decisive had been achieved. I can well imagine our reactions if the process had been reversed! But even more important, was the matter of national opinion and national pride; what would the people of America have said if Montgomery had been given these resources and yet failed? One saw the dangerous situation developing in Normandy when he was being criticised — unfairly, I admit — for slow progress. It might well have led to a crisis between the allies. In the next Chapter I will give an example of what explosive material national prestige can be.

My conclusion is, therefore, that Eisenhower was right when in August he decided that he could not concentrate sufficient administrative resources to allow one strong thrust deep into Germany north of the Rhine with the hope of decisive success. If he had not taken the steps he did to link up at an early date with "Anvil" and had held back Patton, and had diverted the administrative resources so released to the north, I think it possible that we might have obtained a bridgehead over the Rhine before the winter — but not more.

CHAPTER XVI: NORTH-WEST EUROPE — II

I

CRITICS of 21st Army Group's slowness were somewhat shaken when they read of our progress from the Seine into Belgium. The 30th and 12th Corps started advancing from their bridgeheads on August 29th and 30th respectively. Brussels was occupied on September 3rd and Antwerp a day later. The large enemy garrisons holding the various Channel ports were left behind to be dealt with by the First Canadian Army. The thousands of disorganised Germans who were roaming about the area over which we advanced were being rounded up and handed over to the French and Belgian Resistance movements. By the 11th our line ran from Antwerp along the Albert Canal to about Herenthals, and then along the Meuse-Escaut Canal to Bree. We had driven two bridgeheads across the latter waterway, one covering the De Groot bridge and the other north of Gheel.

A pause was now necessary as our administrative difficulties were causing anxiety. In order to maintain the advance of the divisions of 12th and 30th Corps (only the equivalent of about four armoured and two infantry) it was necessary to ground 8th Corps and use all its second line, and at least half its first line transport. The Canadian Army had to resort to similar measures in order to maintain their advance. Our administrative staff directed by Graham did magnificent work during this period, and on September 8th, Dieppe was ready to receive the first ship. By the end of the month, it was handling over 6,000 tons per day.

Montgomery was still determined to cross the Rhine before the enemy had time to re-organise, and ordered Second Army to drive forward between Wesel and Arnhem. Having crossed the river, he proposed to advance into Germany around the northern edge of the industrial area. By the end of the first week of September, the Commander-in-Chief appealed to the Supreme Commander for additional administrative resources, as he felt without them the Second Army's advance would have to be delayed until towards the end of the month — if it could be undertaken at all. Transport aircraft as well as road transport companies were allotted, and this gave us an additional lift of some thousand tons per day. As a result, the date was now fixed for September 17th.

The Supreme Commander had allotted an Airborne Corps of three divisions[40] to 21st Army Group for their next operation. Montgomery decided to use them to accelerate our advance, and to establish a bridgehead across the Rhine. On the 14th he issued orders to Second Army. Crossings over the major river obstacles were to be secured in the vicinity of Grave, Nijmegen and Arnhem. This alignment, which was hardly in the direction of the Ruhr, was chosen because it avoided the Siegfried Line, and was within comfortable range of the U.K. bases for the airborne operations.

The general plan was for 30th Corps to drive northwards as rapidly as possible from their bridgehead over the Meuse-Escaut Canal, and to establish themselves in the area between Arnhem and the Zuider Zee. The airborne troops were to be dropped in the vicinity of the river and canal crossings, in order to capture the bridges and generally facilitate the advance.

---

[40] Two American and one British.

30th Corps was to ignore its flanks, and the intention was that the 8th and 12th Corps would carry out operations to widen the corridor to the east and to the west. Our transport aircraft resources were insufficient to drop the whole Corps in one day. The complete operation, which included reinforcement and re-supply, would take four days in all. Another difficulty was that at Arnhem the country and enemy flak defences necessitated landing the 1st British Airborne Division some eight miles from the town.

I had unfortunately been away sick in England during most of the period of preparation, and only arrived back on the afternoon of the 17th. So I was not in close touch with the existing situation. It was undoubtedly a gamble, but there was a very good dividend to be reaped if it came off. Horrocks was the ideal commander for the task, and morale of the troops was high.

September 17th was fine, and in the early afternoon the airborne troops commenced to drop. First reports were good. Little opposition had been encountered. The Grave bridge had been captured intact by the Americans. The Nijmegen bridge was not blown, but was not in our hands. The Wilhelmina Canal bridge had been destroyed. Two more bridges over the canal between Grave and Nijmegen were in our possession. A message also said that the 1st Airborne Division had some troops holding the northern end of the Arnhem bridge. The 30th Corps advance had started well. So far so good.

Eindhoven was captured on the 18th, and on the 19th the Guards Armoured Division joined up with the Americans at the Grave bridge, and later in the day, elements had reached the Waal river. This important bridge was still intact, but strongly held by the enemy. It was captured, however, on the 20th, after a very gallant Anglo/American attack.

Now what of the British troops at Arnhem? On the 18th the weather was poor, and the reinforcements arrived late and were surrounded. Further, virtually no re-supply had reached the troops. The division was now split up into three parts — elements were, however, still holding on to the road bridge over the river. The Germans were holding Arnhem in strength, and were bringing up reinforcements, including flak. The weather on the 19th was worse and interfered with the airborne operations, as well as cut down the tactical air support available. The 1st Airborne Division were now getting short of supplies, and by mischance the day's effort at re-supply fell into enemy hands. It had been hoped to fly in the Polish Parachute Brigade on this day, but unfortunately the weather prevented this. The intention had been to drop them just south of Arnhem, and so assist the rapid opening up of the route from Nijmegen.

On the 20th things were no better, and it was still found impossible to fly in the Polish Brigade, but some supplies reached the division. Our troops had been forced into a small area near Heveadorp and were being subjected to an increasing amount of artillery and mortar fire. No news came from the paratroops who had been holding the northern end of the bridge.

The weather continued to be bad, but in spite of it, the major portion of the Polish Parachute Brigade was dropped between Arnhem and Nijmegen on the 21st. Nothing could be done on the 22nd, and the balance were flown in on the 23rd.

On the 22nd the 43rd Division and some of the Poles managed to reach the Neder Rijn at a point south-west of Oosterbeek. Enemy fire and the steep banks unfortunately prevented anything but a trickle of supplies being got across.

On the 23rd a couple of hundred Poles were ferried across the river to reinforce the British forces. Further efforts to gain touch and reinforce the 1st Airborne Division were made on the night of the 24th, but these were unsuccessful.

Further to the south, the enemy had twice cut 30th Corps' main axis; this not only interfered with the flow of troops and supplies northwards, but also diverted troops to clear up the situation. All this time the 8th and 12th Corps had been making steady progress in their tasks of widening the corridor. But in spite of all their endeavours the situation at Arnhem was desperate, and so on September 25th, Montgomery decided to withdraw the bridgehead. That night, under conditions of extreme difficulty during which the troops fought with great gallantry, nearly 2,500 troops, with the help of assault boats, were withdrawn across the river.

The enemy made repeated attempts to capture the Nijmegen bridge from us, for he realised the threat it represented to the Fatherland as long as it remained in our hands. Despite bombing attacks, and an attempt to blow up the bridge with charges placed in position by specially trained swimmers, it was not put permanently out of use.

The three main reasons for failure were first the lack of sufficient aircraft to enable the whole force to be carried in one lift; the extremely bad weather which we experienced during the vital period; and lastly, the strength of the enemy's reaction. As regards the weather, we were undoubtedly taking a great risk, but were justified in expecting something very much better. I think we had perhaps underestimated the enemy's powers of recuperation. We were, no doubt, influenced too much by the devastating defeat we had witnessed. Just as the enemy managed to produce forces to organise a defence at Arnhem, so do 1 believe he would have produced an answer to a single thrust into Westphalia as favoured by Montgomery. On the other hand, I consider that we might have held our bridgehead over the Neder Rijn if we had experienced really good weather. But I wouldn't like to bet on it!

It is interesting to consider how far we failed in this operation. It should be remembered that the Arnhem bridgehead was only a part of the whole. We had gained a great deal in spite of this local set-back. The Nijmegen bridge was ours, and it proved of immense value later on. And the brilliant advance by 30th Corps led the way to the liberation of a large part of Holland, not to speak of providing a stepping stone to the successful battles of the Rhineland. But I suppose it is only fair to recall that the primary object was to gain possession of the area between Arnhem and the Zuider Zee, preparatory to crossing the Issel river into Northern Germany. In this we failed. But whilst admitting this, we should also remember that without the measure of success actually achieved, we should not have been able to stage our great advance across the Rhine into Germany when we did. During the winter the Germans flooded the area between Arnhem and Nijmegen, and so for a while removed the potential threat caused by our possession of this bridgehead.

II

I will now explain the evolution of the Supreme Commander's winter strategy.

During the time that 21st Army Group were fighting their way north, the First U.S. Army had broken into the Siegfried defences, and were preparing a thrust that it was hoped would take them as far as Bonn and Cologne. Further south, Patton had driven bridgeheads across the Moselle.

Montgomery was now hoping to launch as early as possible an attack between the Rhine and Meuse from the direction of Nijmegen. Having cleared the left bank of the Rhine it was then hoped to carry out an opposed crossing. It looked as if this new operation might be ready for launching about October 10th. Every day the enemy was increasing his preparedness, and so the longer we waited the harder would be our task. Further, the winter weather was just round the corner, and so we were anxious to get going. The boundary between the two Army Groups was moved north on Montgomery's request, in order that we should have more troops available for offensive action.

Early in October, however, Montgomery came to the conclusion that the proposed offensive was not possible. He had too few troops available for the tasks on hand, and the Scheldt had to be cleared in order that the port of Antwerp could be brought into use. Without it, both 12th Army Group and ourselves would be in difficulties from the maintenance angle. It now looked as if these operations would take some time. Then before an offensive from Nijmegen southwards between the two rivers could be launched, it was imperative that the Germans should be driven over to the east bank of the Meuse. Finally at least two divisions were required to ensure the security of the Nijmegen bridgehead. We could therefore not take on all these tasks at about the same time.

Montgomery also considered that it was necessary for the First U.S. Army to have reached the vicinity of Cologne in order to secure the eventual flank of his proposed Rhineland attack. In fact Montgomery had now discarded any idea of taking risks by thrusting into Germany on a comparatively narrow front.

21st Army Group's first priority became the operations for opening up the Scheldt, and it took the Canadian Army until November 3rd before the southern bank had been cleared. But before the river could be used the island of Walcheren had to be occupied. After the sea dykes had been breached by the R.A.F. and the enemy's defences disrupted and isolated, a well-organised amphibious operation was undertaken, and by November 8th the enemy on the island had been eliminated. It wasn't, however, until November 28th that the first convoy reached Antwerp — nearly three months after the capture of the port. This reinforces my previous argument that a single thrust across the Rhine — the Montgomery plan for August — would ultimately have met major difficulties.

I hope the full tale of these operations in the water-logged country will soon be told. It will then be fully appreciated what an extremely difficult and complex task General Crerar and the troops under his command were saddled with — and how ably they saw the thing through.

The Supreme Commander held an important conference at Brussels on October 18th. Montgomery and Bradley were present; I also attended. It was agreed that 21st Army Group's main task should be to open up Antwerp. After this we were to prepare an offensive from Nijmegen between the two rivers directed on Krefeld. The First U.S. Army's objective was still Cologne, and a new Army — the Ninth U.S. Army — would be brought in on the left of the First Army during the advance eastwards. It was decided that when we approached this new Army during our thrust south-eastwards, it would come under our command. It was also laid down that Bradley would command the operations aimed at the capture of the Ruhr, which still remained the goal for which all these other attacks were necessary preliminaries.

After this meeting Eisenhower decided to undertake yet another offensive, and this by Patton's Third Army, against the Saar.

Before long it became apparent that it would be some time before conditions would be right for launching the Rhineland offensive. In the first place the enemy holding the west side of the Meuse proved to be stronger than anticipated, whilst the First U.S. Army were finding progress difficult. In order to give Twelfth Army Group greater strength we were ordered to extend our boundary southwards again along the Meuse.

Second Army took from November until the early part of December to drive the enemy back to the Meuse — as far south as Roermond.

On the First U.S. Army front the enemy had been fighting desperately, and all his available reinforcements had been brought up to delay the American advance. The offensive was halted in the Roer valley. The weather had been extremely bad, and the country was becoming waterlogged. An added complication was the presence of two dams higher up the river. If these were blown the resultant rush of water would destroy any bridges constructed and flood the countryside. Bradley wisely decided that he must capture these first before attempting a crossing.

Patton's offensive had gone well, and by early December he had reached the Moselle river and had captured Metz. Further south additional offensive operations were being carried out by the 6th U.S. Army Group, which had landed in the south of France, but these thrusts were being maintained by a different L. of C.

After the termination of the Scheldt operations the Canadian Army's boundary was extended to include Nijmegen, and Montgomery gave General Crerar the task of carrying out the attack between the two rivers. Second Army was to study the crossing of the Rhine itself.

This was the situation when the enemy attacked in the Ardennes. But before I draw attention to certain matters of interest in connection with this great German effort, I will sum up my views on the development of our strategy during the autumn.

The question to be answered is "If, after Arnhem, all offensive operations had been restricted to the north, could we have reached the Rhine north of the Ruhr? Might we even have established bridgeheads across that river?"

All were agreed that now the Germans had re-organised their defence and recovered from the shock of their defeat in France, an advance to the Rhine should be on a broader front, i.e. a thrust by the First U.S. Army towards Cologne and Bonn, together with a drive by 21st Army Group south-eastwards from Nijmegen. Let me examine each of these projects in turn.

During the fighting through the Siegfried Line and around Aachen in September and early October, the First U.S. Army were experiencing difficulties regarding their supply. The only satisfactory answer to this was to open the port of Antwerp. Further resources could, however, have been diverted from those then going to Patton's Third Army. I have not sufficient information to be able to assess what such a diversion might have meant in terms of daily tonnages and commodities, but I am pretty certain they could not have amounted to very much. Certainly not sufficient to allow a sustained offensive by the two armies to have taken place in September and October.

In point of fact Patton was getting very little during this period. I discussed the matter on several occasions with Bedell Smith and his experts on my visits to Eisenhower's Headquarters. They used to laugh about the way Patton would wait a few days and accumulate a small reserve of ammunition, and then "have a bang." In this way he edged his way forward. Occasionally he was counter-attacked. So, after leaving the Third U.S. Army with sufficient munitions to give them security, there would not have been much left for diversion elsewhere. The extra distance in carry would certainly have reduced the value of the transport so released. The effect such a policy would have had upon the American commanders and troops had also to be considered. If the Third Army was required eventually for offensive work it could not be allowed to remain in a static and ineffective role for long.

So much for the maintenance factor. Now what about the question of additional divisions?

I must agree with Ingersoll when he says 21st Army Group were short of troops after the Normandy battles. That was one of Montgomery's problems. He was continually feeling the need for more. The Supreme Commander allocated additional resources for particular tasks, and when they could be spared. This did not only apply to divisions, but also to such items as bridging units and equipment.

Montgomery did not have sufficient resources to clear the Scheldt and open Antwerp, and attack up to the Rhine at the same time. Antwerp was the first essential, and so the advance to the Rhine after the failure at Arnhem had to be postponed. It would have been no good Eisenhower allocating the Scheldt area to the Americans. The Army Groups would then have become mixed up — it would not have been a sound arrangement. Then one was also up against the vicious circle of more divisions meaning more maintenance.

So I came to the very definite conclusion that maintenance coupled with the lack of additional divisions forbade us reaching the Rhine in strength during September and October.

Now what of Bradley's "second wind" offensive, which I think started on November 16th? I believe he would have liked more divisions, but the real reason for the advance progressing no further than the Roer river was the weather. His troops had really performed wonders under the most trying conditions. The British and Canadian troops with equal bravery and tenacity fought under somewhat similar conditions in early February, 1945, when we started our real advance to the Rhine.

Eisenhower's strategy of attacking the enemy where resources would permit I feel sure paid a fine dividend. It prepared the way for the great victories in the following year. It is perhaps not realised what a heavy toll was taken of the enemy. I have found an estimate we made which places the enemy casualties during November and December at over a quarter of a million.

III

Early in October the Press were getting very worried as to how things were going and how long the war might last. Several of the war correspondents came to see me about it. They undoubtedly had a very difficult problem to face. The Allied public had been galvanised by events during August and September, and there is no doubt that they were hoping for victory in 1944. After the disasters she had sustained Germany should have given up by all normal rules of war — but she didn't! Now the Press very naturally wanted guidance as to what the public should be told. Would the war be over by Christmas? Early next year — or did another year of fighting lie ahead? These were questions which required answers.

I gave one of my periodical talks to the war correspondents on October 18th and tried to help them. One could not of course be very certain as to how events would shape. I stressed that we had the strength to win at an early date, but administration and the weather were the factors that would delay the end. I gave them an appreciation of the situation as I saw it, and at the end I asked them to do all they could to help the soldier through this difficult period. The main points I made in conclusion were: Remember that we were only one part of the Allied front. The Russians were containing a far larger number of German divisions than we were. It was possible that the decisive battles on the Western front might be fought this year, but it was unlikely that the war would be over until next. I think I was not far wrong, for the defeat of the Ardennes offensive and the loss the Germans suffered in the battles of October, November and December undoubtedly made our early victories in 1945 a certainty.

IV

On December 15th I flew back to England in order to attend a War Office conference on the 18th. I spent the 16th and 17th with my wife at her cottage near Northampton, and on the Sunday turned on the radio and heard that the Germans had attacked on the American Ardennes front. As far as I knew, 12th U.S. Army Group had not been expecting anything on a large scale, and so I did not even trouble to ring up our Headquarters — for which I always had facilities when in England — but decided to wait until I arrived at the War Office the next morning.

It was very foggy the next day and we took a long time to reach London. After clocking in at our hotel I went round to the War Office and asked for the news. I soon realised that a crisis had occurred, and that the German offensive was a formidable and a dangerous affair. I immediately rang up 21st Army Group and spoke to Belchem, my B.G.S. Operations, and then with the Commander-in-Chief. I discussed with Belchem the steps which were being taken to provide road blocks covering Brussels, for by now there was practically nothing in front of the advanced enemy's spearheads. Montgomery appeared to be at the top of his form and really enjoying himself. I told him I would get over as soon as possible, but that the fog might prevent my doing so until the next day. He gave me his views as to the seriousness of the situation, and said he thought there would be an anxious day or two, but was confident the situation could be handled.

The fog was a "pea-souper" and it was impossible to fly back that evening. It was a maddening position in which to find myself, and my temper was not at its best. The next day dawned with the fog as bad as ever, and so I got on to the Admiralty and asked them to help me in getting across the Channel. Arrangements were made for a vessel to take me across from Dover that afternoon about 4 p.m. During the morning my pilot kept on ringing up from Northolt airport to say that no flying was possible. I sat down to lunch at the Savoy about 12.30 p.m. when Culver, my American Aide, came in and said Race had just rung up to say that, provided we came along at once, he would be able to take off, but would have to land somewhere in France, as thick fog extended all over Belgium. Bovill and I said good-bye to our wives and left for the airfield. Here we found two or three hundred yards visibility — just enough to allow a take off.

It was a nasty flight across. Over the Channel we came down low — just skimming the waves. Suddenly out of the mist white cliffs appeared which necessitated a pretty steep turn. We reached the mouth of the Somme. This we were just able to pick up in the failing light, and Race followed the river until Amiens was reached. Here he landed us most skilfully in the fog. We were all I think a little relieved to have finished with the air for a bit. The R.A.F. station commander very kindly put his car at our disposal, and so we started straight off for Brussels, where we arrived late that night. The effect of the Ardennes battle was to be found en route, for we were being stopped continually in order to have our identifications checked.

The next morning, after a talk with the staff, I set out for First U.S. Army Headquarters, where Montgomery was due about 1 p.m.

Before describing this visit I had better give a brief account of the progress of the German attack.

As I have already said it was launched on December 16th and gained complete tactical surprise. The weather was foggy and therefore favoured the enemy in that it hid his movements and intentions, and also prevented us from using the massive air force which would otherwise have been available. Early on it became apparent to the Supreme Commander that this was an all-out blow directed at the junction of the British and American forces. The enemy hoped to capture the great supply centres of Liège, Brussels and even Antwerp. For the final phase of the offensive another attack was being prepared to drive southwards from occupied Holland. The consequences if this plan had succeeded would have been, of course, extremely grave. Our offensive plans would have been seriously upset; Germany would have been able to reinforce her eastern front; and valuable time would have been gained for the production of her latest secret weapons and equipment.

Three Armies were used — the Sixth Panzer, the Fifth Panzer and the Seventh Army. We must acknowledge that the reequipping of these Panzer Armies during the difficult autumn was a masterly effort by such a hard pressed enemy.

He had hoped to capture the crossings over the Meuse between Liège and Givet as a first main objective. To assist the advance of their spearheads, parachute troops were dropped, and in addition a Panzer Brigade using American equipment and parties dressed in civilian or Allied uniforms were employed. These latter troops aimed at spreading alarm and confusion behind our lines, as well as the sabotage of bridges and other vital points. The commander of the parachutists was captured after several days, and he was by that time a sick and disillusioned man. His story of the difficulties which he experienced in obtaining his requirements in equipment and aircraft was most interesting. He had to fight at every stage, and it was obvious from his remarks that he was anything but satisfied with the role he had been given.

The attack broke right through the First U.S. Army's front, and on the 19th a large gap existed with penetrations made as far as Hotton, March and Bastogne. There were few Allied troops available for preventing an advance through to Brussels.

The Allied Command kept very cool during these difficult days. Immediately it was realised that this was a major effort the Supreme Commander ordered all offensive operations to cease. He also gave the Third U.S. Army (Patton) the task of counter-attacking with maximum speed against the southern flank of the salient. To allow this to take place the Seventh U.S. Army was to take over more ground to the north from Third Army.

Then, on the 19th, Eisenhower ordered Montgomery to take command of the Ninth U.S. Army and that part of the First Army north of the enemy's wedge. This was a sound decision made necessary by the fact that Bradley and his Twelfth Army Group Headquarters were out of personal touch with this portion of his Army Group.

When the enemy attacked, Montgomery was in the process of concentrating his forces under the Canadian Army in preparation for the coming offensive between the Meuse and the Rhine. These moves were now stopped, and as a safety precaution 30th Corps was ordered to move to the area north of the Meuse between Louvain and Maastricht. In addition steps were taken to make use of various units in the L. of C. for providing garrisons for the Meuse bridges between Liège and Givet. But even with this assistance our defences were very weak and could hardly have been expected to stop a strong enemy thrust over the river if it materialised in those first two or three days.

V

I arrived at First U.S. Army Headquarters and was glad to see several old friends again, particularly Bill Kean, the Chief of Staff. Hodges, the Commander, was not yet back from visiting his Corps, and Montgomery had not arrived from a visit to Ninth U.S. Army. I found the Americans all very cheerful but rather tired, as some of them had had very few hours' sleep since the enemy offensive began. It was like old times in Normandy having this Army once again under our command. I did some business with Kean, and then Hodges and Montgomery arrived, in that order.

I never admired my Chief more than on occasions like these. He arrived looking supremely cheerful and confident. This was of course just his "cup of tea." He knew just what he wanted and had all the necessary re-grouping clearly defined in his mind. He sat down and asked Hodges to give him the latest situation, and sat and listened whilst this was being explained. He appeared very satisfied with what he heard, and then went on to explain his plan. The first thing was to form a really firm front, and to collect a reserve ready for a counter stroke. Some discussion took place regarding 30th Corps' responsibilities. Hodges wanted help over some of his commitments around Liège and the Meuse, and this was agreed to. Montgomery decided that the U.S. VIIth Corps (Collins) should be withdrawn gradually into reserve and positioned between Durbuy and Ciney. We discussed the plan for this move. I ate my sandwiches, had a talk with Montgomery in his car, and then drove to Maastricht and paid a call on Ninth U.S. Army. They were holding their ground well and appeared quite happy. I must say the situation seemed well in hand, and very much better than it felt when sitting surrounded by a London fog in the Savoy Hotel!

The development of Rundstedt's Ardennes offensive can be described very briefly. The magnificent fighting by the American troops, particularly by their holding the key centres of St. Vith and Bastogne, and the growing power of our air attack, gradually took the punch out of the attack. The enemy never crossed the Meuse, and the nearest point he got was to within four miles of Dinant. I did hear, however, of stories of attempts by isolated jeeps manned by Germans trying to rush one or two of the bridges, but this ruse did not work and they were soon disposed of.

From the 22nd onwards the weather improved and then our air forces taught the enemy that it is not very wise to undertake such ambitious offensives without first having obtained air superiority. During the foggy weather the air forces attacked various railheads and rail centres feeding the Ardennes front, using instruments. After the fog cleared it was found many of these attacks had been most successful. The further back we forced the enemy railheads the more the enemy had to employ road transport to feed his offensive. And this gave our pilots unique opportunities, and the effect of their attacks was crippling.

I'm afraid we worried Supreme Headquarters a great deal during the opening phase of the battle, for we were continually asking for more troops to make certain that the line of the Meuse was well and truly sealed. They responded magnificently, and day by day new units and formations appeared on the scene.

Patton, in accordance with his usual form, lost no time in striking North. He started on the 22nd, and by the 26th had made contact with the heroic defenders of Bastogne, who had been isolated for several days, relying upon airborne supply.

After the relief of Bastogne, the Supreme Commander gave out his orders for our counter-offensive. The plan was to launch attacks from the North and South against Houffalize. The First U.S. Army started on January 3rd, and this was followed by a renewed thrust by Third U.S. Army on the 9th.

In order to release VIIth U.S. Corps for the attack against Houffalize, Montgomery brought some British formations south of the Meuse and these conformed with the American attack. Despite terrible weather good progress was made. On January 10th our two spearheads were only ten miles apart, but it was not until the 16th that actual contact had been made. St. Vith fell on the 23rd, and by the end of the month we had recovered the ground we had lost. The enemy's great effort had been a huge failure, and his losses had been colossal and, what is more, irreplaceable.

Eisenhower decided that on contact being made by the First and Third U.S. Armies at Houffalize, Bradley would take over command of First Army, but that the Ninth U.S. Army would remain with 21st Army Group in order to assist in the coming battle of the Rhineland.

VI

Besides the great effort made by the enemy's army, the German air force produced their maximum contribution during the Ardennes offensive. In the first place they provided tactical support on a larger scale than had been achieved for many months, and they also carried out a somewhat desperate assault against our airfields in Holland and Belgium. This latter operation was certainly a spectacular affair. It happened on January 1st. I was back at our Headquarters in Brussels at the time, and was holding my usual morning staff conference when it took place.

I heard a certain amount of air activity around the building as I was talking, but this was nothing unusual. Then someone said, "These aircraft are dropping things on the town." (These turned out to be extra fuel tanks.) A few heads turned towards the window, but still no one really guessed what was happening. Then suddenly, as one aircraft flew roof-top high past the Headquarters, a shout went up, "Christ, it's a 190!" I'm afraid there was a break in my conference as we went to see what was happening. Bombs and cannon fire were to be heard, and the air was full of German aircraft circling round and round, and then diving down to shoot up the aircraft on the Brussels airfield. Columns of black smoke were rising from that area and, sad to say, there was not a single British plane about. Eventually the attacks ceased, and later that day I went out to see the damage. It was very great — I should hate to have costed the value of the aircraft that had been written off that day. Both Montgomery's Dakota and my own lost their lives! But although a great deal of damage had been sustained, we could afford it, whilst the enemy could not stand the cost of his audacious attack. His losses amounted to over 200 aircraft, which meant a great enemy defeat.

VII

The reason why I have chosen the Ardennes offensive as one of the highlights of the campaign is not only because it was a rather spectacular affair, but also because it led to a certain amount of friction between the Americans and ourselves. It therefore comes under the category of "Lessons for the future."

There were two causes of potential trouble. The first was the little use made of 21st Army Group troops during the period. This was, I know, the subject of some criticism amongst Americans. The second was the danger resulting from the press and public opinion championing Montgomery's or Bradley's part in the battle.

It was only natural that some Americans felt that Montgomery was winning his battle practically entirely at the expense of American casualties. They saw this strong British Corps (30th) echeloned back behind the front but not being used for the fighting. Then when the Supreme Commander's orders arrived for the Allied counter thrusts, he still did not employ this fresh British corps, but pulled out VIIth U.S. Corps for the task. On the face of it, there might appear to have been an unequal distribution of labour. But there were in fact some very sound reasons why Montgomery acted as he did.

To start with, Montgomery's sector of the Ardennes front was the most dangerous. The troops under his command barred the way to the enemy's objectives, e.g. Liège, Brussels and Antwerp. It was, therefore, very necessary that he should have a strong reserve immediately available in case of trouble.

Accepting, therefore, the need for this, there remains the question of whether 30th Corps should have been used at some stage for a more offensive task. Let me mention some of the reasons why Montgomery decided against this.

In the first place, Eisenhower had allotted 21st Army Group the important job of clearing up the area between the Meuse and the Rhine, and then the crossing of the latter river north of the Ruhr. A fresh 30th Corps was vital for this great offensive — without it we should have had insufficient troops — and *there were no new divisions arriving* as was the case with the Americans. Then many complications would arise if a British Corps was injected into the centre of an American Army. Its administrative axis would run right across those of the First and Ninth Armies. Those who witnessed the scenes of congestion on the roads during this period, will understand fully what this would have meant. Again if the counter thrust had developed into a counter offensive, a major move forward of our Corps in an otherwise American sphere, might have proved a difficult matter. Finally the air support of General Horrocks' Corps might have produced complications, for the Americans and ourselves did not have entirely similar methods of control. But I don't say that this last factor could not have been solved.

I suggest, therefore, that bearing in mind the above factors, and also the ultimate success of the operations across the Rhine, Montgomery was justified in his handling of this rather delicate problem.

It was inevitable that the press in England should have made a great deal of the success achieved against the American sector, the re-division of command, and Montgomery's success in his handling of affairs on the northern half of Rundstedt's wedge. It was also inevitable that the writing up of the British hero indirectly cast a shadow on General Bradley. One heard inaccurate interpretations put on the placing of American Armies under Montgomery's command, and there even appeared suggestions that a "Ground Force Commander" was needed in order to prevent another such set-back.

American opinion very rightly resented these suggestions, for not only was Bradley just as much a public figure in the States as Montgomery was in England, but it was appreciated that Eisenhower had no other course but to re-organise the command for a period, in view of the splitting of 12th Army Group in half.

A press Conference Montgomery held did not improve the situation. I was not present, but from all accounts he was rather "naughty," or human enough to adopt the "what a good boy am I" attitude. This, of course, did not help Bradley.

The situation put the Supreme commander in something of a dilemma. There was a danger that Bradley's high prestige *vis-à-vis* his troops might become undermined. And there was also the danger that public opinion in America might become very critical concerning the future employment of U.S. troops under British command. If this happened Eisenhower's hands might have become tied, in that he would not have been allowed to group his forces with complete freedom, irrespective of nationality.

Since I was perhaps in closer touch with opinion in the outside world than my commander could be, I sensed that a difficult stage in Anglo-American relations had been reached, and so I flew down and spent a night with Bedell Smith at Eisenhower's Headquarters in Rheims.

I had a chat to the Chief of Staff and found that the situation was as I had expected, and later in the evening we both went and had a long talk to the Supreme Commander. He was more worried than I had ever seen him, and we discussed the problem in all its aspects. I told him I thought the matter could be put right, and asked him to let me see what could be done to help.

The next morning I flew to Montgomery's Headquarters which then was just North of Hasselt and explained to him the full meaning of the dangerous situation that was arising. His reaction was characteristic of the man. "Give me a writing pad," he said. And then he proceeded to draft a really generous signal to Eisenhower saying that he would do anything to help. After a cup of tea I drove back to Brussels as it was now too dark to fly, where I had arranged to meet the war correspondents committee, of which Alan Moorehead was the Chairman. I arrived there about 8 p.m. and found them waiting for me in my office. I at once explained the dangers if the present trend of press comment persisted, and gave what I hoped was a fair appreciation of Montgomery's and Bradley's part in the Ardennes battle — and also the reasons for Eisenhower's recent re-grouping of First and Ninth U.S. Armies. I also stressed the drawbacks if by any chance the Supreme Commander had restrictions imposed which would limit the flexibility of his command.

From that day I think I can say that the danger subsided, and the re-grouping that took place after contact had been made at Houffalize — i.e. Ninth U.S. Army remaining under 21st Army Group's command — caused no awkward comment.

It is only fair to say that at this time Montgomery did not advocate his being selected as the Ground Force Commander under Eisenhower. He often stressed to me that his place was in command of the 21st Army Group. He certainly considered that the main thrust over the Rhine in the North should be under the direction of one commander. Very naturally he felt that he was well suited and fitted for this role, but on the other hand, he did on several occasions inform Eisenhower that he would willingly serve under Bradley.

I felt very sorry for Bradley during this period for I had a great affection for this modest soldier. From Sicily days we had worked a lot together. Particularly during the months of planning before the landings in Normandy, Bradley had shown me the greatest kindness. I had admired the quiet way in which he tackled the great problems facing him, how he would never admit anything was impossible. This feeling towards the Commander of the 12th U.S. Army Group was shared by all of us at our Headquarters.

The time that Bradley impressed me most was during the vital battle of St. Lô. I happened to be staying with him at his advanced command post at the time. The opening stages were anything but easy and real drive was necessary to achieve the break-through. I liked the quiet and confident way he spoke to his commanders. How he was determined to force the battle his way, and encouraged them with simple words of praise. I was reminded of a passage in a book I had once read about the way Robert E. Lee encouraged his troops after Gettysburg. No wonder his staff liked working under him.

I was delighted to read Eisenhower's tribute to Bradley in his report on the operations in Europe. It reads: —

"I unhesitatingly class General Bradley's tactical operations during February and March, which witnessed the completion of the destruction of the German forces west of the Rhine, as the equal in brilliance of any that American forces have ever conducted."

VIII

I mentioned just now a visit I paid to Eisenhower's Advanced

Headquarters. I made a habit of spending a night there each week or fortnight from October onwards. I invariably stayed with Bedell Smith, and if he was at his Headquarters at the time, I would also see Eisenhower. On these visits I came in contact with many of the other leading American commanders and personalities. In this way I was able to keep fully in the picture, and also could watch for any matters which might disrupt smooth working between the two great Allies.

I think I can claim to have known Eisenhower and his Chief of Staff as well, if not better, than any British officer outside Supreme Headquarters. I would like to take this opportunity of paying a humble tribute to these two men. Eisenhower was always accessible and would talk frankly and openly about anything. More and more was I impressed with the greatness of this man. He was utterly fair in his dealings, and I envied the clarity of his mind, and his power of accepting responsibility. He was always natural, cool and charming, and possessed the secret of making one feel he really wanted to see you, and had plenty of time to talk. Whether it was in his Headquarters in London, in an apple orchard in Normandy, or at SHAEF in France, he was always the same. A lovable, big minded and scrupulously honest soldier — a truly great American.

Amongst the many kindnesses I received from him there is one that I shall for ever cherish. After having left 21st Army Group I received a special invitation, initiated by Eisenhower himself, to sit on the dais on the occasion when he was presented with the Freedom of the City of London. I was very touched by this kindly thought, particularly as I had not been a member of his own staff.

Bedell Smith and I became great friends. I so enjoyed those evenings we spent together at his house either near Versailles or Rheims. We did a lot of business and thrashed out a lot of troubles. He was a most delightful host and is the most generous man I have ever met. He had a wonderful way of creating a pleasant atmosphere around him and rightly or wrongly, I believe this close association between us was responsible for the avoidance of any friction between our two Headquarters.

IX

During the winter I became considerably involved with the Dutch problem. There were in fact really two problems. The first concerned the preparation necessary to be in a position to feed the Dutch whenever the opportunity arose, and the second was the best way to liberate north-western Holland.

The importation and allocation of food for the civilians in Belgium and Holland was one of our Headquarters' responsibilities. It involved a great deal of work with SHAEF and the authorities at home in order to obtain the necessary quantities, as well as the shipping. And once landed on the continent our Civil Affairs organisation handled the distribution in conjunction with the various civil authorities. This was a big task, and when considering the premium there was upon food and all transportation resources at that time, it is easy to realise that great care had to be taken to keep a correct balance between the civil and the military needs. Brigadier Robbins who was in charge of the Civil Affairs branch of the staff, and Graham, are to be congratulated on the way they together solved the problem.

Besides feeding liberated Holland, we were obliged to start accumulating supplies, transport and medical resources for that part still occupied by the enemy. It was not easy to get the amounts required, and eventually we had to give up some of our war-time reserves held in this country for the purpose.

A considerable amount of propaganda and political pressure developed, and this was presumably initiated by the Dutch Government in London. You could not blame them, for naturally they were extremely anxious to ensure that everything possible was being done for their country; from the feeding of the people to the liberation of the occupied area. But I think they were rather inclined to exaggerate the conditions of starvation. Before describing the repercussions from this agitation, I had better explain the policy which we had decided would prove the most effective.

As to the liberation of north-western Holland, Montgomery was in no doubt as to what our policy should be. He very rightly was entirely against undertaking active operations to this end. In his view the best solution was to concentrate all our forces for the purpose of defeating Germany. If we embarked upon a campaign into north-western Holland, the success of our operations across the Rhine would be endangered, as resources required for that purpose would have to be used. Then we knew that the enemy was ready to flood occupied Holland so as to impede our advance. Such action would delay that country's economic recovery for years, and with such flooding the difficulties of the operation would be immense. Another factor was the devastation that would be caused. Dutch towns would be laid low by bomb and shell, for the troops would have to receive all the support which we were able to give them. These arguments were difficult to counter, and there is no doubt that the right course was adopted, and ended in the speediest termination of the Dutch agony. But this policy was not finally agreed to without a fight.

The problem of preparing for the feeding of the Dutch people was so complex that we decided that a special organisation was required to deal with the matter. Graham suggested forming a District Headquarters, and this was agreed to by the War Office, with General Galloway selected as its Commander. A great deal of work was now done, including the concentration of large stock piles of food at convenient points. Detailed plans were prepared for utilising all forms of transport — ships, barges, motor transport, railways and aircraft. In addition a medical organisation was held ready to assist in treating those who were suffering from various stages of starvation. We were well satisfied that we were in a position to meet any demands made upon us when the occasion arose. And indeed this was proved to be the case.

At the height of all this pressure to get us to move against the Germans in occupied Holland, the Dutch Prime Minister came to see me at our Main Headquarters. He was very friendly, but also rather inquisitive as to our future plans. I explained the existing situation, but did not hold out any hopes of the early liberation of the remainder of his country. When I briefly explained what such operations might involve in the way of destruction, he appeared somewhat taken aback, and I felt he expected soldiers to fight without damaging his beloved country. He also complained that we had not given his Government sufficient notice of our intention to bomb the dykes on Walcheren Island. So it can be seen that by and large the interview was not a very satisfactory one.

Shortly after this, the agitation had reached a sufficiently high level to produce a request from the Combined Chiefs of Staff in Washington for an appreciation dealing with the whole business of liberating north-west Holland, and we were asked by Supreme Headquarters for the necessary information. In response we produced a straightforward document bringing out the points which I have already mentioned. We assessed what extra resources would be required, and also stressed the results any operations would have upon Dutch territory. I am glad to say the arguments appeared to satisfy "the great."

But the Dutch Prime Minister could not have been very pleased with the situation as he found it at our headquarters, for when visiting Supreme Headquarters not long afterwards, I was shown a document which suggested that our headquarters, and I personally, were accused of not being sufficiently appreciative of the danger to the Dutch population. I was anything but pleased with this attitude for we had worked very hard on their behalf, and Montgomery's policy was so obviously sound. It was, therefore, with considerable satisfaction that when the end came the Dutch were generous in their acknowledgment of the correctness of our handling of this difficult problem.

The Deputy Prime Minister, Attlee, came over on behalf of the Cabinet to examine the food situation in the liberated countries, and with particular reference to the arrangements for feeding the Dutch. He had a talk with me, and he undoubtedly realised the difficulties with which we were faced. He went into the whole business most thoroughly, and produced a report for his colleagues on his return to England. I am glad to say that he made some very complimentary references to the work of 21st Army Group for the way they had tackled these matters. Grigg, the Secretary of State for War, read me extracts during one of my visits to London.

X

During the battles between the Meuse and the Rhine, Churchill came out for a visit. He lived in Eisenhower's train which was accommodated in a siding not far from Eindhoven. There is a good story told of a visit he paid to General Simpson and the headquarters of the Ninth U.S. Army. He left the train very early and drove to the headquarters. Half-way through the long drive he realised that he had left his dentures behind. But in spite of this inconvenience he started on his programme immediately he arrived. In the middle of the proceedings an interruption took place. Some despatch riders appeared in a cloud of dust, and they were followed by a jeep. Someone jumped out, rushed forward and handed over a sealed packet for the Prime Minister. The onlookers thought that here was a signal of great importance, some critical decision referred to him by the Cabinet. Churchill, however, took the packet and slipped it into his pocket — unread. A ghost of a smile crossed his face. Here were, of course, the missing dentures!

Before he returned Montgomery and I were invited to dinner in the train. It was a good party — excellent food and drink, and interesting company. The C.I.G.S. (Lord Alanbrooke) and General Ismay, Churchill's Chief of Staff, were also there. After dinner was over Montgomery got up, looked at his watch and said, "Well, sir, I must return to my headquarters." The Prime Minister knew the form and made some remark about the austere Field-Marshal. I understood that I was expected to stay on.

After we had talked about various things, the coming battle which was to launch us over the Rhine was discussed. Then Churchill said he wished to see the operations and expected me to help him. He made it crystal clear that this did not mean that he should be located in a safe place far from the crossing places, but that he must have a close-up view, and even pay a visit to the eastern bank. He would like to be allotted a tank and be hitched on to the early waves of the assault. I did not feel too sure of my ground, for I knew Montgomery's views about visitors during battles. I said I would do what I could, and would talk to the Field-Marshal about it, and that I thought something could be arranged. As the evening wore on I realised that the Prime Minister was absolutely determined on this project. He talked about the battles he had been in during the last war, and that he insisted upon being in the thick of it once more. I even began to wonder whether this great man had decided that he would like to end his days in battle, at a time when he knew victory was upon us!

I didn't get away until 1.30 a.m. the next morning. I reported the Prime Minister's wishes to Montgomery, but this was not the last I was to hear about it. A short time afterwards, I was attending a meeting at the War Office, when I received a message saying the Prime Minister wished to see me in his office. On going over I found him sitting in front of a fire in a large arm-chair. He motioned me to sit opposite him. He then asked how the arrangements were going for his viewing of the coming battle. Luckily I could report some progress, but perhaps not quite the amount that he would have liked! We were to give him a tank, but we didn't feel it would be allowed forward quite as early as he had hoped. After discussing dates and timings I left him clutching a big cigar, and grinning gently from his arm-chair.

When the time came Churchill enjoyed himself a great deal. He stayed at Montgomery's Tactical Headquarters and saw the opening stages of the battle from a small aircraft and a tank or some other armoured vehicle. He was delighted, especially as he was "allowed" to visit the east bank of the Rhine on the afternoon of March 24th.[41]

XI

Before turning to the next chapter which deals with the final surrender of the enemy in the west, I will describe very briefly

---

[41] The attack went in on the night of March 23rd/24th.

the pattern of 21st Army Group's operations from the successful conclusion — from our point of view — of the Ardennes offensive.

Directly it became obvious that we had the measure of the German attack Montgomery ordered preparations for the Rhineland battle to go ahead. 30th Corps was moved back under command of the Canadian Army and the target date of February 8th was laid down.

It had been hoped that the attacks by both the Canadian and Ninth U.S. Armies would start simultaneously, but owing to the blowing of the Roer dam, and the consequent flooding, by the enemy, this was not possible.

The object of the operations was to destroy the enemy between the Meuse and the Rhine rivers, and then to close up along the Rhine itself.

The Canadian Army started on February 8th from the Nijmegen area thrusting south-eastwards. Some of the bitterest fighting of the whole campaign in miserable weather conditions took place about the Reichswald Forest. General Crerar fought a fine battle during this difficult period. I stayed with him for a couple of nights and witnessed the cool way in which he handled affairs.

General Simpson sent his army into the attack across the Roer river on February 17th. A successful break through was achieved — made easier no doubt by the drain imposed by the Canadian Army upon the enemy's resources — and a rapid advance north-eastwards was commenced. The Americans brushed aside the enemy's screen and ignoring all opposition on their flanks displayed remarkable dash.

A link up between the two Armies took place on March 3rd in the vicinity of Geldern.

By March 10th there was no enemy in the 21st Army Group's sector west of the Rhine.

During these operations the Second British Army were busy preparing for the crossing of the Rhine. Montgomery had given Dempsey and the Ninth U.S. Army the tasks of the initial assault. The Canadian Army was to join in a bit later. The Supreme Commander had also assigned the Allied Airborne Army to Montgomery.

Eisenhower had laid down that this Anglo-American assault north of the Ruhr was to be the Allied major effort at crossing the Rhine. But it should be remembered that through forceful leadership and "guts" the First U.S. Army had rushed the Remagen bridge before it was completely destroyed, and had already established a bridgehead twenty-five miles long and ten miles deep over the river by the time our attack was ready to start on March 23rd.

Our attack across the Rhine, which was supported by a very large-scale airborne operation, was an outstanding success, and soon we were advancing deep into Germany. Within six weeks the war was won.

XII

In March Field-Marshal Kesselring was appointed to command the Western Front. A prisoner told us that on arrival in his office he said to the assembled staff, "Well, gentlemen, I am the new V.3"!

CHAPTER XVII: THE END

I

IN late March we received reports that the German High Command in Italy were putting out feelers with a view to the cessation of hostilities on that front. It was not, however, until April 13th that we received the first indications that the enemy on the Western Front were beginning to realise that the end was near. These first whisperings came from occupied Holland.

By this date the Second Army's offensive had reached the Weser river, and the great port of Bremen was almost in our hands. The Canadian Army were in possession of most of north-east Holland, and by April 18th had reached the shores of the Zuider Zee.

The result of these operations was that the German garrison in Holland was cut off from their home base. It was, therefore, not surprising that Seyss Inquart began to experience a certain apprehension about the starving Dutch!

On the 13th we started to receive messages through Resistance channels saying that he was prepared to discuss ways and means of feeding the Dutch people. This was followed up by a visit to London of a Resistance leader who had managed to get out of Holland.

The whole matter was being handled by Eisenhower's Headquarters, and it was not until April 28th that the situation had clarified itself sufficiently to allow a first meeting to take place. The Supreme Commander's Chief of Staff, Bedell Smith, instructed me to hold the first meeting in the capacity of the Supreme Commander's representative. My orders were to obtain agreement for the immediate entry of food, and also to sound the enemy as to the possibilities of the capitulation of the German forces in Holland.

Various arrangements had to be made before the meeting could take place. A village school just on our side of the lines was selected for the conference, and agreement had to be obtained for a temporary truce on this particular sector of the front. A rendezvous where the German plenipotentiaries were to be picked up was chosen, and eleven o'clock in the morning was fixed for the deliberations to start.

As I explained in the last chapter, we had all our plans ready for feeding the Dutch directly the right moment arrived, and armed with this plan, and accompanied by a few experts from the staff, I flew off to the Nijmegen airfield early on the morning of the 28th. The Canadian Army sent cars to meet us here, and we drove through Arnhem to our destination.

The commander of the 1st Canadian Corps had made all the arrangements, and he and Mann, Crerar's Chief of Staff, met me at the school, where we ran through the procedure for the coming meeting. There was an atmosphere of subdued excitement around us, for it was obvious to everyone that something of great moment was taking place. It had been arranged that the enemy delegates should be blindfolded when leaving the German lines, and that they should be driven in jeeps by a very roundabout way to the meeting place.

Eventually the convoy arrived with white flags flying on each car, and a rather miserable and cold-looking collection of Germans got out who were then led into the school.

For this meeting Seyss Inquart had sent his right-hand man Schwebel, and Blaskowitz, the German Commander-in-Chief, was represented by one of his staff. A few Dutch civilians had collected in the street, and seeing these uniformed Germans being escorted into the building, must have made them think they were witnessing the preliminaries to the end of their country's ordeal. The unusual silence brought about by the local truce must have appeared to them a significant factor.

I had arranged that the head civilian and the head soldier should be brought into the conference room to see me before the remainder were allowed in. The door opened and the two Germans stepped in, and after saluting I was amazed to see them put out their hands for a handshake! This gesture I ignored, and merely returned their salute, and asked to see their credentials. These having passed inspection, I showed them my authority coming from the Supreme Commander. This over, I ordered in the remaining officers, and the conference started. On our side of the long table there were the following amongst several others — Galloway, who was head of the organisation which was to feed Holland; the Canadian Corps Commander; the Canadian Army Chief of Staff, a sailor from SHAEF, and a staff officer from the 2nd Tactical Air Force.

I started with a little speech in which I explained the situation as we saw it: that Germany had failed in her duties as the occupying power, and the Dutch population were seriously short of food. I said I understood that the German High Command were now willing to allow us to send in food in order to save the Dutch nation from starvation. This being so, General Eisenhower was prepared to help, but the Allied plan must be accepted, and we must be certain that the food would reach the Dutch and not be taken by the Germans.

My opposite number across the table — Schwebel — was one of the most revolting men I have ever seen. A plump, sweating German who possessed the largest red nose I have ever seen, the end of which was like several ripe strawberries sewn together. With him he had Naval, Air and Army representatives as well as a food expert, and a Dutchman was also included in the party. Schwebel explained that he could make no definite commitments until the proposals had been examined by Seyss Inquart, but that generally speaking the situation was as I had described it.

I then said that we would explain the main points in our plan, and demanded that these be examined by his experts in the interval before the next meeting. And that the next conference should be attended by Seyss Inquart himself, Blaskowitz, and sufficient experts to ensure that matters would be finalised without further delay. If we were to save the people from starvation there was not a day to lose.

We then went through the plans for the introduction of food. The German delegation took many notes, and occasionally raised questions — such as an objection to the air dropping scheme. The Dutchman appeared most astonished and delighted at the comprehensiveness of our proposed assistance.

After considerable pressure, Schwebel agreed to the next meeting taking place on April 30th — in two days time. There was considerable discussion as to where this should be. The Germans wanted it to be held on their side of the line, but I refused to agree to this, pointing out that as we were undertaking a commitment which by all the rules of war should have been theirs, therefore they must conform to our wishes. In the end they agreed to meet once again in the school. The only concession I made was that the next party need not be blindfolded.

Having arrived at these decisions we had an interval for some sandwiches whilst documents were drawn up in English and German embodying the agreement reached. A little later I asked Schwebel to come back to the conference room as I had another matter to discuss. I wanted him by himself, but he insisted on bringing the Army representative with him. I realised that these men would not have the necessary authority to discuss the question of a truce, but on the other hand it was useful to test their reactions.

We had received some reports from the Dutch Resistance that suggested the German High Command in Holland realised the hopelessness of their position, and so I approached the matter from this angle. Having stressed the fact that they were now isolated from Germany, and that resistance in that country appeared to be collapsing, I pointed out how difficult the feeding of the Dutch would be if hostilities continued. For our part we were prepared to hold fast on the line of the Grebbe and Eem Rivers. As I expected, I got very little result, and Schwebel looking rather uncomfortable and glancing repeatedly at the soldier next to him, said he was not empowered to discuss such matters. He agreed, however, to convey my remarks to his chief.

There appeared no point in continuing the conference and so as soon as the documents were ready, and had been agreed to by both parties, they were signed, and we departed on our respective ways. On my return to our Main Headquarters near Krefeld, I rang up Bedell Smith and Montgomery and told them what had taken place. Bedell Smith said that he would be attending the next meeting himself, and asked me to come along as well.

Our representation on the 30th was very much larger than on the 28th, for it was necessary to have all the experts with us on this occasion, in order that everything could be settled on the spot. Prince Bernhard of the Netherlands joined the party, and it was a good sight to see how delighted the Dutch people were to have a glimpse of him once again. Some of them lent out of their windows shouting, "How's the Princess?" "It's good to see you again," "Give our love to Juliana." It was all quite touching and very friendly.

On the arrival of the Germans — this time led by Seyss Inquart, who was accompanied by Blaskowitz's Chief of Staff — the meeting started. After his opening remarks Bedell Smith asked me to go through the feeding plan in general. This I did, explaining the various methods which we had prepared, and the amount of food that was available. There was the dropping from the air; supply by ships to Dutch ports; and the movement of food by rail, road and canal. Then there were the medical arrangements for those who were in various stages of starvation. Bedell Smith asked Seyss Inquart if the plan in outline was agreed to and, if so, could the detailed examination commence. The German appeared satisfied, and so the meeting broke up and various syndicates were formed for examining each particular problem.

There was a Naval syndicate for dealing with the question of sailing ships into Dutch ports. The selection of ports, the routing, piloting through the minefields were some of the matters that had to be settled. Then the Air syndicate had to reach agreement about the dropping zones, and the routing of the aircraft. The control of the enemy's anti-aircraft defence was also an important factor. Steps had also to be taken to ensure that the food when dropped would reach the Dutch people. We insisted that the greatest measure of freedom must be given us for these humanitarian missions. And only after a great deal of pressure on our part did the enemy agree to this. And so on — all over the school buildings these small syndicates could be seen discussing their particular business. In most cases the members of the syndicates were drawn from British, Dutch and German representatives. Watching this scene I found it difficult to believe I wasn't dreaming, for all intents and purposes it reminded me of a staff college exercise with the syndicates arguing amongst themselves as to the best way of solving the particular problem.

The result of all these deliberations was most encouraging, and it looked as if we could start the very next day with the entry of food. The Germans agreed to give us all information as to mines in the canals, and said they would repair as soon as possible the bridges to allow through road and rail communication. The Canadian Corps Commander then dealt with the question of "neutral zones" in order to allow the food traffic to move in safety. The finalised front line for both sides was also agreed to and plotted on our maps. Each agreement was committed to writing and signed by those concerned.

Several Dutchmen had arrived with the German delegation, and it was a delight to watch their pleasure at having contact with the Allies and the outside world after all this time. They now saw the end of their sufferings, and they couldn't believe that we were prepared to help to such a large extent. I am sure Galloway and those of his staff who witnessed their simple joy must have felt amply rewarded for all their labours in connection with the feeding arrangements.

During the time the detail was being worked out Bedell Smith decided to tackle Seyss Inquart concerning the question of a general truce, and capitulation. He collected a small party for this purpose, which as far as I recollect consisted of Strong, the Head of SHAEF Intelligence, Prince Bernhard, Williams and myself. Again relying upon my memory, I believe Seyss Inquart attended this meeting alone.

We all sat down in a small huddle around the table and then some drinks and sandwiches were brought in. Bedell Smith poured out the German a stiff glass of gin, and we then all helped ourselves. After this the serious business started. Eisenhower's Chief of Staff explained that his Chief was most disturbed at the plight of the Dutch people, and that he held the German Command directly responsible for any disaster that might befall them. He then went on to describe the general situation. He said that it was only a matter of weeks or perhaps days before Germany must admit complete and absolute defeat. To this Seyss Inquart said, "I entirely agree." This rather surprising admission prompted Bedell Smith to suggest that the time had therefore come for the Germans in Holland to give up and so avoid unnecessary bloodshed and suffering. He pointed out that there was nothing the German garrison could now achieve as they were cut off from Germany.

In reply Seyss Inquart said that he had received no orders which would allow him to take such action, and in any case it was for the Commander-in-Chief, Blaskowitz, to initiate a matter of this sort. To this, Bedell Smith said, "But surely, Reich Kommisar, it is the politician who dictates the policy to the soldier, and in any case our information points to the fact that no real Supreme Headquarters exists any longer in Germany to-day."

The German rather avoided answering the question and merely said, "But what would future generations of Germans say about me if I complied with your suggestion — what would history say about my conduct?"

It was then that Bedell Smith got really tough.

"Now, look here, Reich Marshal" — he called him this by mistake — "General Eisenhower has instructed me to say that he will hold you directly responsible for any further useless bloodshed. You have lost the war, and you know it. And if, through pig-headedness, you cause more loss of life to Allied troops or Dutch civilians, you will have to pay the penalty. And," continued the Chief of Staff, "you know what that will mean — the wall and a firing squad!"

Seyss Inquart slowly turned his watery eyes towards us and said rather quietly and slowly, "I am not afraid — I am a German."

That ended the meeting, and with stiff formality we parted.

I very much doubt whether any of us then realised that the end was quite so near.

The next day the aircraft started dropping supplies and there were no regrettable incidents. Also Galloway began to move the food in by the other routes. About 1,000 tons per day by road started at once, and it was agreed that five ships could be accepted at a time, starting on May 5th. The Germans also undertook to have cleared the rivers and canals of obstructions to allow barges to sail by the same date.

So at long last happier days had started for the suffering Dutch.

II

After our meetings with the Germans in Holland events moved rather more rapidly than we had dared hope. On May 2nd our spearheads had reached the Baltic; Wismar and Lubeck were occupied on that date. Immediately the enemy began overtures for an armistice through Blumentritt's[42] staff. The German Army Commander himself was due to arrive at Second Army's Headquarters the next day. But instead, Admiral Friedeburg, the German Naval Commander-in-Chief, and General Kinzel turned up. The latter was Chief of Staff to Field-Marshal Busch, who commanded the Army Group opposing 21st Army Group. As matters now appeared to have

---

[42] Commander of a German Army, i.e. "Army Staff Blumentritt."

been put on a higher level, Dempsey sent the Germans on to Montgomery's Headquarters at Luneberg Heath.

At first the Admiral tried to get our Commander-in-Chief to accept, within the Anglo-American lines, the soldiers and civilians who were retiring in front of the Russian advance from the east. Montgomery refused to discuss this, saying that since they were fighting the Russians, they must surrender to them.

He then asked the Germans whether they would like to discuss the surrender of their forces facing us. At first Friedeburg said "No," and went on to enquire whether we would agree to an arrangement whereby the German forces could withdraw by stages in front of us with our troops following up.

Again Montgomery said "No." He then said that to him the issue was quite clear and simple. Would they surrender on a tactical basis the troops on 21st Army Group's front and in Denmark? If they would do so, then he would be prepared to discuss the best way of carrying out the surrender. If they would not discuss it, then he would be delighted to continue fighting.

All this took place in the morning. After lunch the discussions continued. Montgomery took Friedeburg into his map lorry and showed him on the battle map the plight of the German forces. The Admiral finally broke down and burst into tears. His whole attitude altogether changed. He decided to return at once to see Keitel and recommend the unconditional surrender of the German forces in Western Holland, Friesland, the Frisian Islands, Heligoland, Schleswig-Holstein and Denmark. He agreed also to ask Keitel whether he would be prepared to surrender in other areas. If so willing, 21st Army Group would make the necessary arrangements to fly the plenipotentiaries to the Supreme Commander's Headquarters for discussions.

Friedeburg returned to our Tactical Headquarters the next day and the surrender was signed that evening. The cease fire was to take place at 0800 hours the next morning — the 5th of May.

I so well remember my feelings when my B.G.S. Operations placed before me the message containing the orders implementing this momentous decision. All our long years of toil had brought victory — total and complete. I felt rather tired and deflated, and my mind went back to the days when I had read in the histories of the great war, about the issuing of the armistice message.[43] How I had envied those who were intimately connected with such doings, and now I found myself in that very position — approving the signal that spelt the consummation of all our endeavours. But I didn't get the kick I might have expected — no, it wasn't "blaséness"; it was just that I was very, very tired.

On the 5th, Friedeburg was flown to Supreme Headquarters from where he sent a signal to Keitel asking for powers to sign a general surrender. I reproduce the answer he received which told him that Jodl was on his way, and that in the meantime he was to hold up further negotiations until Jodl's arrival.

On May 6th, Jodl arrived at Tactical Headquarters and I was asked to fly him in my aircraft to Supreme Headquarters — which was then at Rheims. He looked very drawn and behaved perfectly correctly. It was a queer feeling to be in the same aircraft with the man who had for so long worked in the closest association with Hitler. We were met on the Rheims airfield by officers from Supreme Headquarters, who took charge of Jodl, and so my task was completed. Bedell Smith

---

[43] I was too young to have served in the 1914-18 war.

had, however, asked me to stay the night, and in view of the great event that was soon to take place, I gladly accepted.

I paid a visit to the Chief of Staff at the Headquarters, and as he and others were busy making arrangements for the coming meeting, I drove out to Bedell Smith's house, and then put in an appearance at a cocktail party which was being given by some of the women officers at SHAEF. It was a very cheerful affair, and the excellent dry Martinis coupled with the impending end of the war, produced a distinctly friendly atmosphere! Later on all the great ones turned up — Eisenhower and Tedder amongst them.

After some false starts, when the Germans tried to play for time in order to get as many of their soldiers as possible from the Russian front into our lines, the final surrender was signed at 0241 hours on the morning of May 7th.

After breakfast I flew back to our headquarters in Germany as there was much to do in connection with the enforcing of the terms of surrender.

III

From the staff point of view I believe the problems facing us during those first few days or weeks of peace were nearly as great as anything we had met in war.

Montgomery laid down the broad policy as to how the situation should be handled, and then it was up to the staff to work out all the details in conjunction with the Armies and the Germans.

The first thing I did was to call a very large conference at Tactical Headquarters. This was attended by representatives from Army Group Headquarters (including Military Government), the Chiefs of Staff of both Second and Canadian Armies, our Naval Liaison Officer and my opposite number, Groom, from the 2nd Tactical Air Force. During the first part of the meeting I explained the general plan for dealing with enemy territory and their troops, as well as the operational policy regarding our own forces. We thrashed out any points that required further discussion, and having agreed upon a firm plan, I then had Kinzel, Field-Marshal Busch's Chief of Staff, brought in for a second conference.

It was arranged that Kinzel, with a small staff, should remain with us, and be the channel through which we issued our orders to the German Army. He was undoubtedly a most efficient staff officer, and one could not help being impressed by his attitude and quickness as he sat there opposite me dressed in a magnificent field grey great-coat with scarlet lapels. He wore an eyeglass and was in every respect the typical Prussian General Staff Officer. If he had lived he might have made a fortune in Hollywood.

There was a certain amount of criticism of the way we made use of the German Commanders and staff. I doubt whether anyone outside the Army Group realised what a terrific task we had on hand, or I think they would have appreciated that there was no other possible solution. I will now give as briefly as possible the main problems that were facing us.

Broadly speaking the enemy facing us consisted of C.-in-C. North-West (Busch) with his Headquarters in Holstein; who had under his command the Twenty-Fifth Army in Holland (Blaskowitz), the First Parachute Army between the Ems and Weser, and Army Staff Blumentritt, occupying the area between the Weser and Hamburg and along the Elbe to Lauenburg.

Control

The general policy was to make use of existing German Headquarters to control and administer German troops, and to be based upon the enemy organisation existing on our front at the time of the surrender.

> *21st Army Group* dealt with Field-Marshal Busch's Headquarters.
> *Second Army* dealt with "Army Group" (re-named) Blumentritt.
> *First Canadian* Army dealt with 25th Army (Blaskowitz).
> *The SHAEF Mission to Denmark* dealt with C.-in-C. Denmark (Lindemann).

Then as far as possible our Corps and Divisions, and in some cases Brigades, were allotted lower German formation headquarters with which to work.

All communications between the various German Headquarters had to be carried out in "clear." No codes or cyphers were allowed.

Concentration

It was decided that all the enemy forces were to be concentrated in the peninsulas of Schleswig-Holstein, Cuxhaven and Wilhelmshaven, from where disbandment would take place. Initially steps were taken to obtain large numbers of agricultural workers to deal with the harvest, and also certain German labour units were formed. In these areas full documentation of all the enemy soldiers took place.

In summary our plans catered for the following: —

> *In the Wilhelmshaven-Emden peninsula —*
> Already in the area: 60,000
> To be moved from West Holland: 120,000

Total: 180,000
In the Cuxhaven peninsula —
Already in the area: 160,000
From area north of the Elbe: 100,000
Total: 260,000
In the area south-west Schleswig-Holstein —
From Denmark: 160,000
From North Schleswig-Holstein: 250,000
Total: 410,000
In the area south-east Schleswig-Holstein —
From South Schleswig-Holstein: 134,000
From East Prussia: 75,000
From "Wismar Cushion"[44]: 360,000
Total: 569,000
Overall Total: 1,419,000

In addition to the above there were reported to be about 300,000 German troops in the "Magdeburg Bulge." This area was occupied by the U.S. Ninth Army, but really belonged to our zone. We were responsible therefore for the enemy within it.

It will be seen therefore that we had to handle approximately one and three quarter million German troops.

Besides this vast total we also held on May 19th just under 200,000 German prisoners of war in camps situated in our L. of C. area.

It was arranged that the S.S. troops would be isolated on Nordstrand Island. This was done for security reasons.

Re-deployment

---

[44] An area which really belonged to the Russian zone, and at the time was occupied by U.S. forces under our command.

An added complication was the necessity to re-deploy our forces so that we occupied the agreed British Zone. When the war ended we had entered part of the Russian Zone, and American armies were holding considerable areas that would now become our responsibility. And as the Americans were busy moving formations to the Pacific, it was necessary to avoid delay.

Ex-prisoners of war

We were daily gathering together large numbers of Allied prisoners of war. These had to be sorted out, fed, and moved to their destinations. The numbers ran into many tens of thousands, and besides British there were Russians, Belgians, Yugoslavs, Poles, Italians and others.

Displaced persons

This was one of our greatest problems for there was a great roving population who were living on the country, and committing many crimes in the process. Camps, assembly and transit centres had to be organised before order could be established.

The following is an approximate estimate of the numbers involved as at May 19th: —

West-bound Displaced Persons: 260,000
East-bound Displaced Persons: 360,000
In Denmark —
   East-bound: 300,000 (mostly Germans)
   West-bound: 5,000
Total: 925,000

In addition, at a conference held at Leipzig on May 16th the Russians stated that they held 200,000 west-bound displaced persons who, sooner or later, would arrive in our zone.

Again on top of all this it was estimated that there were about half a million refugees in the British zone of Germany.

The Food Situation

Military Government was faced with the problem of arranging for the feeding of these varied populations. At first it looked as if it would be impossible to make both ends meet before the new harvest became available. Later, however, the situation was found to be better than expected.

Medical

There were several hundreds of thousands of sick and wounded in various parts of the British Zone. The Germans were very short of certain medical supplies, and particularly bandages, anaesthetics and narcotics. The problem had to be dealt with by our Military Government medical staffs.

From the above it is easy to see what a colossal task now faced us. Chaos everywhere — and the problems looked almost insoluble. And yet they were solved and order was rapidly restored. I suggest it provides a good advertisement for our powers of organisation, and for our staff training. In particular General Templer, who was head of our Military Government organisation, working of course in close touch with our administrative staff headed by Graham, deserves special praise for the way he handled this extremely complex situation.

IV

I must describe General Kinzel's ultimate fate. Without

knowing it I no doubt helped him on his way.

Shortly after he set up his small headquarters close to Main Army Group he asked me whether he could carry his pistol. As he was head of the German party and had executive authority over his people, I rather weakly said he could.

Some of our liaison officers who had visited Busch's Headquarters had reported seeing a beautiful blonde who worked in the German Field-Marshal's office.

Well, one day Kinzel asked whether he could have a P.A. (Personal Assistant) on his establishment, as he found the work rather heavy. I agreed to this, but shortly afterwards had to cancel the permission when I received information which showed that the beautiful blonde was the P.A. concerned.

It was not long after I had left 21st Army Group that Kinzel, whilst on a visit to his old headquarters, shot his girl friend and then himself. And so we lost a rather unpleasant but very efficient enemy staff officer. We survived the shock.

V

The day then came when I had to leave 21st Army Group. I had realised more and more as the time drew near how hard this was going to be.

It had been a long journey from the Nile to the Baltic, and not only was I leaving my headquarters that had been involved in such momentous happenings, but I was parting from so many old friends. Several of them belonged to that team that had been together throughout the last three years. There was Graham who had so ably directed our administration, and who had been my constant companion. Belchem, Williams and Richardson, who had blended so well together in the spheres of operations, intelligence and plans. Then there was our tank expert, Richards; White, who somehow kept a smiling face even though burdened with the task of running our communications, and Dennis, our head gunner. And there were many others.

It had been a great chunk out of one's life, but what a chunk — a lifetime's labour and excitement crammed into but a few short years.

An Army Group Headquarters is an unspectacular affair. We received few headlines in the press, no broadcasts were made of our adventures, no toasts were drunk to our achievements. All this so rightly belonged to the formations which we served — to the fighting troops.

And yet this large number of officers and men carried on with their work with efficiency and without complaint, each giving his special contribution towards final victory.

Divisional, Corps and even Army Headquarters had on occasions an easy period, but in an Army Group Headquarters there is no break in the intensity of the work. Somewhere there is fighting, and plans must be prepared so far ahead.

I hope we served those various armies with success. And, what is more important, I hope we gained their confidence. I believe we did. If this was the case then here is all the reward we ask.

It was with a heavy heart that I stepped into my aircraft towards the end of May and said good-bye to the group of friends below. No one had ever been better served, no one ever felt less deserving of such support.

The doors closed, the engines roared, I closed my eyes and tried to forget as we speeded towards England, that vivid realities had now become just memories. But at first I found it impossible to shut out the past, and there flashed through my mind a strange mixture of events and scenes — some important and some so small.

There was the excitement surrounding Hore-Belisha's fall. A last glimpse of dreary half blacked-out Marseilles as I left her on my way to Egypt in early 1940. The sun catching the wings of the Italian bombers high in the sky above Haifa, which told us that war had come to our peaceful area. Bovril and biscuits in the stuffy room at G.H.Q., Cairo, as we worked out plans for the evacuation from Greece. That surge of sympathy that assailed me as I gazed upon the scene of desolation at Larissa after the earthquake; was this a reminder of the tragedy that was to come?

Then a glimpse of the Desert — of a tired-eyed John Harding at Tobruk with chaos around him but remaining calm and undaunted. Critical days in Cairo with Rommel at the gates. That feeling of excitement tinged with loneliness when I reported for duty at the headquarters of the Eighth Army. An evening stroll with Auchinleck when I heard that another was to take his place. This closely followed by that unforgettable meeting with my new Chief at the crossroads outside Alexandria on a hot and sultry August morning. The Ruweisat ridge at sunset when we all heard Montgomery's first address. That moment of acute anticipation as we waited for the guns to open for the battle of El Alamein. The feeling of elation when Rommel started on his long journey back to Tunis.

Bathing in crystal waters that lapped the white sand at Buq Buq on our way to Tobruk. The thrill of meeting green trees and fields about Tripoli after the Desert wastes. What memories to treasure for another day!

The rapid contrast between initial failure and final overwhelming success during Mareth days. Great expectations as I flew back from Tunisia to Cairo in April, 1943, to start planning for our next great adventure — Sicily.

Stepping ashore for the first time in Sicily. An intensely hot evening at Lentini sitting outside our caravans, drinking sweet Italian wine and listening to the radio crooning "Thanks for the memory" as the dust and smoke of battle could be seen rising from the Catanian Plain. The lull before Italy, and bathing in the deep blue waters off Taormina. A bottle of superb sherry flown straight from Gibraltar, drunk in the sunlight at Luchera. Then the mud and frustration around the Sangro. An evening with ENSA on the cliffs near Vasto.

That morning at the close of December as we took off from the runway at the mouth of the Sangro River bound for home and the "Second Front." That first glimpse of war-scarred London, of hard days of planning and then the sailing of the convoys. Eisenhower's order to proceed after hearing what the weather had in store. Great days, busy days, were these. The delight of setting foot again on French soil after a five years' gap. Watching our heavy bombers spell destruction and devastation around Caen on a bright morning in July. The scenes of carnage and the smell of death after Falaise. Our acute optimism as we raced forward to the Dutch frontier. Then disappointment as the winter set in with Germany still undefeated. Caught by the fog in London when Rundstedt attacked. The fleets of aircraft flying overhead en route to stage the greatest airborne operation of all time across the Rhine. That first *parlez* with the enemy in Holland, and then the end of our long journey, and those queer reactions that it entailed. These unforgettable memories — these indelible imprints on my mind.

I stirred myself and glanced down through the window to see a brilliant white carpet of clouds spread beneath us. I allowed them for the moment to screen me from the past, and fell asleep.

CHAPTER XVIII: CONCLUSIONS

I

THIS chapter is in the nature of an afterthought. I had meant to finish the book with the account of my departure from 21st Army Group. It has, however, been suggested that I should try and summarise the conclusions or lessons relating to the higher direction of war, as they have struck me when looking back upon those six momentous years. The selection has not been easy.

It seems hardly necessary to stress the penalties of entering war unprepared. If we find ourselves, however, in this unsatisfactory position, it is more important than ever to ensure that we have first-rate men leading our Services, and if possible men with a public reputation. This is because political pressure and public clamour are so liable in the early stages of a war to force us into unsound military ventures.

The Norwegian and Greek campaigns were both doomed to failure from the start. I know that the politicians were led to believe that the force we sent to Greece had a good chance of carrying out its mission. On the other hand, I do not know what advice Ironside (C.I.G.S.) gave to the government regarding the Norwegian expedition. It would be interesting to know.

I realise that there is the difficulty of public opinion getting out of hand and demanding that we undertake measures which it cannot know are impracticable. This danger must be most carefully watched. With an all-party government in power — a very necessary change immediately we go to war — it should be possible, by employing the maximum frankness compatible with security and by well informed press comment, to prevent the public pressing for action that is not in our best interests.

II

The need for flexibility and the avoidance of rigidity is necessary in all spheres of war direction, but perhaps never so important than in the exercising of high command. The armies with which we fight our wars are mainly comprised of civilians, as well as contingents drawn from our Dominions overseas. It was in the handling of these various components that Montgomery excelled himself. He used great wisdom in his dealings with his individual commanders, just as he did with the different categories of troops — Australian, Canadian, South African, Scotsmen, etc.

I noticed a subtle difference in his handling of Dempsey and Crerar. The Canadian Army Commander was given a slightly greater freedom of action, both with regard to the employment of his army and the handling of his troops. There was complete mutual confidence between them, but Montgomery recognised that there were latent dangers in commanding the forces of a self-governing Dominion, as Crerar owed allegiance to his own government as well as to his Commander-in-Chief. The result was that we all got on very well together. With Dempsey there was a more intimate relationship and a somewhat stricter control.

Then his handling of other Dominion troops was interesting. He recognised the particular characteristics of Freyberg and his New Zealanders, and employed them whenever possible as his mobile shock troops. Freyberg was allowed to have a different organisation from other divisions. He had a tank component and more guns. This complicated some of the staff work, but it paid a handsome dividend. At Alamein, at Mareth, and later, during the advance from the Wadi Akarit, this powerful division played a decisive part. Very soon after taking over Eighth Army Montgomery realised the tough fighting qualities of the Australians, and he cast them for a prominent role in the "dog-fight." They fought the whole time against the best German troops, and their courageous fighting paved the way to the victorious end of the battle.

The South Africans presented Montgomery with yet another problem in the art of command. The loss of the South African Division at Tobruk had been a severe blow to the Union. Not only had their confidence in the High Command been shaken, but the question of adequate man-power was causing anxiety. Not so long before Montgomery's arrival in the Desert a senior South African officer "let his hair down" to me one day concerning this latter difficulty. It was obvious that the South Africans could not afford heavy casualties. They rightly appreciated that a heavy casualty bill during this war might have serious repercussions for the future of their country where a large and growing native population existed.

I was most impressed by the way Montgomery gained their confidence, and how he "coached" them for the coming battle. Their role was an important one, but not likely to be the most expensive in loss of life. The Division fought magnificently and fully justified the Army Commander's confidence in their soldier-like qualities.

Then in his dealings with the various divisions of the British Army serving under him there were distinct differences. The Highland Division was allowed to indulge in every form of publicity in order to foster that invaluable asset — their national *esprit de corps*. They were generally billed for the more methodical and slower roles. Their powers of endurance and native doggedness served them well during their long advance from Alamein to Northern Tunisia. They more or less lived in minefields, as they were usually to be found thrusting down the road axis.

When the battle of Normandy had been won, Montgomery showed his flair for the human or sentimental side of life. In his directive to Crerar dealing with future operations he allotted Dieppe[45] to the Canadians, saying that no doubt they would know how to deal with that objective, and that Scotland would be forever grateful if the Highland Division were directed on St. Valery.[46]

The 50th Division, composed largely of northerners and miners, had proved themselves fine troops for the break-in battle; they were adepts at fighting in organised defensive systems. This of course meant that they were given very "sticky" tasks.

Those fine cavalry armoured car regiments, the 11th Hussars and the 12th Lancers, were great rivals. Montgomery, whenever possible, would exploit this rivalry to everyone's advantage.

And now the soldier. Montgomery understood this "civilian army" as few before him. The rigid old type discipline was not enforced. Human weaknesses were fully appreciated, and the man's lot made as easy for him as possible. This is why he was so lenient as regards dress, and why a certain amount of "personal commandeering" — technically I suppose it might be called "looting" — was winked at. Even when on occasions a unit did not behave in battle as well as it might have done, Montgomery gave them a chance to put things right. All in all

---

[45] Memories of the Canadian raid against Dieppe in 1942.
[46] The original 51st Division was finally surrounded at St. Valery in 1940.

he realised that the Prussian type of discipline was not suited to the "civilian" soldier of the Empire.

III

It struck me that one of the major defects in the preparation of the Army for war was the inadequate training given to our High Commanders.

I admit this is no easy problem, for the size of our peacetime army, its organisation and distribution before the war rarely gave commanders practice in the art of high command. I think it is generally recognised that Montgomery was one of the few of our generals who had really studied the business in peace. Without adequate training and practice it was inevitable that a process of learning by one's errors took place. Montgomery and Slim stand out as really good field commanders, but I doubt whether the others, with the exception of Alexander, will be remembered by the next generation. And the reason for this shortage is, I suggest, the lack of opportunity for learning and practice in time of peace.

Other than the Imperial Defence College, we had no establishment for training those earmarked for high command. And I very much doubt that the syllabus of the I.D.C. before the war was quite what was wanted. I'll wager that now Montgomery is C.I.G.S. he will ensure that this defect in the training of generals is righted.

Rarely in peace did any chances occur for our generals to have opportunities of testing themselves in the command of large forces. Most of the exercises held during our training dealt with the employment of small isolated forces. Excellent for junior commanders, but of little use for those who were to lead our armies in war. When the very occasional large-scale manoeuvres did take place, more often than not the actual commanders of formations and commands would appoint themselves "Directors" for the duration of the exercise, instead of taking every opportunity of getting practical experience.

It is to be hoped that our post-war army will be so organised that Corps at least will be kept alive as such, and will be able to work as a whole instead of its formations and units being scattered at home and abroad in bits and pieces.

IV

Several times during the war the commanders and staff who were ultimately to function in a particular operation were appointed too late. One reason for this was, no doubt, the shortage of suitable officers, but it was certainly not fair on anyone concerned, particularly the fighting troops.

It is only right that the commander who is to lead the troops should be the one who makes the plan. In certain major operations such as our invasion of Europe a tremendous amount of preliminary planning can and should be undertaken, but the ultimate commanders should be the ones who decide upon the actual plan and, if possible, should be appointed in time to superintend the training and detailed planning stages.

On occasions circumstances make all this very difficult, and such was the case when we decided to send a force to Greece. Here Wavell had to use troops who were for the most part being employed elsewhere, and General Wilson was given command just in time to arrive with the leading units of the expedition. The story goes that one of the latter's first requests on arriving at Athens was to ask for maps of the Peloponnese to be sent out. If true, this suggests that the Commander wasn't too pleased or sanguine about the task!

I have described in this book the repercussions resulting from the late availability of Montgomery, Eighth Army

Headquarters, and the formations taking part in the invasion of Sicily. It is difficult to see what other solution could have been found, for as far as I know there was no other Army Headquarters available, and the majority of troops had to be drawn from Eighth Army itself. On the other hand I'm sure a little more foresight would have provided another Army Headquarters, and I can't believe we possessed no other commander capable of achieving successful results in Sicily and Italy. I will say more about the "overworking" of certain personnel a little later. If such action had been taken then Montgomery and Eighth Army staff would have been available to commence planning for the invasion of north-west Europe after a period of rest. As it was, Montgomery and those he brought back with him from Italy were given a terrific task to complete in the time. I am convinced that the delay in announcing the various appointments was quite unjustified. These should have been made in November at the latest, and the reason for not doing so was, I believe, mainly political — Churchill's intense desire to capture Rome before the changes occurred, and also it was thought that the Russians might think we intended to "pipe down" in Italy if Montgomery and others left the theatre too early.

I suppose those who do not agree with my views will argue on the basis that all's well that ends well. To those I would say, "Try being a Chief of Staff during such periods!"

V

This brings me to the over-exploitation of successful commanders and staff. It is obviously very tempting to make use of experience, especially if success has crowned such experience. But if this principle is followed too rigidly, then there is a risk of overworking commanders and others, as well as losing the chance of bringing on those who might prove themselves even more proficient. It seemed to me that more general officers both at home and in India might have been tried out in the Middle East and Central Mediterranean fronts. We were perhaps a little parochial in this respect.

VI

If it is decided to employ a successful commander in a new theatre, it is a decided advantage if he can take certain key officers with him. In fact, where possible "teams" should be kept together. They are so obviously more efficient. Eisenhower and Montgomery appreciated this point and adhered to the team principle and, speaking from the staff point of view alone, it made things so much easier. My Chief in his early days with Eighth Army kept a list of "teams" which he felt would be needed in the winning of the war. It dealt with the high level only, but even so I noticed that gradually certain changes were made in the batting order!

VII

Here are six points which are important for successful generalship. A general must:

(a) Know his "stuff" thoroughly.
(b) Be known and recognised by the troops.
(c) Ensure the troops are given tasks that are within their powers. Success means mutual confidence — failure the reverse.
(d) See that his subordinate commanders are disturbed as little as possible in carrying out their tasks.
(e) Command by personal contact.
(f) Be human and study the human factor.

VIII

There is certainly no black magic about becoming a successful Army staff officer in the field. Youth and brains are the important things. With a comparatively small amount of training and experience most staff appointments can be filled by non-regulars. In 21st Army Group a number of important posts were held by young ex-civilians. One could not have wished for better men.

Montgomery backed youth and the "clever chap,"[47] and this policy paid him enormously.

IX

As an integrated staff for the three Services is not yet to be, it is very necessary that closer working during peace should be attained. This is particularly important with regard to the Army and the R.A.F. I very much favour the establishment of a joint Army/R.A.F. Staff College, and see no insuperable difficulties in implementing such a scheme. In the future more than ever before will our respective activities become intimately involved. Whether a new "Senior" Army/R.A.F. Staff College is required will depend upon the scope and object of the old "Camberley" course. In my opinion the pre-war system whereby one or two R.A.F. officers attended the Camberley Staff College course and vice versa, is nothing like good enough.

X

Many times during the war I have tried to analyse the ingredients of the "big man." The following are the points that I consider important:

---

[47] A favourite expression of Montgomery's

(a) He should be able to sit back and avoid getting immersed in detail.
(b) He must be a good "picker" of men.
(c) He should trust those under him, and let them get on with their job without interference.
(d) He must have the power of clear decision.
(e) He should inspire confidence.
(f) He must not be petty.
(g) He should not be pompous.

APPENDIX A

EIGHTH ARMY
Personal Message from the Army Commander
To be read out to all Troops

1. I have to tell you, with great regret, that the time has come for me to leave the Eighth Army. I have been ordered to take command of the British Armies in England that are to operate under General Eisenhower — the Supreme Commander

2. It is difficult to express to you adequately what this parting means to me. I am leaving officers and men who have been my comrades daring months of hard and victorious fighting, and whose courage and devotion to duty always filled me with admiration. I feel I have many friends among the soldiery of this great Army. I do not know if you will miss me; but I will miss you more than I can say. and especially will I miss the personal contacts, and the cheerful greetings we exchanged together when we passed each other on the road.

3. In all the battles we have fought together we have not had one single failure; we have been successful in everything we have undertaken.

I know that this has been due to the devotion to duty and whole-hearted co-operation of every officer and man, rather than to anything I may have been able to do myself.

But the result has been a mutual confidence between you and me, and mutual confidence between a commander and his troops is a pearl of very great price.

4. I am also very sad at parting from the Desert Air Force. This magnificent air striking force has fought with the Eighth Army throughout the whole of its victorious progress; every

soldier in this Army is proud to acknowledge that the support of this strong and powerful air force has been a battle-winning factor of the first importance. We owe the Allied Air Forces in general, and the Desert Air Force in particular, a very great debt of gratitude.

5. What can 1 say to you as I go away?

When the heart is full it is not easy to speak. But I would say this to you:

"*YOU* have made this Army what it is. *YOU* have made its name a household word all over the world Therefore, *YOU* must uphold its good name and its traditions.

"And I would ask you to give to my successor the same loyal and devoted service that you have never failed to give to me."

6. And so I say GOOD-BYE to you all.

May we meet again soon; and may we serve together again as comrades in arms in the final stages of this war.

B. L. Montgomery
General, Eighth Army

ITALY,
January, 1944.

APPENDIX B (1)

SUPREME HEADQUARTERS
ALLIED EXPEDITIONARY FORCE.

Soldiers, Sailors and Airmen of the Allied Expeditionary Force!

You are about to embark upon the Great Crusade, toward which we have striven these many months. The eyes of the world are upon you. The hopes and prayers of liberty-loving people everywhere march with you. In company with our brave Allies and brothers-in-arms on other Fronts, you will bring about the destruction of the German war machine, the elimination of Nazi tyranny over the oppressed peoples of Europe, and security for ourselves in a free world.

Your task will not be an easy one. Your enemy is well trained, well equipped and battle-hardened. He will fight savagely.

But this is the year 1944! Much has happened since the Nazi triumphs of 1940-41. The United Nations have inflicted upon the Germans great defeats, in open battle, man-to-man. Our air offensive has seriously reduced their strength in the air and their capacity to wage war on the ground. Our Home Fronts have given us an overwhelming superiority in weapons and munitions of war, and placed at our disposal great reserves of trained fighting men. The tide has turned! The free men of the world are marching together to Victory!

I have full confidence in your courage, devotion to duty and skill in battle. We will accept nothing less than full Victory!

Good luck! And let us all beseech the blessing of Almighty God upon this great and noble undertaking.

Signed ... DWIGHT D. EISENHOWER

APPENDIX B (2)

21 ARMY GROUP
PERSONAL MESSAGE FROM THE C-in-C
To be read out to all Troops

1. The time has come to deal the enemy a terrific blow in Western Europe.

The blow will be struck by the combined sea, land, and air forces of the Allies — together constituting one great Allied team, under the supreme command of General Eisenhower.

2. On the eve of this great adventure I send my best wishes to every soldier in the Allied team.

To us is given the honour of striking a blow for freedom which will live in history; and in the better days that lie ahead men will speak with pride of our doings. We have a great and a righteous cause.

Let us pray that "The Lord Mighty in Battle" will go forth with our armies, and that His special providence will aid us in the struggle.

3. I want every soldier to know that I have complete confidence in the successful outcome of the operations that we are now about to begin

With stout hearts, and with enthusiasm for the contest, let us go forward to victory.

4. And, as we enter the battle, let us recall the words of a famous soldier spoken many years ago: —

"He either fears his fate too much,
Or his deserts are small,
Who dare not put it to the touch,
To win or lose it all."

5. Good luck to each one of you. And good hunting on the mainland of Europe.

B. L. Montgomery
General
C-in-C 21 Army Group

1944

APPENDIX B (3)

SPECIAL ORDER OF THE DAY TO THE OFFICERS AND MEN OF THE ALLIED NAVAL EXPEDITIONARY FORCE.

It is to be our privilege to take part in the greatest amphibious operation in history — a necessary preliminary to the opening of the Western Front in Europe which in conjunction with the great Russian advance, will crush the fighting power of Germany.

This is the opportunity which we have long awaited and which must be seized and pursued with relentless determination: the hopes and prayers of the free world and of the enslaved peoples of Europe will be with us and we cannot fail them.

Our task in conjunction with the Merchant Navies of the United Nations, and supported by the Allied Air Forces, is to carry the Allied Expeditionary Force to the Continent, to establish it there in a secure bridgehead and to build it up and maintain it at a rate which will outmatch that of the enemy.

Let no one underestimate the magnitude of this task.

The Germans are desperate and will resist fiercely until we outmanoeuvre and out-fight them, which we can and we will do. To every one of you will be given the opportunity to show by his determination and resource that dauntless spirit of resolution which individually strengthens and inspires and which collectively is irresistible.

I count on every man to do his utmost to ensure the success of this great enterprise which is the climax of the European war.

Good luck to you all and God speed.

B. H. Ramsay
ADMIRAL.
ALLIED NAVAL COMMANDER-IN-CHIEF,
EXPEDITIONARY FORCE.

APPENDIX B (4)

TOP SECRET
HEADQUARTERS
ALLIED EXPEDITIONARY AIR FORCE KESTREL
GROVE, HIVE ROAD, WATFORD, HERTS.

Message from Air Chief Marshal Sir Trafford L. Leigh-Mallory, K.C.B., D.S.O., Air Commander-in-Chief, Allied Expeditionary Air Force,

I wish to congratulate all units of the Allied Expeditionary Air Force on the magnificent work which has been done in preparation for the Invasion. The situation on the eve of the battle has exceeded my highest hopes.

Now we are faced with the greatest operation of its kind ever undertaken. The Air Forces have a vital part to play and a tremendous undertaking in delaying and disorganising the German Armies, as well as in defeating the German Air Force,

I have every confidence that you are well up to the great work that lies before you, I am proud to be with you as a member of the team to fight this great battle. I wish you God Speed and the best of luck in your great task.

ACKNOWLEDGMENTS

Grateful acknowledgment is made to the author and publishers for the quotations taken from *Eclipse* by Alan Moorehead (published by Hamish Hamilton, Ltd.).

Miss Marriott — once a member of 21 Army Group Headquarters — typed the first draft of my book in her spare time, at an astonishing pace. I am indeed grateful to her. To Priscilla Cobb, who worked with me at the War Office, go my thanks for assisting me in many ways.

To Bill Williams I am indebted for several pages of candid and sometimes caustic comment — they helped a lot.

Lastly, the Mooreheads and Charles Richardson have helped in the final proof reading. As I am now in Africa, this has been a tremendous help. I realise the debt I owe them.

F. W. DE G.
Southern Rhodesia, *December*, 1946.

A NOTE TO THE READER

If you have enjoyed this book enough to leave a review on **Amazon** and **Goodreads**, then we would be truly grateful.
Sapere Books

Sapere Books is an exciting new publisher of brilliant fiction and popular history.

To find out more about our latest releases and our monthly bargain books visit our website:
saperebooks.com

www.ingramcontent.com/pod-product-compliance
Lightning Source LLC
Chambersburg PA
CBHW050058170426
43198CB00014B/2383